Lernu. not
Esperantists.

ZAMENHOF
manage differences

Means the
hopeful
one —

a doctor

Communi...
Justice

900 Roots
Handful
affixes
suffices

150 — Books/year
200

Complete Esperanto

Tim Owen and Judith Meyer

Put a
plank across
a stream

The language
belonged to
its users,
not its
inventors

discovering
a common
humanity

replace fear
with
openness
+ acceptance.

~ Million ~ 1000 native
speakers

Numbers
Letters

Conlang
Constructed
language

Complete Esperanto

Tim Owen and Judith Meyer

Teach Yourself®

First published in Great Britain in 2018 by Hodder and Stoughton. An Hachette UK company.

This edition published in 2018 by John Murray Learning

British Library Cataloguing in Publication Data: a catalogue record for this title is available from the British Library.

Library of Congress Catalog Card Number: on file.

ISBN: 9781473669185

4

Cover image © Shutterstock.com

Typeset by Cenveo® Publisher Services.

Printed and bound in Great Britain by CPI Group (UK) Ltd., Croydon, CR0 4YY.

John Murray Learning policy is to use papers that are natural, renewable and recyclable products and made from wood grown in sustainable forests. The logging and manufacturing processes are expected to conform to the environmental regulations of the country of origin.

Carmelite House

50 Victoria Embankment

London EC4Y 0DZ

www.hodder.co.uk

Contents

About the authors

Tim Owen came across Esperanto in a children's encyclopedia one Saturday morning and thought it sounded like a really good idea. Decades later, he has travelled to several countries using the language and held several senior positions in various Esperanto associations, including as Director of Education and Development of the Esperanto Association of Britain.

He runs zamenhof.org, a site about the life of the inventor of Esperanto, and completeesperanto.uk, an unofficial support site for people learning from this course.

Judith Meyer is a computational linguist and author. She grew up near Düsseldorf, Germany, where she learned Esperanto aged only 14. She credits Esperanto with having enabled her to learn many more languages after that – 14 languages at the last count. After completing an MA in Romance Languages and Computational Linguistics, Judith met her partner through Esperanto and together they moved to Berlin, where they live today, enjoying the city's six Esperanto clubs and frequently hosting Esperanto-speaking guests at their apartment.

Judith has extensive experience developing language courses for various companies. Her particular passion lies in finding the smallest and most useful building blocks of a language with which students can quickly build up their ability to speak and understand the language. As a polyglot herself, she is the founder of the Polyglot Gathering (a yearly four-day get-together for around 300 polyglots and language enthusiasts from around the world) and she is part of a team developing the free Amikumu app, which allows anyone to find Esperanto speakers or speakers of any foreign language nearby.

Acknowledgements

Tim Owen: I'm glad to have this opportunity to publicly thank Jagjit Singh Bains and Derek Tatton, two men whom I admire greatly, for being my mentors. And nothing would be possible for me without Clare Hunter, the best thing that Esperanto ever gave me. I'm grateful too for the support which I've received from Ian Carter, Ed Robertson and Edmund Grimley Evans, three of my long-time colleagues in the Esperanto Association of Britain.

Parts of this course have undoubtedly been influenced by contributions elsewhere from other people, particularly from my friends Lee Miller, Bertilo Wennergren, Erin Piateski, John Wells, and Tim Morley. Thank you to all five for the work you've done and continue to do. And thank you to Petro and Dorota at E@I for kindly allowing us to base an exercise on their webpage for the annual event Somera Esperanto-Studado, an unbelievable immersive experience for new learners.

A book can only come to life with the help of unsung heroes on the publishing side and I'm particularly thankful to Emma Green for her enthusiasm and encouragement in making this course a reality, Matthew Duffy, whose sage editorial counsel has improved the book immeasurably, Karyn Bailey, who skillfully navigated the waters from manuscript to typeset book with audio, and Eric Zuarino.

Judith Meyer: I would like to thank Birke Dockhorn, my Esperanto teacher who took me under her wing when I was just 14 years old, as well as Chuck Smith, my partner in everything, who also introduced me to the marvellous world of real-life Esperanto events and who has been my support in writing this course. Finally, I'd like to thank Emma Green for her invaluable support in getting this course published.

How the book works

What you will learn identifies what you should be able to do in Esperanto by the end of the unit.

Culture points present cultural aspects related to the themes in the units, introducing key words and phrases and including follow-up questions.

Vocabulary builder introduces key unit vocabulary grouped by theme and conversation, accompanied by audio. By learning the words and listening to them, your progress in learning Esperanto will be swift.

New expressions introduces the key expressions you will hear in the conversations. Listen to them on the audio and look at how they are expressed as these will aid your comprehension of the conversations. You will have the opportunity to use some of the expressions yourself in exercises and activities.

Conversations are recorded dialogues that you can listen to and practise, beginning with a narrative that helps you understand what you are going to hear, with a focusing question and follow-up activities.

Language discovery draws your attention to key language points in the conversations and to rules of grammar. Read the notes and look at the conversations to see how the language is used in practice.

Practice offers a variety of exercises, including speaking opportunities, to give you a chance to see and use words and phrases in their context.

Speaking and listening sections offer practice in speaking and understanding Esperanto through exercises that let you use what you have learned in previous units.

Reading and writing sections provide practice in reading everyday items and contain mostly vocabulary from the unit. Try to get the main point of the text before you answer the follow-up questions.

Language and culture tip boxes aim to give you extra snippets of vocabulary, cultural tips or helpful pointers for remembering specific expressions.

Test yourself helps you assess what you have learned. You learn more by doing the tests without consulting the text, and only when you have done them check if your answers are the correct ones.

Self-check lets you see what you can do after having completed each unit.

To help you through the course, a system of icons indicates the actions to take:

 Listen to audio

 Figure something out

 Culture tip

 Check your progress

The **Answer key** helps you check your progress by including answers to the activities in the text units.

Once you have completed all 18 units in this course successfully, you may want to proceed with more advanced Esperanto. There are many internet resources for learning Esperanto, some of which you will find listed on library.teachyourself.com.

Learn to learn

The Discovery method

This course incorporates the Discovery method of learning. You will be encouraged throughout the course to engage your mind and figure out the meaning for yourself, through identifying patterns and understanding grammatical concepts, noticing words that are similar to English, and more. As a result of your efforts, you will be able to retain what you have learned, use it with confidence and continue to learn the language on your own after you have finished this course.

Everyone can succeed in learning a language – the key is to know how to learn it. Learning is more than just reading or memorizing grammar and vocabulary. It is about being an active learner, learning in real contexts and using in different situations what you have learned. If you figure something out for yourself, you are more likely to understand it, and when you use what you have learned, you are more likely to remember it.

As many of the essential details, such as grammar rules, are introduced through the Discovery method, you will have more fun while learning. The language will soon start to make sense and you will be relying on your own intuition to construct original sentences independently, not just by listening and repeating.

Happy learning!

Be successful at learning languages

1 MAKE A HABIT OUT OF LEARNING

Study a little every day, between 20 and 30 minutes if possible, rather than two to three hours in one session. **Give yourself short-term goals**, e.g. work out how long you'll spend on a particular unit and work within the time limit. This will help you to **create a study habit**, much in the same way you would a sport or music. You will need to concentrate, so try to **create an environment conducive to learning** which is calm and quiet and free from distractions. As you study, do not worry about your mistakes or the things you can't remember or understand. Languages settle differently in our brains, but gradually the language will become clearer as your brain starts to make new connections. Just **give yourself enough time** and you will succeed.

2 EXPAND YOUR LANGUAGE CONTACT

As part of your study habit try to take other opportunities to expose yourself to the language. As well as using this course you could try listening to music or watching uploaded videos, reading blogs or joining online groups. In time you'll find that your vocabulary and language recognition deepen and you'll become used to a range of writing and speaking styles.

3 VOCABULARY

To organize your study of vocabulary, group new words under:

   a generic categories, e.g. *food*, *feelings*.

   b situations in which they occur, e.g. under *restaurant* you can write *waiter*, *table*, *menu*, *pay*.

   c functions, e.g. greetings, parting, thanks, apologizing.

Say the words out loud as you read them.

▶ Write the words over and over again. Remember that if you want to keep lists on your smartphone or tablet you can usually switch the keyboard language to make sure you are able to include Esperanto's special characters.

▶ Listen to the audio several times.

▶ Cover up the English side of the vocabulary list and see if you remember the meaning of the word.

▶ Associate the words with similar sounding words in English, e.g. **mano** (*a hand*) with *manual*.

▶ Create flash cards, drawings and mind maps.

▶ Write words for objects around your house and stick them to objects.

▶ Pay attention to patterns in words, e.g. adding **mal-** to the start of a word indicates a logical opposite: **bela** – **malbela**, **granda** – **malgranda**.

Experiment with words. You meet lots of affixes during this course which enable you to easily create new words. Once you learn that **-ar-** creates the name for a group of something – **ŝafo** (*sheep*); **ŝafaro** (*flock*) – and that **-eg-** intensifies something – **varma** (*warm*); **varmega** (*hot*) – apply them to other words to help you get a feel for it. Do this with other affixes and you'll find your vocabulary increasing with no real effort.

4 GRAMMAR

To organize the study of grammar write your own grammar glossary and add new information and examples as you go along.

Experiment with grammar rules.

▶ Sit back and reflect on the rules you learn. See how they compare with your own language or other languages you may already speak. Try to find out some rules on your own and be ready to spot the exceptions. By doing this you'll remember the rules better and get a feel for the language.

▶ Try to find examples of grammar in conversations or other articles.

▶ Keep a 'pattern bank' that organizes examples that can be listed under the structures you've learned.

▶ Use old vocabulary to practise new grammar structures.

▶ When you learn a new affix, apply it to words you already know in order to practise building new words.

5 PRONUNCIATION

When organizing the study of pronunciation keep a section of your notebook for pronunciation rules and practise those that trouble you.

▶ Repeat all of the conversations, line by line. Listen to yourself and try to mimic what you hear.
▶ Record yourself and compare yourself to an experienced speaker.
▶ Make a list of words that give you trouble and practise them.
▶ Study individual sounds, then full words.
▶ Make sure you get used to placing the stress on the penultimate syllable.

6 LISTENING AND READING

The conversations in this course include questions to help guide you in your understanding. But you can go further by following some of these tips.

Imagine the situation. When listening to or reading the conversations, try to imagine where the scene is taking place and who the main characters are. Let your experience of the world help you guess the meaning of the conversation, e.g. if a conversation takes place in a snack bar you can predict the kind of vocabulary that is being used.

Concentrate on the main part. When watching a foreign film you usually get the meaning of the whole story from a few individual shots. Understanding a foreign conversation or article is similar. Concentrate on the main parts to get the message and don't worry about individual words.

Guess the key words; if you cannot, ask or look them up. When there are key words you don't understand, try to guess what they mean from the context. If you're listening to an Esperanto speaker and cannot get the gist of a whole passage because of one word or phrase, try to repeat that word with a questioning tone when asking what it means. If for example you wanted to find out the meaning of the word **veturi** (*to go / travel by vehicle*), you would ask **Kion signifas 'veturi'?** (*What does 'veturi' mean?*) or **Kio estas 'veturi'?** (*What is 'veturi'?*).

7 SPEAKING

Rehearse in Esperanto. As all language teachers will assure you, the successful learners are those students who overcome their inhibitions and get into situations where they must speak, write and listen to the foreign language. Here are some useful tips to help you practise speaking Esperanto:

▶ Hold a conversation with yourself, using the conversations of the units as models and the structures you have learned previously.
▶ After you have conducted a transaction with a sales assistant or waiter in your own language, pretend that you have to do it in Esperanto.
▶ Look at objects around you and try to name them in Esperanto.
▶ Look at people around you and try to describe them in detail.
▶ Try to answer all of the questions in the course out loud.

▶ Say the conversations out loud then try to replace sentences with ones that are true for you.

▶ Try to role play different situations in the course.

8 LEARN FROM YOUR ERRORS

Don't let errors interfere with getting your message across. Making errors is part of any normal learning process, but some people get so worried that they won't say anything unless they are sure it is correct. This can lead to a vicious circle as the less they say, the less practice they get and the more mistakes they make.

Many of the errors you will make as a beginner won't make your Esperanto difficult to understand. People will still know what you mean if for example you forget to add an **n**-ending to mark the direct object, accidentally add an **n**-ending after a preposition, or don't make your adjectives agree with their nouns. Concentrate on getting your message across and learning from your mistakes. And remember that nearly everybody who speaks Esperanto used to be a beginner too!

9 LEARN TO COPE WITH UNCERTAINTY

Don't over-use your dictionary. When reading a text in Esperanto, don't be tempted to look up every word you don't know. Underline the words you do not understand and read the passage several times, concentrating on trying to get the gist of the passage. If after the third time there are still words which prevent you from getting the general meaning of the passage, look them up in the dictionary.

Don't panic if you don't understand. If at some point you feel you don't understand what you are told, don't panic or give up listening. Either try to guess what is being said and keep following the conversation or, if you cannot, isolate the expression or words you haven't understood and have them explained to you. The speaker might paraphrase them and the conversation will carry on.

Keep talking. The best way to improve your fluency in Esperanto is to talk every time you have the opportunity to do so: keep the conversations flowing and don't worry about the mistakes. If you get stuck for a particular word, don't let the conversation stop; paraphrase or replace the unknown word with one you do know, even if you have to simplify what you want to say.

About Esperanto

Welcome to Esperanto, unique among the thousands of spoken tongues in the world for being a planned language which developed a speaker community. It started with a single speaker and now extends all around the globe, with the World Esperanto Association having members in over 100 countries. Over the course of a century of usage, Esperanto has become a living language like any other, with new words emerging to reflect the world we all live in and even people being brought up with it as one of their native languages.

Unlike other planned languages, Esperanto was successful in developing a speaker base. This happened because the language was designed to be very accessible for people choosing to learn it, as you'll soon see for yourself. You won't find grammatical gender or silent letters. Its verbs are totally regular and the forms can be learned in minutes. Many learners find Esperanto's grammar refreshingly simple.

Its vocabulary is relatively accessible for people who speak English. You'll be able to work out already what the verbs **havi**, **danci** and **movi** mean, as you will the nouns **problemo**, **momento** and **birdo** and the adjectives **rapida**, **pozitiva** and **delikata**. And if you're familiar with other European languages, you'll find even more of Esperanto's vocabulary to be instantly recognizable. When Ludoviko Zamenhof, a Jewish boy from Białystok, and the creator of Esperanto, was working on his **Lingvo Internacia** (*International Language*), he originally tried using arbitrary, single-syllable words for the vocabulary, and quickly reached the conclusion that it was unworkable. As he grew older and encountered more languages, he picked up a feel for words which were common across several of those he knew and so brought them into Esperanto. So if you know Spanish or Italian, you'll see lots of familiar words in Esperanto because they're related to similar words in French and Latin, both of which were known to Zamenhof.

These linguistic similarities contributed greatly to getting Esperanto off the ground because it made the language more accessible to its learners when it was launched. Thorsten Brants, Research Scientist for Google Translate, acknowledged its accessibility when Google Translate[1] added Esperanto as a language: 'The Google Translate team was actually surprised about the high quality of machine translation for Esperanto … Esperanto was constructed such that it is easy to learn for humans, and this seems to help automatic translation as well.'

Did you notice in the examples that all the nouns ended with **-o**, all the verbs with **-i**, and all the adjectives with **-a**? That's not a coincidence but a deliberate feature. The last letter indicates the grammatical role of the word and you create one form from another by changing the last letter. In English, you have to learn that the adjective corresponding to *hand* is *manual*. In Esperanto, you just replace the relevant ending, creating **mana** from **mano** (*hand*). Learn one word and you learn several others at the same time.

---

1   https://translate.googleblog.com/2012/02/tutmonda-helplingvo-por-ciuj-homoj.html

That approach applies across the board, owing to Esperanto's system of affixes. There's one to create logical opposites, another to denote the place where an activity occurs, one to derive the name of a tool or occupation, and so on. Add them to your word and you create another one, totally predictably. You don't need to learn an extensive list of thematic words which bear no visible tie to each other, such as *to eat*, *meal*, *food*, *cutlery*, *trough*, *to guzzle*, *to nibble*, *to feed*, or *dining room*. Once you know the word **manĝi** (*to eat*) and Esperanto's affix system, you can create all of those words without thinking about it: **manĝi**, **manĝo**, **manĝaĵo**, **manĝilaro**, **manĝujo**, **manĝaĉi**, **manĝeti**, **manĝigi**, **manĝejo**. From one new word come many others.

They might be found all over the world but nobody's quite sure how many Esperanto speakers there are. The language doesn't belong to any nation and Esperanto speakers come from a variety of backgrounds so aren't easy to recognize. (Some individual Esperantists, a name for people who know the language, can claim that their wearing of a green star, the symbol of Esperanto, has occasionally resulted in a fellow Esperantist stopping them for a chat, however!)

What we do know is that Professor Sidney S. Culbert, who was a leading researcher into the speaking population of languages and a long-time contributor to the World Almanac's section on 'Principal Languages of the World', tested for 'professional proficiency' in dozens of countries, estimating a figure of around 2 million Esperanto speakers. This suggests that the vast majority of Esperanto speakers don't join the formal Esperanto associations but instead use and enjoy Esperanto in other ways, whether that's to establish friendships with people from different language backgrounds, to learn it for the simple joy of learning a language, or to indulge their creativity.

For whatever reason you've chosen to learn Esperanto, we're glad that you have and we hope that you enjoy this course. **Bonan lernadon!** (*Happy learning!*)

Pronunciation guide

Esperanto uses the Roman alphabet, as English does. However, it has 28 letters rather than the 26 letters in English. It doesn't contain Q, W, X, or Z, but has six characters which are unique to Esperanto: **Ĉ, Ĝ, Ĥ, Ĵ, Ŝ,** and **Ŭ**.

 00.01 Listen to the whole alphabet on the audio a few times, then try to join in.

Aa	Bb	Cc	Ĉĉ	Dd	Ee	Ff
amiko	bona	certi	ĉokolado	danki	eble	fini
(friend)	*(good)*	*(to be sure)*	*(chocolate)*	*(to thank)*	*(maybe)*	*(to finish)*
Gg	Ĝĝ	Hh	Ĥĥ	Ii	Jj	Ĵĵ
granda	ĝi	havi	ĥoro	instrui	jaro	ĵaluza
(big)	*(it)*	*(to have)*	*(a choir)*	*(to teach)*	*(a year)*	*(jealous)*
Kk	Ll	Mm	Nn	Oo	Pp	Rr
kafo	labori	minuto	nomo	ofte	pluvi	rapida
(coffee)	*(to work)*	*(a minute)*	*(a name)*	*(often)*	*(to rain)*	*(quick)*
Ss	Ŝŝ	Tt	Uu	Ŭŭ	Vv	Zz
studi	ŝati	tablo	unu	aŭ	viziti	zorgi
(to study)	*(to like)*	*(a table)*	*(one)*	*(or)*	*(to visit)*	*(to care for, be anxious about)*

Esperanto is a phonemic language. If you know how to say it you can spell it, and vice versa. Words in Esperanto don't contain any silent letters.

You can usually switch keyboards on your phone or install software on your computer to be able to easily use Esperanto's special letters. If you're unable to do so, there are two common conventions in place to work around the problem. The first is to type the accentless letter and follow it with an **h**, except for after **u: ch, gh, hh, jh, sh, u**. This system dates back to 1888 and is the official alternative. As people started to use computers more frequently, there emerged an alternative scheme, in which the accentless letter was followed by **x: cx, gx, hx, jx, sx, ux**. This has become the most popular system and Esperanto web sites often automatically add the accents if users type an **x** following one of those six letters.

Vowels in Esperanto

The five vowels in Esperanto **A, E, I, O, U** are pronounced pure. Take care not to glide them, as in English. Two vowels next to each other are pronounced separately: the **O**'s in **metroo** are each distinctly pronounced, as are the **I** and **O** at the end of **familio**.

 00.02 Listen to the five vowels and note the way that they are pronounced distinctly in metroo and familio.

Word stress

Words of more than one syllable are pronounced with a slightly stronger stress on the penultimate (i.e. the last but one) syllable: **familio**, **ĉokolado**, **rapida**, **instrui**.

Consonants in Esperanto

Nearly all of the consonants in Esperanto exist in standard English, and there is a one-to-one match between Esperanto and English in the following consonants: **B, D, F, H, K, L, M, N, P, S, T, V, Z**. The letter **G** is always pronounced hard as in *go*.

 00.03 **Listen to the consonants to hear that these sound the same as in English.**

 00.04 **Listen to how the other consonants are pronounced.**

Description	Description
C like *ts* in *bits*	**Ĉ** like *ch* in *church*
Ĝ like *g* in *gym*	**Ĥ** like *ch* in Scottish *loch*
J like *y* in *yes*	**Ĵ** like *s* in *pleasure*
R tapped or trilled as in Spanish *r*	**Ŝ** like *sh* in *shoe*
Ŭ like a *w*, following a vowel	

THE LETTERS C AND R

C and **R** can pose problems for English speakers. The **C** sound can occur in Esperanto in places where it doesn't in English, such as the opening syllable. It becomes trickier for English speakers to pronounce when it is preceded by the letter **S** in common words such as **scii** (*to know*) and **scienco** (*science*). **Mi ne scias** (*I don't know*) is pronounced something like 'mee nest see-as'.

 00.05 **Listen to the pronunciation of scii, scienco and mi ne scias.**

The letter **R** has to be vibrated in Esperanto. This is usually understood to mean trilled or tapped, such as in Spanish or Scottish pronunciation. The key point is that there must be some sort of vibration to make the letter audible; it isn't mute, as it usually is in many flavours of English. Be careful not to pronounce words like **karto** (*card*) and **kato** (*cat*) the same.

00.06 **Listen to the pronunciation of karto and kato and confirm you can hear a difference.**

THE SEMIVOWELS J AND Ŭ

J is pronounced the same as **Y** in English, while **Ŭ** is pronounced like **W**. **J** is often found following the vowels **A, E, O** and **U**, while **Ŭ** normally follows **A** or **E**, causing a glide to be heard. These two letters are counted as consonants in Esperanto, and cannot take an accent or stress, although the vowel preceding them may.

00.07 Listen to the pronunciation of **ĉiu bona knabo** (*every good boy*) and **ĉiuj bonaj knaboj** (*all good boys*) to hear the effect of the **J** when added to a vowel. Compare how **kelo** (*a cellar*) and **kejlo** (*a peg*) sound different, as do **melo** (*a badger*) and **mejlo** (*a mile*). Note how the presence of **Ŭ** causes the sound to change from two distinct vowels into a diphthong in the words **aŭ** (*or*), **Eŭropo** (*Europe*), **hodiaŭ** (*today*) and **baldaŭ** (*soon*).

A FEW TIPS TO HELP YOU ACQUIRE AN AUTHENTIC ACCENT

It is not absolutely vital to acquire a perfect accent. The aim is to be understood. Here are a number of techniques for working on your pronunciation:

1 **Listen carefully to the audio or a competent speaker, especially one who has used Esperanto internationally.**
2 **Record yourself and compare your pronunciation with that of an experienced speaker.**
3 **Ask experienced speakers to listen to your pronunciation and tell you how to improve it.**
4 **Ask experienced speakers how a specific sound is formed. Watch them and practise at home in front of a mirror.**
5 **Make a list of words that give you pronunciation trouble and practise them regularly.**

Useful expressions

NUMBERS

 00.08

0	**nul**		6	**ses**
1	**unu**		7	**sep**
2	**du**		8	**ok**
3	**tri**		9	**naŭ**
4	**kvar**		10	**dek**
5	**kvin**			

DAYS OF THE WEEK

 00.09

Monday	**lundo**
Tuesday	**mardo**
Wednesday	**merkredo**
Thursday	**ĵaŭdo**
Friday	**vendredo**
Saturday	**sabato**
Sunday	**dimanĉo**

EVERYDAY EXPRESSIONS

 00.10

Hi! Hello!	**Saluton!**
I'm called …	**Mi nomiĝas …**
What are you called?	**Kiel vi nomiĝas?**
Thank you!	**Dankon!**
I speak Esperanto a little bit.	**Mi parolas Esperanton iomete.**
I'm a beginner.	**Mi estas komencanto.**
What does that mean?	**Kion tio signifas?**
How do you say … in Esperanto?	**Kiel oni diras … en Esperanto?**
Please say that again / repeat that.	**Bonvolu diri tion denove. / Bonvolu ripeti tion.**
Sorry, I don't understand.	**Pardonu, mi ne komprenas.**
Now I understand.	**Nun mi komprenas.**
Goodbye!	**Ĝis la revido!**

Kiel vi nomiĝas?
What's your name?

In this unit, you will learn how to:
▶ *greet people and present yourself.*
▶ *use the present tense for all verbs.*
▶ *use subject pronouns and ask questions.*
▶ *say what you do for a living.*

CEFR: (A1) *Can use greetings. Can introduce themselves and others and can ask and answer questions about personal details.* **(A2)** *Can understand familiar names, words and very simple sentences (notices and posters in catalogues). Pronunciation is generally clear enough to be understood despite a noticeable foreign accent, but conversational partners will need to ask for repetition from time to time.*

⭐ Interreto *The internet*

People use Esperanto all around **la mondo** (*the world*) and **la interreto** (*the internet*) is an important tool for helping people find other **lernantoj** (*learners*) and **parolantoj** (*speakers*). People use popular **retejoj** (*sites*) and **apoj** (*apps*) to engage with each other and discuss their common interests, using Esperanto as a **pontlingvo** (*bridge language*). It is easy to find other **Esperanto-parolantoj** (*Esperanto speakers*) near you with the free app Amikumu, for example, and arrange to meet them, and once people get a bit more confident they can soon **paroli** (*speak*) with people in other countries using chat programs.

There are lots of free online resources for Esperanto learners, including a version of the most famous **vortaro** (*dictionary*) at vortaro.net, an excellent two-way dictionary at lernu.net/vortaro, plus reference grammars, such as the very detailed bertilow.com/pmeg and its simplified English version at lernu.net/gramatiko.

 What letter do singular nouns (dictionary, internet, world) end with in Esperanto? How do plural nouns (*apps*, *sites*, *learners*) end? What is the Esperanto word for *the*? (There isn't a word for *a* in Esperanto!)

Vocabulary builder 1

01.01 Look at the words and phrases and complete the missing English words and expressions. Then listen and try to imitate the pronunciation of the speakers.

SALUTOJ KAJ ĜISOJ *GREETINGS AND FAREWELLS*

Saluton!	*Hello!*
Bonvenon!	*Welcome!*
Bonan matenon!	*Good morning!*
Bonan tagon!	_____ *day!*
Bonan vesperon!	_____ *evening!*
Bonan nokton!	*Good night!*
Ĝis revido! / Ĝis la revido!	*Goodbye!* (lit. *until the re-seeing*, cf. *au revoir, arrivederci, auf Wiedersehen*)
Ĝis poste!	*See you later!* (lit. *until afterwards*)
Ĝis! / Ĝis la!	*Bye!* (lit. *until / until the*, a shorter form of **ĝis (la) revido**)

Conversation 1

NEW EXPRESSIONS

01.02 Look at and listen to the words and expressions that are used in the following conversation. Note their meanings.

Mi estas …	*I am …*
Dankon!	*Thank you!*
Kiel vi nomiĝas?	*What are you called?* (lit. *How you are named?*)
Mi nomiĝas …	*I am called …*
Mi loĝas en …	*I live in …*
Kaj vi?	*And you?*
el Italio	*from Italy*
ne	*no / not*
mi pardonpetas	*I'm sorry / I apologize*
mi estas komencanto	*I'm a beginner*
Mi venas de …	*I come from …*
ankaŭ	*also, as well, too*
sed	*but*
Ho, nun mi komprenas!	*Oh, now I understand!*

01.03 *Sara has just started learning Esperanto. Today is the first time that she's going to try using her Esperanto with other people. She's logged into an Esperanto chat group and introduces herself.*

1   Why does Sara get confused about what Davido says? What are the Esperanto words for *I* and *you*?

Sara	Saluton! Mi estas Sara.
Roberto	Bonvenon, Sara! Bonan vesperon!
Sara	Dankon! Kiel vi nomiĝas?
Roberto	Mi nomiĝas Roberto. Mi loĝas en Skotlando. Kaj vi?
Sara	Mi loĝas en Londono.
Anna	Bonan vesperon, Sara! Mi estas Anna el Italio.
Davido	Bonan matenon!
Sara	'Bonan matenon'? Ne 'bonan vesperon'? Mi pardonpetas, mi estas komencanto. Mi ne komprenas.
Davido	Ankaŭ mi venas de Britio, sed nun mi loĝas en Aŭstralio, Sara!
Sara	Ho, nun mi komprenas!
Emiljo	Saluton, Sara! Mi estas Emiljo el Brazilo.
Mijoŝi	Bonan matenon! Mi nomiĝas Mijoŝi. Mi venas de Japanio.
Sara	Saluton Emiljo! Saluton Mijoŝi!

2   **Match the English and the Esperanto.**

a Welcome!   **1** Mi estas komencanto.
b I don't understand.   **2** Mi pardonpetas.
c I am a beginner.   **3** Ho, nun mi komprenas.
d What are you called?   **4** Dankon.
e I live in Britain.   **5** Mi ne komprenas.
f I am sorry.   **6** Mi loĝas en Britio.
g Oh, now I understand.   **7** Bonvenon!
h Thank you.   **8** Kiel vi nomiĝas?

3   **Mark the statements based on the conversation either (V) vera *true* or (M) malvera *false*.**

a Roberto lives in Scotland.
b Sara lives in a capital city.
c The Esperanto for *also* is **sed**.
d Emiljo lives in the USA.
e The Esperanto for *but* is **ankaŭ**.
f It's the evening where Davido lives.
g Sara is a beginner.
h The Esperanto for *understand* is **komprenas**.
i Davido lives in Austria.
j The Esperanto for *now* is **nun**.

4

4 **01.04 Now listen to the conversation again line by line and repeat.**

Language discovery 1

1 **Find the words for** *I apologize, I am, I live, I understand* **and** *I am called* **in the conversation.**
2 **Underline all country names in the conversation and guess their English translation.**
3 **Find and remember the expression for** *I am a beginner*. **This will be useful when you start speaking to other people!**

1 PRONUNCIATION BASICS

At the beginning of the course, you will find a guide to Esperanto pronunciation. Use this to compare the sounds to what you hear in the dialogue recording. Pay particular attention to the pronunciation of the accented letters, the **j** in words like **kaj** and the **c** in words like **komencanto**.

2 ESPERANTO VERBS

You've met several Esperanto verbs so far, including the most important one, **esti** *to be*. Verbs in Esperanto all end in the letter **i** when in their basic form, the infinitive. This is the form of the verb given in the dictionary.

To make any Esperanto infinitive into a verb in the present tense, remove the **i**-ending and add **as**: **esti** *to be* > **mi estas** *I am*.

esti	mi estas	havi	mi havas
to be	*I am*	*to have*	*I have*

This is the same for all verbs with no exceptions:

mi estas	mi loĝas	ŝi estas	ŝi loĝas
I am	*I live*	*she is*	*she lives*

To make the meaning negative, add **ne** before the verb:

mi komprenas	mi ne komprenas	mi estas	mi ne estas
I understand	*I don't understand*	*I am*	*I am not*

> **LANGUAGE TIP**
> The **as**-ending in Esperanto is used where English uses both the simple and continuous present: **mi trinkas** *I drink, I am drinking*.

3 PERSONAL PRONOUNS

Personal pronouns such as **mi** *I* and **vi** *you* all end with **i** in Esperanto. When they are used to denote the person carrying out the action of the verb, they're called *subject pronouns*:

mi   vi   li   ŝi   ĝi   ĝi

ni   vi   ili   ili   ili   ili   ili

> **LANGUAGE TIP**
>
> If you've learned other languages, you might be used to the concept of using different words for *you* to denote informality, familiarity, several people rather than one, or respect. Esperanto doesn't use *you* to make any of these distinctions. As with English, the word for *you* is always **vi**.

Practice 1

1 Using the example as a model, fill in the blanks.

Example: she + **esti** *to be*   ŝi estas   she is

a I + **trinki** *to drink*   _____   _____

b you + **ludi** *to play*   _____   _____

c li + **havi** *to have*   _____   _____

d she + _____ *to study*   _____ studas   _____

e _____ + **aĉeti** *to buy*   ni _____   _____

f they + _____ *to greet*   _____ salutas   _____

g it + **dormi** *to* _____   _____   _____ sleeps

h she + **nomiĝi** *to be called*   ŝi _____   _____ is called

2 **Many Esperanto words come from English, or languages from which English also took them. Identify the English meaning of the following verbs.**

    a akcepti

    b danci

    c havi

    d helpi

    e komenci

    f lerni

    g movi

    h preferi

    i rekomendi

    j respondi

    k studi

    l supozi

    m viziti

Vocabulary builder 2

 01.05 Look at the words and complete the missing English words. Then listen and try to imitate the pronunciation of the speakers.

PROFESIOJ *PROFESSIONS*

kuracisto	*doctor* (male)
kuracistino	*doctor* (female)
instruisto	*teacher* (male)
instruistino	*teacher* (female)
programisto	_____
programistino	_____
vendisto	*salesman*
vendistino	_____
kantisto	*singer* (male)
kantistino	*singer* (female)
sciencisto	*scientist* (male)
sciencistino	*scientist* (female)
laboristo	_____
laboristino	_____
verkisto	*writer* (male)
verkistino	*writer* (female)

LANGUAGE TIP

Notice how all of these professions end in **-isto** and the versions for women **-istino**? You can create new words in Esperanto by adding smaller words, called affixes, to another one. A **kantisto** *singer* is someone who **kantas** *sings*: **kant + ist + o**. Not all professions are built this way (a *waiter* is a **kelnero** and a *student* a **studento**) but this is a useful way of naming a profession from a verb.

Another useful affix is **-in-**, which makes something the female version. A **kantistino** is a *female singer*: **kant + ist + in + o**.

Using affixes is a common way of creating new words in Esperanto. There are 41 official affixes. The full list can be found at the end of the course.

Conversation 2

NEW EXPRESSIONS

 01.06 Look at and listen to the words and expressions that are used in the following conversation. Note their meanings.

Ĉu vi laboras?	*Do you work?*
mi instruas en lernejo	*I teach in a school*
Jes, sed ne kiel instruistino.	*Yes, but not as a (female) teacher.*
Mi laboras kiel kelnerino en restoracio.	*I work as a waitress at a restaurant.*
fakte	*in fact*
Kie vi studas?	*Where do you study?*
universitato	*a university*
Kial?	*Why?*
Ĉar …	*Because …*
Mi volas esti …	*I want to be …*
mi ne scias	*I don't know*
vere (Ĉu vere? Mi ne vere scias.)	*really, truly (Oh, really? I don't really know.)*
Ĉu vi ŝatas …?	*Do you like …?*
Mi vere ŝatas …	*I really like …*

 01.07 Sara and Roberto continue their conversation in their online chat group. They're now asking and answering questions. Listen carefully, replaying the dialogue several times if necessary.

1 What is Roberto's profession and what does Sara want to be?

Sara	Ĉu vi laboras, Roberto?
Roberto	Jes, Sara. Mi instruas en lernejo en Edinburgo. Mi estas instruisto. Kaj vi? Ĉu ankaŭ vi laboras?
Sara	Jes, sed ne kiel instruistino. Mi laboras kiel kelnerino en restoracio. Fakte, mi ankaŭ studas.
Roberto	Ĉu? Kie vi studas?
Sara	Mi studas en universitato en Londono.
Roberto	Kial vi studas en Londono?
Sara	Ĉar mi volas esti sciencistino.
Roberto	Kial vi volas esti sciencistino?
Sara	Nu … mi ne vere scias. Kaj vi? Ĉu vi ŝatas esti instruisto?
Roberto	Ho, jes, mi vere ŝatas instrui!

2 Match the English and the Esperanto.

a	I work as a waitress	**1**	Mi instruas en lernejo
b	Do you work too?	**2**	Kie vi studas?
c	Where do you study?	**3**	Ankaŭ mi studas
d	I teach in a school	**4**	Mi laboras kiel kelnerino
e	I really like teaching	**5**	Ĉu ankaŭ vi laboras?
f	I study too	**6**	Mi vere ŝatas instrui

 # Language discovery 2

1 What is the difference between Mi estas instruisto and Mi laboras kiel instruisto?

2 Can you guess the meaning of the following profession names?
Aktoro, futbalisto, studento, politikisto, advokato, muzikisto, profesoro

3 Sara needs to make a change to the word instruisto *teacher* **to show that she's a female. How does she do it?**

ASKING QUESTIONS

There are two ways of asking questions in Esperanto. The first is to use **ĉu**, a word which changes a statement into a question:

Ŝi nomiĝas Anna	Ĉu ŝi nomiĝas Anna?	Li lernas	Ĉu li lernas?
She is called Anna	*Is she called Anna?*	*He is learning*	*Is he learning?*

Ĉu can also be used on its own to mean *Oh?* or *Really?* In English the subject and verb are often inverted and repeated: **Mi estas instruisto** *I am a teacher* **Ĉu?** *Are you?* It can be combined with **vere** *truly, really* as a reinforcement: **Ĉu vere?** *Oh, really?*

The other way is to use a question word. Esperanto has nine of these:

Kio?	Kie?	Kiu?	Kiam?	Kial?	Kiel?	Kiom?	Kies?	Kia?
What?	*Where?*	*Who?*	*When?*	*Why?*	*How?*	*How much / many?*	*Whose?*	*What kind?*

These can be used at the front of a sentence to turn it into a question as with **ĉu**:

| **Ŝi estas Anna.** | *She is Anna.* |
| **Kiu ŝi estas?** | *Who is she?* |

Or you can use them as standalone questions:

| **Kial?** | *Why?* |
| **Kie?** | *Where?* |

Practice 2

1 Turn these sentences into ĉu-questions.

Example: Vi loĝas en Usono. *Ĉu vi loĝas en Usono?*

a Vi komprenas. _____

b Ŝi estas instruistino. _____

c Ŝi studas en Londono. _____

d Ili kantas bele *beautifully*. _____

e Li laboras multe *a lot*. _____

f Mi parolas bone *well*. _____

g Vi volas esti kantisto. _____

h Li laboras kiel kelnero. _____

2 Ask questions that provide the given answer.

a _____? Ne, mi loĝas en Parizo.

b _____? Jes, mi volas esti instruisto.

c _____? Ne, mi laboras kiel kelnerino.

d _____? Jes, li parolas bone kaj kantas bele.

e _____? Mi estas Davido.

f _____? Mi studas en Londono.

g _____? Ĝi estas libro (*a book*).

h _____? Ĉar mi volas esti sciencisto.

3 Match the questions with the appropriate answers.

> 1. Ne, li ne venas el Britio.
> 2. Jes, ŝi estas aktorino.
> 3. Jes, ĝi estas en Usono.
> 4. Jes, ŝi estas verkistino.
> 5. Ne, ĝi ne estas en Italio.
> 6. Ne, ĝi ne estas lando.

a Ĉu Parizo estas en Italio? _____

b Ĉu Meryl Streep estas aktorino? _____

c Ĉu Londono estas lando? _____

d Ĉu J.K. Rowling estas verkistino? _____

e Ĉu Kalifornio estas en Usono? _____

f Ĉu Barack Obama venas el Britio? _____

Reading

Here are some new learners talking in a group chat. Fill in the missing information.

Marko:

Saluton! Mi _____ (*am*) Marko el Italio!

Marko:

Mi _____ (*live*) en Romo.

Marko:

_____ (*who*) vi estas?

Isabel:

Saluton, Marko! Mi _____ (*am called*) Isabel.

Stefano:

Saluton, Marko kaj Isabel. Mi nomiĝas Stefano _____ (*and*) _____ (*also*) mi _____ (*come*) el Italio!

Writing

The people in the chat group seem nice, so you decide to present yourself.

You:	(Type 'Good evening, Marko, Isabel and Stefano! I'm called Laura.')
Marko:	Saluton, Laura!
Isabel:	Saluton!
You:	(Type 'I'm a beginner.')
Isabel:	Ankaŭ mi. De kie vi venas, Laura?
You:	(Type 'I study in London. I want to be an actress.')

Listening

 01.08 **Listen to the conversation between two people who are getting to know each other.**

1 **What are their names?**
2 **Where does the man come from?**
3 **Where does the woman live and what does she do there?**
4 **What is the man's profession?**

Speaking

Record yourself reading out loud the answers you gave in the Writing exercise.

Test yourself

1 Change the following sentences into negatives.
   a Mi loĝas en Usono.
   b Mi nomiĝas Alfredo.
   c Mi laboras kiel instruisto.
   d Mi volas esti sciencistino.
   e Mi ŝatas studi.

2 Change the following statements into questions.
   a Vi estas Mikaelo.
   b Ŝi loĝas en Germanio.
   c Ili nomiĝas sinjoro Smith kaj sinjorino Jones.
   d Parizo estas en Francio.
   e Li volas esti programisto.

3 Use the correct question word so that these questions make sense.
   a _____ vi loĝas?
   b _____ ŝi estas?
   c _____ li nomiĝas?
   d _____ estas tio?
   e _____ vi volas esti futbalisto kaj ne instruisto?

Pluvegas!
It's pouring down!

In this unit, you will learn how to:
▶ *ask people how they're feeling and express how you're feeling.*
▶ *use the prefix* **mal-** *to create logical opposites.*
▶ *use the suffixes* **-eg-** *and* **-et-** *for word building.*
▶ *speak about the weather.*

CEFR: (A1) *Can ask how people are and react to news.* **(A1)** *Can recognize familiar words and basic phrases concerning self, family and concrete surroundings when people speak slowly and clearly.*

 ## Esprimoj en Esperanto *Expressions in Esperanto*

Like all living languages, Esperanto contains idioms which are everyday features. When the time comes, you'll certainly need to know how to ask for the **necesejo** (*toilet*), literally 'place for the necessary'. If you don't know the word and have to ask in English, somebody might say that you're a **krokodilo** (*crocodile*), Esperanto shorthand for speaking one's native language instead of Esperanto. If you try to mitigate that by using somebody else's language … well, you're no longer a **krokodilo** but an **aligatoro** (*alligator*), a person using another language instead of Esperanto. Fingers crossed that somebody calling you that doesn't make you **kabei** (*leave Esperanto*), a word which came into existence after Kazimierz Bein, a prolific early adopter of Esperanto who was known as Kabe (from the first two letters of his first and last names), suddenly gave it up without telling anybody or giving any reasons. Perhaps he didn't think Esperanto was **mojosa** (*cool*) anymore.

 If **krokodili** is the verb for when a person speaks their own language in an Esperanto environment, what is the verb for when a British Esperanto speaker uses French rather than Esperanto?

> **CULTURE TIP**
>
> There is a lot of software available for entering Esperanto's accented characters but if you are not able to access this to add accents, the most popular convention is to follow the letter with **x**, i.e. **gxis** for **ĝis**.

Vocabulary builder 1

 02.01 Look at the words and phrases and complete the missing English words and expressions. Then listen and try to imitate the pronunciation of the speakers.

BONFARTO *WELL-BEING*

farti	*to fare, be (health)*
mi fartas bone / bone fartas	*I'm well / faring well / keeping well*
tre bone / ege bone / bonege	*very well, great*
bedaŭri	*to regret, be sorry*
sana	*healthy*
malsana	*unwell*
malsani	*to be _____*
laca	*tired*
dormi	*to _____*
pli bone	*better (lit. more well)*
feliĉa	*happy*
ĝoji	*to be glad*

> **LANGUAGE TIP**
>
> The adverb **ege** by itself means the same as **tre** *very*. However, it can attach itself to **bone** *well*, producing **bonege** *very well*. Other adjectives and even verbs can also be intensified by including **-eg-**, which you'll meet in more detail later.

Conversation 1

NEW EXPRESSIONS

 02.02 Look at and listen to the words and expressions that are used in the following conversation. Note their meanings.

Kio estas la problemo?	*What is the problem?*
Mi estas ege malsana.	*I am very unwell.*
Mi bedaŭras, ke vi …	*I am sorry that you …*
kvankam mi estas laca	*although / even though I'm tired*
Mi nur dormetas (dorm-et-as)	*I only sleep a little*
tro	*too much, too*
Mi nek … nek … hodiaŭ	*I neither … nor … today*
Ho ve!	*Oh dear! / Alas!*
malpli	*less*
Gratulon!	*Congratulations!*

02.03 *Sara and her new friends are back online and asking each other how they're feeling.*

1   One of them says he is tired. Why?

Sara	Saluton! Kiel vi fartas?
Roberto	Saluton, Sara! Mi fartas bone, dankon. Kaj vi?
Sara	Bonege, dankon.
Mijoŝi	Mi ne fartas tre bone, Sara. Fakte mi malbone fartas.
Sara	Ĉu? Mi bedaŭras. Kial? Kio estas la problemo?
Mijoŝi	Mi estas ege malsana. Malsanega.
Roberto	Ho ve, mi bedaŭras, ke vi malsanas.
Anna	Saluton! Mi bone fartas, dankon, kvankam mi estas laca.
Roberto	Kial vi lacas, Anna? Ĉu vi ne bone dormas?
Anna	Mi ne vere dormas, nur dormetas, ĉar mi tro laboras.
Emiljo	Ankaŭ mi lacegas, ĉar mi tro studas. Fakte mi studegas.
Sara	Mi estas feliĉa, ĉar mi nek studas nek laboras hodiaŭ.
The next day:	
Sara	Saluton, Mijoŝi! Ĉu vi pli bone fartas, hodiaŭ?
Mijoŝi	Ne, Sara. Mi fartas malbonege. Mi estas tre malfeliĉa, ĉar mi estas malsana.
Sara	Ho ve, Mijoŝi. Mi bedaŭregas. Kaj vi, Anna? Ĉu vi lacas?
Anna	Mi nur lacetas hodiaŭ, ĉar mi malpli laboras.
Sara	Ho, gratulon! Mi ĝojas!

2   Match the English and the Esperanto.

a   I'm really sick / unwell

b   How are you doing?

c   Are you doing better?

d   I am extremely unhappy

e   Congratulations!

f   I'm sorry (I regret)

g   I'm neither studying nor working today

h   Why are you tired?

i   I'm working less

j   Oh dear

k   I'm doing extremely badly

l   Even though I'm tired

1   Mi bedaŭras

2   Ĉu vi pli bone fartas?

3   Mi fartas malbonege

4   Kiel vi fartas?

5   Kial vi lacas?

6   Kvankam mi lacas

7   Mi malpli laboras

8   Gratulon!

9   Mi nek studas nek laboras hodiaŭ

10   Ho ve

11   Mi estas ege malsana

12   Mi estas treege malfeliĉa

3   Based on Conversation 1, decide whether these statements are vera (*true*) or malvera (*false*).

a   Mijoŝi fartas tre bone.

b   Anna estas laca.

c   Sara studas hodiaŭ.

d   Emiljo ne estas studento.

4 02.04 **Now listen to the conversation again line by line and repeat.**

> **LANGUAGE TIP**
>
> **Mi fartas bone** and **mi bone fartas** mean the same thing. The word order doesn't make any difference. You can choose to use whichever you prefer.

💡 Language discovery 1

1 **Find the Esperanto for** *happy, sad, I am glad, I'm doing badly* **in the conversation.**

2 **Mijoŝi expresses ege malsana in one word. Similarly, Emiljo expresses that he is** *studying really hard* **in a single word. What words do they use?**

3 **How are the words** *more* **and** *less* **expressed in the dialogue?**

1 WORD ENDINGS

The key to understanding Esperanto is to look at the word endings. As you have seen with verbs, the endings tell you what the grammatical role of a word is:

Ending	-i	-as
Word type	infinitive	present tense
Example	**esti** *to be*	**mi estas** *I am*

The same is true for other grammatical roles too:

Ending	-o	-a	-e
Word type	noun	adjective	adverb

Adjectives are used to describe nouns. Adverbs are used to describe a verb. Adverbs in English usually end *-ly*.

bela kanto	**La kanto estas bela**	**Ŝi kantas bele**
a beautiful song	*The song is beautiful*	*She sings beautifully*

Adjectives may be placed before or after the noun. In practice, people tend to place them before as with English. It is not the word order which determines the meaning but the endings on the words:

bela virino	**virino bela**	**virina belo**	**belo virina**
a beautiful woman		*female beauty*	

Adverbs, as you have seen, can likewise be placed before or after the verb which they modify.

This system in Esperanto means that you can learn a new word and use it however you need to without also having to learn related words:

Ending	-i	-as	-o	-a	-e
Word type	infinitive	present tense	noun	adjective	adverb
Example	**vidi** *to see*	**vidas** *see*	**vido** *sight, vision*	**vida** *visual*	**vide** *visually*

2 BUILDING NEW WORDS WITH AFFIXES

Using affixes such as **-ist-** and **-in-** (introduced in Unit 1) to create new words is a central concept in Esperanto. Some of the affixes go at the front of the word they modify. These are called prefixes. Others, like **-ist-** and **-in**, are attached after the word and are called suffixes.

Forming opposites with mal-

The prefix **mal-** is extremely useful in Esperanto. It makes the word that it modifies into its logical opposite: **bona** *good*, **malbona** *bad*; **juna** *young* **maljuna** *old*; **dekstra** *right*, **maldekstra** *left*; **helpi** *to help*, **malhelpi** *to hinder*; **lumo** *light*, **mallumo** *dark*; **pli** *more*, **malpli** *less*. And it can be used as a word in its own right by adding Esperanto's endings: **la malo** *the opposite*; **male** *conversely, on the contrary*.

Intensifying and softening with -eg- and -et-

The suffix **-eg-** makes something larger, and the suffix **-et-** softens or reduces it. From **bela** *beautiful* you can get **belega** *extremely beautiful* and **beleta** *cute*. You can use it in verbs too: **mi laboregas** *I'm working very hard* gives more detail than the basic **mi laboras** *I'm working*, and **mi studetas** *I'm doing a bit of studying* gives the idea of not being quite so engaged as **mi studas** *I'm studying* does.

Practice 1

1 **Add either the a-ending for adjectives or the e-ending for adverbs in the following sentences:**

   a Ŝi estas malsan_____.
   b Mi studas kaj laboras tro mult_____.
   c Mi estas lac_____, ĉar mi ne bon_____ dormas.
   d Mia instruisto estas maljun_____, sed li instruas tre bon_____.
   e La malsan_____ studento ne fartas bon_____.
   f Mi dancas bon_____, sed ne estas bon_____ kantisto.
   g Ŝi estas feliĉ_____, ĉar hodiaŭ ŝi bon_____ fartas.

2 **Select the correct Esperanto word to reflect the English word:**

   Example: to dance   danco, <u>danci</u>, danca
   a a song   kanto, kanti, kante
   b to thank   danki, danko, danke
   c visual   vidi, vido, vida
   d work (noun)   laboro, labora, labore
   e (I am) learning   lerna, lernas, lerni
   f to cost   koste, kosti, kosto
   g beautifully   bela, belas, bele
   h cool (adjective)   mojoso, mojosa, mojosi
   i (I am) called   nomiĝas, nomi, nome
   j well   bona, bone, bono

3 On the left side is an Esperanto word with its English translation. Change the endings as required to create Esperanto words for the English words listed on the right.

Example: nacio *nation*   national **nacia**

a labori *to work*   work (noun) _____
b helpi *to help*   help (noun) _____
c helpi   helpful _____
d bela *beautiful*   beautifully _____
e problemo *problem*   problematic _____
f mano *hand*   manual _____
g fini *to finish*   end (noun) _____
h fini   final _____
i fakte *in fact*   a fact _____

4 Use **mal-**, **-eg-** and **-et-** to change the meanings as required, as in the example.

Example: ŝi laboras (*working really hard*)   ŝi laboregas

problemo (*a huge problem*)   problemego

a li estas feliĉa (*unhappy*)   _____
b mi fartas bone (*great, very well*)   _____
c la kato (*cat*) dormas (*napping*)   _____
d mi komprenas (*understand a little*)   _____
e granda (*small*)   _____
f granda (*massive*)   _____
g bona (*extremely bad*)   _____
h li nur manĝas (*nibbles*)   _____
i mi lacas (*exhausted*)   _____

Vocabulary builder 2

 02.05 **Look at the words. Then listen and try to imitate the pronunciation of the speakers.**

VETERO *WEATHER*

pluvas	*it's raining / it rains*
neĝas	*it's snowing / it snows*
la suno brilas	*it's sunny / the sun shines*
estas varme/varmege/malvarme	*it's hot / really hot / cold*
estas sufiĉe varme	*it's reasonably warm / warm enough*
forta vento blovas	*a strong wind is blowing*
tondro	*thunder*
fulmo	*lightning*
ŝtormo	*a storm*
vetero	*weather*

> **LANGUAGE TIP**
>
> Don't worry about whether **varma** means *warm* or *hot* and how to decide what temperature something like **malvarma** corresponds to. Things are hot, warm, cold, etc. only in relation to typical values. **Malvarma teo** *cold tea* could well be hotter than **varma biero** *warm beer*, and a **varmega tago** *really hot day* in **Britio** *the UK* could still be considered cold by somebody from **Afriko** *Africa*.

Conversation 2

NEW EXPRESSIONS

 02.06 Look at and listen to the words and expressions that are used in the following conversation. Note their meanings.

denove	*again*
kiel kutime	*as usual*
Nu, ne ĉiam.	*Well, not always.*
Somero en Skotlando okazas …	*Summer in Scotland happens …*
tiam	*then*
Kia estas la vetero en Japanio?	*What is the weather like in Japan?*
Ĝuste!	*Correct!*
Kutime en Brazilo …	*Usually in Brazil …*
Kiel en aŭtuno …	*Like in autumn …*

 02.07 *The group's conversation has moved on and they're discussing what the weather is like in their own countries.*

1   In what seasons does Roberto joke that Scotland usually has downpours?

Roberto	Ho ve. Pluvas denove. Kiel kutime.
Mijoŝi	Ĉu ĉiam pluvas en Skotlando, Roberto?
Roberto	Nu, ne ĉiam. Nur en januaro, februaro, marto, aprilo, majo, septembro, oktobro, novembro kaj decembro!
Mijoŝi	Ha! Somero en Skotlando okazas en junio, julio kaj aŭgusto, do. Tiam la suno brilas, ĉu ne?
Roberto	Nu, briletas.
Sara	Kia estas la vetero en Japanio, Mijoŝi? Ĉu estas varme hodiaŭ?
Mijoŝi	Estas sufiĉe varme, jes.
Anna	En Italio estas varmege. La suno brilas, sed ankaŭ tondras kaj fulmas.
Emiljo	Ho, ŝtormas, ĉu ne?
Anna	Ĝuste.
Emiljo	Kutime en Brazilo la suno brilegas. Sed nun pluvegas.
Roberto	Kiel en aŭtuno, vintro kaj printempo en Skotlando!

2 The names of all 12 months and all four seasons are mentioned in the conversation. List them.

Monatoj: January _____ February _____ March _____
April _____ May _____ June _____
July _____ August _____ September _____
October _____ November _____ December _____

Sezonoj: spring _____ summer _____ autumn _____
winter _____

> **LANGUAGE TIP**
> The names of the days and seasons are normally written without a capital letter. Some Esperanto dictionaries list the names of months with capital letters, but most writers and publications prefer to leave them in lower case.

Language discovery 2

1 **What is the difference between pluvas and pluvegas? How about brilas and briletas?**

2 **Mijoŝi makes a statement into a question by adding an equivalent to English's *isn't it?* to the end. How did he manage to do this?**

3 **English lacks verbs to directly express that *there was thunder and lightning*. Anna takes the words tondro *thunder* and fulmo *lightning* and gives the idea very easily without any additional words. How does she accomplish this?**

1 IMPERSONAL VERBS

Verbs in English must have a subject. This is not the case in Esperanto, which features verbs which do not take a subject, called *impersonal verbs*. This is often the case with verbs associated with the weather. Compare the following sentences with their English translations:

Pluvas	Frostas	Neĝas	Hajlas
It's raining	*It's freezing*	*It's snowing*	*It's hailing*

Because English requires a subject before a verb, it often uses a pronoun *it* which doesn't actually correspond to any noun. Esperanto uses a verb without a subject in those situations.

> **LANGUAGE TIP**
> A useful impersonal verb to know is found in the construction **temi pri** *to be about*: **temas pri Britio** *it's about Britain*. If you wanted to ask *what's it about?*, you would use the question word **kio**: **pri kio temas?**

2 ADDITIONAL SCOPE OF ADVERBS

Esperanto's **a**-ending for adjectives can be used only if there is a subject present or implied. If there isn't one then you have to use the **e**-ending. This applies when there's nothing at all, as in the impersonal verbs you've learned about, or when a verb is acting as though it's a subject. **Estas varme** *it's warm* not '**estas varma**'; **promeni kun leono estas danĝere** *walking with a lion is dangerous / it's dangerous to walk with a lion*, not '**promeni kun leono estas danĝera**'; **bone!** *good!* not '**bona!**'.

> **LANGUAGE TIP**
>
> Using an adverb where in English an adjective would be used can be a hard habit to pick up. Start saying **bone!** *good!* and **bonege!** *great!* as one-word responses to get used to it.

Practice 2

1 **Answer these questions by rewriting them.**

   Example: Ĉu pluvas nun? *Jes, pluvas.*
   a Ĉu estas malvarme en Hispanio?_____
   b Ĉu la suno estas varma?_____
   c Ĉu pluvas en la dezerto?_____
   d Ĉu estas varmege en la dezerto?_____
   e Ĉu neĝas en Brazilo?_____
   f Ĉu la suno brilas en vintro en Skotlando?_____

2 **Choose whether to add the a-ending or the e-ending.**
   a Estas malvarm_____.
   b Boneg_____! Mi ĝojas, ke vi konsentas!
   c Bon_____ instruisto instruas bon_____.
   d Ho, ĉu vi venas el Francio? Mojos_____! Francio estas mojos_____ lando!
   e Ĉu vi scias, ke paroli en Esperanto estas amuz_____ (*fun*)?
   f Loĝi en Italio estas boneg _____!

> **LANGUAGE TIP**
>
> Esperanto's affixes give you enormous scope to expand your vocabulary and add nuances. **Pluvegas** has been used as an equivalent to *raining cats and dogs, bucketing it down* and so on. What if you wanted to say you only spoke a smattering of Esperanto? Why not **paroleti**? It doesn't exist in the dictionary, but you would be understood perfectly, even if the person you're speaking to had never heard it before.

Reading

Look at the information in the text message about the weather and answer the questions.

Estas malvarmega tago en Skotlando. Neĝas en la nordo, kaj en la sudo fulmas kaj tondras. Ankaŭ en la nordo de Anglio la vetero estas malbona, ĉar pluvas. En la sudo de Anglio estas varme. La suno brilas. Sed en Kimrio la vetero ne estas bona. Estas ventego.

1 Does the speaker think the weather in Scotland is a little bit cold, fairly cold, or very cold?

2 Does the speaker say that it's warm everywhere in England?

3 Does the speaker like the weather in Wales?

Writing

Write a text message to a friend about the weather in the United Kingdom, using the map below as a guide.

Listening

 02.08 Listen to Ramona from Romania speaking with Ann from England about what the weather is like in her country and answer the following questions.

1   In what months is winter?
2   Does it snow in winter in Romania?
3   What's the weather like in April?
4   How does Ramona feel in summer?

Listening and speaking

 02.09 Now Ramona wants to know about the weather in England, so she asks Ann some questions in return. During the gaps in the recording, say Ann's responses out loud.

Ramona:	Kia estas la vintro en Britio? Ĉu neĝas?
You:	(Say 'No, it doesn't snow. It's cold but it doesn't snow. It usually rains.')
Ramona:	Ĉu pluvas en printempo?
You:	(Say 'Yes, in April. There are showers.') (Use **-et-**.)

Ramona:	Ĉu somero en Britio estas varma?
You:	(Say 'Yes, it's warm. It's not extremely hot but it's warm. Normally it's sunny. I am happy in summer.')
Ramona:	Ankaŭ mi estas feliĉa en somero. Tamen ne tro en aŭtuno.
You:	(Say 'I am also happy in autumn. It's a beautiful season.')

Test yourself

1 Form opposites to the following words. What do the words you've created mean?

  a bona

  b juna

  c feliĉa

  d bela

  e mojosa

2 Use suffixes to create new weather words which would mean the following:

  a heavy snow

  b a shower

  c a gale

3 Fill in the crossword with the days of the week and the seasons. Note that the **o**-endings have been removed, so **lundo** is **lund**, for example.

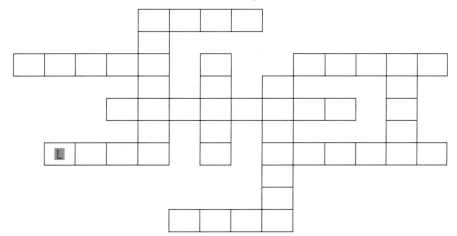

Paroli kun amiko
Speaking with a friend

In this unit, you will learn how to:

▶ *say what you are doing using the present tense.*
▶ *string verbs in a sequence to create longer sentences.*
▶ *talk about your family.*
▶ *state your opinions using expressions like I think and I believe.*

CEFR: (A1) *Can ask and answer questions about people they know.* **(A1)** *Can recognize familiar words and basic phrases concerning self and family.* **(A1)** *Can produce simple, mainly isolated phrases and sentences to describe where they live and people they know.*

⭐ Esperantaj familioj *Esperanto families*

It's **eble** (*perhaps / maybe*) inevitable that **junuloj** (*young people*) from **malsamaj landoj** (*different countries*) meet at Esperanto events and fall in love. It has been known for one to move to live with the other, and you may soon have an **edzo** (*husband*), an **edzino** (*wife*), and then **infanoj** (*children*). If the **gepatroj** (*parents*) had Esperanto as their **komuna lingvo** (*common language*), then it may well remain the **hejma lingvo** (*domestic language*) of the **familianoj** (*family members*).

It's in this environment that **denaskaj Esperanto-parolantoj** (*native Esperanto speakers*) **aperas** (*appear*). The children aren't **unulingvanoj** (*monolingual people*) but often **senprobleme** (*without a problem*) speak **pluraj lingvoj** (*several languages*): **tiu** (*that*) of their **patro** (*father*) with him, of their **patrino** (*mother*) with her, and Esperanto when the **gepatroj** (*parents*) and **gefiloj** (*sons and daughters*) are **kune** (*together*). And just like in other cultures, they have affectionate names for each other, referring to their **paĉjo** (*dad / daddy*), **panjo** (*mum / mummy*) and other **geamikoj** (*friends*) and **parencoj** (*relatives*) by shortened names, **ĝuste kiel ni faras** (*just as we do*).

 What do you notice about Esperanto's **a**-ending when it is used with a plural noun, such as in *several languages* and *different countries?* Can you spot how the word for *parents* is formed from *father?* If so, what do you think the word for *son* might be?

Vocabulary builder 1

 03.01 Look at the words and phrases and complete the missing English words and expressions. Then listen and try to imitate the pronunciation of the speakers.

ĈIUTAGAJ AGADOJ *EVERYDAY ACTIVITIES*

babili	*to chat*
paroli	*to speak*
legi	*to read*
kanti	*to sing*
danci	_____
manĝi	*to eat*
ludi	*to play*
viziti	_____
pensi	*to think*
fari	*to do, to make*
iri al	*to go to*
foriri / iri for	*to leave / go away*

> **LANGUAGE TIP**
>
> The preposition **al** corresponds to English's *to* with movement: **iri al la restoracio** *to go to the restaurant*. It is used in other cases too, including in **mi donas X al vi** *I give you X*, where it introduces the person or thing receiving. The particle **for** means *away* and can be combined with verbs as in **foriri** *to go away*, **foresti** *to be absent*.

Conversation 1

NEW EXPRESSIONS

 03.02 Look at and listen to the words and expressions that are used in the following conversation. Note their meanings.

Kion vi volas fari?	*What do you want to do?*
kun mi	*with me*
plani	*to plan*
devi	*must, to have to*
Jam estas vespero ĉi tie.	*It's already evening here.*
aŭ eble	*or maybe*
Mi ne devas labori	*I don't have to work*
Ĉu hodiaŭ vi intencas danci?	*Do you intend to dance today?*
do	*so*
poste	*later, afterwards*
frue	*early*
morgaŭ	*tomorrow*
Mi esperas resti hejme	*I hope to stay at home*
same por mi	*same for me*

Sara wants to practise her Esperanto, so she decides to start a video chat with Lan, a Vietnamese Esperanto speaker.

1 What does Lan want to do?

Sara	Saluton, Lan! Ĉu vi volas babili kun mi nun?
Lan	Saluton, Sara! Jes, mi ĉiam ŝatas paroli kun vi.
Sara	Bone! Kion vi planas fari hodiaŭ? Ĉu vi devas labori?
Lan	Ho ne, mi ne devas labori. Jam estas vespero ĉi tie. Mi ne laboras en la vespero. Mi nur legas, aŭ eble iras danci vespere.
Sara	Ĉu hodiaŭ vi intencas danci, Lan?
Lan	Ne, mi jam estas tro laca hodiaŭ. Mi esperas resti hejme kaj kanti kun mia amikino. Ŝi volas viziti min, kaj mi ŝategas kanti! Ĉu ankaŭ vi ŝatas kanti?.
Sara	Mi ŝatas kanti, sed ne bone kantas.
Lan	Do, kion vi faras hodiaŭ?
Sara	Nun mi studas. Mi devas iri al mia familia hejmo poste. Mi planas manĝi kun mia familio.
Lan	Ho, bone! Kaj kion vi pensas fari en la vespero?
Sara	Mi ne scias. Eble iri al la teatro. Tamen mi volas dormi frue. Mi devas labori morgaŭ.
Lan	Same por mi. Nu, mi devas foriri nun. Ĝis!
Sara	Ĝis!

2 Match the English and the Esperanto.

a	I don't know	**1**	Same por mi
b	What do you hope to do afterwards?	**2**	Eble iri al la teatro
c	I don't sing well	**3**	Mi jam estas tro laca hodiaŭ
d	It's already evening here.	**4**	Kion vi pensas fari en la vespero?
e	It's the same for me	**5**	Mi ĉiam ŝatas paroli kun vi
f	I have to go (away) now	**6**	Kion vi esperas fari poste?
g	What are you thinking about doing in the evening?	**7**	Mi ne scias
h	Do you have to work?	**8**	Kio estas tio?
i	Maybe go to the theatre	**9**	Jam estas vespero ĉi tie
j	I always like to speak with you	**10**	Mi ne bone kantas
k	What is that?	**11**	Ĉu vi devas labori?
l	I am already too tired today	**12**	Mi devas foriri nun

> **LANGUAGE TIP**
>
> In the conversation you met **mi ne scias** *I don't know*. Esperanto has two words for *to know*: **scii** is used to refer to knowledge, information which you have in your head. The other, **koni**, is when there's some degree of acquaintance: **vi scias fakton** *you know a fact* and **konas homon** *know a person*.

3 **Based on Conversation 1, decide whether these statements are vera (*true*) or malvera (*false*).**

   a Sara estas bona kantistino.

   b La familio de Sara estas ĉi tie.

   c Lan devas labori morgaŭ.

   d Lan ege ŝatas kanti.

> **LANGUAGE TIP**
>
> **Se** *if* cannot be used in constructions like *I don't know if* … Instead, use **ĉu**: **mi ne scias, ĉu vi volas manĝi kukon** *I don't know if / whether you want to eat cake*. A good rule of thumb is to ask yourself whether English could take *whether* as well as *if*. If it could, then you need to use **ĉu**. In the dialogue, Lan could have said **mi ne scias, ĉu iri al la teatro** *I don't know whether to go to the theatre*.

 4 03.04 **Now listen to the conversation again line by line and repeat.**

 # Language discovery 1

1 **Find the words for *evening, today, to sing, to eat, to sleep* and *to go to the theatre* in the conversation.**

2 **Select the words which have been modified with suffixes in the conversation and guess their English translation.**

3 **How do you say *I've got to go now* in Esperanto?**

1 PLACING VERBS TOGETHER

In Unit 1 you saw **Ĉu vi ŝatas esti instruisto?** This formula of **-as** + **-i** is very common in Esperanto. It occurs where two verbs follow each other, as in *I want to play* where *I want* is followed by a second verb *to play*. Switch from *I* to *he* and you'll see what's happening: *he wants to play*. The first verb is in the present tense and the second is the infinitive.

In Esperanto we would write this as **li volas ludi**, the first verb **voli** getting the **as**-ending and any subsequent ones staying as **-i**. This is the rule whenever you have more than one verb, no matter whether you are talking about **mi**, **li** or anyone else.

2 SAYING WHAT YOU THINK

To change a statement into a thought or opinion, start it with a form of **pensi** *to think*, **kredi** *to believe* or **opinii** *to think, have an opinion*:

La viro estas inteligenta	Mi pensas, ke la viro estas inteligenta	Ŝi ŝatas danci	Mi kredas, ke ŝi ŝatas danci
The man is intelligent	*I think that the man is intelligent*	*She likes to dance*	*I believe she likes to dance*

Whereas in English the relative pronoun *that* is optional, **ke** must always be used in Esperanto.

To state your opinion you can also use the expression **laŭ mi** *according to me, in my opinion*:

Laŭ mi tio estas tre bona ideo *In my opinion that is a very good idea*

Practice 1

1 **Convert the following statements into opinions. Then add words like *can* and *must* to make longer sentences.**

   Example: Ŝi amas lin – use **kredi** to get *I think she loves him.*   Mi kredas, ke ŝi amas lin.

   Mi manĝas la kukon – use **devi** to get *I must eat the cake.*   Mi devas manĝi la kukon.

   a Mi lernas Esperanton – use **ŝati** to get *I like learning Esperanto.*
   b Lerni Esperanton estas amuze – use **kredi** to get *I think learning Esperanto is fun.*
   c La viro ŝatas bicikli – use **pensi** to get *I think that the man likes to ride a bike.*
   d Mi sendas leteron al mia patrino – use **devi** to get *I have to send a letter to my mother.*
   e Li ne volas vojaĝi al Britio – use **laŭ** to get *In my opinion, he doesn't want to travel to the United Kingdom.*
   f Vi ne volas helpi – use **scii** to get *I know that you don't want to help.*
   g Mi ne movas la tablon – use **povi** to get *I can't move the table.*
   h Mi komencas studi – use **devi** to get *I have to start studying.*
   i Li volas uzi la forkon por manĝi la spagetojn – use **pensi** to get *I think that he wants to use a fork to eat the spaghetti.*

2 **Fill in the blanks, adding -as or -i.**

   a Mi vol_____ ir_____ al la teatro.
   b Ŝi kred_____, ke mi vol_____ est_____ instruisto.
   c Kion vi vol_____ far_____ poste?
   d Anna dev_____ stud_____ morgaŭ.
   e Roberto loĝ_____ en Skotlando, sed li vol_____ loĝ_____ en Francio.
   f Mijoŝi pensas, ke lern_____ Esperanton estas malfacile (*difficult*)
   g Davido kant_____, danc_____ kaj manĝ_____ tre bone.
   h Ili dev_____ iri al la universitato por stud_____ kaj poste labor_____.

Vocabulary builder 2

 03.05 Look at the words and complete the missing words that follow the same patterns. Then listen and try to imitate the pronunciation of the speakers.

FAMILIANOJ *FAMILY MEMBERS*

patro / patrino / gepatroj	*father / mother / parents*
frato / fratino / gefratoj	*brother / _____ / siblings*
filo / _____ / gefiloj	*son / daughter / children*
avo / avino / geavoj	*grandfather / grandmother / grandparents*
onklo / _____ / _____	*uncle / aunt / uncles and aunts*
_____ / kuzino / gekuzoj	*cousin / _____ / cousins*
nevo / nevino / genevoj	*nephew / niece / nephews and nieces*
nepo / nepino / genepoj	*grandson / granddaughter / _____*
bopatro / bopatrino / bogepatroj	*father-in-law / mother-in-law / parents-in-law*
edzo / edzino / _____	*husband / wife / spouses*
parenco	*relative*
familio	*family*
familiano	*family member*
infano	*child*
knabo / knabino / _____	*boy / girl / boys and girls*
paĉjo / panjo	*dad / mum*
avĉjo / avinjo	*grandad / grandma*

> **LANGUAGE TIP**
>
> Note how often **-in-** is used to create feminine forms, and that the plural in Esperanto is formed by adding **-j** to the usual **o**-ending on nouns: **homo** *a person* becomes **homoj** *people*. Although using **-in-** for females has become optional for professions, it remains compulsory for a small set of words, including female family members.

Conversation 2

NEW EXPRESSIONS

 03.06 Look at and listen to the words and expressions that are used in the following conversation. Note their meanings.

por li ne eblas	*for him it is not possible* (**ebli** = *be possible*)
kune (**kun** *with* + **-e**)	*together*
mia bofratino devas resti hejme	*my sister-in-law has to stay at home*
unu	*one*
mi ne certas	*I am not certain / sure*
Mi kredas, ke …	*I believe that …*
Jen bona ideo!	*That's a good idea!*
malfacila	*difficult*
ambaŭ	*both*

fari ambaŭ ne estas eble	*it's not possible to do both*
unu post la alia	*one after the other*
solvo	*solution*

 03.07 *Sara and Lan catch each other again a day later and discuss their families.*

1 What does Lan suggest Sara should do?

Lan	Saluton denove, Sara! Kiel fartas via familio?
Sara	Bone, dankon. Mia fratino estas kun mia patrino. Ili volas iri kune al restoracio por manĝi kune. Mi esperas iri kun ili.
Lan	Ĉu ankaŭ via frato intencas iri kun vi?
Sara	Ne, por li ne eblas veni hodiaŭ, ĉar li devas labori. Kaj lia edzino ne planas manĝi kun ni, ĉar ŝi devas resti hejme kun la infanoj. Kaj vi, Lan: kion vi pensas fari kun via familio?
Lan	Nu, kiel via bofratino, ankaŭ mi devas resti hejme. Mia avino vizitas, kaj ŝi nun estas laca. Avĉjo parolas kun paĉjo, do mi esperas legi kaj baldaŭ dormi. Mi volas iri al la biblioteko kun mia kuzino morgaŭ.
Sara	Kion faras via patrino?
Lan	Ŝi estas kun la genepoj: unu knabo kaj unu knabino. Mi ne certas, sed mi kredas, ke ili intencas iri al la parko por ludi.
Sara	Ho, jen bona ideo! Mi tre ŝatas iri al la parko! Ho, fakte ne … nun mi devas decidi: ĉu iri al la restoracio kun mia patrino, aŭ ĉu iri al la parko.
Lan	Jen malfacila decido, ĉu ne? Kion vi preferas fari?
Sara	Fari ambaŭ! Sed fari ambaŭ ne estas eble, ĉu ne?
Lan	Kial ne? Eblas fari unu post la alia. Jen la solvo!

> **LANGUAGE TIP**
>
> The suffix **-ebl-** works like its lookalike in English, expressing
> that something could be done: **komprenebla** *understandable*,
> **kompreneble** *understandably, of course.*

2 Match the English and the Esperanto.

a What does your mother do?	**1** Jen la solvo
b I want to go tomorrow	**2** Por li ne eblas
c There's the answer	**3** Ankaŭ ni devas resti hejme
d It's not possible for him	**4** Kiel fartas via familio?
e How is your family?	**5** Kion faras via patrino?
f We have to stay home too	**6** Mi volas iri morgaŭ

🔆 Language discovery 2

1 **What is the difference between kuzo and kuzino?**

2 **Can you guess the meaning of praavo from this description?**
Mia praavo estas la patro de mia avo.

3 **How does Sara say doing both isn't possible, is it? / it's not possible to do both, is it?**

1 Creating family words with affixes

Affixes make it very easy to create family words without having to learn lots of vocabulary. **Ge-** is a common prefix which means *including both sexes*: **gepatroj** *parents (father and mother)*, **geknaboj** *boys and girls*, **gefratoj** *siblings*. **Bo-** establishes that it's a relation via marriage; **patro** is *a father* but **bopatro** is *a father-in-law*.

You've also seen the suffix **-an-** used in **familiano** *a family member*. It denotes that somebody is a member of something, an adherent of an idea or doctrine, or a resident of a place: **klubano** *member of a club*, **islamano** *Muslim*, **vilaĝano** *villager*.

2 POSSESSIVE PRONOUNS

Possessive pronouns like **mia** *my* and **lia** *his* behave as adjectives in Esperanto, since their role is to describe a noun. Like all adjectives in Esperanto, they take the **a**-ending, which is applied to the subject pronouns to give:

mia   via   lia   ŝia   ĝia   ĝia

nia   via   ilia   ilia   ilia   ilia   ilia

> **LANGUAGE TIP**
>
> To show possession where English uses its *apostrophe-s* construction use **de** in Esperanto: **la patrino de Anna** *Anna's mother*, literally *the mother of Anna*.

Practice 2

1 Here is Paŭlo's family tree. Complete these sentences about Paŭlo's family using the items in the list. Each item is used once, except for one, which is used in two responses.

Example: La _____ de Olivia estas Samĉjo. _____ _____ estas Bo. La frato de Olivia estas Samĉjo. Lia kuzo estas Bo.

La familio de Paŭlo

Karlo Sofia

Andreo Sali Paŭlo Maria

Olivia Samĉjo Lunjo Bo Anjo

> patro onklino gepatroj
> nevino fratino onklo
> geavoj edzino gefiloj
> bogepatroj frato filo kuzino
> geedzoj edzo bofratoj filino

a Olivia estas la _____ de Samĉjo kaj la _____ de Lunjo.

b La _____ de Anjo nomiĝas Karlo kaj Sofia.

c Andreo kaj Paŭlo estas _____. Paŭlo estas la _____ de Sali. Ŝia_____ nomiĝas Andreo.

d La _____ de Sofia estas Sali. Ŝia_____ nomiĝas Lunjo.

e Paŭlo estas la _____ de Samĉjo, la _____ de Bo, kaj la _____ de Karlo.

f Maria estas la _____ de Paŭlo. Ili estas _____. Iliaj_____ estas Lunja, Bo kaj Anjo.

g La _____ de Olivia nomiĝas Maria.

h La _____ de Lunjo nomiĝas Karlo kaj Sofia. Ili estas la _____ de Sali kaj Paŭlo kaj la _____ de Andreo kaj Maria.

2 Fill in the correct pronoun.

a Mi estas brito. _____ nomo estas X .

b Ĉu vi pensas, ke _____ (his) patro dormas nun?

c Laura estas bona kuiristino. _____ kuko gustas tre bone!

d Davido kaj _____ edzino dancas tre ofte.

e _____ (*our*) domo estas granda. Ankaŭ _____ (*your*) domo estas granda.

CULTURE TIP

Esperanto has two suffixes which allow you to create familiar forms like *mum* and *dad* in English: **-ĉj-** for male names, **-nj-** for female: **avo** *grandfather*, **avĉjo** *grandad*; **patrino** *mother*, **panjo** *mum*. These suffixes are added after the first few letters of a word, not to the whole word, because the aim is to come up with something shorter.

These two forms are also used with people's names to create nicknames: **Vilhelmo** *William*, **Vilĉjo** *Bill, Billy*.

Reading

Look at Paŭlo's family tree again from Practice 2. Answer the questions with full sentences.

Example: Who is Paŭlo's wife? *Maria estas la edzino de Paŭlo.*

1 **What is Olivia's (male) cousin called?**

2 **What is the grandfather called?**

3 **Who is Karlo's son-in-law?**

4 **Whose brother is Paŭlo?**

5 **Who are sisters-in-law?**

Writing

Draw your own family tree and write short descriptions such as *Mia patro nomiĝas Bob. Lia edzino estas mia patrino. Ŝi nomiĝas Mary.*

Listening

 03.08 **Listen to Petro and Bill trying to make plans to meet up and answer the questions.**

1 **Where does Petro propose they go?**

2 **Why can't Bill make it?**

3 **Why can't Petro make it the next day?**

4 **Why does Bill think Petro could make it?**

Speaking

Take part in a conversation with Harry. He can see you're dressed nicely and wants to know what your plans are.

Harry:	Saluton! Ĉu vi iras al la teatro?
You:	(Tell him you're not going to the theatre, you're going to the restaurant.)
Harry:	Ho, kun kiu? Kun via edzino, ĉu ne?
You:	(Tell him not with your wife, you're going with your parents.)
Harry:	Ĉu vi ofte iras al la restoracio kun viaj gepatroj?
You:	(Tell him you don't often go to the restaurant with your parents because they live in France.)
Harry:	Ĉu vi planas iri al Francio?
You:	(Tell him you don't intend to go to France … you intend to go to the restaurant! Say goodbye.)

Test yourself

1 Use suffixes to create a word meaning the following:
   a big brother
   b little brother
   c small child
   d small girl

2 Unscramble the following words related to family members
   a atropin
   b pjongee
   c rtobapo
   d agovej
   e ĉapjo
   f ukoz
   g nafino
   h fragteoj
   i pjano
   j ennvio

SELF-CHECK

I CAN ...
... say what I'm doing using the present tense.
... string verbs in a sequence to create longer sentences.
... talk about my family.
... give my opinions using expressions like *I think* and *I believe*.

Ĉu vi volas teon aŭ kafon?

Do you want tea or coffee?

In this unit, you will learn how to:

▶ *offer and accept food and drink.*
▶ *ask for more when you're still hungry or thirsty.*
▶ *use conjuctions to lengthen your sentences.*
▶ *use Esperanto's n-ending to mark the direct object in a sentence.*

CEFR: (A1) *Can ask people for things and give people things.* **(A1)** *Can get an idea of the content of simpler informational material (brochures) and short simple descriptions, especially if there is visual support.* **(A2)** *Can communicate in simple and routine tasks requiring a simple and direct exchange of information on familiar and routine matters.* **(A2)** *Can find specific, predictable information in simple everyday material such as advertisements, prospectuses, menus and timetables on familiar topics.*

⭐ Kluboj por Esperantistoj *Esperanto clubs*

Since **la plej fruaj tagoj** (*the earliest days*) of the language people **kunvenis** (*have got together*) to practise Esperanto with each other. **La klubo** (*the club*) is the **loko** (*place*) where **novuloj** (*new people*) can mix with **spertuloj** (*experienced people*), swapping **libroj** (*books*) and **gazetoj** (*magazines*).

The internet has **eĉ** (*even*) given **nova vivo** (*new life*) to the concept of clubs. **Dank' al** (*thanks to*) sites like meetup.com, people have the **eblo** (*possibility*) of finding other Esperanto speakers in their **propraj urboj** *own towns*.

 What is the only set expression in Esperanto which has its final **-e** removed and replaced by an apostrophe? (This is just a case of established usage; you can keep the **-e** if you prefer to.)

Vocabulary builder 1

 04.01 Look at the words and phrases and complete the missing English expressions. Then listen and try to imitate the pronunciation of the speakers.

MANĜAĴOJ KAJ TRINKAĴOJ *FOOD AND DRINK*

MANĜAĴOJ *FOOD*

pastaĵoj	*pasta*
rizo	*rice*
pano	*bread*
butero	_____
viando	*meat*
kokaĵo	*chicken*
legomo	*vegetable*
frukto / fruktoj	*a fruit / fruit* (collectively)
kuko	*cake*
kuketo / biskvito / kekso	*a biscuit*
malsata / malsati	*hungry /* _____
sukero	*sugar*

TRINKAĴOJ *DRINK*

soifi	*to be thirsty*
akvo	*water*
suko	*juice*
teo	*tea*
kafo	*coffee*
biero	*beer*
vino	*wine*
koktelo	_____
lakto	*milk*
alkoholo / alkoholaĵo	*alcohol / an alcoholic drink*

Conversation 1

NEW EXPRESSIONS

 04.02 Look at and listen to the words and expressions that are used in the following conversation. Note their meanings.

kara	*dear*
koni	*to know (a person), be familiar with*
al la klubo	*to the club*
vi pravas	*you're right*
Jen la unua fojo, ke mi …	*This is the first time that I've …*
Estas plezuro renkonti vin.	*It's a pleasure to meet you.*
Ĉu vi havas ion por -i?	*Do you have anything to …?*
nova klubano (klub-ano)	*new club member*
serĉi	*to look for*
tamen	*however*
juna	*young*
kun aŭ sen	*with or without*

 04.03 *Sara has discovered that a group of Esperanto speakers meets up not far from where she lives. Although she's nervous, she decides to go to the next club meeting.*

1   How does Sara take her tea?

Klara	Saluton, kara! Mi ne konas vin. Bonvenon al la klubo! Mi estas Klara.
Sara	Saluton, Klara! Mi nomiĝas Sara. Vi pravas, mi estas komencanto. Jen la unua fojo, ke mi vizitas la klubon.
Klara	Do, estas plezuro renkonti vin, Sara. Ĉu vi bone fartas?
Sara	Fakte, mi soifas. Ĉu vi havas ion por trinki?
Klara	Certe. Ni havas akvon kaj sukon. Aŭ ĉu vi volas teon aŭ kafon?
Sara	Teon. Mi ne ŝatas kafon. Mi preferas teon.
Klara	Tre bone, ankaŭ mi preferas teon. Do, mi prezentas vin al Alano … Alano, jen nova klubano. Ŝi nomiĝas Sara.
Alano	Estas plezuro por mi renkonti vin, Sara. Ĉu vi volas trinki ion? Ni havas bieron. Eĉ koktelon.
Sara	Dankon, Alano, sed ne. Mi ne trinkas alkoholaĵojn. Fakte Klara nun serĉas por mi teon.
Alano	Ho, teon ankaŭ mi trinkas. Mi tamen preferas manĝi kukon kun ĝi. Ĉu vi volas manĝi kukon? Ĉu biskviton eble?
Sara	Ho, vi havas kukon! Kaj mi ja malsatas. Jes, kial ne?
Alano	Jes ja, kial ne? Ho, jen Olivia. Kiel vi, ŝi estas juna klubano. Ĉu vi konas ŝin?
Sara	Ne, mi ne konas ŝin. Saluton, Olivia.
Olivia	Saluton! Ĉu vi estas Sara? Klara faras por vi nun teon kaj volas scii, ĉu vi volas ĝin kun aŭ sen sukero kaj lakto.
Sara	Mi preferas teon kun lakto, sed sen sukero. Dankon!
Alano	Kaj ankaŭ kun kuko!

2 **Match the English and the Esperanto.**

a	A biscuit, maybe?	**1**	Ĉu vi konas ŝin?
b	I prefer tea too	**2**	Klara serĉas teon
c	I don't know you	**3**	Ĉu biskviton eble?
d	Do you know her?	**4**	Mi ne ŝatas kafon
e	I don't like coffee	**5**	Ankaŭ mi preferas teon
f	Klara's looking for a tea	**6**	Mi ne konas vin

3 **Based on Conversation 1, decide whether these statements are vera (*true*) or malvera (*false*).**

  a **Soifi** means *to be thirsty*.
  b The Esperanto for *why not?* is **kial ne?**
  c **La unua fojo** means *the last time*.
  d Olivia is an older person.
  e The Esperanto word for *to be full* is **sati**.
  f **Ĉu vi volas trinki ion?** means *You're not hungry, are you?*

 4 04.04 **Now listen to the conversation again line by line and repeat.**

Language discovery 1

1 **Find the words for *alcoholic drinks, beer, tea, coffee, cocktail* in the conversation.**

2 **How does Sara say *with milk* and *without sugar*?**

3 **If Alan didn't know a word for *biscuit*, he could create one from kuko *cake* and a suffix. What word would he create?**

1 IDENTIFYING AND MARKING THE DIRECT OBJECTS

You're familiar with sentences which contain subjects (nouns or the subject pronouns) and verbs:

mi estas   *I am*   **mi iras**   *I go*   **mi scias**   *I know*

Most sentences in Esperanto will also require something called a direct object, which isn't the thing doing the action (that's the subject) but the thing receiving it, the thing that the action is being done to:

Mi	manĝas	kukon.	Ŝi	amas	min.
(subject)	(verb)	(object)	(subject)	(verb)	(object)
I	*eat*	*cake.*	*She*	*loves*	*me.*

In Esperanto the direct object is shown with the **n**-ending, marking what in formal grammar is called the accusative case or 'the accusative' for short. The meaning is the same in all six of these sentences:

Mi manĝas kukon.   **Mi kukon manĝas.**

Manĝas mi kukon.   **Manĝas kukon mi.**

Kukon mi manĝas.   **Kukon manĝas mi.**

Changing the word order is a handy tool for adding emphasis and nuance: **kukon li manĝas** *he's eating cake* (not something else), **manĝas kukon li** *he's the one eating cake* (not me).

> **LANGUAGE TIP**
> Marking direct objects with the **n**-ending allows Esperanto to have a relatively free word order. In practice, people are most likely to use the ordering subject-verb-object, as in English and many other languages.

2 NOUNS FOLLOWING VERBS BUT NO N-ENDING

Nouns which follow prepositions (words such as *in, out, with, from, of* …) do not normally receive the n-ending in Esperanto. Even though in English you say *with him*, in Esperanto it's **kun li** and not 'kun lin'. This is why in the text Sara says **Mi preferas teon kun lakto sed sen sukero. Teon** is the object of **mi preferas**, and so has an **n**-ending. **Lakto** and **sukero** follow the prepositions **kun** *with* and **sen** *without*, and so haven't been changed.

> **LANGUAGE TIP**
> There is a special circumstance when the **n**-ending is used with prepositions, which you will meet in Unit 11.

After the verb **esti** the **n**-ending is never needed.

Mi estas komencanto.	Mia patrino estas kuiristino.
I am a beginner.	*My mother is a cook.*

There is a handful of verbs like **esti** in Esperanto which describe or rename the subject. What follows these linking verbs isn't an object but something called a subject complement.

Li fariĝas fama kantisto.	Malgraŭ la malbona vetero li restas seka.
He's becoming a famous singer.	*He's remaining dry despite the bad weather.*

Practice 1

1 **Decide whether there should be an -n in the blanks in the sentences or nothing.**

    a Mi___ estas Alano___. Mi ne trinkas akvo___.

    b Mi___ preferas teo___ kun lakto___.

    c Mi___ ŝatas legi mia___ gazeto___. Ĝia___ nomo___ estas *The Esperanto Times*.

    d Kio___ vi volas fari hodiaŭ?

    e Mi___ havas frato___ kaj fratino___. Mia___ fratino___ estas studento___. Ŝi___ studas biologio___ kaj fiziko___ en universitato___.

    f Ĉu vi___ konas la viro___? Mi ŝatas li___ sed ne scias lia___ nomo___. Ĉu vi___ kredas, ke li___ ŝatas mi___?

    g Ili___ ne volas iri al la muzeo kun mi___, do mi devas iri sen ili___.

    h Mi___ ne memoras ŝia___ nomo___, sed mi___ renkontis ŝi___ en la loka___ klubo___. Ŝi___ ne volis paroli kun mi___. Mi___ pensas, ke ŝi___ estas malafabla___ kaj mi___ ne ŝatas ŝi___.

2 **Translate the following to Esperanto and decide whether the n-ending is needed or not.**

    a I am a boy and she is a girl.

    b I study science.

    c I live in Scotland and he lives in France.

    d I like to drink tea but I don't like coffee.

    e He is my friend. He has a sister. Her name is Matilda.

    f I really like David. It's fun (estas amuze) to talk with him.

    g My mother is a very good cook. She likes to bake cakes … and I like to eat them!

    h What do you want to eat today? Do you want (to eat) a cake?

    i What do you like to drink? (Do you like to drink) beer?

    j Do you think that he prefers coffee or tea? With or without milk?

Vocabulary builder 2

04.05 **Look at the words and complete the missing English words. Then listen and try to imitate the pronunciation of the speakers.**

MANGETAĴOJ *SNACKS*

manĝaĵoj	*food*
trinkaĵo	a *drink*
sandviĉo	_____
burgero	_____
pico	*pizza*
fritoj / frititaj terpomoj / terpomfritoj	*chips*
ĉipsoj / terpomflokoj	*crisps*
ĉokolado	*chocolate*

FRUKTOJ *FRUIT*

banano	_____
pomo	*apple*
piro	*pear*
beroj	*berries*
vinberoj	*grapes*
oranĝo	_____
citrono	*lemon*
frago	*strawberry*
frambo	*raspberry*

LEGOMOJ *VEGETABLES*

karoto	_____
brasiko	*cabbage*
pizoj	_____
tomato	_____
cepo	*onion*
brokolo	_____
ajlo	*garlic*
kapsiko	*pepper*

Conversation 2

NEW EXPRESSIONS

 04.06 Look at and listen to the words and expressions that are used in the following conversation. Note their meanings.

afabla viro	*kind man*
doni	*to give*
ne plu	*not any more*
tie	*there*
Li montras gazeton al …	*He's showing a magazine to …*
Mi ne volas ĝeni …	*I don't want to be a nuisance …*
aĉeti	*to buy*
Mi vere ĝuas …	*I'm really enjoying …*
en la reala vivo	*in real life*
Kutime mi uzas Interreton.	*Normally I use the internet.*
Kiun trinkaĵon vi preferas?	*Which drink do you prefer?*
mi preferas trinki plian teon	*I prefer to drink another tea*
se tio ne ĝenas vin	*if it doesn't bother you*

04.07 *Sara is enjoying being at the club and is chatting with Olivia, while Alano has wandered off.*

1 What does Olivia suggest doing?

Olivia	Vi konas Alanon, ĉu ne? Li estas tre afabla viro. Li ĉiam donas kukon al mi!
Sara	Jes, mi ja havas ideon, ke li tre ŝatas manĝi kukojn. Tamen mi ne plu vidas Alanon.
Olivia	Ho, mi vidas lin tie! Li montras gazeton al Klara. Ĝi nomiĝas 'Esperanto'. Ĉu vi legas ĝin?
Sara	Ne, sed mi ja volas legi ĝin. Tamen mi ne volas ĝeni Alanon aŭ Klaran.
Olivia	Kial ne iri manĝi ion? Ĉu vi malsatas? Mi konas bonan restoracion, kie eblas aĉeti manĝaĵojn kaj trinkaĵojn. Ĉu vi volas manĝi sandviĉon? Burgeron? Picon? Fritojn?
Sara	Mi malsatetas, sed mi ne volas foriri, ĉar mi vere ĝuas esti en la klubo. Estas plezuro renkonti vin, Alanon kaj Klaran kaj mi tre ŝatas paroli kun vi. Hodiaŭ estas la unua fojo, ke mi parolas Esperanton en la reala vivo. Kutime mi uzas Interreton.
Klara	Saluton, denove! Vi estas malsata kaj soifa, ĉu ne? Mi havas manĝaĵojn, se vi volas manĝi ion.
Sara	Fakte mi ne vere estas malsata. Mi tamen estas tre soifa, ĉar mi parolas tro! Mi ege ŝatas paroli Esperanton!
Klara	Kiun trinkaĵon vi preferas? Ĉu sukon? Ĉu akvon?
Sara	Fakte mi preferas trinki plian teon, se tio ne ĝenas vin.
Klara	Ne estas problemo. Jen via teo!

> **LANGUAGE TIP**
>
> It is traditional to place a comma before phrases beginning with **ke** or conjunctions like **sed** *but* and **ĉar** *because*: **Ŝi diras, ke ŝi ne trinkas teon, ĉar ŝi ne ŝatas ĝin** *She says that she doesn't drink tea because she doesn't like it.*

2 Match the English and the Esperanto.

a I see him there   1 Mi ne vere estas malsata

b In real life   2 Kiun trinkaĵon vi preferas?

c I'm not really hungry   3 Li ĉiam donas kukon al mi

d Which drink do you prefer?   4 En la vera vivo

e If it doesn't bother you   5 Mi vidas lin tie

f He always gives me cake   6 Se tio ne ĝenas vin

Language discovery 2

1 Why are Alano and Klara's names written **Alanon** and **Klaran** when Sara says it's nice to meet them?

2 How does Sara say that she can't see Alano any more?

CREATING 'THINGS' WITH -AĴ-

The suffix **-aĵ-** denotes a physical – or occasionally an abstract – object related in some way to the word it is attached to:

trinki	trinkaĵo	havi	havaĵo
to drink	*a drink*	*to have*	*a possession*
bela	**belaĵo**	**diri**	**diraĵo**
beautiful	*something beautiful*	*to say*	*a saying*
nova	**novaĵo**	**sensenca**	**sensencaĵo**
new	*something new*, for example, *a piece of news*	*making no sense* (**sen** + **senco** *sense*)	*nonsense*

There's a particular meaning of **-aĵ-** when used with animal names; it gives the name of the meat:

porko	*pork*	**kokaĵo**	*chicken*
bovo	*cow*	**bovaĵo**	*beef*

By applying the **o**-ending you can create **aĵo**, used to mean a physical thing of some undefined type, *a thingy*.

Practice 2

1 What might these **-aĵo** words mean?
   a amuzaĵo
   b havaĵo
   c utilaĵo (utili *to be of use, to be useful*)
   d stultaĵo (stulta *stupid, foolish*)
   e infanaĵo
   f bakaĵo (baki *to bake*)
   g skribaĵo
   h kreskaĵo (kreski *to grow*)

> **LANGUAGE TIP**
>
> There is another word, **afero**, in Esperanto which means *thing*. **Mi treege ŝatas tri aferojn pri Italio: la veteron, la manĝaĵojn kaj la vinon.** *I really like three things about Italy: the weather, the food and the wine.*

2 **Using -aĵ- can be really useful when you haven't learned more specific vocabulary yet. How would you translate the following sentences, using -aĵ- instead of specific words?**

   a I don't think I want the brown thingy. (*brown* = **bruna**)

   b Being unhappy is a terrible thing. (*terrible* = **terura**)

   c I think that it's sawdust. (*to saw* = **segi**)

   d I don't know the name but it's a noisy thing. (*noise* = **bruo**)

> **CULTURE TIP**
>
> Larger Esperanto events usually have a **drinkejo**, a place serving alcoholic drinks such as a bar. Not everybody likes the noise that often comes with that environment, so they may prefer to go to the **gufujo**, a room where people drink tea and coffee, chat quietly, and maybe read or listen to poetry. The name comes from **gufo** *eagle owl* (which is nocturnal) and **-uj-** *a container*, so the **gufujo** is the place where you'll find the night owls.

Reading

You and Alice are out in town and both feeling hungry, so you have a look at the menu in a nearby restaurant. Read the menu and answer the questions.

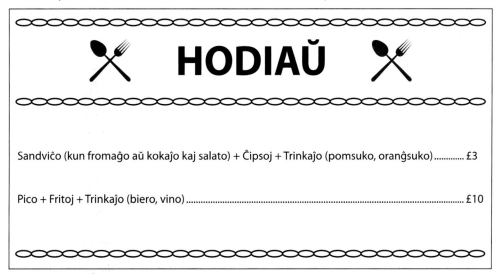

✗ HODIAŬ ✗

Sandviĉo (kun fromaĝo aŭ kokaĵo kaj salato) + Ĉipsoj + Trinkaĵo (pomsuko, oranĝsuko) £3

Pico + Fritoj + Trinkaĵo (biero, vino) £10

1 **Alice is a vegetarian. Will she be able to eat the sandwich?**

2 **What types of juices are available with the sandwich option?**

3 **Could a child order the pizza option?**

Writing

Create a simple menu containing food that you like.

Listening

04.08 Listen to this conversation between a man, who is out with his wife, and a waiter.

1 What does the man ask for but the waiter no longer has?

2 The man asks for vegetables but expresses regret when the waiter says he has some. What does he prefer to eat?

3 The waiter offers to bring him some junk food if that's what he wants. But the man knows his doctor will find out that he's acting against orders if he does that. How will the doctor know?

Listening and speaking

04.09 You're a first-timer at your local Esperanto club. The first person to welcome you is Phillip, who takes good care of you when you arrive. Listen to the dialogue and say out loud the missing parts.

Phillip:	Saluton kaj bonvenon al la klubo! Mi ne konas vin. Kiel vi nomiĝas?
You:	(Tell him what your name is and then say 'I'm a beginner'.)
Phillip:	Nu, estas plezuro por mi renkonti vin. Ĉu vi volas ion por trinki? Ni havas kafon.
You:	(Say 'I'm sorry but I don't like coffee. Do you have tea, maybe?')
Phillip:	Ho, jes, kompreneble. Teon ni havas. Ĉu kun sukero?
You:	(Say 'Thank you but without sugar. Do you have milk?')
Phillip:	Mi kredas, ke jes.
You:	(Say 'Thank you. Tea with milk but no sugar if it doesn't bother you.')
Phillip:	Tio tute ne ĝenas min. Mi iras nun serĉi por vi vian teon.

Test yourself

1 Unscramble the following to form different words related to food and drink:

   a tuebro

   b mnaĝaĵo

   c pajatsĵo

   d vasdniĉo

   e ipoc

   f ĉoldokao

   g kuso

h ukroft

i kniartĵo

j zori

k apon

l avndio

m akokĵo

n lgmoeo

2 Add the missing letters to create the names of fruit and vegetables. The **o**-ending on all the words has been removed, so **vinbero** would be **vinber**, for example.

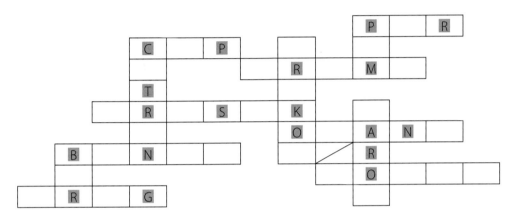

3 Complete the sentences with either **scii** or **koni**.

  a Mi _____ Andreon. Li _____ kiel baki belegan kukon tre dolĉan.

  b Ĉu vi _____, ĉu la ĉokolado estas bona?

  c Mi ne _____, ĉu mi _____ ŝin. Ĉu vi _____, kiel ŝi nomiĝas?

  d Ŝi volas _____, ĉu mi preferas mian teon kun aŭ sen sukero. Vi _____ min, do jam _____ la ĝustan respondon, ĉu ne?

5 Mi legas multajn librojn
I read a lot of books

In this unit, you will learn how to:
▸ *talk about your hobbies and interests, particularly things that might define your nature.*
▸ *create words to describe people based on their characteristics and tendencies.*
▸ *present another person to someone.*

CEFR: (A2) *Can use a series of phrases and sentences to describe family, other people, living conditions, daily routines, educational background and present or most recent job.* **(A2)** *Can describe in simple terms aspects of background, immediate environment and matters in areas of immediate need.* **(A2)** *Can explain likes or dislikes.*

⭐ Libroj en Esperanto *Books in Esperanto*

Esperanto was born with a **libro** (*book*) when a Jewish doctor, hiding his identity behind the name Doktoro Esperanto, published a **libreto** (*booklet*) about his **internacia lingvo** (*international language*). That was in 1887 and Ludoviko Zamenhof became the language's first **verkisto** (*author*). The **plena verkaro** (*complete works*) of Zamenhof spans 58 volumes!

Around 150 **novaj libroj** (*new books*) **aperas** (*appear*) every year in Esperanto, including translations, original fiction, current affairs, **ktp** (*etc.*). Esperanto author Kalle Kniivilä has even won national prizes in Sweden and Finland for the translations of his books about the lives of ordinary people in Russia and the Baltic countries.

The ease of producing electronic books has made older books **alireblaj** (*accessible*) again and new books easier to find. On the downside, it also means that some stores sometimes sell things with modern dates on that are a century old or uploads of people's own books translated **malbone** (*poorly*) by machine. **Atentu** (*be careful*) and check the reviews, ask somebody **pli sperta** (*more experienced*), or use established Esperanto organizations such as the **Universala Esperanto-Asocio** (uea.org.uk). You can find dozens of older Esperanto texts available **senkoste** (*at no cost*) at Project Gutenberg (gutenberg.org).

What do you do in Esperanto to make **kaj tiel plu** *and so on* into an equivalent to *etc.* in English?

Vocabulary builder 1

 05.01 Look at the words and phrases and complete the missing English words and expressions. Then listen and try to imitate the pronunciation of the speakers.

INTERESOJ *INTERESTS*

legi librojn	*to read books*
filmo	*film*
spekti filmojn	*watch films*
televido	*television*
ĵurnalo	*newspaper*
studi literaturon	_____
aŭskulti muzikon	_____
kulturo	_____
interesiĝi pri arto	_____

Use a dictionary and add a few of your own interests:

_____ _____

_____ _____

_____ _____

Conversation 1

NEW EXPRESSIONS

 05.02 Look at and listen to the words and expressions that are used in the following conversation. Note their meanings.

multaj libroj / multe da libroj	*many books*
Kion alian vi faras?	*What else do you do?*
danci multe plaĉas al mi	*I like dancing a lot*
ofte	*often*
kosti	*to cost*
dum la tago	*during the day*
ĉe	*at*
loka (**loko** = *place*)	*local*
multa libera tempo	*a lot of free time*
propra	*own*

> **LANGUAGE TIP**
>
> Esperanto frequently uses the construction **multe da** to mean *a lot of*:
> **Mi legas multe da libroj** *I read a lot of books*, **Mi havas malmulte da libera tempo** *I don't have a lot of free time*.

05.03 *Sara's finding it really easy to speak to people at the club, so she has moved beyond the basics and on to finding out more about the people she has just met.*

1 Why does Alano have time to teach Esperanto?

Sara	Do, vi parolas Esperanton, Olivia. Tion mi scias. Sed kion alian vi faras en la vivo?
Olivia	Mi tre ŝatas spekti bonajn filmojn kun miaj amikoj. Kaj danci multe plaĉas al mi.
Sara	Al mi ne. Mi estas malbona dancistino. Sed kiel vi, ankaŭ mi ŝatas spekti bonajn filmojn, tamen ne tre ofte. Spekti filmojn kostas multe. Kaj mi preferas legi.
Alano	Ho, ankaŭ mi, Sara! Mi legas multajn librojn. Librojn kaj gazetojn.
Olivia	Mi ne povas legi hejme – mi devas tro legi dum la tago en la universitato, ĉar mi studas. Do legi ne plu estas plezuro por mi.
Sara	Ankaŭ mi estas studento! Kion vi studas? Kie?
Olivia	Mi studas literaturon ĉe la Universitato de Manĉestro. Kaj vi?
Sara	Sciencon ĉe mia loka universitato. Kaj vi, Alano? Mi ne kredas, ke vi estas studento. Kion vi faras en la vivo? Ĉu vi laboras?
Alano	Ne, mi ne plu laboras. Tio donas al mi multan liberan tempon por instrui Esperanton. Do mi havas miajn proprajn studentojn!
Sara	Ĉu ili venas ĉe vi por studi? Kion vi faras?
Alano	Jes, ĝuste. Ni ne uzas Interreton, do ili venas al mia domo. Ni parolas kune, legas novajn gazetojn, ĵurnalojn, malnovajn librojn, ktp. Ili estas tre afablaj, kaj bonaj studentoj. Instrui bonajn estas plezure.
Sara	Ho, do vi estas Esperanto-instruisto kaj havas bonajn studentojn! Bonege!

LANGUAGE TIP

Since it's not possible to use a noun to describe another noun, Sara cannot say **'Esperanto instruisto'** to mean *Esperanto teacher*. One solution is to combine the two nouns to make a new noun. In many cases the **o**-ending on the first noun is removed. Sara chose to combine them with a hyphen, since it is much easier to pronounce and read **Esperanto-instruisto** than **'Esperantinstruisto'**.

---

2 Match the Esperanto and the English.

a	Spekti filmojn kostas multe		**1**	I read old books
b	Tio donas al mi tempon		**2**	Watching films costs a lot
c	Mi legas malnovajn librojn		**3**	They come to my house
d	Tamen ne tre ofte		**4**	I reckon you're a student
e	Mi kredas, ke vi estas studento		**5**	Not very often, though
f	Ili venas al mia domo		**6**	This gives me time

 3 05.04 Now listen to the conversation again line by line and repeat.

Language discovery 1

1 **Find the expressions for** *free time, reading is no longer a pleasure for me* **and** *what do you study?* **in the conversation.**

2 **In the sentences Ni legas novajn gazetojn, ĵurnalojn, malnovajn librojn, Ili estas tre afablaj, and bonaj studentoj, why do you think novajn and malnovajn end in -jn but afablaj and bonaj end in -j?**

3 **How does Sara say** *at university*? **How does she say** *to yours / to your house* **to Alano?**

ADJECTIVAL AGREEMENT

In Esperanto, just like nouns, adjectives change their ending depending on whether they correspond to something plural or not. And just like nouns, the plural is marked with a **-j**. In English, you say *a new table* and *new tables*, where only the noun is marked. In Esperanto, however, you say **nova tablo** and **novaj tabloj**. Adjectives also take the **n**-ending if required: **mi havas novan tablon** and **mi havas novajn tablojn**.

This is true even when the adjectives and nouns are separated, such as when **esti** is used:

La montoj en Francio estas belaj kaj la manĝaĵoj estas bonegaj.	*The mountains in France are beautiful and the food is wonderful.*

Sometimes an adjective applies to several singular nouns. In that case, the adjective is plural, just like the verb is in English:

Mia patrino kaj mia fratino estas belaj.	My mother and my sister are beautiful.

Practice 1

1 **In the conversation, identify all adjectives and the nouns they belong to.**

2 **Match the adjectives on the left with the nouns on the right.**

a bela	**1** viron		
b maljunaj	**2** virinojn		
c grandan	**3** familianoj		
d afablajn	**4** kato		

3 Place the correct endings on the adjectives if they need one.

   a Ŝi havas bel_____ katon.

   b La infanoj estas tre jun_____.

   c Estas bone, spekti nov_____ filmon.

   d Mi ŝatas drinki bon_____ bieron kun mi_____ patro.

   e Mi_____ fratino kaj ŝi_____ amikino estas inteligent_____
   kaj ĉarm_____.

   f Mi estas feliĉ_____ kiam mi aĉetas nov_____ librojn kaj havas
   liber_____ tempon por legi ilin.

4 Select the correct forms of the adjectives.

   a Mia patrino estas (bona / bonaj / bonan / bonajn) (kuiristino / kuiristinoj / kuiristinon /
   kuiristinojn).

   b Ŝi ŝatas legi (amuza / amuzan / amuzaj / amuzajn) (libro / libron / libroj / librojn) kaj
   legas ilin ofte.

   c Mi kaj mia fratino havas (multa / multaj / multan / multajn) (afabla / afablaj / afablan /
   afablajn) (geamiko / geamikoj / geamikon / geamikojn).

   d Ĉu vi kredas, ke mi estas (bela / belan / belaj / belajn)?

Vocabulary builder 2

**05.05 Look at the words and complete the missing English words. Then listen and try
to imitate the pronunciation of the speakers.**

HOBIOJ *HOBBIES*

baki belajn kukojn	*to bake* _____
pentri	*to paint*
retumi	*to surf the internet*
programi	_____
kolekti malnovajn fotojn	_____ *photos*
fari sporton	_____
naĝi	*to swim*
bicikli	_____
ludi futbalon, piedpilkon	*play football*
(pied-pilko)	

> **LANGUAGE TIP**
>
> Word order can matter. **Tute ne** *absolutely not* doesn't mean the
> same as **ne tute** *not entirely*: **Mi tute ne / ne tute komprenas**
> *I absolutely don't / don't entirely understand.* Words like **nur** *only* and
> **ankaŭ** *too, also, as well* can change the meaning depending on
> where you place them.

Conversation 2

NEW EXPRESSIONS

 05.06 Look at and listen to the words and expressions that are used in the following conversation. Note their meanings.

sperto / sperta	*experience / experienced*
spertulo	*expert*
diri	*to say*
tute ne	*not at all*
aŭskulti	*listen to*
interesaj hobioj	*interesting hobbies*
supozi	*to suppose*
kiam mi vidas kukon …	*when I see cake …*
ĉarma	*charming*
malfrua	*late (**frua** = early)*

 05.07 *Sara is chatting quite happily with the club members about their hobbies.*

1 It seems that Ĝejmzo (James) might be attracted to Olivia. What gives it away?

Alano	Ho, jen plia nova amiko, Sara. Mi prezentas al vi Ĝejmzon. Ĝejmzo: Sara estas novulino.
Ĝejmzo	Dankon, spertulo! Saluton kaj bonvenon, Sara. Mi esperas, ke mi ne ĝenas vin. Mia patrino ĉiam diras, ke mi estas tro parolema.
Sara	Tute ne, vi ne ĝenas min. Ankaŭ mi ŝatas babili. Kaj mia patrino ĉiam diras, ke mi estas tro babilema. Sed mi pensas, ke mi ankaŭ estas aŭskultema. Mi ĝojas renkonti vin.
Ĝejmzo	Kion vi ŝatas fari, Sara? Ĉu vi havas interesajn hobiojn?
Sara	Ne vere. Mi supozas, ke mi estas legemulino (leg-em-ul-in-o).
Ĝejmzo	Ho, kiel Alano. Ankaŭ li estas legemulo.
Sara	Jes, mi scias. Kaj kiel Alano, kiam mi vidas kukon, mi estas manĝemulino!
Alano	Ho jes, mi ĉiam estas manĝema.
Ĝejmzo	Do, Sara, mi komprenas, ke vi estas legema. Ĉu aliajn hobiojn vi havas? Ĉu vi ŝatas bicikli, naĝi, danci? Ĉu vi estas sportema, dancema?
Sara	Nu … ne vere. Mi malofte faras sporton. Olivia estas dancemulino, sed ne mi.
Ĝejmzo	Ho, ĉu vi konas la ĉarmulinon? Jes, ŝi ĝuas danci. Ho, jen Andreo, nia malfruemulo!
Andreo	Nu, mi nur estas malfrua, ĉar mi ĉiam tro laboras.
Ĝejmzo	Mi pardonpetas: "nia laboregemulo!"

2 Decide whether these statements are vera (*true*) or malvera (*false*).

   a Sara likes to dance.

   b Sara's mother thinks she's shy.

   c Andreo is lazy.

   d Ĝejmzo thinks that Olivia is very nice.

💡 Language discovery 2

1 Why does Sara say that she's a **dancemulino** and not a **dancemulo?**

2 Can you guess the meaning of **studema, parolema, belulo** and **novulo?**

3 How does Ĝejmzo give the impression that Andreo is a workaholic?

4 How does Alano express *another new friend*?

DESCRIBING PEOPLE

You have previously seen how to use adjectives to describe people: **juna viro, bela virino.** With the suffix **-em-** you can create adjectives from other word forms because **-em-** indicates a characteristic or tendency. Somebody who likes to **paroli** is **parolema**, and somebody who likes to **danci** is **dancema**.

Where **-em-** can create an adjective, **-ul-** describes a person characterized by something. You can describe a **bela viro** as a **belulo** and an **inteligenta homo** *intelligent person* as an **inteligentulo**. You can add **-in-** if you like: **belulo** *handsome man*, **belulino** *beautiful woman*.

It is possible to combine both these forms too: somebody who **studas** is **studema** *studious*, and a *studious person* is a **studemulo**. Combining affixes is a powerful tool in Esperanto. For example, a word for *hospital* **malsanulejo** is created from the word **sana** *healthy*, plus two affixes which you already know (**mal-, -ul-**), and a third one which you've met in earlier conversations and will learn formally in Unit 15 (**-ej-**, the location for X, such as **lernejo** *school*): **mal-san-ul-ej-o.**

Practice 2

1 **What kind of people would you describe with the following Esperanto words? Match the English with the Esperanto.**

1	a joker, prankster	**a**	forgesemulo
2	a fearful person	**b**	manĝemulo
3	an unwell person	**c**	bonulo
4	a forgetful person	**d**	amemulo
5	a moaner	**e**	timemulo (**timi** = *to be afraid, to fear*)
6	a loving person	**f**	kritikemulo
7	a glutton	**g**	plendemulo (**plendi** = *to complain*)
8	someone who criticizes all the time	**h**	malsanulo
9	a good person	**i**	ŝercemulo (**ŝerci** = *to joke*)

2 **Finish each sentence with an appropriate adjective built with -em-.**

a Mi ĉiam forgesas mian poŝtelefonon. Mi estas tre _____.

b Vi tro multe laboras kaj neniam festas. Vi estas tro _____.

c Mia patrino estas tre feliĉa kaj ĉiam ridas. Ŝi estas _____.

d Ho, mi konas lin. Li parolas ĉiam. Li estas tre _____.

3 Finish each sentence with an appropriate noun built with -ul-.

 a Mia nova amiko estas tre bela. Li estas _____.

 b Mi kredas, ke ŝi estas ege inteligenta. Ŝi estas _____.

 c Mi konas ŝin. Ŝi estas tre bonkora (**koro** = *heart*). Ŝi ja estas _____.

 d Mi bedaŭras, sed li estas malsana. Li estas _____.

> **CULTURE TIP**
>
> People with shared interests have used Esperanto as their working language since the language was published. There have been peace associations, environmental groups, even an association for international Esperanto-speaking railway workers. The Czech Wikipedia was a result of **kunlaboro** (*collaboration*) between Chuck Smith, an American who founded Vikipedio, the Esperanto version of Wikipedia, and Miroslav Malovec, an Esperanto speaker from Brno.

Reading

Read this dating app profile and answer the questions.

Saluton, mi estas John el Ĉiĉester. Mi estas sportema; nu, mi tre ŝatas spekti futbalon, rugbeon kaj tenison en la drinkejo. Sportspektema, ĉu ne? Mi estas kuiremulo; mi bonege kuiras fritojn kaj burgerojn.

Vi vidas, ĉu ne, ke mi bezonas vian helpon. Mi serĉas bonkorulinon, kiu interesiĝas pri ŝercemulo vojaĝema kaj deziras vojaĝi kun mi. Dankon!

 1 John describes himself as sporty but later refines that. What does he amend it to?

 2 He gives the impression that he loves cooking but it might be a bluff. What does he specialize in?

 3 What does John say to give the impression that perhaps we shouldn't take what he's saying seriously?

 4 He finally indicates a serious hobby at the end. What does he like to do?

Writing

Write a social media post about your own hobbies. Don't forget to use -em- and -ul- so that people get an idea of what you're like!

Listening

 05.08 **Listen to the conversation between Geoff and Bob at the Esperanto club.**

 1 What's the first reason Bob gives for his recent disappearance?

 2 Bob then claims to have got a new interest. What is it?

 3 What's the real reason that Bob's not been coming out?

Speaking

You also know Geoff and Bob, and you want to introduce them to Elaine. She's a lady who is about their age and wants to learn Esperanto, but she's very shy, so you make the introductions. Say out loud the missing lines.

Geoff:	Saluton, Derek! Kiel vi fartas, malnova amiko?
You:	(Say 'Good morning, Geoff. I want to speak with you if you don't mind.')
Geoff:	Ĉu? Pri kio?
You:	(Say 'I know a lady. Her name is Elaine and she wants to learn Esperanto. But she's very shy.')
Geoff:	Kia ŝi estas?
You:	(Say 'Very kind hearted and intelligent. You're a helpful person, Geoff. Can you help her?')
Geoff:	Kun plezuro. Ĉu ŝi intencas veni al la klubo hodiaŭ?
You:	(Say 'She's not planning to come because she doesn't speak Esperanto well. Well, she doesn't think she speaks Esperanto well.')
Geoff:	Tio ne estas problemo. Mi povas telefoni al ŝi. Ĉu vi havas ŝian telefon-numeron?
You:	(Say 'No, but I can give her yours.')
Geoff:	En ordo. Ĝis!

🄌 Test yourself

1 Change the following sentences which use **ŝati** into ones which express the same thing using **plaĉi**:
   a mi ŝatas ludi tenison
   b li tre ŝatas aŭskulti la radion
   c ŝi ŝategas kolekti artaĵojn

2 Use **-em-** and **-ul-** to create words which would mean a person who is:
   a a keen participant of sports
   b an avid follower of all things football
   c a bookworm

3 George has listed his favourite hobbies. Unscramble them to identify what George likes to do in his spare time.
   a eigl blnoijr
   b duli olufnatb
   c anĝi
   d skpeti elneivotd
   e aŭstliku iomuznk
   f kiestp fjilmon

I CAN …
○ … talk about my hobbies and interests, particularly things that define my nature.
○ … create words to describe people based on their characteristics and tendencies.
○ … present another person to someone.

6 Interŝanĝi telefon-numerojn
Exchanging phone numbers

In this unit, you will learn how to:
▶ *use numbers.*
▶ *give your phone number.*
▶ *ask what something costs.*
▶ *ask how old somebody is and give your own age.*

CEFR: (A1) *Can handle numbers, quantities, cost.* **(A2)** *Can agree and disagree.* **(A2)** *Can understand short, simple texts containing the highest frequency vocabulary, including a portion of shared international vocabulary items (menus).* **(A2)** *Can order a meal.* **(B1)** *Can obtain more detailed information.*

 ## Esperanto en nombroj *Esperanto by numbers*

Nobody knows **kiom da homoj** (*how many people*) speak Esperanto in the whole world, but we have some interesting **informoj** (*information*) about the **kvanto** (*quantity*) of Esperanto speakers in Hungary, where 8397 (**ok mil tricent naŭdek sep**) people indicated in the census of 2011 (**du mil dek unu**) that they speak Esperanto, which equals **unu** (*one*) person for each 1183 (**mil cent okdek tri**) people, or 485 (**kvarcent okdek kvin**) for each **miliono** *million*. The **nombro** (*number*) is so high because students can take an exam in Esperanto. In 2007, 6163 (**ses mil cent sesdek tri**) took a CEFR exam. In most years this is **inter** (*between*) two and five **elcentoj** (*per cent*) of the **sumo** (*total*) of language exams in the country, which puts it at **tria loko** (*third place*) behind English and German, and slightly ahead of French.

It took **tri** (*three*) **jaroj** (*years*) for Esperanto to register its first **mil** (*thousand*) users, when their names were published in 1890 (**mil okcent naŭdek**). The first Esperanto wedding took place in 1899 (**mil okcent naŭdek naŭ**) when Valdemar Langlet from Sweden and Signe Blomberg from Finland tied the knot, and the first **denaska parolanto** (*native speaker*) of Esperanto, Emilia Gastón, was born in 1904 (**mil naŭcent kvar**). The **sekva jaro** (*following year*) the first **Universala Kongreso** (*World Congress*) took place in France. It took place **ĉiujare** (*every year*) until the **Unua** (*First*) World War interrupted it, when 3739 (**tri mil sepcent tridek naŭ**) people had signed up for the **deka** (*tenth*).

Esperanto is also the 64th (**sesdek-kvara**) language which Google translated, back in 2012 (**du mil dek du**).

 What letter do ordinal numbers (*first*, *second*, *third* …) end with? How are they formed?

Vocabulary builder 1

06.01 **Look at the words and phrases and complete the missing English words and expressions. Then listen and try to imitate the pronunciation of the speakers.**

KOLOROJ *COLOURS*

nigra	*black*
blanka	_____
griza	*grey*
flava	*yellow*
ruĝa	*red*
verda	*green*
blua	_____
bruna	*brown*
koloro	_____

Conversation 1

NEW EXPRESSIONS

06.02 **Look at and listen to the words and expressions that are used in the following conversation. Note their meanings.**

revidi vin ĉiujn	*to see you all again* (**ĉiuj** = *all*)
Kiu estas via telefon-numero?	*What's your phone number?*
elekti kaj ŝanĝi	*to choose and change*
foje	*sometimes* (**dufoje** = *twice*, **trifoje** = *three times*)
La ruĝa kostas dek pundojn.	*The red one costs ten pounds.*
Ĉu vi estas preta?	*Are you ready?*
multe tro rapida	*much too fast*
Bonvolu ripeti.	*Please repeat.*
Mi esperas aŭdi de vi baldaŭ!	*I hope to hear from you soon!*

06.03 *The meeting at the club is coming to a close. Sara has enjoyed her first time meeting other Esperanto speakers and would like to see them again, so they end up swapping phone numbers.*

1   How much did Sara's red phone case cost?

Olivia	Kiel vi fartas, Sara? Ĉu vi ĝuas la klubon?
Sara	Jes, dankon. Vi ĉiuj estas tre afablaj. Mi esperas reveni al la klubo kaj revidi vin ĉiujn.
Olivia	Bonege! Eble ni povas kontakti nin. Kiu estas via telefon-numero? Ĉu vi scias ĝin?
Sara	Mi ne certas, sed se vi donas al mi vian numeron, mi povas telefoni vin nun.
Olivia	Via telefono estas belega! Mi tre ŝatas ĝian koloron! Tio estas la unua fojo, ke mi vidas ruĝan telefonon. Bele!
Sara	Dankon. Fakte, mi povas facile elekti kaj ŝanĝi ĝian koloron. Do hodiaŭ ĝi estas ruĝa, sed foje ĝi estas blua aŭ flava. Kaj eĉ verda, kiel la koloro de Esperanto! Kaj tio ne kostas multe.
Olivia	Kiom kostas la ruĝa?
Sara	Ne multon. La ruĝa kostas dek pundojn. Kaj la kosto de la verda estas nur kvin pundoj.
Olivia	Ĝi tre plaĉas al mi. Do, mia numero estas … ĉu vi estas preta?
Sara	Jes, mi pretas.
Olivia	Ĝi estas nul sep sep du tri kvin unu ses kvar naŭ ok.
Sara	Mi pardonpetas, Olivia, sed tio estas multe tro rapida! Bonvolu ripeti, sed malrapide.
Olivia	Nul sep sep … du tri kvin … unu ses kvar … naŭ ok.
Sara	Nul, sepdek sep, dudek tri, kvindek unu, sesdek kvar, naŭdek ok. Ĉu ĝuste?
Olivia	Ĝuste. Ho, jen Ĝejmzo kaj Andreo.
Ĝejmzo	Saluton! Kion vi faras?
Olivia	Sara devas foriri baldaŭ, do mi diras al ŝi mian telefon-numeron.
Ĝejmzo	Bele! Mia estas nul, sepdek kvar, okdek du, kvindek tri, naŭdek kvin, sesdek ses. Mi esperas aŭdi de vi baldaŭ!

> **LANGUAGE TIP**
>
> The prefix **re-** works like its English lookalike, meaning *to happen* or *do something again* or *to make as it was before*. It is used with verbs such as **reveni** *to come back* and **revidi** *to see again*. You'll have seen the latter before in the Esperanto expression for *goodbye*: **ĝis (la) revido** *until we see each other again*.

2 Match the English and the Esperanto.

a How much does the red one cost? **1** Mia estas

b (It costs) not much **2** Mi tre ŝatas ĝian koloron

c I really like its colour **3** Ne multon

d What's your phone number? **4** Ĉu vi pretas?

e Mine is **5** Kiu estas via telefon-numero

f Are you ready? **6** Kiom kostas la ruĝa?

> **LANGUAGE TIP**
>
> Notice that there is no word for *one* when Olivia asks **kiom kostas la ruĝa?** *how much is the red one?* In Esperanto you don't need to add a pronoun as in English; it's perfectly normal to mention the adjective without mentioning the noun or a pronoun representing it.

 3 06.04 **Now listen to the conversation line by line and repeat.**

 Language discovery 1

1 How does Olivia ask for Sara's phone number?

2 Find the words for the numbers 0–9 in the conversation. Based on related English words like *duo, trio, quarter* and so on, can you guess which word means which?

3 How do you ask how much something costs?

> **LANGUAGE TIP**
>
> It's natural to find that people speak a bit too quickly for you when you're a beginner or use words that you don't understand. Nobody will mind if you ask them to **bonvolu ripeti** *please repeat* or **bonvolu paroli pli malrapide** *please speak more slowly*. And if you don't understand the word, you can always ask people **kion signifas X?** *what does X mean?*

NOMBROJ *NUMBERS*

Nombroj *numbers* in Esperanto are extremely easy. The **ciferoj** *digits* are the same as those used in English. Here are 0 to 9:

nul	0
unu	1
du	2
tri	3
kvar	4
kvin	5
ses	6
sep	7
ok	8
naŭ	9

You may recognize some of these words from *triple*, *quartet*, *quintuplets*, etc.

The higher numbers are created by combining these numbers with others corresponding to ten, hundred, thousand, and so on. The word for *ten* is **dek**; *hundred* is **cent**; *thousand* is **mil**. These numerals can be combined to create other numbers. The number 13, for example, is thought of as 10 plus 3 and so is called **dek tri**. Note the space between the numerals which are added together:

dek unu	11
dek du	12
dek tri	13
dek kvar	14
dek kvin	15
dek ses	16
dek sep	17
dek ok	18
dek naŭ	19

The **dekoj** *tens* are multiples of ten, so 20 is 'twoten'. Note that with multiples there is no space: **dudek** not **'du dek'**:

dek	10
dudek	20
tridek	30
kvardek	40
kvindek	50
sesdek	60
sepdek	70
okdek	80
naŭdek	90

The **centoj** *hundreds* work in exactly the same way:

cent	100
ducent	200
tricent	300
kvarcent	400
kvincent	500
sescent	600
sepcent	700
okcent	800
naŭcent	900

The **miloj** *thousands* are formed in the same way, although there are spaces between the elements here:

mil	1000
du mil	2000
tri mil	3000
kvar mil	4000
kvin mil	5000
ses mil	6000
sep mil	7000
ok mil	8000
naŭ mil	9000

Note that **unu** does not come before **dek**, **cent** or **mil**. They keep their basic form, not 'unudek', 'unucent', etc. The **dekoj** and **centoj** are written as single words, whereas the **miloj** are written with spaces.

The numbers which don't end in a zero use both techniques, with multiplication of tens, hundreds, thousands plus the addition of 1 to 9 as needed:

dudek du	22		
dudek tri	23		
dudek kvar	24		
tridek sep	37		
kvardek ok	48		
kvindek naŭ	59		
cent tri	103	**ducent tridek sep**	237
mil unu	1001	**okdek tri mil kvarcent kvindek ses**	83,456

Years should be read out in full; they don't follow the English convention of breaking them down into smaller parts. 1985 is **mil naŭcent okdek kvin** not '**dek naŭ okdek kvin**'.

Note that the convention in Esperanto is to use a space or a **punkto** *full stop* rather than a **komo** *comma* to separate thousands. Usually people don't separate if there are only four digits.

LANGUAGE TIP

Giving your age in Esperanto is as simple as saying **mi aĝas 18 (jarojn)** or **mi estas 18-jara /18-jaraĝa**. Some people also make use of the verb **havi**: **mi havas 18 jarojn**. To find out someone's age you can ask them **kiom vi aĝas?**, **kiom jaraĝa vi estas?**, **kiom da jaroj vi havas?** and so on.

Practice 1

1 **Look at the list of historical events. The box contains the years when these events happened. Match the year to the event and write it out in words.**

Example: Birth of the Prophet Mohammed: 570 (kvincent sepdek)

> 1600 aK (antaŭ Kristo)   753 aK   29
> 476   1066   1492
> 1776   1789   1887   1969   1990

   a Man lands on the Moon
   b Dawn of Greek civilization
   c The US declares independence
   d The Normans invade England
   e Jesus Christ dies
   f The Roman Empire collapses
   g Colombus discovers America
   h The World Wide Web is created
   i Foundation of Rome
   j The French Revolution
   k Esperanto is born!

2 **How would you say the following song titles in Esperanto?**
   a *Nine to five* (Sheena Easton) (*to* = **ĝis**; you can add **de** = *from* at the beginning too)
   b *Thirteen days* (J.J. Cale)
   c *Summer of 69* (Bryan Adams)
   d *Fourteen years* (Guns N' Roses)
   e *24 hours* (Joy Division)
   f *When I'm 64* (The Beatles)
   g *99 red balloons* (Nena) (*balloon* = **balono**)
   h *She's only 18* (Red Hot Chili Peppers)

 3 **06.05 Listen to the recording of someone giving their phone number and write it down.**

> **LANGUAGE TIP**
>
> Both **nombro** and **numero** mean *number*. A **nombro** is the unit for counting: 1, 2, 3, etc. A **numero** is more like a label, a name for something based on its place in a line, such as how you identify your house among others on the street or a particular page in a book – number 12, for example.

Vocabulary builder 2

06.06 Look at the words and complete the missing English words. Then listen and try to imitate the pronunciation of the speakers.

MANĜADO KAJ TRINKADO *FOOD AND DRINK*

salato	_____
supo	_____
terpomo	*potato (**ter-pomo** = earth apple)*
fiŝo / fiŝaĵo	*fish (the animal) / fish (the food)*
kareo	*curry*
saŭco	_____
fromaĝo	*cheese*
deserto	_____
torto	*tart, torte*
glaciaĵo	*ice cream*
sengasa/gasa akvo	*still, natural / sparkling, fizzy water*
botelo da ruĝa vino	*a bottle of _____*
glaso da biero	*_____ of beer*
taso da teo	*a cup of _____*

> **LANGUAGE TIP**
>
> The preposition **da** is used to link an expression of quantity with a noun expressing the substance, hence **botelo da vino** *a bottle (a bottle's worth) of wine*. It occurs most commonly in expressions such as **pli da mono** *more money* and **multe da mono** *a lot of money*.

Conversation 2

NEW EXPRESSIONS

06.07 Look at and listen to the words and expressions that are used in the following conversation. Note their meanings.

gusto	*taste*
bongusta	*tasty, delicious*
Kia surprizo!	*What a surprise!*
loko	*place*
ie	*somewhere*
tiu, ĉi tiu	*that, this*
Ĉio vere bongustas.	*Everything tastes really good.*
Tial mi rekomendas ĝin	*That's why I recommend it.*
ŝajni	*to seem*
kompreneble	*of course, understandably*

06.08 *Two days after she went to the Esperanto club, Sara is shopping in the city centre when she sees Olivia in the street.*

1   Why doesn't Olivia think she'd make good recommendations in the restaurant?

Olivia	Ho, Sara! Estas bele vidi vin!
Sara	Ho, Olivia! Kia surprizo! Kion vi faras?
Olivia	Ne multon. Vi?
Sara	Mi serĉas bonan lokon por manĝi. Devas esti bona restoracio ie.
Olivia	Ĝuste, mi konas bonan. Ni povas manĝi kune, se vi volas. Tie eblas manĝi ĉion. Kion vi preferas manĝi? Picon? Pastaĵojn? Salaton? Kareon kaj rizon?
Sara	Ĉion! Kie estas la restoracio?
Olivia	Tie. *(Olivia points at a restaurant.)* Ĉu vi vidas ĝin?
Sara	Ĉu tiu restoracio? Aŭ ĉu ĉi tiu? *(Sara points at a restaurant and then at a slightly closer one.)*

They go to the restaurant and sit down. The waiter comes over to them and they ask for some time before they order, so that they can choose what to have.

Sara	Do, kion vi rekomendas manĝi?
Olivia	Nu, mi ne certas, ĉu mi povas ĝuste rekomendi, ĉar mi ne manĝas viandon. Nu, mi povas rekomendi malviandaĵojn …
Sara	Ho, vi estas vegetarano, ĉu ne? Devas esti malfacile manĝi vegetare.
Olivia	Nu, ne ĉiam estas facile trovi bonan vegetaran manĝaĵon, sed ĉi tie en ĉi tiu restoracio eblas bone manĝi. Kiam mi estas ĉi tie mi bonege manĝas. Ĉio vere bongustas. Tial mi rekomendas ĝin. Sed ne ĝenas min se vi volas manĝi viandon.
Sara	Dankon. Mi ne certas … Ho, kion manĝas tiu virino? Kio estas tio?
Olivia	Kiu virino? Ĉi tiu, ĉu? Ŝi manĝas fiŝaĵon, ĉu ne?
Sara	Ĉu? Mi ne kredas tion. Eble, se ja estas fiŝaĵo, tiam mi ne volas ĝin.
Olivia	Mi konsentas. Ĝi ne ŝajnas al mi bona. Mi ne rekomendas ĝin!
Sara	Jes, kompreneble! Vi ne manĝas viandon! Bone – tiuj pastaĵoj kun legomoj, tomata saŭco kaj fromaĝo ŝajnas bonaj. Ĉi tiu manĝaĵo ne multe kostas. Kaj ĝi estas senvianda, ĉu vi vidas?
Olivia	Jen do manĝaĵo, kiun mi rekomendas!

> **LANGUAGE TIP**
>
> Olivia says **mi ne certas, ĉu mi povas** *I don't know if I can.* As you've seen already with **scii** *to know*, Esperanto would use **ĉu** *if, whether* or **ke** *that* in this sort of construction, but never **se** *if.* If an English statement uses *if* and could take *whether*, **ĉu** is needed in Esperanto.

2 Go through the conversation and find the following phrases for agreeing and disagreeing:

a I agree

b yes, of course

c I am unsure / I'm not sure

d I don't think so

e that doesn't sound good

f I don't recommend it

 # Language discovery 2

1 **Can you guess the meaning of vegetarano and manĝi vegetare?**

2 **How does Sara express the idea that her meal doesn't contain meat?**

3 **What is the difference between tiu restoracio and ĉi tiu restoracio?**

ESPERANTO'S 'TABLE WORDS'

Kio?	Kie?	Kiu?	Kiam?	Kial?	Kiel?	Kiom?	Kies?	Kia?
What?	Where?	Who? Which?	When?	Why?	How?	How much / many?	Whose?	What kind?

These question words are examples of Esperanto's **tabelvortoj** *table words*, so called because they can be set out in a table, arranged by what letter they start with and what their endings are. Notice that all of these start with the letter **k**, which indicates that these words are either questions or relative pronouns.

Kie vi loĝas? (Kie = question word)	Mi volas loĝi en la sama urbo, kie vi loĝas.
Where do you live?	*I want to live in the same town where you live.*

The endings of the **tabelvortoj** have specific meanings:

-o	-e	-u	-am	-al	-el	-om	-es	-a
a noun (an **o**-word)	location	a specific one, a person	time	cause	manner	quantity, amount	association, possession	quality, kind, sort

This means that once you know the meaning of the initial letter, you can predictably derive the meaning of the specific **tabelvorto**. **Tabelvortoj** ending in **-u** and **-a** can take Esperanto's **j-** and **n-**endings if appropriate. The ones ending in **-o** can take the **n-**ending, as can those ending in **-e** in an additional use of the **n-**ending which you will learn about in Unit 11:

Kion li volas? Ĉu li volas librojn?	Kiujn librojn vi volas?
What does he want? Does he want books?	*Which books does he want?*

Tabelvortoj which start with the letter **t** indicate something specific:

kio	kie	kiu	kiam	kial	kiel	kiom	kies	kia
tio	tie	tiu	tiam	tial	tiel	tiom	ties	tia
that thing, that	*there, in that place*	*that person, that one*	*then, at that time*	*therefore, for that reason*	*in that way / manner, thus*	*so much, so many*	*that one's*	*that kind*

There are five different combinations of letters, so all together 45 different **tabelvortoj**. You will meet individual words as they come up in conversations and learn the remaining three rows formally in Unit 10.

> **LANGUAGE TIP**
>
> The **tabelvortoj** can take the particle **ĉi** to distinguish closeness: **Ne tiu kuko, sed ĉi tiu** *Not that cake, but this one.* You'll see it most often in the construction **ĉi tie** *here*, as opposed to **tie** *there*. Sometimes people put **ĉi** after the **tabelvorto**. The order is not important and does not change the meaning.

Practice 2

1 Answer these questions by using the equivalent tabelvorto with ti-. Add n- and j-endings where appropriate.

Example: Kie vi laboras? Mi laboras tie.

a Kio estas tio? _____ estas kafo.

b Kie vi loĝas? Mi loĝas _____.

c Kiu estas via patrino? _____ virino estas mia patrino.

d Kial vi demandas min? Mi ne komprenas, _____ mi demandas vin.

e Kiun sandviĉon vi preferas? Mi preferas _____ sandviĉon.

2 Give the correct tabelvortoj so that the sentences make sense. Add n- and j-endings where appropriate.

a Mi loĝas _____ (*there*), en la granda domo.

b Mi ne scias _____ (*how*) paroli la francan.

c Mi ne komprenas _____ (*why*) ŝi estas tiel malbona.

d Mi volas fari _____ (*that thing*), sed ne havas la tempon.

e _____ (*who*) scias fari _____ (*that thing*)?

f Ŝi loĝas _____ (*there*), _____ (*where*) estas la restoracio.

g _____ (*what*) vi volas fari morgaŭ?

h Mi ne ŝatas _____ (*that*) bieron. Mi preferas _____ (*this one*).

Reading

Alice is with friends at an Esperanto Café. Read the transcript of her conversation with the waiter.

Kelnero	Bonan tagon, sinjorino. Kion mi povas fari por helpi vin? Vi serĉas ion por manĝi eble.
Alice	Bonan tagon, sinjoro. Nu, estas tro malfrue por tagmanĝi kaj tro frue por vespermanĝi. Do mi serĉas nur ion por trinki.
Kelnero	Laŭ via prefero, sinjorino. Kion vi preferas trinki?
Alice	Kiom kostas glaso da vino? Prefere la ruĝa?
Kelnero	Vino kostas tri pundojn por eta, kvar pundojn por meza, kaj kvin pundojn por granda.
Alice	Do, tri grandajn mi petas.
Kelnero	Certe. Ĉu ion alian? Ion por manĝi eble?
Alice	Nur iom da pano. Tio kostas du pundojn, ĉu ne?
Kelnero	Ĝuste. Do, tri glasojn da vino kaj iom da pano. Ĉu ion alian?
Alice	Ne dankon. Kiom do mi devas pagi?

1 **Why doesn't Alice order food?**

2 **What does Alice order?**

3 **How much does her order cost her?**

Writing

Your local Esperanto club is having a meal out this evening but one of the guests can no longer attend. Send a message to the group giving details of the meal that needs to be cancelled.

Listening

 06.09 Listen to the lottery numbers and tick off the numbers as you hear them. Then answer the questions.

1   How much is the prize for winning?

2   How much have you won (**gajni**)?

Listening and speaking

 06.10 Complete your part of the conversation, giving your phone number and other details.

Ĵenja:	Do, kion manĝi? Mi estas malsatega. Kion pri vi?
You:	(Say 'Yes, I'm also extremely hungry. I want to eat lots of food.')
Ĵenja:	Por komenci mi pensas pri salato. Ĉu estas same por vi?
You:	(Say 'I'm too hungry to eat only salad. I prefer bread and soup.')
Ĵenja:	Bona ideo. Kaj poste? Ĉu rizo kun karea saŭco kaj kokaĵo, eble?
You:	(Say 'Preferably meat with potatoes and vegetables.')
Ĵenja:	Kaj por deserto? Ĉu frukto? Eble fromaĝo?
You:	(Say 'The tart looks tasty. Maybe with a cup of coffee.')
Ĵenja:	Kaj litro da vino, ĉu ne?
You:	(Say 'I like wine but a litre is too much!')

? Test yourself

1 Ask somebody's age using two different ways: one with **esti**, one with **havi**.

2 Write the answers to these maths questions:
  a unu plus unu faras
  b dek plus dek faras
  c tridek sep minus dudek tri faras
  d kvardek kvar minus dek ses faras
  e naŭdek naŭ plus naŭdek naŭ faras
  f dek tri plus dek du minus tri faras

3 Write the Esperanto for the following, remembering that a preposition is needed when you use a word relating to quantity of a substance:
  a a glass of wine
  b two bottles of beer
  c lots of cake
  d more tea

SELF-CHECK

I CAN ...
... use numbers.
... give my phone number.
... ask what something costs.
... ask how old somebody is and give my own age.

Review for Units 1–6

Grammar

Here is a summary of the grammar covered in Units 1–6.

Basic word types	
-o	Nouns, e.g. **patro**, **vetero**
-a	Adjectives, e.g. **bona**, **bela**
-e	Adverbs, e.g. **rapide**, **ofte**
-i	Verbs in the infinitive, e.g. **iri**, **manĝi**
Basic endings	
-j	Plural, e.g. **belaj katoj**
-n	Accusative, e.g. **mi ŝatas nigran ĉokoladon**
-as	Present tense, e.g. **mi iras**, **mi manĝas**
Creating new words	
mal-	Opposite, e.g. **malbona**, **malhelpi**
ge-	Groups including both genders, e.g. **gepatroj**, **geamikoj**
-aĵ-	Concrete things, e.g. **manĝaĵo**, **verdaĵo**
-eg-	Intensifies, e.g. **bonege**, **sandviĉego**
-et-	Weakens, e.g. **manĝeti**, **malvarmeta**
-em-	Propensity, e.g. **manĝema**, **dancema**
-in-	Female, e.g. **programistino**, **patrino**
-ul-	Person, e.g. **fortulo**, **inteligentulo**

▶ If the noun ends in **-j**, **-n** or **-jn**, the adjective has to match it.

▶ **-j** and **-n** can be used simultaneously: **Mi ŝatas belajn katojn**.

▶ Only the first verb in the sentence will end in **-as**. All other verbs will end in **-i**: **Mi ŝatas manĝi. Mi devas iri kaj paroli kun li.**

▶ The affixes can be stacked: **malbonega, malbonegulo, malbonegulino**.

ASKING QUESTIONS

Yes / No questions use the word **ĉu**:

Mi iras al la klubo.   **Ĉu vi iras al la klubo? Vi iras al la klubo, ĉu ne?**

W-questions use **kiu(j / n / jn), kio(n), kiam, kie, kiel, kial, kiom, kies, kia(j / n / jn)**:

Kiam vi iras al la klubo? Kial vi iras?

PERSONAL PRONOUNS

As a subject: **mi, vi, li / ŝi / ĝi, ni, vi, ili**

As an object: **min, vin, lin / ŝin / ĝin, nin, vin, ilin**

As indicating possession: **mia, via, lia / ŝia / ĝia, nia, via, ilia**

Pronouns indicating possession behave like adjectives, i.e. they also receive the **-j**, **-n** or **-jn** endings to match the noun they belong to: **miaj gepatroj ŝatas mian novan hobion**.

NUMBERS

nul, unu, du, tri, kvar, kvin, ses, sep, ok, naŭ, dek, dek unu, dek du …

dudek, dudek unu … dudek ok, dudek naŭ

tridek, tridek unu …

kvardek, kvindek, sesdek, sepdek, okdek, naŭdek

cent, cent unu … cent naŭdek naŭ

ducent, tricent, kvarcent, kvincent, sescent, sepcent, okcent, naŭcent

mil … mil naŭcent kvardek kvin …

du mil … du mil dek ok, du mil dek naŭ, du mil dudek, du mil dudek unu …

tri mil, kvar mil, kvin mil, ses mil, sep mil, ok mil, naŭ mil, dek mil …

Practice

1 **Write self-introductions for Lingling and François, based on their profiles.**

Nomo:	Lingling Wang
Loĝloko:	Ŝanhajo, Ĉinio
Lernejo:	Universitato de Ŝanhajo
Familio:	2 gepatroj, 1 frateto
Hobioj:	legi, danci
Nomo:	François Dufour
Loĝloko:	Parizo, Francio
Laborejo:	Volkswagen en Parizo
Familio:	1 edzino, 1 filo
Hobioj:	kuiri, manĝi bone, trinki vinon

2 **Fill in the blanks with suitable words. Apply -as, -j, -n or -jn if necessary. To help you, the first letter of each missing word has been given.**

Hodiaŭ mia f_____ kuiras por miaj g_____ kaj mi. Ni ĝ_____ ĉar ŝi estas tre bona k_____. Ŝi laboras en r_____. Kiam mi devas kuiri, la m_____ kutime ne bongustas. Mi vere ne ŝ_____ kuiri, do mi ofte nur a_____ burgerojn aŭ f_____. Jen f_____ solvo!

3 **The cafeteria has three lunch offers today. Your friend is vegetarian. Help her pick a dish.**

   a Terpoma supo kun fiŝaĵo.

   b Flava tajlanda kareo kun bovaĵo, aziaj legomoj kaj rizo.

   c Pastaĵoj kun ruĝa saŭco el tomatoj kaj fromaĝo.

4 **Using the affixes at the beginning of this review section, create Esperanto words that mean the following:**

   a slow

   b a big beer

   c thinker

   d to be late

   e someone who is late

   f a female person who is late

   g someone who likes beer

   h unnecessary

   i something that is unnecessary

   j someone really ugly

   k aunts and uncles, taken together

5 **Write out these numbers in Esperanto.**

   a 17

   b 23

   c 99

   d 164

   e 256

   f 1001

   g 1984

   h 2040

   i 45,000

6 **Chuck has joined the local Esperanto group tonight. Almost everyone is happy and excited to see him, except one person. Read the conversation and decide who it is.**

Julia:	Bonvenon, Chuck!
Sandro:	Ni tre ĝojas, ke vi estas ĉi tie.
Petro:	Saluton kaj bonvenon.
Mary:	Mi ŝatas komencantojn. Mi ankaŭ instruas lingvokurson.
Kevin:	Ĉu vi volas kafon aŭ teon?
Anjo:	Ni havas kukon. Ĉu vi ŝatas ĉokoladan kukon?
Katerina:	Ĉu vi volas ekzerci vian kun mi? (**ekzerci** = *to exercise, to practise*)
Chuck:	Vi estas tre afablaj, dankon!
Tom:	Mi malŝatas novulojn. Ili ĉiam krokodilas.

7 Translate the following sentences into Esperanto.

   a The cocktail has an interesting colour.

   b It is late now.

   c The kids are already sleeping.

   d A strong wind is blowing and it is raining.

   e I am staying home and eating.

8 Decide if the following sentences are correct without the accusative or if you need to add an -n somewhere.

   a Ni estas en lernejo.

   b La instruisto instruas al la infanoj.

   c La infanoj aŭskultas la instruisto.

   d Ili diras 'Ni ne komprenas vi.'

   e Matematiko estas tro malfacila.

   f Ni ne volas lerni ĝi.

   g La instruisto malesperas.

   h La gepatroj ne ĝojas, ke la infanoj ne lernas matematiko.

9 Now, prepare some phrases for a conversation in Esperanto. Fill in the blanks with Esperanto phrases.

   a I understand.   _____.

   b I don't understand.   _____.

   c Great idea!   _____!

   d I have a problem.   _____.

   e I am a beginner.   _____.

   f I don't understand you.   _____.

   g Yes / No / Maybe   _____ / _____ / _____

   h Really?   _____?

   i Can you help me?   _____?

   j You are speaking too quickly. _____.

   k Can you speak more (**pli**) slowly? _____?

   l Can you repeat that?   _____?

   m Do you know?   _____?

   n I know.   _____.

   o Later   _____.

   p I don't have time now.   _____.

   q See you!   _____!

Kiam vi havos tempon vendrede?
When will you have time on Friday?

In this unit, you will learn how to:
▶ *tell the time.*
▶ *use the days of the week and the months of the year.*
▶ *make arrangements to meet.*
▶ *talk about the future.*

CEFR: (A1) *Can indicate time by such phrases as next week, last Friday, in November, 3:00.* **(A2)** *Can make arrangements to meet, decide where to go and what to do.* **(A2)** *Can make and respond to suggestions.* **(A2)** *Can locate specific information in lists and isolate the information required (e.g. an online directory to find a tradesman, times and dates in a schedule).*

⭐ Esperanto ĉirkaŭ la mondo *Esperanto around the world*

It's not surprising that in its early years Esperanto wasn't as **tutmonda** (*global*) as hoped; of the first 1,000 Esperantists, 919 **loĝis en la Rusa Imperio** (*lived in the Russian Empire*) and 30 were from Germany, **la dua plej populara lando** (*the second most popular country*). **Sume** (*all together*) those Esperantists **reprezentis 266 urbojn en 12 landoj** (*represented 266 towns in 12 countries*). **Hodiaŭ** (*today*) the **Universala Esperanto-Asocio** has members in over 100 countries **ĉirkaŭ la tuta mondo** (*around the whole world*).

The **Universala Kongreso** is a week-long event and is held in a different country every year. The first took place in 1905 and it headed **ekster Eŭropo** (*outside Europe*) **unuafoje** (*for the first time*) in 1910 when it was held in San Francisco, although the **nombro de partoprenantoj** (*number of participants*) there was much smaller than it had been **antaŭe** (*previously*). **Aferoj pliboniĝis** (*things have improved*), though, and subsequent **Universalaj Kongresoj** have taken place successfully in countries such as **Japanio** (*Japan*), **Kubo** (*Cuba*), **Brazilo** (*Brazil*), **Kanado** (*Canada*), **Vjetnamio** (*Vietnam*) and **Sud-Koreio** (*South Korea*). The first **Internacia Junulara Kongreso** (*International Youth Congress*), the **Universala Kongreso** for younger people, to take place in **Afriko** (*Africa*) was held in **Togolando** (*Togo*) in 2017.

For the first time could have been translated literally as **por la unua fojo**. In the text it has been written as one word instead of those four. What is the word?

Vocabulary builder 1

 07.01 Look at the words and phrases and complete the missing English words and expressions. Then listen and try to imitate the pronunciation of the speakers.

TAGOJ DE LA SEMAJNO *DAYS OF THE WEEK*

lundo	*Monday*
mardo	*Tuesday*
merkredo	_____
ĵaŭdo	*Thursday*
vendredo	*Friday*
sabato	_____
dimanĉo	*Sunday*

ESPRIMOJ POR TEMPO *PHRASES FOR TIME*

postmorgaŭ	*day after tomorrow*
post du semajnoj	*in (after) two weeks*
dum la semajnfino	*at the weekend*
en la mateno / matene	*in the morning*
en la vespero post la sesa	*in the evening after six* (lit. *after the sixth*)
ĝis tagmezo	*until noon*
posttagmeze	*in the afternoon* (lit. *afternoon-ly*)
antaŭ tri jaroj	*three years ago*

> **LANGUAGE TIP**
> You'll notice different forms of the days in the conversation. The basic form is, for example, **merkredo** *Wednesday*. The forms **je merkredo** and **merkredon** both mean *on Wednesday*; **merkrede** means *on Wednesdays* but is increasingly used to mean *on Wednesday* too.

Conversation 1

NEW EXPRESSIONS

 07.02 Look at and listen to the words and expressions that are used in the following conversation. Note their meanings.

Mi demandas min, ĉu …	*I wonder … (I am asking myself whether …)*
Estos utile …	*It will be useful …*
Mi havos libertempon.	*I'll have free time.*
Kion vi pensas pri …?	*What do you think about …?*
inter la oka kaj la deka	*between 8 and 10 o'clock* (lit. *between the 8th and the 10th*)
lerni Esperanton	*to learn Esperanto*
dum la tuta tago	*during the whole day*
Momenton!	*Just a moment!*
temas pri …	*it's about …, it's a matter/question of*
je kioma horo?	*What time? (At what hour?)*

07.03 *Sara phones Olivia to find a convenient time to meet and practise Esperanto together. But it's not as easy as she thought, since both Olivia and she are quite busy.*

1   **Olivia initially thinks that Sara's proposal to meet at ten on Saturday is too late. Why is this?**

Sara	Saluton, parolas Sara. Ĉu vi estas Olivia?
Olivia	Saluton, Sara! Kiel vi?
Sara	Bone, dankon. Do, mi demandas min, ĉu vi estos libera en la semajno? Estos utile vidi nin por paroli kune, ĉu ne?
Olivia	En la semajno … Nu, libertempon mi havos. Kiam ni vidos nin? Kiam vi havos tempon? Ĉu morgaŭ?
Sara	Ne, morgaŭ kaj postmorgaŭ mi studos. Kion vi pensas pri merkredo? Mi estos libera inter la oka kaj deka.
Olivia	Ne eblas por mi en la mateno, sed mi estos libera en la vespero post la sesa.
Sara	Ne, mi ne povos vidi vin vespere, nur matene. En la vespero mi vizitos mian fratinon … kaj ŝi ne lernas Esperanton.
Olivia	Eble unu tagon ŝi lernos ĝin! Nu … vendredon? Kion vi faros dum la tago?
Sara	Ne, dum la tuta tago mi studos denove.
Olivia	Kaj kvankam mi estos libera dumtage, en la vespero mi manĝos kun miaj geamikoj je la oka, do ne havos tempon vidi ankaŭ vin. Kion vi faros semajnfine?
Sara	Sabaton mi estos libera post la deka.
Olivia	Ne, tro malfrue.
Sara	Ĉu? Ho, momenton! Temas pri la deka matene, ne pri la dudek-dua.
Olivia	Ho, ne la deka vespere! Bone, nun mi komprenas.
Sara	Do, mi estos libera de la deka matene ĝis tagmezo. Posttagmeze venos vidi min miaj geonkloj. Ili foriros je la kvara, do vespere mi estos libera. Same dimanĉe.
Olivia	Dimanĉon mi ne estos libera, sed mi havos du-tri liberajn horojn sabaton vespere. Do, kion pri sabato en la restoracio?
Sara	Je kioma horo?
Olivia	Je la sepa vespere?
Sara	Do, je la deknaŭa, ĉu ne? Bonege! Mi vidos vin tiam!

> **LANGUAGE TIP**
>
> Olivia mentions **mi estos libera dumtage** *I'll be available in the daytime*, which is a neat way of expressing **dum la tago** in one word. Combining prepositions with nouns and verbs to create new words is a common occurrence in Esperanto.

2   **Match the English and the Esperanto.**

a I will be free in the evening	**1** Nu … vendredon?
b Will you be free in the week?	**2** mi estos libera en la vespero
c Maybe one day she'll learn it	**3** Kiam ni vidos nin?
d In the morning isn't possible for me	**4** Ĉu vi estos libera en la semajno?
e Well … on Friday?	**5** Sabaton mi estos libera post la deka

f	I'll have 2–3 free hours on Saturday	**6**	je la oka
g	At what time?	**7**	Ne eblas por mi en la mateno
h	tomorrow and the day after	**8**	Ho, ne la deka vespere!
i	at eight	**9**	morgaŭ kaj postmorgaŭ
j	When will we see each other?	**10**	Je kioma horo?
k	Oh, not 10 p.m.!	**11**	Eble unu tagon ŝi lernos ĝin
l	On Saturday I'll be free after ten	**12**	mi havos du–tri liberajn horojn sabaton

3 Complete the gaps in the sentences so that they reflect what was said in the conversation.

> geamikoj   vendredon   manĝos
> semajno   lernas   libertempon
> posttagmeze   fratinon   kion
> vespero   geonkloj

a Anna havas _____, kiu ne _____ Esperanton.

b La _____ vizitos Annan _____.

c Olivia havos _____ en la _____.

d Olivia volas scii _____ Anna faros _____.

e La _____ de Olivia _____ kun ŝi en la _____.

 4 07.04 Now listen to the conversation again line by line and repeat.

Language discovery 1

1 **This conversation contains a lot of verbs ending in -os rather than -as. What does this change mean?**

2 **How do Sara and Olivia specify that they mean a time in the morning or in the evening?**

3 **Underline the words in the conversation which relate to days and times. What are the English equivalents?**

1 FUTURE TENSE

To form the future tense, change the present tense ending in **-as** to **-os:**

mi estas	*I am*	**mi estos**	*I will be, I am going to be*
ŝi havas	*she has*	**ŝi havos**	*she will have, she is going to have*

> **LANGUAGE TIP**
>
> Be careful not to automatically use the **os**-ending whenever you see *going to* in English. *I am going to the restaurant* **mi iras al la restoracio** is not the same as *I am going to go to the restaurant / I will go to the restaurant* **mi iros al la restoracio**.

2 ORDINAL NUMBERS

When ordinal numbers such as **first** and **second** describe a noun (**Unua Libro** *First Book*) they have an **a**-ending, which is applied to the number: **deka** *tenth*. If used in a plural context, the number will also take the **j**-ending: **la unuaj homoj sur la Luno** *the first people on the Moon*.

It is not necessary to write the full name of the number; digits can be used, followed by the **a**-ending (optionally with a hyphen): **en la 12a / 12-a jarcento ne ekzistis Interreto** *the internet didn't exist in the 12th century*.

Numbers which are written with spaces (**dek tri**, **kvindek sep**) are usually collapsed into one unit (sometimes with hyphens to split the elements for ease of reading) before the **a**-ending is added: **dektria / dek-tria**, **kvindeksepa / kvindek-sepa**.

3 DATES

Ordinal numbers are crucial for giving dates in Esperanto, working like in English: **la 31a de decembro estas la lasta tago de la jaro** *the 31st of December is the last day of the year*. Esperanto uses the same approach for hours; the 12th hour of the day is **la 12a horo** (*12:00*).

4 WRITING DATES

The norm in Esperanto when expressing dates on their own, such as in a letter, is to use the **n**-ending or the preposition **je**.

Sabaton la 5-an de junio

Varmajn salutojn el Britio, kara Hiroŝi!

Whether to use a hyphen between the number and the **an**-ending is a case of personal preference.

> **CULTURE TIP**
>
> Is 06/07/23 July 6th or June 7th? One solution to avoid confusion is to use letters rather than numbers for the month: 06/jul/23. Another option is YYYY-MM-DD: 2023-07-06..

Practice 1

1 **Complete the sentences with the appropriate forms of the endings -as, -os or -i.**

  a Mi est_____ kontenta, ke mia fratino vizit_____ min merkredon.

  b Ŝi vol_____ sci_____, ĉu mi ven_____ lundon aŭ mardon.

  c Mi est_____ studento nun sed unu tagon mi est_____ fama kantisto.

  d Se ne pluv_____ morgaŭ, ni pov_____ ludi tenison.

  e Kiam li sci_____ la respondon, li dir_____ al mi, kaj tiam mi ripet_____ ĝin al vi.

  f Se vi ne manĝ_____ vian kokaĵon, vi malsat_____ vespere!

  g Kutime mi prefer_____ manĝ_____ picon, sed ili ne plu hav_____, do mi manĝ_____ spagetojn, kiam mi ir_____ al la restoracio ĵaŭdon vespere.

2 Write the days of the week into the blanks on the calendar.

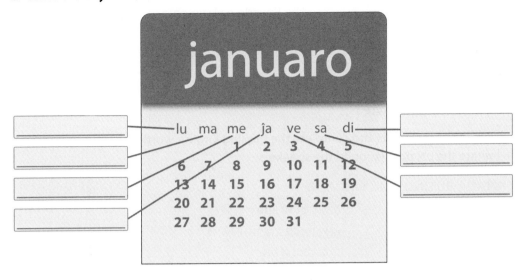

	lu	ma	me	ĵa	ve	sa	di
			1	2	3	4	5
	6	7	8	9	10	11	12
	13	14	15	16	17	18	19
	20	21	22	23	24	25	26
	27	28	29	30	31		

> **LANGUAGE TIP**
>
> You can use prepositions with dates and times to convey various meanings. Use **de ... ĝis** (*from ... to*) or **inter** (*between*) to say in one sentence what would take you several otherwise.

3 Sara's drawn up her to-do list for the coming week. Complete the sentences based on the list, making sure to use je or the n-ending as appropriate for the date. Use the future tense for the verb and an appropriate preposition (je, de, ĝis, inter) for the time phrase.

Example: Vendredo: Teatro (19:00–21:00)   Vendredon Sara iros al la teatro inter la deknaŭa kaj la dudekunua.

> Sabato: Manĝi kun Olivia en restoracio (19:00)
> Dimanĉo: Laboro (10:00-16:00)
> Dimanĉo: Studi Esperanton (18:00)
> Lundo: Universitato (08:00-14:00)
> Lundo: Paroli kun Roberto (vespere)
> Mardo: Universitato (08:00-12:00)
> Mardo: Laboro (14:00-22:00)
> Merkredo: Studi Esperanton kun Roberto (vespere)

   a Sabato_____ Sara _____ kun Olivia en restoracio _____ la 19:00.

   b _____ dimanĉo Sara _____ _____ la 10:00 ĝis la 16:00 kaj

      poste _____ Esperanton _____ la 18:00.

   c Lundo_____ Sara ir_____ al la universitato _____ la 8:00 ĝis
      la 14:00 kaj poste _____ kun Roberto en la vespero.

   d _____ mardo Sara ir_____ al la universitato _____ la 08:00
      kaj la 12:00. Poste ŝi _____ de la 14:00 _____ la 22:00.

   e Merkredo_____ Sara _____ Esperanton kun Roberto vespere.

Vocabulary builder 2

 07.05 **Look at the words and complete the missing English words. Then listen and try
to imitate the pronunciation of the speakers.**

ĈIUTAGA RUTINO *DAILY ROUTINE*

enlitiĝi	*to go to bed (***lito** *= bed)*
vekiĝi	*to wake up*
ellitiĝi	*to get out of bed*
leviĝi	*to get up, rise*
mi ekzercas min	*I exercise (lit. I exercise myself)*
mi lavas miajn manojn	*I wash my hands*
mi duŝas min	*I shower (lit. I shower myself)*
mi vestas _____	*I get dressed (lit. I dress myself)*
mi ludas kun la hundo	*I play with the dog*
matenmanĝo	*breakfast*
brosi dentojn/harojn	_____ *teeth/hair*
prepari lunĉon	_____
vespermanĝi	*to eat dinner*
skribi en taglibro	*to write in one's diary*

Conversation 2

NEW EXPRESSIONS

 07.06 **Look at and listen to the words and expressions that are used in the following
conversation. Note their meanings.**

alveni (al + veni)	*to arrive*
Ĉu mi malpravas?	*Am I wrong?*
Mi bezonas ok horojn da dormado	*I need eight hours of sleep*
kompare kun vi	*compared to you*
pli longe	*longer*
ne eblas, alie …	*it's not possible, otherwise …*
mi rompos mian rutinon	*I will break my routine*
Nekredeble!	*Unbelievable!*

… aŭ io tia?	… or something like that?
almenaŭ ĝis la unua kafo	at least until the first coffee
mi daŭre ne komprenas	I still don't understand
esti ĉe la bushaltejo ĝustatempe	to be at the bus stop on time
la sekva buso	the following bus

 07.07 *Davido and Mijoŝi are chatting online and talking about their routines.*

1 Why does Mijoŝi have to be out of the house so early?

Mijoŝi	Alvenas la dormo-horo. Mi devas foriri nun por dormi. Ĝis!
Davido	Jam? Kioma horo estas nun en Japanio? Mi kredis, ke la horo en Japanio estas sama kiel en Adelajdo. Sed estas ĉi tie nur la dudeka kvardek kvin. Ĉu mi malpravas?
Mijoŝi	Ne, vi pravas. Sed mi ĉiam enlitiĝas je la dudekunua.
Davido	Ĉu?! Nu, mi ĉiam pensas, ke mi bezonas dormi longe, sed kompare kun vi … Ĉu vi ne povas resti pli longe? Kial ne enlitiĝi je la dudekunua kaj duono? Ne ĝenos paroli dum pliaj 20–30 minutoj, ĉu ne?
Mijoŝi	Ne, ne eblas, alie mi rompos mian rutinon.
Davido	Vian rutinon? Mi eĉ ne havas. Kiam mi volas dormi, mi dormas.
Mijoŝi	Nu, mi ja estas dormema! Mi ĉiam enlitiĝas je la dudekunua por povi dormi sufiĉe longe. Mi bezonas ok horojn da dormado. Kaj mi vekiĝas je la kvina ĉiutage.
Davido	Nekredeble! Kial vi vekiĝas tiel frue? Kial ne enlitiĝi je la dudekunua kaj duono, je la dudekunua kaj tri kvaronoj, aŭ io tia? Tiel vi povos vekiĝi je pli normala horo.
Mijoŝi	Sed kion pri la rutino? Mi ĉiam vekiĝas je la kvina, ellitiĝas je la kvina kaj kvin. Je la kvina kaj dek mi kaj la hundo ludas dum kvin minutoj, kaj je la kvarono mi donas al ĝi ĝian matenmanĝon. Poste mi kutime preparas mian tagmanĝon kvankam foje mi aĉetas ion por manĝi ĉe la laborejo.
Davido	Mi leviĝas, kiam leviĝas la suno, kaj ne kapablas eĉ pensi … almenaŭ ĝis la unua kafo de la tago. Sed kial vi vekiĝas tiel frue? Mi daŭre ne komprenas.
Mijoŝi	Nu, ĉar je la duono mi ekzercas min dum kvaronhoro, kaj je la kvina kvardek kvin mi duŝas min. Je la sesa mi vestas min, je la sesa kaj dek mi matenmanĝas, kaj poste mi brosas la dentojn. Tiel mi povas esti ĉe la bushaltejo ĝustatempe por la buso, kiam ĝi alvenas je la sesa kaj kvindek du. La sekva ne venas ĝis la sepa kaj dudek du, ja tro malfrue por alveni ĝustatempe en la laborejo.
Davido	Ho, nun mi komprenas. Do, bonan nokton!

> **LANGUAGE TIP**
>
> Mijoŝi tells Davido that **mi vekiĝas je la kvina ĉiutage** *I wake up at five every day*. This is an alternative version of **ĉiun tagon**, and can be used with other time phrases too, such as **ĉiujare** (**ĉiun jaron**). It comes in particularly handy for descriptions, since you can add an **a**-ending: **ĉiutaga vivo** *daily life*.

2 **Match the English and the Esperanto.**

a I always wake up at five

b I have to go away now to sleep

c I shower at 5:45

d I brush my teeth afterwards

e I get up with the sun

f I need eight hours' sleep

1 Poste mi brosas la dentojn

2 Je la kvina kvardek kvin mi duŝas min

3 Mi bezonas ok horojn da dormado

4 Mi ĉiam vekiĝas je la kvina

5 Mi devas foriri nun por dormi

6 Mi leviĝas, kiam leviĝas la suno

3 **Match the left-hand column with the correct ending in the right-hand column to show Mijoŝi and Davido's routines.**

a Post kiam li vekiĝas, Davido

b Mijoŝi enlitiĝas

c Mijoŝi bezonas buson

d Mijoŝi vekiĝas

e Davido leviĝas

f Mijoŝi devas dormi

1 por iri al la laborejo

2 samtempe kiel la suno

3 ĉiam je la sama horo

4 bezonas kafon

5 dum ok horoj

6 je la 21:00

Language discovery 2

1 **Underline all the times in the dialogue and note the digital time in the margins.**

2 **What are the words for *a half* and *a quarter*?**

3 **How does Mijoŝi say *I exercise for a quarter of an hour*?**

> **LANGUAGE TIP**
>
> The suffix **-on-** allows you to form fractions: **duono** *half*, **triono** *third*, **kvarono** *quarter*. This is useful for telling the time, to say *half past*, etc. Similar affixes are **-obl-**, which gives you multiples (**duobla** *double*), and **-op-**, which gives you a group of x people (**duopo** *a pair, a couple*).

1 THE N-ENDING WITH TIME PHRASES

The **n**-ending can replace **je** when speaking about days:

sabaton = je sabato   *on Saturday*

It can replace other prepositions in time phrases too:

la tutan tagon = dum la tuta tago   *(during) the whole day*

This is another feature of the **n**-ending and in some instances it's the preferred approach to indicate time:

Unu fojon li eĉ donis al mi monon!   *He even gave me money once!*

Mi nur renkontis lin du fojojn.   *I've only met him twice (on two occasions).*

Ĉiun jaron ni vizitas nian fratinon en Aŭstralio.   *We visit our sister in Australia every year.*

If it's not playing the role of subject in a sentence or it doesn't follow a preposition, the time phrase has the **n**-ending:

Unu tago estas kiel ĉiu alia.	*One day is like any other.* (**unu tago** is the subject of **estas**)
Unu tagon mi estos riĉa.	*One day I'll be rich.* (**unu tagon** is a time phrase in the sentence; **mi** is the subject)

> **LANGUAGE TIP**
>
> You can still use other prepositions besides **je** where it's logical to do so, such as **dum la semajnfino** *during the weekend*, **en somero** *in summer*, **ĝis novembro** *until November*.

2 TELLING THE TIME

Ordinal numbers are used to give the hour:

estas la deka (horo)	*it's 10 o'clock*
je la tria (horo)	*at 3 o'clock*

Minutes are given using numbers:

estas la naŭa tridek	*it's 9:30*

which is short for **estas la naŭa horo kaj tridek minutoj**.

> **LANGUAGE TIP**
>
> To find out the time you would ask somebody **kioma horo estas?**, which translates as something like *which hour is it?*

15, 30 and 45 minutes can be given as numbers or as fractions:

Estas la oka kaj duono.	*It's half past eight.*
La koncerto okazos je la dudeka kaj duono.	*The concert takes place at 8:30 p.m.*
Mi renkontos mian fratinon je la naŭa kaj kvarono.	*I'll meet my sister at a quarter past nine.*

It's possible to change the structure to talk about minutes past or to the hour:

estas dek kvin post la sesa	*it's a quarter past 6 / 6:15*
estas dek kvin antaŭ la naŭa	*it's a quarter to nine / 8:45*

> **LANGUAGE TIP**
>
> The 24-hour clock is a useful aid for preventing misunderstandings but you can always clarify by adding details such as **matene** *in the morning*, **posttagmeze** *in the afternoon*, **vespere** *in the evening*, if required. **Antaŭtagmeze (atm)** and **posttagmeze (ptm)** are equivalents to *a.m.* and *p.m.*

Practice 2

1 Apply the n-ending to these times as appropriate.

  a Mi vidos vin je sabato_____, Charlie!

  b Sabato_____ estas la plej bona tago en la semajno, ĉar mi ne devas labori.

  c Mi ne povas vidi vin nun, sed mi ja povos veni sabato_____.

  d Unu tago_____ mi tute bone povos paroli Esperanton senprobleme.

  e Mi preferas vojaĝi en somero_____ kaj ne dum la vintro_____.

  f Mi lacegas, ĉar mi devis studi la tuta_____ tago_____.

  g Estas ja malplaĉe studi dum la tuta_____ tago_____, ĉu ne?

  h Mi renkontis ŝin por la unua fojo_____ unu tago_____ antaŭ ol mi renkontis vin.

2 Write the time given on these clocks.

(a)

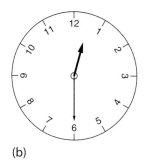

(b)

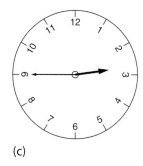

(c)

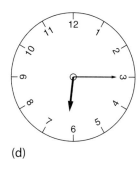

(d)

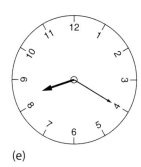

(e)

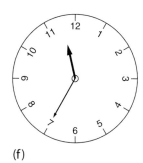

(f)

Reading

Answer the following questions using full sentences. If a verb is not provided, use okazi to mean *take place*.

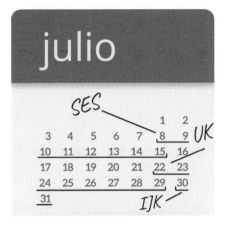

Example: When is Somera Esperanto-Studado from and to? *Somera Esperanto-Studado okazos de la 8-a ĝis la 15-a de julio.*

1 What dates does the **Universala Kongreso** take place between?

2 When is the **Internacia Junulara Kongreso** from and to?

3 What date does the **Internacia Junulara Semajno** start (**komenciĝi**)?

4 What date does the **Somera Esperanto-Studado** finish (**finiĝi**)?

5 On what dates does the **Junulara E-Semajno** start and finish?

Writing

What does the week ahead look like for you? Draw up a diary showing what you've got on this week.

Listening

 07.08 Listen to a phone conversation between Sara and Olivia. On what day and at what time will they meet?

Listening and speaking

 07.09 Join in the conversation, saying that you'd like to meet and arranging a time.

Amiko:	Saluton! Kiel vi fartas?
You:	(Say you're doing fine and ask him how's he doing.)
Amiko:	Mi fartas tre bone, dankon! Ĉu vi havas libertempon? Mi deziras paroli kun vi.
You:	(Say you have free time and ask him what you will do.)
Amiko:	Manĝi kune? Ĉu vi estos libera lundon vespere?
You:	(Say no, but you will be free on Tuesday evening.)
Amiko:	Ankaŭ mi! Bonege! Ni manĝos kune tiam.
You:	(Ask at what time.)
Amiko:	Ĉu estos bone por vi je la oka?
You:	(Say, using the 24-hour clock, that 8 o'clock is fine for you and that you'll see him then.)
Amiko:	Ĝis tiam!

Test yourself

1 Write out the following times of the day:
   - **a** 9:00 a.m.
   - **b** 10:15 a.m.
   - **c** 1:55 p.m.
   - **d** 6:03 p.m.
   - **e** 11:30 p.m.

2 Unscramble the letters to discover words relating to time:
   - **a** vspeeer
   - **b** donul
   - **c** ofijnasemn
   - **d** rlbipeotem
   - **e** ttogpasmeze

3 In which order would the following activities take place during the day? Put them in the right order:

a ellitiĝi

b vekiĝi

c lunĉi

d duŝi

e vespermanĝi

f enlitiĝi

g spekti televidon

h labori

8 Kion vi faris ĉe la kunveno?

What did you do at the meeting?

In this unit, you will learn how to:

▶ *talk about something that happened in the past.*
▶ *describe someone's character.*
▶ *talk about the body.*
▶ *describe illness.*

CEFR: (A2) *Can write about past events (describe life).* **(A2)** *Can exchange relevant information and give opinions on practical problems when asked directly, provided some help is received with formulation, and can ask for repetition of key points if necessary (e.g. making complaints).*

 PIV kaj PMEG *PIV and PMEG: the main Esperanto reference works*

When Ludoviko Zamenhof **publikigis** (*published*) the first Esperanto book in 1887, it came with a **vortolisto** (*wordlist*) at the back, containing a mere 900 words. **Nacilingvaj vortaroj** (*national-language dictionaries*) were soon published by the **unuaj pioniroj** (*first pioneers*), containing **pli kaj pli da vortoj** (*more and more words*) as people started translating and using the language. When Zamenhof **eldonis** (*published*) his **Universalan Vortaron** in 1894, he **listigis** (*listed*) 1640 words.

The **majstroverko** (*masterpiece*) of Esperanto dictionaries was not produced until 1970, under the editorship of the eminent French Esperantist Gaston Waringhien. The **Plena Ilustrita Vortaro** (*Complete Illustrated Dictionary*), more commonly known as **PIV**, contained **pli ol** (*more than*) 15,000 **kapvortojn** (*headwords*) and **preskaŭ** (*nearly*) 40,000 lexical units. **PIV** was revised in 2002 and 2005, and in 2012 an online version was introduced. You can access it at vortaro.net.

Just as the size of Esperanto dictionaries has increased **multoble** (*multiple times over*) since the language first appeared, so has the number of pages in its grammar books. The **Unua Libro** listed 16 rules of Esperanto grammar, a number **fifame** (*infamously*) quoted by Esperanto enthusiasts ever since. By far the **plej bona** (*best*) resource for Esperanto grammar is widely considered to be Bertilo Wennergren's **Plena Manlibro de Esperanta Gramatiko** (*Complete Handbook of Esperanto Grammar*), which he has kindly made **senpage** (*freely*) available on his **retejo** (*site*), bertilow.com/pmeg.

 What are the two ways we've translated *to publish*, one meaning *to make public* and the other *to give out*?

Vocabulary builder 1

 08.01 Look at the words and phrases and complete the missing English words and expressions. Then listen and try to imitate the pronunciation of the speakers.

KARAKTERO *CHARACTER TRAITS*

amuza	*amusing, fun*
avara	*mean, miserly*
brila	*brilliant*
bonveniga	*welcoming*
fidela	*loyal*
freneza	*crazy*
inteligenta	_____
modesta	_____
nervoza	_____
pasia	*passionate*
serioza	*serious*
timema	*fearful (**timi** = to fear)*
trankvila	_____

> **LANGUAGE TIP**
> The conversation uses **ĉeesti** as an alternative to **estis tie** *were there*. You can often find alternative words in various contexts to prevent overuse of **esti**, such as **partopreni** *to take part in* and **troviĝi** *to be found*, from **trovi** *to find*.

Conversation 1

NEW EXPRESSIONS

 08.02 Look at and listen to the words and expressions that are used in the following conversation. Note their meanings.

Kion vi faris lastatempe?	*What did you do/have you been doing recently?*
unuafoje en la reala vivo	*for the first time in real life*
mi trovis lokan klubon	*I found a local club*
ili havis kunvenon antaŭ du semajnoj	*they had a meeting two weeks ago*
Mi decidis partopreni	*I decided to participate*
iu parto – prelego pri trajnoj – estis teda	*some part – a lecture on trains – was boring*
la aliaj homoj	*the other people*
dudek homoj ĉeestis	*20 people were present (**ĉe-esti** = be at)*
Kiaj estis la junuloj?	*How were the young people?*
pli-malpli	*more or less*
tute hazarde	*completely randomly*

08.03 *Sara is catching up with her Esperanto teacher, Lisa, online, and tells her all about the club meeting she went to as well as the chance encounter with Olivia.*

1   How many people does Sara think were at the club?

Lisa	Kion bonan vi faris lastatempe? Ĉu ion amuzan?
Sara	Vi ne kredos min, sed mi parolis unuafoje Esperanton en la reala vivo kun veraj homoj!
Lisa	Ĉu vere? Kiel tio okazis? Kion vi faris?
Sara	Mi trovis en la interreto lokan klubon. Ili havis kunvenon antaŭ du semajnoj kaj do mi decidis partopreni.
Lisa	Bonege, Sara, mi gratulas vin! Kia estis la kunveno?
Sara	Brila! Kaj tre bonveniga! Nu, iu parto – prelego pri trajnoj – estis teda, sed ĉio alia estis bonega.
Lisa	Kaj kiaj estis la aliaj homoj?
Sara	Tre amikemaj kaj tre afablaj – mi ŝatis ilin ĉiujn. Eble dudek homoj ĉeestis; mi renkontis kaj junajn kaj maljunajn.
Lisa	Ho, do partoprenis junuloj? Kiaj ili estis?
Sara	Inteligentaj, parolemaj kaj helpemaj. Mi renkontis du junajn virojn. Ili nomiĝas Ĝejmzo kaj Andreo. Kaj mi multe parolis kun alia virino, Olivia. Ĝejmzo sekrete ŝategas ŝin – estas ege evidente.
Lisa	Kion vi faris ĉe la kunveno?
Sara	Parolis multe! Kaj multe aŭskultis. Estis nekredeble povi aŭdi homojn, kiam ili parolis Esperanton tiel perfekte. Kaj mi pli-malpli ĉion komprenis! Tamen ne estis por mi tiel facile paroli.
Lisa	Tio estas normala. Kion vi pensis antaŭe?
Sara	Antaŭ ol iri? Mi estis tre nervoza kaj timema antaŭe, ĝis mi alvenis kaj renkontis ĉiujn. Post kiam mi parolis kun la unuaj afabluloj, mi ne plu estis tia.
Lisa	Do vi esperas revidi ilin, ĉu ne?
Sara	Tion mi jam faris! Tute hazarde mi vidis Olivian lastan semajnon, do ni decidis manĝi kune. Kaj tiel denove mi sukcesis paroli Esperanton!

2   Match the English and the Esperanto.

a	I've already done that!	**1**	Antaŭ du semajnoj
b	Didn't always come when I spoke	**2**	Mi komprenis pli-malpli ĉion
c	Two weeks ago	**3**	Kion vi pensis antaŭe?
d	I understood just about everything	**4**	Ne ĉiam venis kiam mi parolis
e	By chance I saw Olivia	**5**	Kiaj ili estis?
f	Until I arrived and met everybody	**6**	Hazarde mi vidis Olivian
g	What did you think before?	**7**	Tion mi jam faris!
h	What were they like?	**8**	Ĝis mi alvenis kaj renkontis ĉiujn

3 **Based on the conversation, only one of the three statements in each part is true. Which?**

a 1 Sara jam parolis Esperanton en la reala vivo kun homoj.
   2 Ne partoprenis la kunvenon junuloj, nur maljunuloj.
   3 Sara poste estis maltimema kaj malnervoza.

b 1 Sara trovis la klubon en Interreto.
   2 Sara tre ŝatis la prelegon pri trajnoj.
   3 Pli-malpli 12 homoj ĉeestis la kunvenon.

c 1 Sara ne bone komprenis, kiam la aliaj parolis.
   2 Sara parolis en Esperanto kun Olivia antaŭ unu semajno.
   3 Okazis la kunveno antaŭ du tagoj.

 4 08.04 **Now listen again to the conversation line by line and repeat.**

> **LANGUAGE TIP**
>
> In the conversation Sara says that she met several people: **kaj junajn kaj maljunajn** *both young and old.* **kaj … kaj** can be used to mean *both … and.* Esperanto also has **aŭ … aŭ** *either … or,* **nek … nek** *neither … nor,* **ĉu … ĉu** *whether … or.*

Language discovery 1

1 **This conversation included a lot of verbs with the -is ending instead of -as. What do you think this means?**

2 **The conversation included the words sekrete, evidente and perfekte. Why do they have the e-ending and how would you translate them to English?**

3 **Here are two partial sentences said by Sara: Mi renkontis du _____ and Kaj mi multe parolis kun _____. The endings of these two sentences are junajn virojn and alia virino. Why could the ending of one sentence not be applied to the other?**

1 TALKING ABOUT THE PAST

Verbs in the past tense take the ending **-is**:

mi trinkas	**mi trinkos**	**mi trinkis**
I drink	*I will drink*	*I drank*

En 2013 mortis Nelson Mandela. *In 2013 Nelson Mandela died.*

Kiam mi estis juna, mi ŝatis ludi tenison. *I used to like playing tennis when I was young.*

Antaŭ tri monatoj mi komencis lerni Esperanton. *Three months ago I started learning Esperanto.*

And you can use **ĵus** just like English uses *just* to mean *very shortly before:*

Mi ĵus manĝis, do ne volas iri al restoracio nun. *I've just finished eating so don't want to go to a restaurant now.*

2 BEFORE AND AFTER: ANTAŬ(E) AND POST(E)

The prepositions **antaŭ** *before* and **post** *after* are useful in conversations about time:

Antaŭ ducent jaroj ne ekzistis Esperanto.	*200 years ago Esperanto didn't exist.*
Post ducent jaroj daŭre ekzistos Esperanto.	*After 200 years (in 200 years' time), Esperanto will still exist.*

When they are used without a time phrase following them, use the **e**-ending for adverbs:

Mi konis lin antaŭe, sed ne rekonis lin, ĉar lia vizaĝo ŝanĝiĝis poste.	*I knew him before but didn't recognize him because his face had changed afterwards.*

In English you can often replace **antaŭe** with *beforehand* and **poste** with *afterwards*.

When they're introducing a dependent clause, **antaŭ** and **post** take the forms **antaŭ ol** and **post kiam**.

Antaŭ ol mi lernis Esperanton, mi provis lerni la francan kaj la kimran.	*Before I learned Esperanto I tried to learn French and Welsh.*
Antaŭ ol viziti la gepatrojn, li adiaŭis la edzinon.	*Before visiting his parents he said goodbye to his wife.*
Post kiam mi trovis pomon, mi manĝis ĝin.	*After I found an apple, I ate it.*

Practice 1

1 **Give the correct endings (-is, -as, -os, -i) so that the following sentences make sense.**

  a George Washington est_____ prezidento de Usono.

  b Mi vizit_____ mian patrinon antaŭhieraŭ, sed ŝi jam forir_____ do mi ne vid_____ ŝin.

  c Mi ne memor_____, kiam mi unue aŭd_____ pri Esperanto, sed mi komenc_____ lern_____ ĝin antaŭ ses monatoj.

  d Kiam mi est_____ juna, mi loĝ_____ en Italio. Mi esper_____ vizit_____ Italion en la somero.

  e Nelson Mandela est_____ bonega homo. Mi esper_____, ke kiam mi est_____ pli maljuna ankaŭ mi est_____ bona homo kiel li.

2 Match the sentence halves to form complete sentences.

a Mi loĝas en Londono nun, sed kiam mi estis infano   **1** sensukcese provis lerni la francan.

b Hodiaŭ estas mardo. Antaŭhieraŭ   **2** mi loĝis en Germanio.

c Antaŭ du mil jaroj   **3** poste ŝi diris al mi la veron.

d Antaŭ ol komenci lerni Esperanton mi   **4** estis dimanĉo.

e Mi volis legi mian novan libron, sed mi ne povis,   **5** li petis mian telefon-numeron.

f Mi antaŭe ne sciis kion diri, sed   **6** vivis Jesuo Kristo.

g Mi unue demandis ŝin kaj   **7** mia amikino donis al mi bonan ideon ĝustatempe.

h Post kiam mi parolis al li,   **8** ĉar miaj gepatroj venis viziti min.

3 Translate the following sentences into Esperanto.

a I was an actor when I was young.

b My father was a teacher but now he's a scientist.

c I knew him before he was a musician.

d After we ate at the restaurant we visited my parents.

e I said goodbye but then I saw him again afterwards.

f I used to play football and tennis.

g When we were children we would eat chocolate all day.

h Before I ate breakfast, I read my magazine.

Vocabulary builder 2

 08.05 **Look at the words and complete the missing English words. Then listen and try to imitate the pronunciation of the speakers.**

PARTOJ DE LA KORPO *PARTS OF THE BODY*

korpo	*body*
kapo	*head*
vizaĝo	*face*
okuloj	*eyes*
nazo	_____
oreloj	*ears*
buŝo	*mouth*
lipoj	_____
dentoj	_____
lango	*tongue*
kolo	*neck*
dorso	*back*
brusto	*chest*
koro	*heart*

ŝultro	*shoulder*
brako	*arm*
mano	*hand*
fingro	_____
kruro	*leg*
piedo	*foot*

DOLORO KAJ MALSANOJ *PAIN AND AILMENTS*

mia brako doloras	*my arm is hurting*
mi dolorigis al mi la piedon	*I've hurt my foot*
bruligita mano	*burned hand*
rompitaj fingroj	*broken fingers*
malsana (mal-sana)	*sick (un-healthy)*
suferi pro doloro / malsato / soifo	*suffer from pain / hunger / thirst*
dento komencis dolori	*a tooth started hurting*
mi havas gripon / malvarmumon / doloron	*I have the flu / a cold / pain*
dentodoloro / kapdoloro / ventrodoloro	*toothache / a headache / stomach ache*

Conversation 2

NEW EXPRESSIONS

 08.06 Look at and listen to the words and expressions, some of which are used in the following conversation. Note their meanings.

tajpi malrapide	*to type slowly*
la respondo aperas	*the response appears*
kelkajn horojn poste	*several hours afterwards*
hieraŭ mi falis	*yesterday I fell*
mi apenaŭ povas -i	*I can hardly*
tio estas terura	*that is horrible, terrible*
ŝia unua paciento	*her first patient*

> **LANGUAGE TIP**
>
> The preposition **pro** introduces the cause of something, like *because of* or *owing to*. You will see it most often with **dankon**: **Dankon pro via helpo** *Thank you for your help*. Here it has been used with the verb **suferi**: **suferi pro soifo** *to suffer from thirst*.

08.07 *Sara and her friends are chatting online again and it turns out that not everybody is feeling 100 per cent well.*

1 Why is Emiljo having trouble typing?

Roberto	Vi tajpas tiel malrapide hodiaŭ, Emiljo! Aperas via respondo kelkajn horojn post la demando. Kion vi uzas por tajpi? Ĉu vian kapon? Vian nazon?
Emiljo	Tre amuze, Roberto, dankon. Mi tajpis malrapide, ĉar mi povas uzi nur unu manon.
Sara	Ho, Emiljo, kio okazis? Ĉu via mano estas bruligita? Ĉu viaj fingroj estas rompitaj?
Emiljo	Temas pri mia brako; ĝi doloregas! Hieraŭ mi falis kaj nun mi apenaŭ kapablas movi mian tutan brakon.
Sara	Ho, mi tre bedaŭras. Io tia okazis ankaŭ al mi, kiam mi estis juna. Mi rompis miajn antaŭbrakon kaj ŝultron. Pro la rompitaj antaŭbrako kaj ŝultro mi povis nek skribi nek ludi dum kelkaj semajnoj.
Emiljo	Ho, tio estas terura por infano. Tamen mi ne kredas, ke mia brako estas rompita. Morgaŭ aŭ postmorgaŭ mi esperas povi uzi ĝin denove. Sed ĝis tiam, mi tajpos malrapide!
Mijoŝi	Antaŭ ne longe mi estis terure malsana. Mia kapo doloris tiom, ke mi eĉ ne kapablis pensi.
Roberto	Ĉu ĉiu alia bone fartas? Neniu alia havas rompitajn manon aŭ fingrojn, ĉu ne?
Sara	Nu, mi havas nenion rompitan, sed ĉar vi demandis … ankaŭ mi suferas pro doloro!
Roberto	Ĉu? Kion doloran vi havas? Ĉu ankaŭ la kapon, kiel Mijoŝi?
Sara	Unu mia dento doloras. Kutime miaj dentoj estas tute bonaj, sed antaŭhieraŭ unu dento komencis dolori. Mi loĝas kun dentistino, do kiam ŝi revenos ĉi tiun vesperon, mi demandos, ĉu ŝi kredas ĝin rompita.
Roberto	Ĉu vi ĵus diris, ke vi loĝas kun dentistino? Mi kredis, ke vi loĝas kun alia junulino. Ĉu mi malpravas dum tiom da tempo?
Sara	Nu, mi nomas ŝin dentistino, sed fakte ŝi estas studento. Sed unu tagon ŝi estos dentistino, kaj mi ĉi-vespere estos ŝia unua paciento. Baldaŭ mi scios, ĉu ŝi kredas mian doloran denton rompita.

> **LANGUAGE TIP**
>
> Sara says **mi ĉi-vespere estos ŝia unua paciento** *this evening I'll be her first patient*. **Ĉi-vespere** is a common way of saying **ĉi tiun vesperon**. It works with other time phrases too, such as **ĉi-jare** (**ĉi tiun jaron**), **ĉi-semajne** (**ĉi tiun semajnon**), **ĉi-monate** (**ĉi tiun monaton**) and so on.

2 Answer the following questions based on the conversation.

  a What couldn't Sara do for several weeks?
  b When does Emiljo hope to be able to use his arm again?
  c When did Sara's tooth start to hurt?
  d What does Sara live with?

💡 Language discovery 2

1 If **postmorgaŭ** is *day after tomorrow*, can you work out what **antaŭhieraŭ** means?
2 Sometimes our friends use **rompita, rompitaj, rompitan** and **rompitajn** to mean *broken*. Why are there several forms for the same thing?
3 How does Sara say *soon I'll know whether she believes my painful tooth to be broken*?

1 MORE ON ADJECTIVE AGREEMENT

Adjectives in Esperanto agree in case and number with the nouns they describe:

Ĉu via mano estas bruligita?   **Ĉu viaj fingroj estas rompitaj?**

Is your hand burnt?   *Are your fingers broken?*

Sometimes an adjective applies to more than one noun. It can either be repeated before each noun or written in the plural, even if the nouns it describes are in the singular:

Mi rompis mian antaŭbrakon kaj mian ŝultron   **Mi rompis miajn antaŭbrakon kaj ŝultron**

I broke my forearm and my shoulder   *I broke my forearm and shoulder*

2 AGREEMENTS WITH AN IMPLIED ESTI

Verbs which link to a noun or adjective describing the subject like **esti** *to be*, **ŝajni** *to seem*, **fariĝi** *to become* are known as linking verbs. The noun or adjective used for description is called the predicate and is not expressed with the **n**-ending which direct objects take.

Li fariĝis fama kantisto   **Ili ŝajnis bonaj amikoj**

He became a famous singer   *They seemed good friends*

Just as nouns and adjectives following **esti** don't accept an **n**-ending, neither do they when **esti** is implied.

La viro farbas la bluan pordon   **La viro farbas la bluan pordon blanka**

The man is painting the blue door   *The man is painting the blue door white*

There are several examples in the text where there is an implied **esti**, in other words where the noun or adjective is a predicate:

Mi nomas ŝin dentistino   **Ŝi kredas mian denton (esti) rompita**

I call her a dentist   *She believes my tooth (to be) broken*

> **LANGUAGE TIP**
> Don't worry if these new new aspects of agreement seem complicated. You're already doing well to cope with making adjectives agree, considering that the concept doesn't exist in English.

3 ONGOING ACTIONS WHICH STARTED IN THE PAST

English uses past forms to indicate that an action started in the past and is continuing in the present. In Esperanto, since the action is still taking place, it is considered to be in the present, so the **as**-form is used:

Mi atendas la buson dum la tuta tago.   *I've been waiting for the bus all day.*

Mi lernas Esperanton dum tri monatoj.   *I've been learning Esperanto for three years.*

You can use **ekde** (**ek-** + **de**) *since* to give the point in the past when the action started:

Mi loĝas en Francio ekde 2015.   *I've been living in France since 2015.*

Mi atendas vin ekde la kvara.   *I've been waiting for you since four o'clock.*

Practice 2

1 Complete the adjectives with the correct endings so that they agree with the nouns.

    a La plej bon_____ biero estas senpag_____ biero!

    b Mi memoras, ke la maljun_____ virino preferas trinki varm_____ teon kun bongust_____ kuko.

    c Mi rompis mi_____ fingrojn kiam mi estis jun_____ knabo.

    d Mi_____ brako kaj mi_____ piedo estas dolor_____.

    e Mi_____ brako kaj piedo estas rompit_____.

    f Doloras mi_____ et_____ piedfingro kaj nazo.

    g Li_____ okuloj estas strang_____; unu estas blu_____ kaj la alia verd_____.

    h Mi vidis li_____ strang_____ okulojn; mi preferas la blu_____.

    i Mi_____ pli jun_____ frato demandis mi_____ et_____ fratinon.

    j La nov_____ ideo estas bon_____, sed mi preferas la antaŭ_____.

2 Fill in the blanks in the following sentences with either an as-verb or an is-verb as appropriate.

    a Mia piedo treege dolor_____ ekde hieraŭ

    b Vi kon_____ mian fratinon jam dum sep jaroj, ĉu ne?

    c Mia brako dolor_____ dum la tuta semajno, sed nun ĉio estas en ordo

    d Mi apenaŭ povas paroli, ĉar mi jam parol_____ dum preskaŭ du horoj sen trinki akvon!

    e Mi atend_____ vin dum longa tempo, sed decidis iri sen vi, ĉar vi ne venis

    f Ŝi loĝ_____ en Italio, kiam ŝi estis juna, sed nun ŝi loĝ_____ en Londono dum ses jaroj

    g Li komenc_____ studi la latinan, kiam li estis 18-jara, do li stud_____ ĝin jam dum dek jaroj

Reading

Read the email that Sara sent to Lisa shortly after they spoke in Conversation 1.

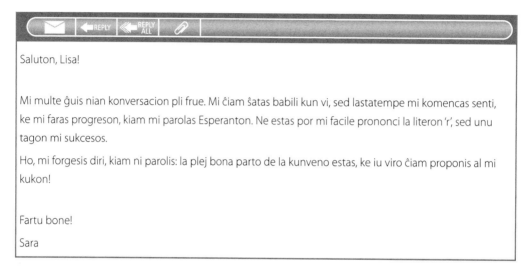

Saluton, Lisa!

Mi multe ĝuis nian konversacion pli frue. Mi ĉiam ŝatas babili kun vi, sed lastatempe mi komencas senti, ke mi faras progreson, kiam mi parolas Esperanton. Ne estas por mi facile prononci la literon 'r', sed unu tagon mi sukcesos.

Ho, mi forgesis diri, kiam ni parolis: la plej bona parto de la kunveno estas, ke iu viro ĉiam proponis al mi kukon!

Fartu bone!

Sara

1 **Does Sara think she's getting better at Esperanto?**
2 **What doesn't Sara find easy?**
3 **What does Sara say her favourite part of the meeting was?**

Writing

Use some vocabulary from the unit to write a short text describing your best friend. Include a description of your friend's character and what they look like.

Speaking

Record yourself describing a friend or family member and request feedback on your accent from your Esperanto friends.

Listening and speaking

 08.08 Imagine that you are Sara and that you're meeting a friend for coffee. He is very curious about what Esperanto clubs are like, so answer his questions.

Amiko: Ĉu via kafo estas bongusta?

You: (Thank him and confirm that your coffee tastes good.)

Amiko: Do, vi iris al Esperanto-klubo, ĉu ne?

You: (Tell him that you did and that you enjoyed being there.)

Amiko: Bone. Do, kiaj estis la homoj?

You: (Tell him that they were nice and friendly.)

Amiko: Kion vi faris?

You: (Tell him that you spoke in Esperanto.)

Amiko: Ĉu vere? Ĉu tio estis malfacila por vi?

You: (Tell him yes, it was hard for you beforehand but was easier (more + easy) afterwards.)

Amiko: Do, ĉu vi iros denove?

You: (Tell him that because you enjoyed it and the people were nice, you will go the next (**sekvan**) time.)

Test yourself

1 Match the Esperanto body parts with the English translations.

a okulo	**1** lips
b koro	**2** ear
c fingro	**3** tongue
d orelo	**4** eye
e piedo	**5** nose
f lipoj	**6** finger
g mano	**7** face
h vizaĝo	**8** heart
i dorso	**9** leg
j dentoj	**10** foot
k kruro	**11** mouth
l nazo	**12** teeth
m buŝo	**13** hand
n lango	**14** back

2 Decide which verb ending to use in the following sentences:

    a Hodiaŭ mia kapo ege dolor_____.

    b Ĝi jam dolor_____ hieraŭ, do mi ne pov_____ labori dum du tagoj.

    c Tamen hieraŭ vespere mi sent_____ min pli bone, do mi ir_____ al festo.

    d Ĉe la festo mi drink_____ multe.

    e Mi est_____ malsana ekde hieraŭ.

    f Mi esper_____ ke morgaŭ mi sent_____ min pli bone, ĉar morgaŭ est_____ sabato.

3 Mark the following character traits with (+) if they're positive and (-) if they're negative:

    a honesta _____

    b avara _____

    c fidela _____

    d brila _____

    e freneza _____

    f amuza _____

    g malmodesta _____

SELF-CHECK

I CAN ...
... talk about something that happened in the past.
... describe someone's character.
... talk about the body.
... describe illness.

9 Aligatorejo

Where the alligators are – speaking other languages

In this unit, you will learn how to:
▶ *talk about languages and your learning routine.*
▶ *ask for people to help you without resorting to English.*
▶ *describe your workplace.*

CEFR: (A2) *Can indicate when he/she is not following a conversation.* **(A2)** *Can ask for clarification about key words using stock phrases.* **(A2)** *Can describe plans, arrangements, habits and routines, past activities and personal experiences.* **(B1)** *Can ask someone to clarify or elaborate on what they have just said.*

⭐ Lingvemularo *A collection of language aficionados*

Esperanto speakers are usually, **laŭ difino** (*by definition*), at least bilingual and many are keen **lingvemuloj** (*language enthusiasts*). **Internaciaj kunvenoj** (*international get-togethers*) give them a chance to use **ne nur** (*not only*) their Esperanto, **sed ankaŭ** (*but also*) other languages **kiujn ili lernis** (*which they've learned*). Events often have an **aligatorejo** (*alligator place*), a **loko** (*place*) where people can use other languages besides Esperanto. Its name comes from an Esperanto idiom meaning *to speak in a language which is neither your native one nor Esperanto*.

If you go to **eksterlandaj aranĝoj** (*events abroad*), you'll often find a **lokulo** (*native*) giving classes about the **loka lingvo** (*local language*), using Esperanto as the teaching language. If you are one of the **plurlingvuloj** (*multilingual people, polyglots*) who start learning Esperanto, then this is a great way to add the **bazoj** (*basics*) of **plia** (*another*) language to your **kolekto** (*collection*).

How were words to mean *a language enthusiast, a native / local, somebody who speaks several languages* created in the text?

106

Vocabulary builder 1

 09.01 Look at the words and phrases and complete the missing English words and expressions. Then listen and try to imitate the pronunciation of the speakers.

LINGVOJ *LANGUAGES*

la angla	*English*
la franca	*French*
la ĉina	*Chinese*
la japana	_____
la araba	_____
mi sensukcese provis lerni la rusan	*I unsuccessfully tried to learn Russian*
mi iam lernis la germanan	*I once learned* _____
mi parolas la italan iomete	*I speak a little* _____
mia denaska lingvo estas la hispana	*my native language is Spanish*
mi flue parolas la portugalan	*I speak Portuguese fluently*
mi tute ne konas la polan	*I don't know Polish at all*
mi sukcesis bone lerni la grekan	*I managed to learn Greek well*

Conversation 1

NEW EXPRESSIONS

 09.02 Look at and listen to the words and expressions that are used in the following conversation. Note their meanings.

Dankon, ke vi akceptis helpi min.	*Thanks for agreeing to help me.*
Ne dankinde.	*Don't mention it. / You're welcome.* (lit. *not thank-worthy*)
Mi pardonpetas, sed mi ne komprenas.	*Sorry, but I don't understand.*
alilandano (ali-land-ano)	*foreigner* (lit. *other-country member*)
samlandano (sam-land-ano)	*compatriot* (lit. *same-country member*)
Kia honoro!	*What an honour!*
fremda akĉento	*foreign accent*
viaj frazoj estas komplikaj	*your sentences are complicated*
komence mi uzis kurson en la reto	*at the beginning I used a course on the web*
mi lernis tutsole (tut-sole)	*I learned all by myself (all alone)*
ekzistas grupo en granda retejo	*there is a group on a big website*
en la tuta mondo	*in the whole world, all over the world*
mesaĝejo (mesaĝ-ejo)	*messenger, chat room (message place)*
foje uzi anglajn vortojn	*sometimes use English words*

09.03 *After her recent successes, Sara is feeling more confident in her Esperanto and has decided to try a new teacher, Kimiko, a Japanese Esperanto speaker.*

1   What has Sara never heard out loud before?

Kimiko	Saluton, Sara. Estas plezuro paroli kun vi.
Sara	Kaj same por mi, Kimiko. Dankon, ke vi akceptis helpi min lerni Esperanton.
Kimiko	Ne dankinde. Do, pri kio plaĉas al vi paroli?
Sara	Mi pardonpetas, sed mi ne komprenas. Tio estas la unua fojo, ke mi parolas Esperanton kun alilandano. Vi parolas tro rapide kaj mi ne bone komprenas. Mi bedaŭras ĝeni, sed ĉu vi povas paroli malpli rapide?
Kimiko	Ĉu vere mi estas la unua, kun kiu vi parolis? Kia honoro!
Sara	Nu, mi 'parolis' kun homoj el aliaj landoj interrete. Mi havas amikojn italan, brazilan, japanan ktp. Sed mi nur parolis Esperanton unu aŭ du fojojn en la reala vivo, kaj ĉiam kun samlandanoj. Do mi neniam antaŭe aŭdis fremdan akĉenton en Esperanto.
Kimiko	Vi tamen tre bone parolas, Sara. Ĉi tiuj ne estas facilaj frazoj. Ili estas sufiĉe komplikaj. Kiel vi lernis Esperanton?
Sara	Bonvolu diri denove, Kimiko. Mi ne certas, ke mi bone aŭdis ĉion.
Kimiko	Viaj frazoj estas komplikaj, ne facilaj. Mi volis scii, kiel vi lernis Esperanton.
Sara	Mi aŭdis pri Esperanto kaj komence mi uzis kurson en la reto. Kvankam mi lernis tutsole komence, mi baldaŭ poste uzis help-grupon.
Kimiko	Kion tio signifas, 'help-grupo'? Mi ne vere konas Interreton.
Sara	Tio signifas, ke ekzistas grupo en granda retejo, nur por homoj, kiuj lernas Esperanton per tiu kurso. Tie oni povas fari demandojn kaj ricevi respondojn de spertuloj. Tio vere helpegis. Kaj ankaŭ eblis vidi, ke homoj en la tuta mondo uzas Esperanton.
Kimiko	Sed vi bone parolas nun. Ĉu eblis lerni vere per tiu kurso kaj help-grupo?
Sara	Nu, poste mi komencis uzi mesaĝejon, do unuafoje havis konversaciojn pri la ĉiutaga vivo. Tio multe helpis. Mi tie renkontis geamikojn el la tuta mondo. Kaj post tio, mi komencis babili per Interreto kun homoj. Tiuj ĉiuj parolis la anglan, tamen, do eblis foje uzi anglajn vortojn, kiam ni ne sciis la vortojn en Esperanto. Poste mi partoprenis klubon kaj tie vere aŭskultis homojn, kiuj flue parolas Esperanton.
Kimiko	Do, mi gratulas vin. Ŝajnas al mi, ke vi jam perfekte komprenas Esperanton!
Sara	Mi pardonpetas denove, Kimiko – bonvolu ripeti!

LANGUAGE TIP

Note expressions like **kun kiu** *with whom* and **al kiu** *to whom*. You can't finish clauses or sentences with them in Esperanto and you can't split them, so you have to structure things like **la knabo, al kiu mi donis la pomon** *the boy I gave the apple to*, **la unua homo, kun kiu mi parolis** *the first person I spoke with*.

2 Match the English and the Esperanto.

a	I managed to speak Esperanto	**1**	Ĉu vere mi estas la unua, kun kiu vi parolis?
b	You speak too quickly	**2**	Mi lernis tutsole komence
c	Say it again, please	**3**	Mi tie renkontis geamikojn el la tuta mondo
d	I learned all by myself at the beginning	**4**	mi sukcesis paroli Esperanton
e	Please repeat	**5**	Vi parolas tro rapide
f	At the beginning I used an online course	**6**	Mi aŭskultis homojn, kiuj flue parolas Esperanton
g	Am I really the first you've spoken with?	**7**	Bonvolu ripeti!
h	I listened to people who speak Esperanto fluently	**8**	Mi aŭdis pri Esperanto
i	I met friends from all around the world there	**9**	Bonvolu diri denove!
j	I heard about Esperanto	**10**	Komence mi uzis kurson en la reto

3 Match the sentence beginnings to the most likely sentence endings.

a	Sara komence lernis tutsole	**1**	kun kiu Sara parolis en Esperanto.
b	Kimiko estas la unua fremdulo	**2**	kiuj parolas Esperanton flue.
c	Ĝis nun Sara nur parolis Esperanton	**3**	ricevi respondojn de spertuloj.
d	En la klubo Sara aŭskultis homojn	**4**	sed poste ricevis helpon de reta help-grupo.
e	Ĉe la reta grupo eblas	**5**	uzi anglajn vortojn, kiam Sara ne sciis la ĝustajn.
f	Kun la aliaj eblis	**6**	kun samlandanoj.

 4 09.04 **Now listen to the conversation again line by line and repeat.**

Language discovery 1

1 Find the words for *foreign accent, a person from the same country* **and** *someone from another country* **in the conversation.**

2 You know dankon pro as a way of expressing *thank you for …* **What form does Sara use for** *thank you for x-ing* **in thanking Kimiko for helping her?**

3 Sara says that she learned Esperanto all by herself at the beginning. How does she take the words tuta *whole, entire* **and sola** *alone, sole* **to say** *all by myself* **in one word?**

4 Sara asks Ĉu vi povas paroli malpli rapide? *Can you speak less quickly?* **How would you alter that request to** *Can you speak more slowly?*

1 COUNTRIES AND NATIONALITIES

Country names and nationalities are closely linked in Esperanto. There are two separate approaches which guide you in how to work out one from the other.

Approach 1: Name the country, derive the inhabitant

The first is that a country is given a name (**Peruo** *Peru*, **Irako** *Iraq*, **Brazilo** *Brazil*, **Usono** *the USA*), which then changes its form according to the usual rules of Esperanto grammar: **sambo estas brazila danco** *samba is a Brazilian dance*. The names of the people who come from these countries are derived from the country name using the suffix **-an-**:

Usono	*the USA*	**usonano**	*an American*
Kanado	*Canada*	**kanadano**	*a Canadian*

With this approach, the adjective is based on the country name:

usona futbalo	*American football*

Approach 2: Name the inhabitant, derive the country

The alternative approach is to name the inhabitants, and then derive the country name from that. In modern Esperanto this is typically done by inserting **-i-**:

brito	*a Brit, a Briton*	**Britio**	*Great Britain*
franco	*a French person*	**Francio**	*France*

Francoj ŝatas francan vinon kaj loĝas en Francio.	*Frenchmen like French wine and live in France.*

In this case, just as the country name is derived from the inhabitant, so is the adjective:

germana ŝinko	*German ham*

Unfortunately, you can't pick and choose which approach to take. Some countries have their own names on which the name of the inhabitants is based, using a suffix. In other cases, it works the other way around: the inhabitants have a name from which the country name is derived. You just have to learn which is which as you come across them.

> **LANGUAGE TIP**
>
> Take your hints from the endings **-io** and **-ano** when you see them. If you see a country ending with **-io**, you know that it's probably named after the inhabitant.

2 ALTERNATIVE FORMS FOR COUNTRY NAMES

Although forms such as **Britio** and **Francio**, which have been derived from the names of the inhabitants, are very popular for country names, they are not the official names. The suffix **-uj-** was originally used for this role, meaning that **Britujo** and **Francujo** were used and still continue to be in use alongside the alternatives. The versions with **-uj-** hold an advantage over the alternatives with **-i-**: if you see a country ending with **-ujo**, you know you can remove **-uj-** to derive the inhabitant. This approach doesn't always work with countries ending with **-io** because the **-i-** is sometimes part of the name rather than something which has been added, such as with **Niĝerio** (where **niĝerianoj** live) and **Ĉilio** (home to **ĉilianoj**).

The **io**-forms were introduced in the first decade of the 20th century and have become the dominant version. It is correct to use the original forms with **-uj-**, although it may sound a bit old-fashioned because of how widespread the use of **-io** has become.

Some countries could theoretically take one of these two approaches but rarely do because they are established with having a word meaning *country* appended rather than a suffix. Adding **-lando** to the name of the inhabitant works the same as it does in English:

Skotlando = la lando de la skotoj   *Scotland = the land of the Scots*

Finnlando = la lando de la finnoj   *Finland = the land of the Finns*

> **LANGUAGE TIP**
>
> Some countries, such as **Nederlando** *the Netherlands* and **Irlando** *Ireland*, coincidentally look as though **land** has been added to their names when in fact it's actually part of the name. Don't make the mistake of removing **land** and adding **-i-** or **-uj-**!

> **CULTURE TIP**
>
> Where is Esperanto spoken? In **Esperantujo!** Even though **Esperantio** and **Esperantolando** exist as words, they're barely ever used.

Practice 1

1 Read the following text about Africa. List the names of as many countries as you can. What are the Esperanto words for *north*, *south*, *east* and *west*?

Afriko estas la due plej granda (*largest*) kontinento. Troviĝas tie la plej alta (*tallest*) besto en la mondo, la ĝirafo. En la oriento (*east*) de Afriko eblas aĉeti bananan bieron!

Eblas paroli la francan en multaj afrikaj landoj, inkluzive de (*including*) Alĝerio, Tunizio kaj Maroko en la nordo (*north*), kaj Senegalo, Malio, Togolando, Niĝero kaj la Eburbordo en la okcidento (*west*).

En aliaj landoj, ekzemple (*for example*) Egiptio, Sud-Afriko, Niĝerio, Malavio, Svazilando kaj Zanzibaro, la homoj parolas pli bone la anglan ol la francan. Ili parolas multajn aliajn lingvojn, komprenebl: en Niĝerio ekzistas pli ol (*more than*) 500 lingvoj! Kelkaj homoj diras, ke ekzistas pli ol (*more than*) 3.000 lingvoj en la tuta Afriko!

2 Hidden in the text in Exercise 1 are the words for the four points on a compass. Label the blanks in the diagram.

n

o

s

o

3 Complete the table with the correct forms of the words for inhabitants and adjectives, deriving them from the names of the countries.

a Rusio
b Danio
c Meksiko
d Islando
e Kroatio
f Aŭstralio

g Japanio
h Gvatemalo
i Skotlando
j Kanado
k Nov-Zelando
l Pollando

Country	Inhabitant	Adjective
Rusio *Russia*		
Danio *Denmark*		
Meksiko *Mexico*		
Islando *Iceland*		islanda
Kroatio *Croatia*		
Aŭstralio *Australia*		aŭstralia
Japanio *Japan*		
Gvatemalo *Guatemala*		
Skotlando *Scotland*		skota
Kanado *Canada*		
Nov-Zelando *New Zealand*		novzelanda
Pollando *Poland*		pola

Vocabulary builder 2

 09.05 **Look at the words and complete the missing English words. Then listen and try to imitate the pronunciation of the speakers.**

LABORO EN OFICEJO *AT THE OFFICE*

(labor)posteno	*job*
plentempa	*full-time*
partatempa	_____
kolego	*colleague*
labortablo	*desk ('work table')*
oficejo	_____
ricevi telefonvokojn	*to receive phone calls*
aranĝi kunvenojn	*to set up meetings*
sidi en kunvenoj	*to attend meetings*
fari fotokopiojn de dokumentoj	*to make photocopies of documents*
fotokopiilo	*a photocopier*
sendi retpoŝton	*to send emails*
financa raporto	*financial report*
mia ĉefo	*my boss*
horaro (hor-ar-o)	*schedule ('set of hours')*

Conversation 2

NEW EXPRESSIONS

 09.06 **Look at and listen to the words and expressions that are used in the following conversation. Note their meanings.**

senpaga (sen-paga) kontribuo	*unpaid contribution*
ne longe for de mia domo	*not far from my house*
mi forgesis diri	*I forgot to say*
ne plu funkcias la lifto	*the lift no longer works*
mi ĉiam devas uzi la ŝtuparon	*I always have to use the stairs*
porti skribilojn	*to carry pens*
jen ekzemplo	*here's an example*
ju pli … des pli …	*the more … the more …*
tuta aro da ĝenuloj	*a whole bunch of irritating people*
Kion faras via kolegaro?	*What does your group of colleagues do?*
kelkaj paroladas la tutan tagon	*some keep talking all day long*
preskaŭ ĉiuj alvenas malfrue	*nearly all of them arrive late*
neniu lavas la trinkilaron	*nobody washes up the items for drinking*

kiu havas treege malbonan odoron	*which has an extremely bad smell*
la tutan tagon kelkaj plendadas	*some keep complaining the whole day*
vi havos malpli da problemoj	*you'll have fewer problems*
la ĝenularo ĉiam uzis ĝin senbezone	*the gang of irritating people always needlessly used it*

 09.07 *Kimiko doesn't think her job is very interesting and finds her colleagues to be a bit irritating.*

1   Kimiko doubts that the lift will be useful to her even if it gets fixed. Why is that?

Sara	Kion vi faras en la vivo, Kimiko? Ĉu vi laboras?
Kimiko	Komprenebla. Instrui Esperanton ne estas plentempa laboro, nur senpaga kontribuo en mia libera tempo, do laborpostenon mi devas havi. Mi laboras en oficejo ne longe for de mia domo.
Sara	Kion vi faras? Ĉu ion interesan?
Kimiko	Ho, ne, ne la laboro. Ĉiam mi devas ricevi telefonvokojn, aranĝi kunvenojn, fari fotokopiojn de dokumentoj. Okazas nenio interesa.
Sara	Ho, mi malĝojas aŭdi tion. Vi faras nur tion, ĉu? Ĉu nenion alian?
Kimiko	Ne, ne nur tion. Mi forgesis diri, ke mi ĉiam devas ricevi kaj sendi retpoŝton, sidi en kunvenoj, prepari la dokumentaron antaŭ kunvenoj. Ho – kaj ne plu funkcias la lifto, do mi ĉiam devas uzi la ŝtuparon, dum mi portas financajn raportojn … kaj la skribilaron de mia ĉefo, ĉar li ĉiam forgesas.
Sara	Kiel malbone. Mi vere bedaŭras tion.
Kimiko	Ju pli da tempo mi laboras tie, des pli mi demandas min, kial mi ne forlasas la postenon. Miaj kolegoj vere ĝenas min. Estas tie tuta aro da ĝenuloj!
Sara	Ĉu? Kion faras via kolegaro por tiel multe ĝeni vin?
Kimiko	Kie komenci? Jen ekzemplo: kelkaj paroladas ĉe telefono la tutan tagon dum estas laboro por fari. Neniam estas papero en la fotokopiilo. Preskaŭ ĉiuj alvenas malfrue kaj foriras frue; ne gravas la horaro. La kuirejo estas en malordo, ĉar la trinkilaron neniu lavas.
Sara	Trinkilaron? Kion vi celas?
Kimiko	Kaftasojn ktp. Ho, kelkaj manĝas fiŝaĵon, kiu havas treege malbonan odoron. Kaj la tutan tagon kelkaj plendadas, ke estas tro varme, dum aliaj plendadas, ke malvarmas!
Sara	Nu, mi esperas, ke baldaŭ funkcios denove la lifto! Almenaŭ tiel, vi havos malpli da problemoj!
Kimiko	Dankon – sed mi ne certas pri tio. Eĉ kiam ĝi ja ĝuste funkciis, mi kutime devis uzi la ŝtuparon, ĉar la ĝenularo ĉiam uzis la lifton senbezone!

2 Match the English to the Esperanto.

a Nothing interesting happens	**1** Ne plu funkcias la lifto
b I always have to	**2** Ju pli da tempo mi laboras tie …
c The lift doesn't work any more	**3** Okazas nenio interesa
d Things for drinking? What do you mean?	**4** Paroladas la tutan tagon
e Keep talking all day	**5** Plendadas, ke malvarmas
f Keep complaining it's cold	**6** Trinkilaron? Kion vi celas?
g The longer I work there …	**7** Laborpostenon mi devas havi
h I've got to have a job	**8** Mi ĉiam devas

> **LANGUAGE TIP**
>
> The English construction *the more … the more* is given by **ju pli … des pli …** in Esperanto: **ju pli mi vidas lin, des pli mi amas lin** *the more I see him, the more I love him.* You can use **malpli** if required too.

Language discovery 2

1 **The dictionary translates both labori and funkcii as *to work*. What's the difference?**

2 **What expression does Kimiko use to say *not far away from*?**

3 **A dokumento is *a document* and dokumentaro is *a set of documents*. How is horo *hour* made into *a set of hours*? And if a ŝtuparo is *a staircase*, what do you think a ŝtupo is?**

1 MEMBERS AND GROUPS

Showing association with -an-

The suffix **-an-** shows a person's association to something. This could be as a member, as an adherent to an idea or doctrine, or as a resident:

Member	**klubano** *a member of a club*
Adherent	**islamano** *a Muslim*
Resident	**vilaĝano** *a villager*

In the conversations, Sara uses **-an-** to create new words, Esperanto's system of affixes helping her to express herself easily without having to develop an extensive vocabulary (**samlandano** *compatriot*) or use a wordy description (**alilandano** *somebody resident in another country*).

> **LANGUAGE TIP**
>
> If speaking about a woman, it is not necessary to mark **-an-** with **-in-**, although some people do. A **brazilano** could be either male or female, just as a **franco** or **italo** is.

Creating groups with -ar-

The affix **-ar-** can be used to express a group or collection of something. It can be the name given when something consists of lots of the same thing:

haro	*a hair*	**hararo**	*hair (the collection on one's head)*
arbo	*a tree*	**arbaro**	*a forest*

And it also works when something is chiefly composed of lots of the same thing, even if it contains other things too:

vorto	*a word*	**vortaro**	*a dictionary* (consists of a list of words but also definitions, etc.)
ŝtupo	*a step*	**ŝtuparo**	*a staircase* (not just a number of steps, but set out in an ordered fashion and with bannisters, etc.)
horo	*an hour*	**horaro**	*a timetable* (a list of hours set out to be consulted)
demando	*a question*	**demandaro**	*a questionnaire* (a sequence of questions)

Sometimes the affix is used to convey all of something general:

homo	*a person*	**homaro**	*mankind*
gazeto	*a magazine, newspaper, periodical*	**gazetaro**	*the press*

You can also create a standalone word from it:

aro da libroj	*a collection / pile / assortment / set of books*

> **LANGUAGE TIP**
>
> The **-ar-** affix means it is not necessary to learn collective nouns for animals, such as *a flock of sheep, a herd of cows, a pride of lions, a school of fish, a murder of crows*, and so on. If you know the name of the animal, you know what the group is called: **leono** *a lion*, **leonaro** *a pride of lions*.

2 RELATIVE KI-TABELVORTOJ

The **ki-tabelvortoj** can be used to form relative pronouns:

Mi konas la viron, _kiu_ aĉetis la panon.	*I know the man who bought the bread.*
Mi vidis la virinojn, _kiujn_ vi ŝatas.	*I saw the women (who(m)) you like.*
Jen la knabo, kun _kiu_ mia filo ludis.	*There's the boy my son played with.*
Mi vekiĝis, _kiam_ mia patrino telefonis.	*I woke up when my mother phoned.*

All of the **ki-tabelvortoj** can assume this role of relative pronoun. There are occasions when an **n**-ending is needed; it all depends on the role that the relative pronoun has:

Mi konas la viron, kiu aĉetis la panon *I know the man who bought the bread.* **Kiu** represents **la viro**.

Mi vidas la panon, kiun aĉetis la viro *I see the bread that the man bought.* **Kiun** represents **la panon**.

Practice 2

1 **Translate these words into Esperanto using -an- and -ar-. The two can be combined when appropriate.**

   Example: a group of club members   klubanaro

   a a group of friends
   b a set of teeth
   c a display of cakes
   d a member of a club
   e hair (the collection on the head)
   f a family member
   g a group of family members
   h a congress attendee
   i a collection of congress attendees
   j somebody from another country

2 **Match the beginnings and endings of the sentences to create phrases with relative clauses.**

   a Mi tre volas loĝi en la urbo,
   b Ŝi ĉiam memoras la viron,
   c Ili estas la legemaj infanoj,
   d Li ne ŝatis la unuan bieron,
   e Tio ne okazis
   f Jen la knaboj,
   g Vi estas la sola Esperantisto
   h Mi bone memoras la tagon,

   1 kiujn mi vidis antaŭhieraŭ
   2 kiel li memoris ĝin
   3 kiu unue kuiris manĝaĵon por ŝi
   4 kie loĝas mia frato
   5 kiam ni unue renkontis nin
   6 kiun mi konas
   7 kiun li trinkis
   8 al kiuj mi legis libron

> **CULTURE TIP**
>
> At the first **Universala Kongreso** in 1905 Ludoviko Zamenhof gave a speech in which he stated that he felt the participants were relating to each other '**ne francoj kun angloj, ne rusoj kun poloj, sed homoj kun homoj**'. He perceived himself as a **homarano** (**hom-ar-an-o**), an **ano** *member* of the **homaro** *human race,* and called his philosophy **homaranismo** (**hom-ar-an-ism-o**).

Reading

Read Alicia's email and then tick which activities she did in the list below.

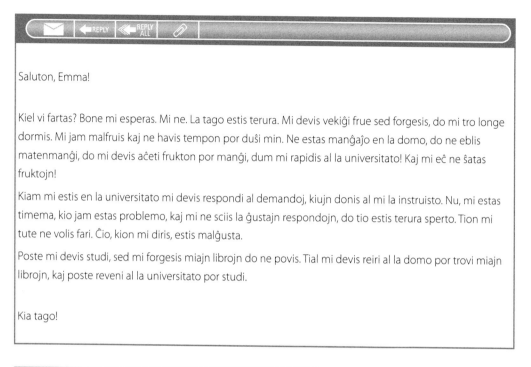

Saluton, Emma!

Kiel vi fartas? Bone mi esperas. Mi ne. La tago estis terura. Mi devis vekiĝi frue sed forgesis, do mi tro longe dormis. Mi jam malfruis kaj ne havis tempon por duŝi min. Ne estas manĝaĵo en la domo, do ne eblis matenmanĝi, do mi devis aĉeti frukton por manĝi, dum mi rapidis al la universitato! Kaj mi eĉ ne ŝatas fruktojn!

Kiam mi estis en la universitato mi devis respondi al demandoj, kiujn donis al mi la instruisto. Nu, mi estas timema, kio jam estas problemo, kaj mi ne sciis la ĝustajn respondojn, do tio estis terura sperto. Tion mi tute ne volis fari. Ĉio, kion mi diris, estis malĝusta.

Poste mi devis studi, sed mi forgesis miajn librojn do ne povis. Tial mi devis reiri al la domo por trovi miajn librojn, kaj poste reveni al la universitato por studi.

Kia tago!

Woke up early	
Had a shower	
Bought fruit on the way to university	
Had to answer questions from her tutor	
Gave a presentation	
Had to study	
Had to go back home	
Worked a shift at her job	
Went back to university to study	

Writing

Write an email to a friend describing your daily routine. Did you get up early? Was there anything memorable in the day?

Listening

🎧 **09.08 Listen to these self-introductions by participants at an Esperanto event. What are their nationalities? Which languages do they speak?**

1 _____

2 _____

3 _____

4 _____

5 _____

6 _____

Speaking

Practise reading out loud the email you prepared in the writing exercise.

⁉️ Test yourself

1 Name the native inhabitants of the following countries:

   Irlando, Francio, Germanio, Japanio, Meksiko, Togolando, Usono, Ĉinio, Rusio, Brazilo, Nov-Zelando, Aŭstralio, Kanado

2 Translate the following requests into Esperanto.
   a Speak slowly, please!
   b Can you repeat that?
   c Can you write that?
   d How do you say X in your language?
   e I don't understand. Do you speak Esperanto?

3 Which of these would NOT commonly be found in an office?

   horaro, avo, fotokopio, kareo, kolego, dentobroso, dokumento, ĉefo

---

SELF-CHECK

I CAN ...
⚪ ... talk about languages and my learning routine.
⚪ ... ask people to help me without resorting to English.
⚪ ... describe my workplace.

10 Mi iros al la Universala Kongreso!
I'll go to the World Congress!

In this unit, you will learn how to:
▶ *describe how you feel.*
▶ *correctly use Esperanto exclamations.*
▶ *talk about holiday and travel.*
▶ *book a trip to an Esperanto event.*

CEFR: (B1) *Can write short, simple essays on topics of interest (describe holiday / hotel stay).*
(B1) *Can make opinions and reactions understood as regards solutions to problems or practical questions of where to go, or how to organize an event.* **(B1)** *Can express and respond to feelings such as surprise, happiness, sadness, interest and indifference.*

★ Ĉiujaraj Esperanto-eventoj *Annual Esperanto events*

The earliest Esperantists didn't have much opportunity to meet with people from other countries. That **ekŝanĝiĝis** (*began to change*) in 1904, when English and French Esperantists **kunvenis** (*got together*) in Dover and Calais. Witnessing for himself the event, Alfred Michaux, a French lawyer, invited people to return **la sekvan jaron** (*the following year*) to Boulogne-sur-Mer, for what would be the first **Universala Kongreso de Esperanto** (*World Esperanto Congress*). This was and remains **la plej granda** (*the largest*) **ĉiujara** (*annual*) **Esperanto-evento** (*Esperanto event*) in the world. The **centa** (*100th*) UK **okazis** (*took place*) in Lille, France in 2015 and was attended by 2698 people.

The **junularo de la Esperanto-movado** (*Esperanto movement's young people*) decided in 1938 to **starigi** (*set up*) something **pli taŭga** (*more suited*) to them. The first **Internacia Junulara Kongreso** (*International Youth Congress*) was held in the Dutch village Groet. Like its big brother, the **IJK** is an **unusemajna** (*week-long*) event and is held in a different country every year, usually in either the same one as the UK or in a neighbouring country.

There are several smaller annual Esperanto events that have run for several years, including **Somera-Esperanto Studado**, which is always held in a different town in Slovakia and mixes educational courses with cultural activities; the **Junulara E-Semajno**, which **daŭras unu semajnon** (*lasts a week*) and spans New Year, usually in Germany or Poland; and the **Internacia Junulara Semajno**, a week-long summer event in Hungary, which was first held in Esperanto's **jubilea jaro** (*jubilee year*), 1987.

 How can you say that something takes place every year in Esperanto? How about expressing that something lasts for a week?

Vocabulary builder 1

10.01 Look at the words and phrases and listen to the pronunciation. Then, imagine one situation for each in which you'd say each phrase.

EKKRIOJ *EXCLAMATIONS*

Kiom / kiel tede!	*How boring!*
Ne gravas!	*Doesn't matter!*
Ho mia dio!	*Oh my God!*
Finfine!	*Finally!*
Kiel timige!	*How frightening!*
Aĉe!	*Ugh!*
Terure!	*Terrible!*
Domaĝe!	*That's a pity / shame!*
Mojose!	*Cool!*
Nekredeble!	*Unbelievable!*
Kompreneble!	*Of course!*
En ordo!	*OK! Alright!*
Brile!	*Brilliant!*
Fi!	*Shame!*

Conversation 1

NEW EXPRESSIONS

10.02 Look at and listen to the words and expressions that are used in the following conversation. Note their meanings.

unuflanke … aliflanke …	*on the one hand … on the other hand …*
dum la somera paŭzo	*during the summer break*
Mi enuas!	*I am bored!*
eĉ ne unu vorton	*not even one word*
mi neniam pripensis vojaĝi	*I've never thought about travelling*
verŝajne (ver-ŝajne)	*probably (true-seemingly)*
mi iel kapablos paroli	*I will somehow be able to speak*
Kion vi celas?	*What do you mean? (**celo** = goal, aim)*
ĉies komuna lingvo	*everyone's common language*
la plej granda evento	*the biggest event*
preskaŭ ĉiu alia	*almost everyone else*
nenies lingvo sed samtempe ĉies	*nobody's language but at the same time everyone's*
estas neniu kialo timi	*there is no reason to be afraid*
kiom ajn vi pezas	*however much you weigh*
kiun ajn vi amas	*whoever you love*
ajna kialo	*any reason*
priskribi	*to describe*
plenigi la aliĝilon	*to fill out the registration form*
eksterlande (ekster-land-e)	*abroad (outside-country-ly)*

> **CULTURE TIP**
>
> **Nenies kaj ĉies** *nobody's and everybody's* is a traditional way of speaking about Esperanto's neutrality making it suitable for adoption as an international language. It doesn't have a historical homeland and very few native speakers, so it's **nenies lingvo** *nobody's language* and therefore can be said to be **ĉies** *everybody's* equally.

 10.03 *Sara is chatting with Roberto, who suggests that she goes to Slovakia, where the* **Universala Kongreso** *is being held.*

1   What does Sara exclaim when she realizes what Roberto is talking about?

Sara	Unuflanke estas bone, ne devi iri al universitato dum la somera paŭzo; aliflanke, mi havas nenion por fari. Mi enuas! Kiom tede! Ĉiuj miaj amikoj reiris al la gepatroj, same mia samdomano. Restas neniu ajn, kun kiu mi povas paroli. Feliĉe mi havas Esperanton; almenaŭ pro ĝi mi povas paroli kun vi!
Roberto	Se ĉio estas teda, kial ne vojaĝi? Post du semajnoj mi iros al Slovakio. Kial ne veni kun mi? Almenaŭ en Slovakio estos multe da homoj, kun kiuj vi povos paroli.
Sara	Kion? Kiel 'kun kiuj mi povos paroli'? La slovakan mi tute ne parolas. Neniom. Eĉ ne unu vorton! Kaj mi eĉ neniam pripensis vojaĝi al Slovakio. Kies ideo tio estis?
Roberto	Verŝajne vi havas neniun ideon, do, pri tio, kio okazos en Slovakio post du semajnoj. Ne gravas, ke neniel vi lernis la slovakan; vi ne bezonos ĝin.
Sara	Ĉu? Mi ial iros al Slovakio kaj iel kapablos paroli kun multaj homoj, kies lingvon mi ne scias, ĉu ne? Do viajn vortojn mi komprenas, Roberto, sed neniom el tio, kion vi celas.
Roberto	Ĉu vi parolas Esperanton, Sara? Evidente. Same kiel la aliaj homoj, kiuj kunvenos en Slovakio. Ĝi estos ĉies komuna lingvo tie.
Sara	Ho mia dio! Vi parolas pri la Universala Kongreso! Kiel mi forgesis?
Roberto	Finfine! Mi ne estos en Slovakio nenial ajn, sed ĝuste ĉar tie okazos la plej granda Esperanto-evento en la mondo. Ne gravas, ke mi kaj preskaŭ ĉiu alia tie ne parolos la slovakan, ĉar ni ĉiuj parolos Esperanton. Kiel oni diras: nenies lingvo sed samtempe ĉies.
Sara	Sed … kiel timige! Ĉu vi ne timas? Kion vi manĝos kaj trinkos? Kion vi faros, se vi povos trovi nenion ajn, kion vi ŝatas por manĝi? Ĉu vi jam konas iun, kun kiu vi povos paroli?
Roberto	Kion mi manĝos? La lokajn manĝaĵojn, kompreneble. Tiom, kiom mi povos! Ĉiom! Sed … serioze, Sara. Estas neniu kialo timi. Oni salutas ĉiujn. Kiu ajn kaj kia ajn vi estas, de kie ajn vi venas, kiom ajn vi pezas, kiun ajn vi amas … tio ne gravas. Ĉiuj estas bonvenaj ĉe la UK.
Sara	Nu … mi ne povas pensi pri ajna kialo ne partopreni, kiam vi priskribas ĝin tiel! Ĉu estas iu, kun kiu mi devas paroli? Ĉu mi devas fari ion?
Roberto	Necesas nur iri al la kongresa retejo kaj tie plenigi la aliĝilon. Kial ne fari tion nun? Via Esperanto jam estas tre bona, kaj vi ĝis nun neniam ajn parolis Esperanton eksterlande. Jam temp' está!

2 Match the English and the Esperanto.

a It will be everybody there's common language

b Whose idea was that?

c Whoever you love

d There's nobody at all left who I could speak with

e You have no idea

f Wherever you come from

g Is there anybody I have to speak to?

h Nobody's language and at the same time everybody's

i Whoever you are and whatever you're like

j I'll somehow be able to speak

k On one hand … on the other

l You've never spoken Esperanto abroad

1 Vi havas neniun ideon

2 Restas neniu ajn, kun kiu mi povas paroli

3 Ĉu estas iu, kun kiu mi devas paroli?

4 Kies ideo tio estis?

5 Ĝi estos ĉies komuna lingvo tie

6 Mi iel kapablos paroli

7 Nenies lingvo kaj samtempe ĉies

8 Unuflanke … aliflanke

9 De kie ajn vi venas

10 Kiu ajn kaj kia ajn vi estas

11 Vi neniam parolis Esperanton eksterlande

12 Kiun ajn vi amas

3 Based on the conversation, decide whether these statements are true or false. If false, give a corrected version.

Example: Post unu monato Roberto iros al Slovakio. *Post du semajnoj Roberto iros al Slovakio.*

a Sara iam komencis lerni la slovakan.

b Roberto intencas neniom manĝi.

c Sara havas tro por fari.

d Neniu parolos Esperanton tie.

e Sara havis bonan ideon pri tio, kio okazos.

f Neniu estas bonvena ĉe la UK.

 4 10.04 Now listen to the conversation again line by line and repeat.

Language discovery 1

1 **What phrases does Sara use to present the two sides of an argument?**

2 **What do you notice about the word for *a reason*?**

3 **The conversation uses a verb salutas *greets*. If saluton is *hello*, what does saluti mean? What's a saluto?**

4 **Find the words for *nobody, everybody's, never, somehow, nobody's* and *for some reason* in the conversation.**

1 THE REST OF THE 'TABLE WORDS'

In addition to the **ki-** and **ti-tabelvortoj** (Unit 6), there are three other rows to the table: the **neni-**, the **ĉi-** and the **i-tabelvortoj**.

The endings are:

-o	-e	-u	-am	-al	-el	-om	-es	-a
a thing (an **o**-word)	place	a specific -**o**, a person	time	cause	manner	quantity, amount	possession	quality, kind, sort

Once you know that the **neni-tabelvortoj** are all negatives, then you can work out the meanings of the words:

nenio	nenie	neniu	neniam	nenial	neniel	neniom	nenies	nenia
nothing	*nowhere*	*nobody*	*never*	*for no reason*	*in no way*	*none, no quantity*	*nobody's*	*no kind*

Similarly, the meanings of the **ĉi-tabelvortoj** become clear once you know that they mean *every, each, all*:

ĉio	ĉie	ĉiu	ĉiam	ĉial	ĉiel	ĉiom	ĉies	ĉia
all, everything	*everywhere*	*each, everybody*	*always*	*for every reason*	*in every way*	*the whole quantity, all of it*	*everybody's*	*every kind*

The **tabelvortoj** beginning with **i-** refer to indefinites, something indeterminate:

Io	Ie	Iu	Iam	Ial	Iel	Iom	Ies	Ia
something	*somewhere*	*somebody, some (person or thing)*	*at some time, ever*	*for some reason*	*in some way, somehow*	*some quantity*	*somebody's*	*some kind*

The pattern is as follows:

nenio	nenie	neniu	neniam	nenial	neniel	neniom	nenies	nenia
ĉio	ĉie	ĉiu	ĉiam	ĉial	ĉiel	ĉiom	ĉies	ĉia
io	ie	iu	iam	ial	iel	om	ies	ia

2 AJN

Ajn is chiefly used with **ki-tabelvortoj**:

Kiu ajn venos estos bonvena.	*Whoever comes will be welcome.*
Kiom ajn mi laboris, mi neniam havis sufiĉe da mono.	*I never had enough money, however much I worked.*

You'll also see it used with other **tabelvortoj**:

Mi estas tiel malsata, ke mi manĝos ion ajn.	*I'm so hungry that I'll eat anything (at all).*
Ne gravas la horo. Venu iam ajn.	*The time doesn't matter. Come whenever you like.*
Estas simpla tasko. Iu ajn povas fari ĝin.	*It's an easy job. Anyone (at all) can do it.*

3 RELATIVE KI-TABELVORTOJ WITH OTHER TABELVORTOJ

You've seen the **ki-tabelvortoj** used as relative pronouns:

la viro, kiu legas la libron	*the man who is reading the book*
la virino, kun kiu ŝi parolas	*the woman she's speaking with*

The **ki-tabelvorto** can also follow other **tabelvortoj**:

Mi tre ŝatas tion, kion vi faris.	*I really like what you did.*
La restoracio troviĝas tie, kie antaŭe estis lernejo.	*The restaurant is where the school used to be.*
Li estas ĝuste tia, kia mi memoras lin!	*He's exactly like I remember him!*
Manĝu tiom, kiom vi volas!	*Eat as much as you like!*

It is acceptable to drop the initial **tabelvorto**, leaving just the **ki-tabelvorto**, so you will often see **Mi tre ŝatas, kion vi faris** and **La restoracio troviĝas, kie antaŭe estis lernejo.**

Practice 1

1 Give the meaning of the table words in the sentences below.

   a Neniel eblas, ke mi estos lia edzino. Estas nenia kialo fari tion.

   b Mi manĝis tiom da kuko, ke restas preskaŭ neniom por la aliaj.

   c Ĉiaj homoj estas fratoj, eĉ tiuj, kiujn mi ne ŝatas.

   d Ĉiel ajn mi provis fari ĝin, mi ne sukcesis.

   e Mia mano estas rompita, tial mi tiel malbone skribas.

   f Ĉiu virino estas ies filino.

2 Fill in the gaps with an appropriate tabelvorto from the box to answer the questions correctly.

ial	ĉiom	iam	iel	iom	tiel

   a Kiam vi pensas vojaĝi al Usono? – Mi ne certas. _____ baldaŭ, eble en somero

   b Ĉu vi parolas la portugalan? – Mi parolas ĝin _____ sed ne multe.

   c Kial li faris ĝin tiel? – _____ sed mi ne certas, fakte.

   d Ĉu vi ŝatis la koncerton? – Jes! Ĝi estis _____ bona, ke mi volas iri denove!

   e Kiom da kuko restis? – _____! Ĝi estis tro malbongusta por manĝi!

   f Kiel vi faros ĝin? – Mi ne scias, sed _____ mi sukcesos fari ĝin.

3 Read the text and fill in the gaps.

Jen rakonto pri kvar homoj, kiuj nomiĝas Ĉiu, Iu, Iu Ajn, kaj Neniu.

Estis grava tasko por fari. (*Everybody*) _____ certis, ke faros ĝin (*somebody*) _____. Povus fari ĝin (*anybody*) _____, sed (*nobody*) _____ faris ĝin. (*Somebody*) _____ koleris pri tio, ĉar estis la devo de (*everybody*) _____. (*Everybody*) _____ kredis, ke (*anybody*) _____ povus fari ĝin, sed (*nobody*) _____ eksciis, ke faros ĝin (*nobody*) _____. Rezulte, (*everybody*) _____ plendis pri (*somebody*) _____, kiam (*nobody*) _____ faris tion, kion povus fari (*anybody*) _____.

Vocabulary builder 2

 10.05 Look at the words and complete the missing English words. Then listen and try to imitate the pronunciation of the speakers.

SENTOJ *FEELINGS*

senti sin X	*to feel X* (lit. *to feel oneself X*)
konfuzita	*confused*
koleri / ekkoleri	*to be angry / get angry*
embarasita	*embarrassed*
kulpa	*guilty*
honti	*to be ashamed*

esti kontenta	to be _____
dubi	to doubt
malcerta	_____
sociema	sociable
memfida	self-confident
trista	sad
streĉita	stressed
deprimita	depressed
superŝutita	overwhelmed
ekscitita	_____
amata	loved

LANGUAGE TIP

You'll notice in the conversation that Sara says things like **Mi sentas min nervoza** *I feel nervous*. Saying *to feel* in Esperanto is **senti sin**, which is an example of a reflexive verb, where the action is done to oneself. Use **min** with **mi**, **vin** with **vi** and **ni** with **nin**, but **sin** *him / her / itself / themselves* with **li**, **ŝi**, **ĝi** and **ili**.

Conversation 2

NEW EXPRESSIONS

 10.06 Look at and listen to the words and expressions that are used in the following conversation. Note their meanings.

la pag-sistemo povas esti konfuza	the payment system can be confusing
riĉaj kaj proksimaj landoj	rich and nearby countries
elekti la unuan kategorion	choose the first category
maljusta	unfair
bonŝanca	lucky
peti monon	to ask for money
ĵus	just now
organizanto	organizer
simile	similarly
viziti restoracion	visit a restaurant
ĉiaokaze	in any event
(kun)kanti	to sing (along)
amuzado	fun, amusement
turismado	sightseeing, tourism
mi tuj konfirmos mian	I will immediately confirm my pre-order
antaŭmendon kaj antaŭpagos	and pay in advance
flugi el … al …	to fly from … to …
antaŭĝui viziti Slovakion	to look forward to visiting Slovakia

10.07 *Sara is filling out her* **aliĝilo** *while talking to Roberto about the Congress.*

1 Why is Roberto relaxed about not knowing how to get from the airport to the congress venue?

Sara	Roberto, mi bezonas vian helpon. Mi ne scias kiel ĝuste plenigi la aliĝilon. Mi sentas min nervoza, ĉar mi ne komprenas ĉion. Mi ektimas nun. Ekzemple, mi eĉ ne komprenas, kiom mi devas pagi.
Roberto	Ho jes, la pag-sistemo povas esti konfuza. Estas normale, ke vi estas konfuzita. Nu, temas pri tio, ke homoj, kiuj loĝas en riĉaj kaj proksimaj landoj, devas pagi pli. Do vi devas elekti la unuan kategorion, ĉar vi venas el Britio.
Sara	Sed kial? Mi opinias tion tre maljusta! Mi ne estas riĉa! Nun mi ekkoleras!
Roberto	Nu, vi ne sentas vin riĉa, eble. Sed kion pri homoj en Afriko, aŭ malriĉaj landoj? Ili ne havas monon, foje eĉ ne havas domon. Do kompare kun ili, vi ja estas riĉa, ĉu ne?
Sara	Ho, mi ekkomprenas! Vi pravas. Mi estas kaj riĉa kaj bonŝanca. Mi ne devas laboradi dum la tuta semajno aŭ petadi monon aŭ manĝaĵon. Kiel embarasita kaj kulpa mi sentas min.
Roberto	Ne gravas, Sara. Do, denove al la aliĝilo …
Sara	Fakte, mi ekhontas nun! Nu, pro tio, kion mi ĵus diris, komprenelbe, sed ankaŭ ĉar mi ne komprenas kion elekti por loĝado kaj manĝado. Tiel malfacila mi ne imagis tion.
Roberto	Pri loĝado vi havas la elekton aŭ resti en hotelo, kiun aranĝis la organizantoj, aŭ aranĝi vian propran. Kostas malpli, se vi estas kontenta kunloĝi kun iu alia. Simile pri manĝado; aŭ vi pagas pli kaj ricevos ĝin ĉe la kongreso, aŭ vi trovos vian propran en la urbo.
Sara	Nu, mi estas tro timema por kunloĝi kun homoj, kiujn mi ne konas. Sed mi dubas, ĉu mi povos aranĝi mem hotelon en lando, kiun mi ne konas. Do mi pagos pli por resti sola en oficiala hotelo. Pri manĝado mi sentas min malcerta. Unuflanke mi preferas esti certa, kie mi manĝos. Sed plaĉas al mi la ideo, ke mi povos iradi de unu restoracio al alia, kaj ne devos vizitadi ĉiam la saman.
Roberto	Kutime mi elektas resti en la sama loko, ĉar mi estas socioema kaj kunmanĝema.
Sara	Ho, mi ĵus vidis la tutan koston por partopreni la kongreson, resti en oficiala hotelo, kaj manĝi en la tiea restoracio. Estas tro por komencanto, ĉu ne? Mi ne tiel bone povas paroli Esperanton.
Roberto	Vi estas tro malmemfida, Sara! Vi ja bone komprenas la lingvon. Ĉiaokaze, estos pli ol simpla parolado: okazos dancado, kunkantado, kunlaborado, kuntrinkado, amuzado, turismado, kaj multe pli.
Sara	Ĉu tiom? Do, mi tuj konfirmos mian antaŭmendon kaj antaŭpagos. Ho ne, mi ĵus ekhavis plian penson! Kiel ni vojaĝos al la kongresejo? Ni tute ne konas Slovakion.
Roberto	Estas facile. Ni flugos el Londono al Bratislavo. Iu renkontos nin tie kaj diros al ni kiel vojaĝi poste. Ĉiam estas iu organizanto por renkonti homojn, kiam ili alvenas.
Sara	Bonege! Nu, nun vi ekscias, ke mi ĵus konfirmis! Mi ekvojaĝos post du semajnoj kaj antaŭĝuas viziti Slovakion!

128

2 Match the English and the Esperanto.

a I don't have to work all week long	**1** Mi ekkoleras
b I don't speak Esperanto so well	**2** Ho, mi ekkomprenas!
c I'm getting angry	**3** Mi ne devas petadi monon aŭ manĝaĵon
d Well, now you know that I've confirmed!	**4** Manĝi en la tiea restoracio
e I just had another thought!	**5** Mi ne devas laboradi dum la tuta semajno
f Oh, I get it!	**6** Mi ne parolas Esperanton tiel bone
g I don't have to ask for money or food	**7** Nu, nun vi ekscias, ke mi ĵus konfirmis!
h Eat in the restaurant there	**8** Mi ekvojaĝos post du semajnoj
i There'll be dancing and drinking together	**9** Mi ĵus ekhavis plian penson!
j I set off in two weeks' time	**10** Okazos dancado kaj kuntrinkado

Language discovery 2

1 **The preposition kun** *with* **is often used as though it were a prefix and gives the effect of doing something together. In this conversation you saw kunlabori, kunloĝi kun iu alia and kuntrinki. What do you think they mean?**

2 **What could Roberto mean when he says he's kunmanĝema (kun-manĝ-ema)?**

3 **How would you translate la tiea restoracio (tie-a), la tiama (tiam-a) prezidento estis Barack Obama, and kioma (kiom-a) horo estas?**

EK- AND -AD-

Starting with ek-

The prefix **ek-** indicates the start of an action:

ekdormi	*to fall asleep*	**ekvidi**	*to catch sight of*

Sometimes it indicates that you're not talking about a prolonged activity, but an action that was sudden and then over:

ekbrili / ekfulmi	*to flash*	**ekkrii**	*to exclaim*

There is a crossover between **ek-** and **komenci**:

Mi eklernis / komencis lerni Esperanton,   *I started learning Esperanto when I was 20.*
kiam mi estis 20-jara.

Prolonging with -ad-

The suffix **-ad-**, in contrast, is used to indicate that an action takes longer:

Li parolis pri la milito.	*He talked about the war.*
Li paroladis pri la milito.	*He gave a speech about the war.*

It generally gives the idea that the action is continuous, repeated or habitual:

Continuous	**Mi kuradis, ĝis mi ne plu povis.** *I ran (kept on running) until I couldn't any more.*
Repeated	**Mia filino petadis, ĝis finfine mi donis al ŝi dolĉaĵon.** *My daughter kept on asking until I finally gave her a sweet.*
Habitual	**Kiam mi estis juna, mi ludadis futbalon, sed nun mi nur spektas ĝin.** *When I was young I used to play (would play) football but now I only watch it.*

Another one of its uses is to express an activity when the usual **o**-form indicates an isolated act. This occurs when the basic form of a word is a verb:

kanti	*to sing*	**kanto**	*a song*	**kantado**	*singing*
paroli	*to speak*	**parolo**	*an utterance*	**parolado**	*a speech*
pensi	*to think*	**penso**	*a thought*	**pensado**	*thinking, contemplation*

It plays a similar role when the main form of the word is a noun and you need to express the idea of action:

broso	*a brush*	**brosi**	*to brush*	**brosado**	*brushing*
martelo	*a hammer*	**marteli**	*to hammer*	**martelado**	*hammering*

Practice 2

1 **By applying affixes to the following roots you will be able to create an equivalent to the English word. Sometimes you will need to apply more than one to a single word. Identify which ones you need from the following list.**

> ek- x 4   -ar- x 4
> -ad- x 2   -et- x 1

    Example: dormi (*to nap*)   *dormeti*
    a   manĝi (*to start eating*)
    b   amiko (*a group of friends*)
    c   dormi (*sleeping*)
    d   dormi (*to start napping*)

e papero (*a ream of paper*)

f pluvi (*to start raining*)

g scii (*to find out*)

h manĝi (*eating*)

i Esperantisto (*community of Esperanto speakers*)

j haro (*hair (collection on the head)*)

CULTURE TIP

To make it easier to attend the large Esperanto events, there are often groups travelling together called **karavanoj** *caravans*, with details of the route appearing on the relevant websites. All you have to do is head to one of the spots on the route at the right time. If two events occur in quick succession near to each other, you'll often find a **karavano** or two set up.

---

2 Enter the correct ki-tabelvorto in the following sentences.

a Mi aĉetis tiom, _____ eblis aĉeti, ĉar mi treege ŝatas ĝin.

b Ŝi ne estas tia, _____ vi imagas ŝin. Ŝi fakte estas tre afabla.

c Mi faris ĝin tiel, _____ vi diris, sed ĝi ne funkcias.

d Mi ĝis nun ne komprenas tion, _____ vi celas. Bonvolu diri alivorte.

e Jen iu, _____ alvenas ĝuste nun.

f Jen iu, _____ mi konas.

Reading

Read these reviews of hotels near the Universala Kongreso and rank them from most positive to most negative.

a Aĉe! Ĉio estas aĉa!

b Mi sentas min kiel honorulo, tiel bone estas ĉio. La manĝaĵo ege bongustas, kaj la homoj, kiuj laboras tie, estas treege helpemaj. Mi tre rekomendas!

c Unuflanke la hotelo kostis malmulte. Aliflanke, mi ne tre ŝatis ĝin. Pro la malgranda kosto, mi povas iom rekomendi ĝin.

d Sufiĉe bona hotelo, dankon! Ne ĉio estis perfekta, sed ĉio estis almenaŭ bona.

_____ *Best hotel*

_____

_____

_____ *Worst hotel*

Writing

Fill in the aliĝilo for the Universala Kongreso.

Via persona nomo: _____

Via familia nomo: _____

Via loĝlando: _____

Via retadreso: _____

Ĉu vi estas membro de UEA? (J / N)

Ĉu vi volas kongresan loĝadon (J / N)_____, aŭ ĉu vi organizos propran (J / N)_____?

Ĉu vi volas kongresan manĝadon (J / N)_____, aŭ ĉu vi aranĝas propran (J / N)_____?

Ĉu vi estas vegetarano? (J / N)

Ĉu vi partoprenos la post-kongresan viziton al la ĉefurbo? (J / N)

Listening

 10.08 Listen to this conversation, in which Erik asks Georgo what he thinks about going to Japan. Georgo thinks it's out of the question for him to go. Why? What makes him change his mind?

Listening and speaking

 10.09 Your friend is talking at length about his last holiday. You only need to give a few reactions. Practise reacting.

Amiko:	Kaj post tiam ni iris al alia hotelo. Sed ankaŭ ĉi tiun ni ne ŝatis. Ĝi estis longe for de la urbo, kaj ni ne povis bone vidi dum la vespero, kiam ni revenis. Mi vere timis.
You:	(Say 'How frightening!')
Amiko:	Ĝuste! Do ni decidis resti en la hotelo kaj ne iri al aliaj lokoj. Ĉio estis do tre teda.
You:	(Say 'That's terrible! How boring!')
Amiko:	Sed ne ĉiam teda, tamen. Ĉu vi scias, kiun ni vidis en la hotelo unu tagon? Tiun kantiston, kiun vi amas!
You:	(Say 'Oh my god! Cool!')
Amiko:	Kaj ĉu vi vidas? Li skribis mesaĝon por vi en mia libro.
You:	(Say 'Unbelievable!')

? Test yourself

1 How would you translate the following into English?

   a pensado

   b ludado

   c dancado

   d studado

   e eklabori

   f ekdormi

   g ekbrili

2 Unscramble these words for feelings.

   a ikerol

   b pulka

   c stairt

   d ĉitarest

   e ataam

   f fuoknizat

   g tkoennat

   h imfeamd

   i esrupŝtiaut

   j rbmsaeatia

3 Find the correct word (related to Esperanto travel) based on the description.

   Example: homoj, kiuj vojaĝas kune al kongreso   *Karavano*

   a la homoj, kiuj organizas eventon

   b dokumento por aliĝi

   c loko, kie vi ricevas nomŝildon kaj manĝkuponojn

   d ĉambro, en kiu vi povas paroli aliajn lingvojn

SELF-CHECK

I CAN ...
○ ... describe how I feel.
○ ... correctly use Esperanto exclamations.
○ ... talk about holiday and travel.
○ ... book a trip to an Esperanto event.

En la flughaveno
At the airport

In this unit, you will learn how to:
▶ *give instructions, orders and requests.*
▶ *request information about using public transport.*
▶ *ask for and understand directions.*
▶ *describe positions and movement from one place to another.*
▶ *explain what you used to do.*

CEFR: (A2) *Can understand everyday signs and notices: in public places, such as streets, restaurants, railway stations and work places, such as instructions, directions, warnings.* **(A2)** *Can get simple information about travel, use of public transport, give directions and buy tickets.* **(A2) Can ask for and give directions referring to a map or plan.* **(B1)** *Can give detailed instructions.*

⭐ Pasporta Servo *Passport Service*

Before there was CouchSurfing or AirBNB, for example, Esperanto had its **Pasporta Servo** (*Passport Service*). Today, over 1000 **gastigantoj** (*hosts*) in more than 80 **landoj** (*countries*) welcome people **en siajn hejmojn** (*into their homes*). Speaking Esperanto is usually the only requirement, although some hosts may attach certain conditions, such as not accepting **fumantoj** (*smokers*).

Some hosts are happy to meet their **gastoj** (*guests*) at the **flughaveno** (*airport*) and to act as a **ĉiĉerono** (*tour guide*) for them. Others get on with **ĉiutaga vivo** (*daily life*), while their guests go **en la urbon** (*into town*) by themselves and **reveni hejmen** (*come back home*) to **tranokti** (*sleep overnight*). But you can always ask them in advance for directions and to tell you about the **vidindaĵoj** (*sights*) and they'll be happy to tell you **kien iri** (*where to go*) to see the best places that their town has to offer.

You can search for hosts in your chosen destination on the **Pasporta Servo** website pasportaservo.org or by buying its book. **Serĉu** (*look for*) the town you want to visit, **kontaktu** (*contact*) the host, and **mendu vian bileton** (*book your ticket*)!

 The last sentence is asking you to do something. What letter do verbs end with if they're instructions, orders, commands or requests?

Vocabulary builder 1

11.01 Look at the words and phrases and complete the missing English words and expressions. Then listen and try to imitate the pronunciation of the speakers.

VOJAĜADO *TRAVEL*

flughaveno	*airport*
taksio	_____
stacidomo	*a train station*
trajno	*a train*
metroo (subtertrajno)	*metro (underground train)*
marŝi	*to walk, stride, march*
piediri	*to go by foot*
aviadilo	*plane*
flugi (flugo)	*to fly (a flight)*
veturi	*to go (when using a vehicle)*
buso	_____
bileto	*ticket*
halti (haltejo)	*to stop (a stop)*
vojo	*way, route*

Conversation 1

NEW EXPRESSIONS

11.02 Look at and listen to the words and expressions that are used in the following conversation. Note their meanings.

Ni atendu ankoraŭ iom.	*Let's wait a bit longer.*
Ni parolu laŭte en Esperanto.	*Let's talk loudly in Esperanto.*
Ni atendu, ĝis ni vidos lin.	*Let's wait until we see him.*
Pardonu, ke mi ne venis ĝustatempe.	*Sorry (excuse, forgive) that I didn't arrive on time.*
mi montros al vi la vojon	*I'll show you the route, the way*
kiel atingi la kongresejon	*how to reach / get to the congress venue*
plej rapide estas …	*fastest is …*
Vi bezonos eĉ ne du minutojn por atingi ĝin.	*It won't even take two minutes to reach it.*
aĉetu viajn biletojn per la maŝino	*buy your tickets using the machine*

11.03 *Sara and Roberto have arrived at Bratislava airport and are expecting somebody to be waiting for them.*

1 How do they recognize Miro? How long will it take them to reach the bus stop?

Sara	Atendas nin iu viro, Roberto, sed mi vidas neniun. Ĉu vi?
Roberto	Ankoraŭ ne. Nu, mi vidas multajn homojn, sed ne la ĝustan. Ni atendu ankoraŭ iom. Eble iu venos baldaŭ.
Sara	Kiel rekoni lin? Kiel li rekonos nin? Ho, mi ekhavis ideon, Roberto! Ni parolu laŭte en Esperanto!
Roberto	Ne, ni ne faru tion! Estas tro multaj homoj ĉi tie. Ni atendu, ĝis ni vidos lin.
Sara	Ho, rigardu! Jen viro kun Esperanto-flago en la mano! Venu! Ni parolu al li!
Roberto	Saluton! Pardonu nin … sed ĉu vi atendas nin?
Miro	Ĝuste! Pardonu, ke mi ne venis ĝustatempe. Bonvolu veni kun mi kaj mi montros al vi kiel atingi la kongresejon. Plej rapide estas iri al la urbo per taksio ĝis la stacidomo. Poste vi veturos per trajno.
Sara	Mi preferas marŝi al la urbo, se eblas. Ni estis en aviadilo kaj devis sidi dum la tuta flugo. Ĝenas min tiom da sidado.
Miro	Bone, mi tute komprenas, tamen estas tro longa distanco por marŝi la tutan vojon. Mi povas fari al vi la jenan rekomendon: marŝu al la bushaltejo, poste veturu per la buso ĝis la stacidomo, kaj poste piediru al la kongresejo. La bushaltejo estas ekster la flughaveno, sed ne longe for. Estas nur mallonga distanco. Vi bezonos eĉ ne du minutojn por atingi ĝin. Aĉetu viajn biletojn per la maŝino ĉe la haltejo!

> **LANGUAGE TIP**
>
> Even **jen** *there is, there are, look!* can be used in other roles by adding Esperanto endings. Miro gives it an **a**-ending and uses it to mean something like *the following* when he says **la jena rekomendo** *the following recommendation*.

2 Match the Esperanto and the English.

a	Maybe someone will come soon	**1**	Kiel rekoni lin?
b	Oh, look!	**2**	Ni parolu al li
c	Some man is waiting for us	**3**	Veturu per buso
d	How to recognize him?	**4**	Kiel li rekonos nin?
e	No, let's not do that	**5**	Pardonu, ke mi ne venis ĝustatempe
f	Sorry I didn't come on time	**6**	Piediru al la kongresejo
g	Let's speak to him	**7**	Atendas nin iu viro
h	How will he recognize us?	**8**	Ho, rigardu!
i	Go by bus	**9**	Eble iu venos baldaŭ
j	Go by foot to the congress venue	**10**	Ne, ni ne faru tion

136

3 Decide whether these statements are correct (**ĝuste**) or incorrect (**malĝuste**).

   a Only Sara and Roberto are at the airport.
   b Miro arrived on time.
   c Miro was carrying an Esperanto flag.
   d Miro left them behind.
   e Sara wants to travel by taxi.
   f The bus stop is close.

 4 11.04 **Now listen again to the conversation line by line and repeat.**

Language discovery 1

1 **How does Sara say *look!* and *come on!* in the conversation?**

2 **How does Roberto say *we shouldn't do that / let's not do that*?**

3 **Esperanto uses the same word for *by / with / using / from* when these refer to a tool or a means of transport. Which word is it? Find it in these expressions from the conversation:**

   a Plej rapide estas iri al la urbo per taksio. (*The quickest is to go to town by taxi.*)
   b Tiam veturi per la buso ĝis la stacidomo. (*Then travel by bus as far as the station.*)
   c Aĉetu viajn biletojn per la maŝino. (*Buy your tickets from the machine.*)

1 GIVING INSTRUCTIONS USING THE U-ENDING

The **u**-ending in Esperanto indicates an expression of a wish, such as requesting or inviting somebody to do something:

Bonvolu ripeti tion.	*Please repeat that.*
Manĝu tiom, kiom vi volas.	*Eat as much as you like.*

When the **u**-ending is used with **ni**, the speaker is included and it's no longer an instruction but a suggestion or exhortation about a wished-for outcome, a desired state:

Ni manĝu du pliajn.	*Let's eat two more. / We should eat two more.*
Ĉu ni iru?	*Shall we go? / Should we go?*

Negations are formed by putting **ne** before the verb:

Ne fumu!	*Don't smoke!*	**Ne mensogu!**	*Don't lie!*

Ni diru la veron; ni ne mensogu.   *Let's tell the truth; let's not lie. / We should tell the truth; we shouldn't lie.*

> **LANGUAGE TIP**
>
> Grammar books often refer to using the **u**-ending to command, invite or request as the imperative. The **u**-ending in Esperanto covers more ground than that, but it's helpful to think about it as a way of giving instructions. You'll see further uses of the **u**-ending in Unit 12.

2 WORKING WITH *PLEASE*

Bonvolu, *please*, comes from **bonvoli** (**bona** *good* + **voli** *to want*) and takes the **u**-ending to form a polite request.

Manĝu!   *Eat!*   **Bonvolu manĝi!**   *Please eat!*

> **LANGUAGE TIP**
>
> Be careful not to put two **u**-endings together: if you're using **bonvolu**, then that verb is already in the **u**-form and the one indicating the action stays with its **i**-ending: **bonvolu trinki** not **bonvolu trinku**. Alternatively, use **bonvole** (literally *good-willingly*), which goes with **-u**: **bonvole trinku**. Both **bonvolu trinki** and **bonvole trinku** can be translated as *please drink*.

Practice 1

1 Match the English and Esperanto.

a Drink your coffee!

b Be happy!

c Let's learn Esperanto!

d Don't drink!

e Let's go dancing!

f Don't eat too much!

g Be more talkative!

h Let's be friends!

i Let's not be enemies!

j Let's go to the World Esperanto Congress!

1 Ne trinku!

2 Estu pli parolema!

3 Ne manĝu tro!

4 Ni ne estu malamikoj!

5 Estu feliĉa!

6 Ni iru al la Universala Kongreso!

7 Ni iru danci

8 Trinku vian kafon!

9 Ni lernu Esperanton!

10 Ni estu amikoj!

2 Change each instruction into a polite form using bonvolu and then rewrite it using the alternative bonvole.

Example: Parolu malrapide!   Bonvolu paroli malrapide.
                                   Bonvole parolu malrapide.

a Venu viziti min!

b Aĉetu du biletojn!

c Renkontu min ĉe la flughaveno!

d Ne forgesu vian flugon!

e Vojaĝu per buso ĝis la stacidomo!

f Veturu al la stacidomo por trovi min!

3 Add the correct verb ending to these sentences.

a Bonvolu don_____ al mi la monon por la bileto.

b Bonvole ne parol_____ rapide – mi estas komencanto.

c Se vi bonvolos respond_____ al mia demando, tio multe helpos min.

d Bonvol_____ paroli al mia frato, ĉar li estas timema.

e Bonvol_____ diru al mi, kiel vi nomiĝas.

Vocabulary builder 2

11.05 Look at the words and phrases and complete the missing English words and expressions. Then listen and try to imitate the pronunciation of the speakers.

POZICIOJ *POSITIONS*

apud la monumento	*beside the monument*
antaŭ /malantaŭ la domo	*in front of / _____ the house*
dekstre / maldekstre	*on the right / _____*
dekstre de la pordo	*on the right of the door*
sur la tablo	*on the table*
sub la akvo	*_____ the water*
super la arboj	*above the trees*
ĉirkaŭ la mondo	*around the world*
inter vi kaj mi	*_____ you and me*
preter la limoj	*beyond the limits*
ĉe mi, ĉe universitato	*at mine / at my house, at university*
ekster la lernejo	*outside the school*
trans la rivero	*across the river*
tra la fenestro	*through the window*
supre de la monto	*on top of the mountain*

Conversation 2

NEW EXPRESSIONS

11.06 Look at and listen to the words and expressions that are used in the following conversation. Note their meanings.

Kie ĝi troviĝas? Kien ni iru?	*Where's it found? Where should we go?*
per tiu ne eblas eliri	*it's not possible to go out using that one*
apud ĝi troviĝas la ĝusta	*the right one's next to it*
dekstre / dekstre de la enirpordo	*on the right / on the right of the entrance*
iru trans la taksihaltejon	*go across the taxi rank*
poste iru dekstren	*then head right*
marŝu preter la unuajn	*walk past the first ones*
eniru la buson / eliru el la buso	*get on / off the bus*
bushaltejen	*to the bus stop*
trairu la pordon	*go through the door*
ni iris laŭ tio, kion diris Katalina	*we went how Katalina said*
nek indikiloj, nek vojmontriloj	*neither something for indicating, nor something for showing the way*
ĉe la dekstra flanko	*on the right side*
tre helpa ilo por mi	*a very useful tool for me*
kie vi tranoktos (tra + nokto)	*where you will spend the night*
mi mian ricevis retpoŝte	*I got mine by email*
mi havas la detalojn surpapere	*I have the details on paper*

11.07 *Sara and Roberto need Miro's help to guide them out of the airport and to the bus stop, so that they can make it to the venue.*

1 Which bus stop do they head to?

Roberto	Bone, ni iru al la bushaltejo. Kie ĝi troviĝas, Miro? Kien ni iru?
Miro	Ĉu vi vidas la grandan pordon? Kelkaj homoj trairas ĝin nun, ĉu vi vidas?
Roberto	Ĉu ĉi tiun pordegon?
Miro	Ne, ne tiun. Per tiu ne eblas eliri, nur eniri. Sed apud ĝi troviĝas la ĝusta, per kiu eblas iri el la flughaveno. Ĉu vi vidas? Jen, dekstre. Dekstre de la enirpordo.
Roberto	Ho, jes! Jen la elirpordo! Mi ne vidis ĝin ĝis nun, ĉar kelkaj homoj estis inter ĝi kaj mi.
Miro	Nu, trairu ĝin kaj tiam transiru la taksihaltejon. Poste iru dekstren kaj vi vidos plurajn bushaltejojn. Vi bezonos ne la unuajn, sed la plej foran. Do marŝu preter la unuajn, ĝis vi atingos la finan.
Sara	Kion mi devos diri, kiam mi aĉetos la bileton, Miro? Mi tute ne kapablas paroli la slovakan.
Miro	Ne gravas, ĉar vi aĉetos la bileton per maŝino, kiu estas ĉe la haltejo. Eniru la buson kaj post duonhoro vi iros en la urbon kaj atingos la stacidomon. Tio estas la lasta haltejo, do vi ne iros preter ĝin. Eliru tie kaj trovu la aliajn esperantistojn, kiuj atendas tie. Ili scias, kien vi devos iri por atingi la kongresejon.
Roberto	Do, ni devos trairi la pordon, transiri la taksihaltejon, kaj poste ni iru dekstren preter la bushaltejojn, ĝis ni atingos la lastan, ĉe kiu ni trovos maŝinon, per kiu ni aĉetos bileton, ĉu ne? Ĉu en ordo? Bone – nun, bushaltejen!

Sure enough, there's a lady with an Esperanto flag waiting when they get off …

Katarina	Bonvenon! Ĉu vi longe vojaĝis por veni ĉi tien?
Sara	Sufiĉe longe, jes. Unue ni flugis per aviadilo, poste ni veturis per buso.
Katarina	Vi veturis jam aviadile kaj buse? Do, restas nur iri marŝe. Bonvolu sekvi min!

A few minutes later …

Katarina	Kaj jen la kongresejo! Mi devos nun reiri al la stacidomo, sed por vi estos facile trovi la akceptejon. Simple eniru la kongresejon kaj iru tuj maldekstren. Trairu la pordon, sur kiu vi vidos la afiŝon 'Bonvenon!' kaj vi atingos la akceptejon.

Unfortunately, something seems to have gone wrong …

Sara	Nu, ni iris laŭ tio, kion diris Katarina, sed mi vidas nenion ajn. Nek indikilojn, nek vojmontrilojn.

They approach a friendly-looking man and explain the problem.

Marko	Ho, la akceptejon vi volas! Ŝajne gvidis vin Katarina, ĉu ne? Ĉiam ŝi havas problemojn rekoni la diferencon inter dekstra kaj maldekstra. Troviĝas la akceptejo ĉe la dekstra flanko, ne la maldekstra!

At the reception …

Akceptejisto	Saluton! Ĉu vi havas vian konfirmilon?

Roberto	Mian kion?
Akceptejisto	Vian konfirmilon. Paperon, kiu konfirmas, ke vi pagis vian kotizon. Per ĝi mi scios, ĉu doni al vi manĝkuponojn, kie vi tranoktos, kaj tiel plu. Tre helpa ilo por mi.
Roberto	Mi ne sciis, ke eĉ ekzistas ĉi tiu afero! Mi ne legis pri tio en la informilo. Ĉu vi havas, Sara?
Sara	Mi mian ricevis retpoŝte, post kiam mi aliĝis. Per la aliĝilo eblas pagi kaj indiki, ĉu vi volas manĝi en la kongresejo kaj ricevi loĝadon, aŭ ĉu vi mem trovos manĝojn kaj loĝadon. Poste per retmesaĝo eblas konfirmi la detalojn. Vi do ne ricevis la konfirmilon, ĉu?
Akceptejisto	Mi helpos vin. Mi havas la detalojn surpapere en ĉi tiu longa listo. Ĉu vi vidas vian nomon?
Roberto	Nu … jes, ĉi tiu nomo estas mia, la jena. Kaj nun mi komprenas, kial mi ne ricevis la konfirmilon: mi ne donis ĝuste mian retpoŝtadreson!

CULTURE TIP

When you **aliĝi** *sign up* for an Esperanto event, you'll often be asked whether you want to **mendi** *book* the event's own **loĝado** *accommodation* and food, or whether you'll sort out your own arrangements. You'll receive **konfirmo** *confirmation* in a **konfirmilo** *confirmation letter* afterwards.

2 Match the English and Esperanto.

a You'll buy the ticket using a machine

b I can't see anything at all

c The registration area is found on the right side

d I got mine by email

e You'll need the furthest away

f Some people are going through it now

g A really useful tool for me

h You can only enter through it, not exit

i Some people are between it and me

j Where shall (should) we go?

k Get on the bus

l You've already travelled by plane and bus?

m To the bus stop

1 Tre helpa ilo por mi

2 Kelkaj homoj trairas ĝin nun

3 Per ĝi eblas nur eniri, ne eliri

4 Kien ni iru?

5 Kelkaj homoj estas inter ĝi kaj mi

6 Mi vidas nenion ajn

7 Vi jam veturis aviadile kaj buse?

8 Troviĝas la akceptejo ĉe la dekstra flanko

9 Vi bezonos la plej foran

10 Bushaltejen

11 Vi aĉetos la bileton per maŝino

12 Mi mian ricevis retpoŝte

13 Eniru la buson

Language discovery 2

1 Sara uses **per** to show her means of travel. Katarina doesn't. How does she say *travelled by plane and by bus*?

2 Roberto doesn't use **kie** but **kien** for *where* when he asks *where shall we go / should we go*? Miro doesn't use **dekstre** *on the right* but **dekstren** in **iru dekstren** *go to the right*. Which letter can be added to words to indicate that there's motion from one location towards another?

3 The conversation contains **maŝino, kiu estas ĉe la haltejo, ni atingos la lastan, ĉe kiu ni trovos maŝinon** and **troviĝas ĉe la dekstra flanko**. Which preposition in Esperanto shows that something is located close by something or in the general proximity?

1 INDICATING MOTION WITH THE N-ENDING

Some prepositions take the **n**-ending to indicate motion from one location towards another. Compare:

La infanoj kuras en la ĝardeno.	*The children are running in the garden.*
La infanoj kuras en la ĝardenon.	*The children are running into the garden.*
La kato saltas sur la tablo.	*The cat is jumping on the table.*
La kato saltas sur la tablon.	*The cat is jumping onto the table.*

Words like **kie** *where* and **tie** *there* also take the **n**-ending to indicate motion:

Kien vi volas iri por manĝi morgaŭ?	*Where do you want to go to eat tomorrow?*
Ni iru tien por manĝi, ĉu ne?	*We'll go there to eat, shall we?*

Since Esperanto can use adverbs to indicate places, they too take the **n**-ending when they need to show movement:

Mi iris nenien. Mi restis hejme la tutan tagon.	*I went nowhere. I stayed home all day.*
Baldaŭ mi iros hejmen.	*I'll go home soon.*

2 CREATING VERBS FROM PREPOSITIONS AND ADVERBS

Verbs can be created from constructions which use prepositions and adverbs. Roberto does this when he summarizes the directions given to him by Miro: **ni devos trairi la pordon** and **transiri la taksihaltejon**. These verbs are **trairi** *to go through* and **transiri** *to cross*.

There are many words constructed like this in regular use in Esperanto, such as **eniri** *to enter*, **eliri** *to exit*, **travivi** *to live through, to experience* and **postvivi** *to survive*.

If an adverb originally took an **n**-ending to indicate motion, then this form is collapsed into the verb rather than the **n**-less version:

Mi iros hejmen morgaŭ.   *I'll go back home tomorrow.*   **Mi hejmeniros morgaŭ.**

> **LANGUAGE TIP**
> Because the prepositions **al**, **ĝis** and **el** already indicate motion, they can never be followed by the **n**-ending.

3 PER AND -IL-: THE MEANS OF DOING THINGS

The preposition **per** shows the means to do something. It is often represented in English by *using*, *by* or *with*:

Ni veturis per buso.	*We travelled by bus.*
Mi aĉetis bileton per maŝino.	*I bought a ticket from / using a machine.*
Mi pagas per monbiletoj.	*I'm paying with cash (banknotes).*

The suffix **-il-** plays a similar role, indicating the tool used to do something:

Mi skribas per skribilo.	*I write with a pen.*

kuraci	*to cure*	**kuracilo**	*something for curing, such as a medicine*
montri la vojon	*to show the way*	**vojmontrilo**	*something which shows the way*
manĝi	*to eat*	**manĝilo**	*a utensil for eating, an item of cutlery*

You can use **ilo** as a standalone word meaning *a tool*.

> **LANGUAGE TIP**
>
> Because they were travelling inside the vehicles, Sara would also have been correct if she'd said **Unue ni flugis en aviadilo, poste ni veturis en buso**. It is also possible to avoid **per** and use the **e**-ending: **iri piede** *to go on foot*, **veturi buse** *to travel by bus*.

Practice 2

1 Select which of the forms is the correct one in the following sentences.

   a La infanoj kuras en la (ĉambro / ĉambron). *The children are running in the room.*
   b La infanoj kuras en la (ĉambro / ĉambron). *The children are running into the room.*
   c La knabino parolas kun la virino en la (trajno / trajnon). *The girl is speaking to the woman on the train.*
   d La knabo devas iri en la (trajno / trajnon). *The boy must go into the train.*
   e Ni iros en la (urbo / urbon) por manĝi morgaŭ. *We will go into town to eat tomorrow.*
   f Iru al la (vendejo / vendejon) kaj aĉetu fromaĝon. *Go to the shop and buy cheese.*
   g La viro staras (tie / tien), apud la (monumento / monumenton). *The man is standing there beside the monument.*
   h Bonvolu iri (tie / tien) kaj aĉeti ion por manĝi. *Please go there and buy something to eat.*
   i En la (mondo / mondon) venis nova sento. *A new feeling came into the world.*
   j La knabino devas meti la ludilon en la (skatolo / skatolon). *The girl must put the toy into the box.*
   k Revenu (hejme / hejmen) antaŭ la oka! *Come home before eight!*
   l La viro eniras la (ĉambro / ĉambron). *The man enters the room.*
   m Mi vidas la viron tra la (pordo / pordon). *I see the man through the door.*

2 Change the following constructions as required.

Example: La infano **iras en** la trajnon.   La infano *eniras* la trajnon.

a La knabino **iras el** la ĉambro. La knabino _____ el la ĉambro.

b La trajno **iris for.** La trajno _____.

c La knabo **iros hejmen** sabaton. La knabo _____ sabaton.

d La bona infano **iris supren** La bona knabo _____.

e **Iru preter** tiun arbon kaj vi vidos lin _____ tiun arbon kaj vi vidos lin.

f La Luno (*Moon*) **iras ĉirkaŭ** la Teron (*Earth*). La Luno _____ la Teron.

g Atentu (*be careful*), kiam vi **iros trans** la straton. Atentu, kiam vi _____ la straton.

h La Tero _____ la Suno. La Tero ĉirkaŭiras la Sunon.

3 Translate the following into Esperanto using per or -il- where appropriate:

a I bought it with cash.

b I will travel there by bus.

c He learned Esperanto using a great book.

d a vehicle (from **veturi**)

e a computer (from **komputi**)

f a wing (from **flugi** *to fly*)

Reading

Read the conversation between the man and the volunteer at the airport ahead of the Universala Kongreso.

Viro	Saluton! Mia hotelo estas en la ĉefa strato de la urbo. Kiel plej bone atingi ĝin?
Virino	Kiel vi preferas veturi? Per taksio? Troviĝas taksioj ne longe for. Eliru kaj iru maldekstren.
Viro	Mi ne volas pagi tiom da mono, tamen. Ĉu estas stacidomo ie?
Virino	Jes, certe. Por atingi ĝin iru suben laŭ la ŝtuparo. Ĉu vi jam havas bileton?
Viro	Bileton? Kompreneble ne. Mi ĵus alvenis.
Virino	Bedaŭrinde nun estas tro malfrue por aĉeti bileton. Sed foriros buso post dek minutoj, kiu alvenos en la urbon post unu horo. Ĝi estas sufiĉe malmultekosta.
Viro	Ĉu? Bone. Kie la bushaltejo troviĝas?
Virino	Vi devas eliri tra la pordego, kaj poste iri dekstren, ĝis vi atingos la finon de la strato.

1 **What direction should the man turn if he wants a taxi?**

2 **To get to the train station does the man need to go up or down?**

3 **What will the man find at the end of the street?**

Writing

Read Olivia's text message to Sara and fill in the blanks using the words in the box.

> kongresejon per eliris
> flughaveno buse rekomendis
> biletojn bushaltejon

Mi kaj Roberto sukcese flugis al la _____, kie nin renkontis loka viro, Miroslav. Li _____ veturi _____ taksio, sed ni preferis iri _____. Li do montris al ni la _____. Ne gravis, ke mi ne parolas la slovakan, ĉar eblis aĉeti _____ per maŝino. Alia homo renkontis nin, post kiam ni _____ el la buso, kaj baldaŭ ni sukcese atingis la _____.

Listening

 11.08 **Listen to Miro's directions while consulting the map. Where do you end up? Use the restaurant as a starting point.**

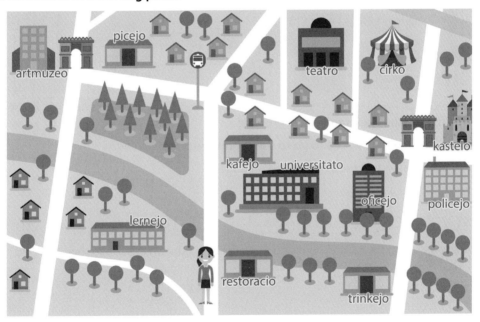

Speaking

Using the map, give some directions to some new arrivals at the Universala Kongreso telling them how to reach the places below.

1 The first person wants to go to the circus.
2 The second person wants to go to the art museum.
3 The third person wants to go to the restaurant.

Test yourself

1 Imagine that you're training your dog to respond to Esperanto. Tell him the following:
   a Go!
   b Come here!
   c Don't do that!
   d Don't eat that!
   e Be a good boy!

2 Add the **n**-ending where appropriate:

Ni vojaĝis al Bratislavo_____ por partopreni la Universala___ _____ Kongreso_____ _____. Kiam ni alvenis al la kongresejo_____, ni trairis granda_____ pordo_____ kaj trovis la akceptejo_____. Ni iris en ĝi_____ kaj ricevis niaj_____ manĝkuponoj_____ ĝustatempe por iri al la manĝejo_____. Do, ni tuj iris manĝeje_____!

3 Change the positional words in these examples to their opposites.

    a La infano ludas en la domo.

    b La kato dormas sub la tablo.

    c La viro staras antaŭ la arbo.

SELF-CHECK

I CAN ...
... give instructions, orders and requests.
... request information about using public transport.
... ask for and understand directions.
... describe positions and movement from one place to another.
... explain what I used to do.

12 Ĉe la Universala Kongreso
At the World Congress

In this unit, you will learn how to:
▶ *make a purchase and get a discount.*
▶ *talk about books.*
▶ *express wishes and recommendations.*

CEFR: (A2) *Can make simple purchases by stating what is wanted and asking the price.* **(B1)** *Can narrate a story or relate the plot of a book or film and describe reactions.* **(B1)** *Can exploit a basic repertoire of language and strategies to help keep a conversation or discussion going.*

⭐ Literaturo en Esperanto *Literature in Esperanto*

Sensurprize (*unsurprisingly*) the first Esperanto author was its initiator, Ludoviko Zamenhof, who wrote masterful **poezio** (*poetry*), **tradukoj** (*translations*) of Andersen and Shakespeare's *Hamlet*, and even the entire **Malnova Testamento** (*Old Testament*). Other authors, themselves really still learners, started writing poetry and some limited prose in those early days. The first Esperanto crime novel, **Pro Kio?**, was written in 1920.

By the 1920s, the style of Esperanto's authors had matured, and in Britain the magazine **Literaturo** (*Literature*) ran from 1919 to 1925. Budapest, and in particular the magazine **Literatura Mondo** (*Literary World*), saw the emergence of two of Esperanto's most eminent poets, 'the Poets' Poet' Kálmán Kalocsay and 'the People's Poet' Julio Baghy.

Stellan Engholm wrote the first Esperanto trilogy with his **Infanoj en Torento** (1936, 1939 and 1946) and Scottish poet William Auld wrote what is considered by many to be the finest piece of Esperanto literature, **La infana raso** (*The Mewling Race*) in 1956, for which he was nominated for the Nobel Prize for Literature. **Baldaŭ poste** (*soon afterwards*), Auld produced another masterpiece of Esperanto literature, **ĉi-foje** (*this time*) the 1958 **Esperanta Antologio** (*Esperanto Anthology*) 1887–1957. Tibor Sekelj became a crossover success when his travelogue **Nepalo malfermas la pordon** was translated into English as *Window on Nepal* in 1959, and his **Kumeŭaŭa, la filo de la ĝangalo** (*Kumewawa, the son of the jungle*) has been translated into over 20 languages, and is still a set text in Japanese schools.

Is it possible to give an idea of how much original Esperanto literature there is? **Certe** (*certainly*), if we consider the content of some specialist periodicals, such as **Fonto** (*Source*), which published 991 original poems by 138 authors between 1980 and 1993. The *Concise Encyclopedia of the Original Literature of Esperanto*, at 740 pages long, tells its own story about just how much literature Esperanto's writers have produced.

 Why isn't the **Malnova Testamento** called the **Maljuna Testamento**?

Vocabulary builder 1

12.01 Look at the words and phrases and complete the missing English words and expressions. Then listen and try to imitate the pronunciation of the speakers.

LIBROJ KAJ LEGADO *BOOKS AND READING*

mistera romano	*mystery novel*
krima / krim-romano	*crime novel*
fikcia	*fictional*
antologio	*anthology*
traduko	*translation*
nacilingva (= en nacia lingvo)	*in a national language*
poezio	_____
prozo	*prose*
fama verko	*famous work*
plena verkaro	*complete works*
komikso	_____
kolekto de poemoj de hispana poeto	*collection of poems by a Spanish poet*
proponi / rekomendi bonan libron	*recommend a good book*
rakonti rakonton	*to tell a story*

Conversation 1

NEW EXPRESSIONS

12.02 Look at and listen to the words and expressions that are used in the following conversation. Note their meanings.

libroservo (libro-servo)	*book service*
(ne) nepre	*(not) necessarily*
pli facile legebla	*more readable, easier to read*
ekde mia infanaĝo	*from / since my childhood*
ili postulas tro da lingvoscio	*they require too much language knowledge*
ili aspektas iom malnovaj	*they look a bit old*
serio da libroj pri nuntempa Rusio	*a series of books about current-day Russia*
la libroj ricevis premiojn	*the books received awards*
tre konata	*very well-known*
Mi konsilas, ke vi trafoliumu ĝin	*I advise you to leaf through it*
La fono estas Britio en la unua jarcento	*the background is Britain in the first century*
Mi ĵus konstatis, ke porkomencantan lernolibron mi ja bezonas	*I just realized that I do need a coursebook for beginners after all*

12.03 *Sara and Roberto are in the UK having a look in the* **libroservo.**

1   Why does Sara decide to buy a beginners' book?

Sara	Nekredeble! Mi ne kredas miajn okulojn, Roberto! Ĉieas esperantaj libroj! Ni butikumu!
Roberto	Kie komenci? Mi povas fari kelkajn rekomendojn, proponi bonajn librojn. Mi multajn librojn aĉetis de la libroservo interrete. Kiajn librojn vi ŝatas?
Sara	Ĉiajn. Misterajn, krimajn, fikciajn …
Roberto	Ĉu vi preferas, ke la libroj estu por komencantoj por ke vi komprenu ilin pli facile?
Sara	Ne nepre. Porkomencantaj libroj estos pli facile legeblaj, sed plej gravas, ke ili estu bonaj.
Roberto	Nu, unue ni iru tien, kie mi vidas la antologiojn. Tiuj estas tradukoj de nacilingvaj poezio kaj prozo. Homoj tradukis de la nacia lingvo en Esperanton, kaj nun ne plu necesas, ke vi komprenu la hungaran aŭ la makedonan por legi famajn verkojn de la tieaj kulturoj.
Sara	Kiel bona ideo! Kaj jen la Slovaka Antologio, ĉu vi vidas? Nu, ŝajnas al mi necese, ke la unua esperanta libro, kiun mi aĉetas, estu ĉi tiu, ĉu ne? Ho, rigardu; mi ĵus ekvidis kelkajn komiksojn, kiujn mi tre ŝatas … kaj ĉi tiun mi legas ekde mia infanaĝo!
Roberto	Do, nepras, ke vi aĉetu la tradukon, ĉu ne? Kion vi opinias pri historio kaj geografio? Mi vidas plurajn librojn pri tiuj temoj.
Sara	Mi ne tiom interesiĝas. Kaj mi pensas, ke ili postulas tro da lingvoscio. Plie ili aspektas iom malnovaj.
Roberto	Ne ĉiuj. Jen libro de Kalle Kniivilä, ĵurnalisto kiu verkis serion da libroj pri nuntempa Rusio. Mi vere rekomendas, ke vi aĉetu almenaŭ unu. Liaj libroj ricevis premiojn, en Esperantujo sed ankaŭ en diversaj landoj pro la nacilingvaj tradukoj.
Sara	Bonege! Do, mi aĉetos ĝin laŭ via rekomendo. Kion alian vi konas?
Roberto	Jen kolekto de poemoj de Jorge Camacho, hispana poeto. Li estas tre konata en Esperantujo. Mi konsilas, ke vi provu ĉi tiun. Trafoliumu por ekscii, ĉu plaĉas al vi.
Sara	Bele! Kion vi scias pri fikcio? Kion vi rekomendas? Ĉu vi konas bonajn krim-romanojn?
Roberto	Mi aŭdis pri kelkaj, sed ne legis. Sed ĉi tiun libron mi konas kaj rekomendas. Verkis ĝin Anna Lowenstein.
Sara	Pri kio temas?
Roberto	La fono estas Britio en la unua jarcento. Estas rakonto pri iu virino, kiu vojaĝas al Romo, kie ŝi renkontas la fruajn kristanojn. Mi opiniis ĝin treege ekscita.

Sara	Bone, post tia rekomendo, nepras, ke mi aĉetu ankaŭ ĝin! Ni iru al la libroservisto kaj petu, ke li vendu tiujn librojn al mi. Ho, mi ĵus konstatis, ke porkomencantan lernolibron mi ja bezonas.
Roberto	Ĉu? Sed vi jam decidis aĉeti tiujn aliajn. Porkomencantan vi ne bezonas.
Sara	Ne por mi … Sed mi deziras, ke mia fratino eklernu Esperanton. Tia libro helpos!

> **LANGUAGE TIP**
>
> Roberto speaks about **libro por komencantoj** *a book for beginners*. When referring to these books, Sara calls them **porkomencantaj libroj**, since prepositions can be used as prefixes, for example with verbs like **antaŭĝui** *to look forward to* and **ne povi ĝisatendi** *to be so excited that you can't wait*. They can also be used to create adjectives.

2 Match the English and the Esperanto.

a They require too much language knowledge

b Moreover, they seem a bit old

c The most important is that they be good

d It's necessary that I buy that too

e I want my sister to start learning Esperanto

f It's no longer necessary to understand every possible language

g It's necessary to buy the translation

h … so that you understand them more easily

1 Nepras, ke mi aĉetu ankaŭ ĝin

2 … por ke vi komprenu ilin pli facile

3 Plie ili aspektas iom malnovaj

4 Ne plu necesas, ke vi komprenu ĉiun eblan lingvon

5 Ili postulas tro da lingvoscio

6 Estas necese, ke vi aĉetu la tradukon

7 Mi deziras, ke mia fratino eklernu Esperanton

8 Plej gravas, ke ili estu bonaj

> **LANGUAGE TIP**
>
> **-Um-** can be useful for creating new words. **Butikumi** means *to go shopping*, built on **butiko** *a shop* with the suffix **-um-**, which has no fixed meaning. This is handy for when you need to associate with a word but the link isn't perfectly clear. How can you say *to sunbathe*? It's something to do with **la suno** but what? **Sunumi** solves the problem, just as **akvumi** does when you want to water the garden.

3 Based on Conversation 1, decide whether these statements are **vera** (*true*) or **malvera** (*false*).

   a Sara neniam antaŭe legis libron en Esperanto.

   b Kalle Kniivilä verkas pri la 1917-a revolucio en Rusio.

   c La antologioj estas tradukoj de nacilingvaĵoj.

   d Jorge Camacho verkas poezion.

   e Sara opinias, ke libroj pri historio estas tro malfacilaj.

   f La libro de Anna Lowenstein temas pri la nuntempo.

 4 12.04 **Now listen to the conversation again line by line and repeat.**

Language discovery 1

1 **There are examples in the conversation of a tabelvorto which has been changed into an adjective, one which is used as a verb, and another which indicates motion. Can you spot them?**

2 **Mi opiniis ĝin tre ekscit_____. Does the adjective have an n-ending? If not, can you think of the reason?**

3 **What ending does the verb take in these excerpts from the conversation?**
Mi vere rekomendas, ke vi aĉet_____ almenaŭ unu; Nepras, ke mi aĉet_____ ĝin; Mi deziras, ke mia fratino eklern_____ Esperanton.

THE U-ENDING AFTER KE

In Conversation 1 the **u**-ending, used for giving instructions, often occurs, particularly in parts of the sentence which follow **ke** *that*. In these instances the speakers are indicating a wished-for state or action, just as when you ask somebody to do something. In situations where the initial verb is **voli**, **deziri**, **ordoni**, **proponi**, **postuli**, **peti** and others, what follows the **ke** is usually a wished-for outcome and therefore takes the **u**-ending:

Mi volas, ke vi manĝu ĉion.   *I want you to eat everything.*

La reĝo ordonis, ke la viro estu liberigita.   *The king ordered that the man be set free.*

When a clause follows **por ke** *in order that*, its verb takes the **u**-ending:

Mi parolas malrapide, por ke vi   *I speak slowly in order that you understand me*
komprenu min.   */ so that you understand me.*

> **LANGUAGE TIP**
>
> Don't get confused by the presence of **ke** and automatically add the **u**-ending. Sentences like **Mi opinias, ke li estas inteligenta** and **Dankon, ke vi venis** are the default. The **u**-ending appears only when the initial verb indicates that what follows is a desired outcome. If in doubt, stick with what you know until you develop a feel for it.

Practice 1

1 **Look at the following English sentences and decide whether their Esperanto translations require the u-ending.**

  a *Tell him not to speak!* Diru al li, ke li ne parol_____!

  b *Ask him to sell me the book!* Petu lin, ke li vend_____ al mi la libron!

  c *I see that he has a new girlfriend.* Mi vidas, ke li hav_____ novan koramikinon.

  d *I wanted him to come earlier but he didn't.* Mi volis, ke li ven_____ pli frue, sed tion li ne faris.

  e *They prefer that I not go there.* Ili preferas, ke mi ne ir_____ tien.

  f *I forgot that my mother doesn't eat fish.* Mi forgesis, ke mia patrino ne manĝ_____ fiŝaĵon.

  g *It's necessary for everybody to learn to read.* Estas necese, ke ĉiu lern_____ legi.

  h *Dad told me not to do it but I did it anyway.* Paĉjo ordonis, ke mi ne far_____ tion, sed mi faris ĉiaokaze.

2 **Complete the sentences with the appropriate verb endings, choosing from -as, -is, -os, -u and -i:**

  a Kiam mi est_____ pli maljuna, mi est_____ futbalisto.

  b La eta knabino vol_____ manĝ_____ ĉokoladon hieraŭ, sed ŝia frato jam ĉiom manĝ_____, tial ŝi dev_____ manĝ_____ frukton.

  c La knabineto koler_____ nun, ĉar hieraŭ ŝi dev_____ manĝ_____ frukton anstataŭ ĉokolado.

  d Ŝi ne vol_____, ke li manĝ_____ la ĉokoladon, sed tion li far_____.

  e Krom futbalo li ankaŭ ŝat_____ lud_____ tenison.

  f Nepr_____ manĝ_____ bone kaj necesas trink_____ multe da akvo ĉiutage.

  g Nepr_____, ke vi manĝ_____ frukton hodiaŭ anstataŭ ĉokolado.

  h Unu tagon mi ir_____ al la Universala Kongreso, kred_____ min!

  i Mi ne sci_____, kiam li reven_____. Ĉiuokaze, mi ne vol_____, ke li reven_____, do ne est_____ grave, ke li ankoraŭ ne est_____ ĉi tie.

3 **Complete the sentences with the appropriate verb from the list, applying the necessary verb endings.**

> **deziri   konsili   proponi**
> **necesi   rekomendi   peti   diri**

  a Mi _____ aĉet_____ novan libron de tiu fama aŭtoro (*I recommend*)

  b _____ leg_____ kaj fikcion kaj komiksojn. (*It's necessary*)

  c Mi _____, ke vi ne leg_____ ĉi tiun libron. La traduko estas malbona. (*I advise*)

d Ĉu vi _____, ke la aŭtoro verk_____ plian en la serio? (*Do you wish*)

e _____ al li, ke vi prefer_____, ke li traduk_____ ĝin en Esperanton. (*Tell him*)

f Ŝi _____, ke mi aĉet_____ por ŝi la novan poezion, kiun verkis la konata kroata poeto. (*She asked*)

g Li _____, ke mi leg_____ ĉi tiun libron, antaŭ ol spekti la filmon. (*He suggested*)

Vocabulary builder 2

 12.05 Look at the words and complete the missing English words. Then listen and try to imitate the pronunciation of the speakers.

BUTIKUMADO *SHOPPING*

aĉeti	*to buy*
vendi, vendejo	*to sell, a shop*
deziri	*to desire, wish*
oferto	*offer*
senpaga (sen-paga)	*free (without-pay)*
rabato	*discount*
Kiom mi ŝuldas al vi?	*How much do I owe you?*
sume tio faras … eŭrojn	*all together / in total that's … euros*
mono, monero, monbileto	*money, coin, banknote*
kreditkarto	_____
dolaroj	*dollars*
pundoj	*pounds*
multekosta	_____

Conversation 2

NEW EXPRESSIONS

 12.06 Look at and listen to the words and expressions that are used in the following conversation. Note their meanings.

precipe ĉi tiujn librojn	*especially these books*
ĉi tiu romano estas tre populara	*this novel is very popular*
Kiu aĉetas du, tiu ricevas ĉiujn tri	*someone buying two gets all three*
kiu …, tiu …	*he who … (see Cultural tip)*
Ili kostas po 12€	*They cost 12€ each*
sume 120€	*120€ in total*
membro de la Universala Esperanto-Asocio (UEA)	*member of the World Esperanto Association*
eblas uzi … anstataŭ …	*it's possible to use … instead of …*
pli malmultekosta/malpli kosta	*cheaper*

12.07 *Sara and Roberto make their way to Johano, the **libroservisto**, so that they can pay for their new books.*

1 **How would Roberto have benefitted had he been a member of the *Universala Esperanto-Asocio*?**

Johano	Saluton! Ĉu mi povas helpi vin? Nur diru. Kion vi deziras? Ke mi rekomendu ion?
Roberto	Ke vi vendu ion, fakte amiko, precipe ĉi tiujn librojn.
Johano	Tre bone. Ho, ĉi tiu romano estas tre populara. Ĉu vi jam legis la aliajn en la serio?
Roberto	Ne, la aliajn mi ne legis. Mi aŭdis pri la serio, sed ĉi tiu estos la unua, kiun mi legos.
Johano	Nu, ni havas proponon eble interesan por vi. Kiu aĉetas du, tiu ricevas ĉiujn tri. La tria do estas senpaga.
Roberto	Dankon, mi faros! Ho, tiujn komiksojn mi konas. Mi jam havas plurajn en la angla. Kiom ili kostas?
Johano	Ili kostas po 12€. Kutime ĉiuj dek do kostas sume 120€, sed dum la Universala Kongreso ni proponas rabaton 20 eŭran.
Roberto	Ja bonega oferto, sed tro da mono. Bone, kiom mi ŝuldas al vi?
Johano	Sume tio faras … 88€. Ĉu vi estas membro de la Universala Esperanto-Asocio?
Roberto	Ankoraŭ ne. Kial?
Johano	Ĉar membroj ricevas 10%-an rabaton. Do, 88€ mi petas. Ni preferas, ke vi pagu per monbiletoj, se eble.
Roberto	Sufiĉe da monbiletoj mi ne havas kun mi. Ĉu eblas pagi alie?
Johano	Jes, eblas uzi kreditkarton anstataŭ monbiletoj. Dankon!
Sara	Saluton! Jen miaj libroj. Mi serĉas ankaŭ porkomencantajn lernolibrojn. Kion vi rekomendas?
Johano	Tiuj du estas inter la plej bonaj. Ili kostas po 15€. Krom ili, ankaŭ tiuj estas tre bonaj kaj kostas nur po 10€.
Sara	Do, mi preferas unu el la pli malmultekostaj. Dankon!

2 **Match the English and the Esperanto.**

a	How much does it cost?	**1**	Kiom mi ŝuldas?
b	They cost £100 each	**2**	Ke mi rekomendu ion
c	How much do I owe?	**3**	Ni ofertas rabaton
d	I prefer the cheap one	**4**	Kiu aĉetas du, tiu ricevas trian senpage
e	That I recommend something	**5**	Ili kostas po cent pundojn
f	We offer a discount	**6**	Eblas pagi per kreditkarto anstataŭ monbiletoj
g	Buy two, get one free	**7**	Ke mi vendu ion
h	You can pay by card instead of notes	**8**	Krom tiuj, ankaŭ ĉi tiuj estas bonaj
i	That I sell something	**9**	Mi preferas la malmultekostan
j	As well as those, these ones are good too	**10**	Kiom (ĝi) kostas?

ⓘ Language discovery 2

1 How does Johano differentiate between a single price (12€ each) and a total price (120€ all together)?

2 You've seen that **mono** *money* gives **monero** *coin*. If **pluvero** means *raindrop* and **neĝero** *snowflake*, what do you think Esperanto's **-er-** suffix does?

> **CULTURE TIP**
>
> The **Proverbaro Esperanta** contains 2,630 proverbs. They often take a form like **Kiu ne krimas, tiu ne timas**, corresponding to English's construction in *He who laughs last laughs longest*. You can use this construction yourself in everyday use too, such as **Kiu aĉetas du, (tiu) ricevas trian senpage** *Buy two, get one free.*

PO, ANSTATAŬ AND KROM

Po is used to show how quantities are distributed and is always placed before a number or some expression of quantity.

Mi donis al la knaboj po 2 librojn.	*I gave the boys two books each.*
La libroj kostas po 12€.	*The books cost 12€ each.*
La viando kostas po 4€ por kilogramo.	*The meat costs 4€ per kilogram.*

Po was traditionally considered to be a preposition and so wasn't followed by an object with the **n**-ending. However, it behaves much more like an adverb, which would be followed by an **n**-ending. Treating **po** as an adverb rather than a preposition has become normal usage so you will usually see **po** followed by the **n**-ending. The traditional approach, although increasingly uncommon, is also correct, so you have some freedom as to whether to use the **n**-ending or not.

Anstataŭ means *in place of, instead of*:

Eblas uzi kreditkarton anstataŭ monbiletoj.	*It's possible to use a credit card instead of cash.*

It also exists as a verb, **anstataŭi**:

La kreditkarto anstataŭis la monbiletojn.	*The credit card replaced the cash.*

Be careful, though: **anstataŭas** is the thing taking the place of something else. If you replace one thing with something else, use **anstataŭigi**:

Mi anstataŭigis la monbiletojn per la kreditkarto.	*I replaced the cash with the credit card.*

Krom indicates something which is considered apart or distinct. It has two separate meanings which appear to be contradictory; there's an exclusive and an inclusive version.

The exclusive **krom** shows something for which the rest of the sentence isn't valid, like *except*, *except for* or *but*. If the sentence is positive, then **krom** is negative:

Mi ŝatas ĉion pri Esperanto, krom la akuzativo.	*I like everything about Esperanto except for the accusative.*
Ĉiuj miaj amikoj venis krom Roberto.	*All of my friends came except for Roberto.*

Conversely, if the sentence is negative, then **krom** is positive:

Mi tute ne ŝatas italajn manĝaĵojn, krom pico.	*I really don't like Italian food except for pizza.*
Neniu venis, krom mia fratino.	*Nobody came except for my sister.*

When the inclusive **krom** is used, the word following is still separated but shares the same attributes as other things in the sentence, as with English's *moreover* or *besides*:

Krom bela ŝi estas inteligenta.	*Besides being beautiful she's intelligent.*

There is a lot of scope for misunderstanding because of the opposite effects of the two uses of **krom**. For example, **krom pico mi ŝatas ĉiujn italajn manĝaĵojn** *besides pizza I like all Italian food* could mean that the person likes or dislikes pizza. For this reason, people using **krom** tend also to use other words to remove the ambiguity: **Krom pico mi ŝatas ankaŭ ĉiujn italajn manĝaĵojn.**

> **LANGUAGE TIP**
>
> Neither **krom** nor **anstataŭ** should take the **n**-ending because they're prepositions. Many people use the **n**-endings with them, though, often with the justification there's an implied verb: **Krom (ŝati) picon mi ŝatas ĉiujn italajn manĝaĵojn** *Besides (liking) pizza I like all Italian food* and **mi manĝis panon anstataŭ (manĝi]) picon** *I ate bread instead of (eating) pizza*. If you happen to overtly include that verb, then the **n**-ending is necessary: **mi gratulis ilin ĉiujn krom gratuli Davidon** *I congratulated them all except for (congratulating) David*.

Practice 2

1 Fill in the blanks with either po, anstataŭ or krom.

    a _____ la manĝaĵo, ĉio estis bonega.

    b Mi volis manĝi kokaĵon, sed ili ne havis. Do, _____ kokaĵo mi manĝis porkaĵon.

    c _____ *The Beatles* mi ŝatas ankaŭ *The Rolling Stones*, *The Who* … ĉion!

    d _____ la verdaj ŝi aĉetis la bluajn, ĉar ili kostis nur _____ £5.

    e Post la rabato la vino kostis _____ £3 por glaso _____ £5. Bonega rabato!

    f Mi ŝatas ĉiajn legomojn _____ pizoj. Ilin mi tute ne ŝatas.

g Mi dankis ilin ĉiujn _____ mia frato, ĉar li faris nenion por helpi.

h _____ facila Esperanto estas bela. Mi ĝojas, ke mi decidis lerni ĝin _____ lerni latinon.

2 **Decide whether the n-ending is necessary, normal or possible (but not necessarily normal) in the following sentences.**

	Necessary	Normal	Possible
a Mi kaj mia frato ricevis po dek pundoj_____			
b Ŝi ŝatas ĉian ĉinan manĝaĵon, krom ĉi tiu_____			
c Ŝi ricevis promeson anstataŭ mono_____!			
d Anstataŭ ricevi mono_____ ŝi ricevis promeson!			
e Krom mi_____, ŝi ŝatas mian tutan familion			
f Ili kostas po kvin pundoj_____.			
g Krom kisi mi_____, li ankaŭ kisis ĉiun alian virinon en la urbo!			

> **CULTURE TIP**
>
> The **Universala Esperanto-Asocio** has the largest **libroservo** in all of **Esperantujo** at its headquarters. You can purchase online and members receive a discount too. If you attend a UK, you'll find that the **libroservo** has been boxed up and brought to you!

Reading

Read the description of a book and answer the questions.

La romano 'Vojaĝo al la Universala Kongreso', kiun verkis Sara Feliĉulino originale en Esperanto, temas pri juna virino, kiu havas nenion por fari dum la universitata somerpaŭzo. Dum la geamikoj malaperas en ĉiun parton de la lando, nia heroino devas resti tutsola kaj senamika. Ne ĉio estas senespera, tamen, pro ia stranga ideo, kiun havas ŝia amiko, Roberto: 'Ni iru al Slovakio!', lando kiun Anna tute ne konas. Kio sekvos estas ekscita semajno, kiun ŝi neniam forgesos. Nek vi. Legu, ĝuu, esperantumu.

1 Which relative pronouns are used in the text?

2 Where has -**um**-been used?

3 How would you interpret the word written with -**um**-?

Writing

Describe your favourite book using the prompts below to help you:

Who is the author? Is it the author's first book? Are you reading a translation? What genre is it?

Listening

12.08 **Listen to the conversation.**

1   **What does the hungry man buy?**

2   **What do they cost each?**

3   **How many does he buy?**

4   **How much does he pay?**

Listening and speaking

12.09 **Join in the following conversation with the bookseller.**

Librovendisto:	Bonan vesperon, sinjoro. Kion mi povas fari por helpi vin?
You:	(Greet the bookseller and say that you're a bookworm, so you wish to buy a new book.)
Librovendisto:	Ho, vi estas legema, ĉu ne? Do, vi estas en la ĝusta loko. Kiajn librojn vi preferas legi?
You:	(Say you usually read fiction but today your mother has asked you to buy a poetry book for her.)
Librovendisto:	Do mi rekomendas, ke vi aĉetu por ŝi ĉi tiun. Ĝi estas tute nova, kaj la aŭtoro tre bona. Ĉiuj aĉetas ĝin lastatempe, kaj ne restas multaj.
You:	(Say you'll buy it and ask whether the shopkeeper can recommend a good mystery novel to you.)
Librovendisto:	Misteran romanon ne, sed mi rekomendas ĉi tiun krimromanon.
You:	(Ask how much it costs.)
Librovendisto:	Por vi nur 8 pundojn. Kaj la poezia libro por via patrino kostas 10 pundojn, do 18 pundojn sume. Mi preferas, ke vi pagu per monbiletoj, se vi havas.
You:	(Say that you only have a credit card.)
Librovendisto:	Dankon. Jen viaj libroj. Agrablan tagon!

Test yourself

1 Fill in the correct verb endings.

Antaŭhieraŭ mi vizit_____ Petron. Li ne est_____ hejme, sed lia edzino diris, ke mi atend_____, ĉar li nur ir_____ ekzerc_____ sin. Mi ne sci_____ kion mi far_____ dum atendado, do mi propon_____, ke ni babil_____ iomete. Feliĉe Petro reven_____ antaŭ ol ni ne plu hav_____ temojn.

2 Match the book and its description.

a	*Harry Potter*	**1**	krima romano
b	*Sherlock Holmes*	**2**	komikso
c	*Pride and Prejudice* (Fiereco kaj antaŭjuĝemo)	**3**	dramo
d	*Tintin*	**4**	fantazia rakonto
e	*Star Wars*	**5**	historia
f	*Romeo and Juliet*	**6**	sciencfikcia
g	*The Silence of the Lambs*	**7**	romantika romano
h	*The Decline and Fall of the Roman Empire*	**8**	horora

3 Complete these sentences with the missing verb and then add the correct verb ending.

a Mi _____, ke vi prov_____ ĉi tiun ĉokoladon. (suggest)

b Mi tiom _____, ke li est_____ mia edzo! (wish, desire)

c Mi _____, ke vi vojaĝ_____ al Francio unue. (think, have the opinion)

d Mi _____, ke vi respond_____ poste, sed ne nun. (advise)

e Mi vere _____, ke vi aĉet_____ lian novan libron. (recommend)

SELF-CHECK

I CAN ...
○ ... make a purchase and get a discount.
○ ... talk about books.
○ ... express wishes and recommendations.

Grammar

Here is a summary of the new grammar covered in Units 7–12.

Basic endings	
-as	Present tense, e.g. **mi iras, mi manĝas**
-is	Past tense, e.g. **mi iris, mi manĝis**
-os	Future tense, e.g. **mi iros, mi manĝos**
-u	Wishes, commands, exhortations: **Venu! Ni iru! Mi volas, ke vi manĝu**
-n	For showing motion towards, e.g. **dekstren, en la domon**
-a	For ordinal numbers, e.g. **unua, dua**

Creating new words	
ek-	Starting, e.g. **ekvidi, ekparoli**
kun-	Doing something together, e.g. **kunkanti, kunmanĝi**
-ad-	Longer duration, e.g. **paroladi, pensado**
-an-	Member of a group or citizen of a country, e.g. **klubano, peruano**
-ar-	Collection, e.g. **arbaro, fiŝaro**
-il-	Tools, means, e.g. **skribilo, aliĝilo**
-on-	Fractions, e.g. **duono, kvarono**
-uj-	Name of a country from the inhabitant, **Franco, Francujo**
-um-	No particular meaning, e.g. **brakumi, akvumi la arbojn**

GIVING DATES

Use the ordinal number for the day: **la unua de majo, la dudek-kvina de decembro**. If you want to say on such-and-such a date, either use the the **n**-ending or the preposition **je**:

Ni renkontiĝis mardon, la unuan de majo 2015. = **Ni renkontiĝis je mardo, la unua de majo 2015.**

In writing, the ordinal number is often shortened: **la 1-a de majo / la 1-an de majo**.

TELLING THE TIME

Hours are also referred to using ordinal numbers (*the first (hour), the second (hour)*, etc.). This is why the question **Kioma horo estas?** *What's the time?* involves the word **kioma** (**kiom** (*how much, how many?*) with the a-ending, so something like '*how-many-th*') and the answer might be **Estas la tria posttagmeze**. The preposition **je** is the equivalent of *on*: **ni renkontiĝos je la kvara kaj duono, aŭ je la kvara kaj kvardek kvin**.

COUNTRIES, NATIONALITIES, LANGUAGES

When the country name ends in **...io**, then usually the people living there are called **...oj**, the adjective is **...a** and the main language (if any) is **la ...a**. For example:

En Francio loĝas la francoj, kiuj ŝatas francan fromaĝon kaj kiuj parolas la francan.

When the country name ends in ...**o**, the people living there are called ...**anoj**, the adjective is ...**a**. For example:

En Barato loĝas la baratanoj, kiuj ŝatas baratan kareon. La lingvoj de Barato estas la hindia, la angla, la bengala, la telugua, kaj tiel plu.

'TABLE WORDS'

Review the new **tabelvortoj** you learned in Unit 10.

Practice

1 **Sara recently participated in a city-wide charity run. She was 131st out of more than 20,000 participants. How would she say this, and what would her friends say to congratulate her?**

2 **Describe a typical Monday morning: at what time do you wake up, get out of bed, shower, have breakfast and so on?**

3 **Fill in the blanks with suitable words, adding the appropriate verb endings. To help you, the first letter of each missing word has been given.**

   Komencanto estas ekscitita: 'Vi ne k_____ min, sed mi p_____ unuafoje Esperanton en la reala vivo! Hieraŭ mi hazarde e_____ en la urbocentro por aĉeti aferojn, kiam mi eka_____ du homojn paroli malantaŭ mi. La unua viro d_____ ion kiel 'Mi p_____ en la JES ĉi-jare' kaj la dua viro d_____ 'Ho, kiam la JES o_____?', do mi s_____, ke ili ambaŭ p_____ paroli Esperanton. Mi do turnis min malantaŭen kaj d_____ 'Saluton!'. Kia surprizo por ĉiuj!'

4 **Here are some invented band names. What would they be in Esperanto?**
   a The green bananas
   b The mysterious Russians
   c The dangerous summer
   d The crazy doctors

5 Using the affixes listed at the beginning of this review section, create Esperanto words that mean the following:

a a circle of friends

b a member of a circle of friends

c to drink something together

d the country which **italoj** come from

e fifths

f cutlery

g to write a really long text

h to suddenly hear

6 Complete the gaps in the conversation below.

Example: Kion ni faru?   Ion ajn!

Ŝi	Kien ni iru?
Via amiko	_____ ajn!
Ŝi	Nu, mi volas manĝi, do ni iru al restoracio. Al kiu restoracio ni iru?
Via amiko	_____ ajn!
Ŝi	Mi konas tre bonan japanan restoracion, la 'Fukuoka'.
Via amiko	Ho, bone.
Ŝi	Kiam ni iru tien?
Via amiko	_____ ajn!

7 Complete the table with the names of countries, nationalities and languages.

Lando	Loĝantoj	Adjektivo	Lingvo
Francio (Francujo)	francoj	franca	la franca
Germanio (Germanujo)			
			la angla
	italoj		
		hispana	
			la ĉina
Japanio (Japanujo)			
Kanado			
			la (_____) angla, la franca
Irlando			la _____, la (_____) angla

8 Solve this crossword puzzle, which uses vocabulary you've learned in recent units. Use a dictionary to find the translation if you need to.

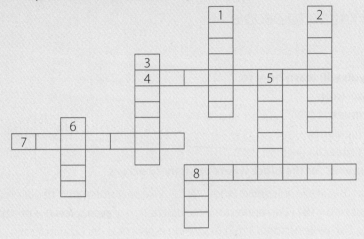

Across

4. Jen bona _____ de la akuzativo. (example)

7. Ni bezonas _____n el la franca. (translation)

8. Mia brako _____. (hurts)

Down

1. Ŝi havas novan labor _____n. (job)

2. Mi ne kredas vin! Vi _____! (lie)

3. Li estas _____ parolanto de Esperanto. (native / from birth)

5. Instruisto faras interesan _____n. (lecture / lesson)

6. Mi ne _____ la kotizon. (paid)

8. Ne _____! Li estas lojala. (doubt)

9 Complete the blanks with expressions or sentences in Esperanto.

  a Cool! _____!

  b This is tasty. _____.

  c Ugh! _____!

  d Help me! _____!

  e Please show me. _____.

  f 10€ each, 50€ total _____.

  g Really? That was five years ago! _____!

  h Unbelievable! _____!

  i It's possible. _____.

  j You're right. _____.

Skribi al homoj
Writing to people

In this unit, you will learn how to:

▶ *make comparisons.*
▶ *use superlatives.*
▶ *talk about incidents.*
▶ *use indirect speech.*
▶ *create the names for the place where an activity occurs.*

CEFR: (A2) *Can use simple descriptive language to make brief statements about and compare objects and possession.* **(B1)** *Can understand the description of events, feelings and wishes in personal letters. Can write personal letters describing experiences and impressions.*

Internaciaj kontaktoj per Esperanto *International contacts through Esperanto*

The first **idealistoj** (*idealists*) who learned Esperanto had **apenaŭ** (*hardly*) anybody to speak it with. Ludoviko Zamenhof had a little contact with the early learners, but most of them were from the Russian Empire, as was he. **Fariĝis pli facile** (*it became easier*) to use Esperanto as a **pontlingvo** (*bridge language*) **inter alilingvuloj** (*between people with different languages*) with the **alveno** (*arrival*) of the **unuaj du** (*first two*) magazines, **La Esperantisto** and **Lingvo Internacia**. Now people could contact other **samideanoj** (*like-minded people*) and become **plumamikoj** (*penpals*).

It was in the early part of the 20th **jarcento** (*century*) when those international contacts became **verviva** (*real-life*) ones and lifelong friendships were formed. The **fondiĝo** (*establishment*) of the **Universala Esperanto-Asocio** (**UEA**) in 1908 was the result of this **internacieco** (*internationalism*), and it soon introduced its **delegita reto** (*network of delegates*), publishing the details in its members' **jarlibro** (*yearbook*). Now Esperantists had access to a host of names of people who were happy to be approached by other Esperantists for help and information. Some people **ofertis** (*offered*) guided tours of their cities, while others **proponis** (*proposed*) free **faka konsilado** (*specialist advice*) about their areas of interest.

This system stood the test of time for a century but it contained only the contact details of **UEA** members or groups affiliated to it. The arrival of the app **Amikumu** in 2017 **ĝustigis** (*rectified*) this. Now it's possible to find Esperantists all around you, **kie ajn vi troviĝas** (*wherever you are*). You no longer need to consult a book well in advance and then engage in written correspondence prior to meeting in person; you can arrive at your destination and arrange to meet up in seconds.

 How is the word for *a century* formed in Esperanto? How do you think *decade* would be written? How do you express *people with different languages*?

Vocabulary builder 1

13.01 Look at the words and phrases and complete the missing English words and expressions. Then listen and try to imitate the pronunciation of the speakers.

LETEROJ KAJ RETMESAĜOJ *LETTERS AND EMAILS*

Informal

kara X	*dear X*
mi esperas, ke vi bone fartas	*I hope you're well*
dankon pro la letero / poŝtkarto, kiun mi ricevis la [date]	*thank you for the letter / postcard, which I received on* [date]
amike	*with friendly greetings*
bondezirojn / bondezire	*best wishes*
kore / korajn salutojn	*with hearty greetings*
ame / kun amo	*with love*
ĉion bonan!	*all the best!*
fartu bone!	*look after yourself!*

Formal

estimata X	*dear X*
estimataj gesinjoroj	_____ *ladies and gentlemen*
rilate vian leteron de la [date]	*in respect of your letter of* [date]
rilate nian antaŭan korespondadon	*with regards to our earlier correspondence*
sincere	*sincerely*

Conversation 1

NEW EXPRESSIONS

13.02 Look at and listen to the words and expressions that are used in the following conversation. Note their meanings.

Bratislavo estas multe pli bela ol mi pensis	*Bratislava is much more beautiful than I thought*
ĝi estas eble la plej bela urbo, kiun mi iam ajn vizitis	*it's maybe the most beautiful town (city) I've ever visited*
multe malpli granda ol mi atendis	*much smaller (less big) than I expected*
certe multe pli amuza ol resti en Britio	*certainly much more fun than staying in Britain*
Mi esperas, ke vi ricevos ĉi tiun poŝtkarton	*I hope you get this postcard*
la afranko por sendi alilanden kostas pli ol sendi ene de Slovakio	*the postage for sending abroad costs more than for within Slovakia*
peti ĝustan poŝtmarkon	*to ask for the right stamp*
aparte plaĉas al mi	*I particularly like (particularly pleases me)*
biero en Slovakio estas multe malpli kosta ol kutime	*beer in Slovakia is much cheaper (less expensive) than usual*

la malplej kosta biero	*the cheapest (least expensive) beer*
ĉiaokaze mi jam havas la librojn, kiujn mi plej volas legi	*in any case I already have the books which I most want to read*
same kiel en Francio	*just like in France*

 13.03 *Sara writes a postcard to her friend, Karla, while Roberto sends a text to his friend, Stefano. Read the messages and listen to Karla and Stefano reading them out loud.*

1 **What precaution did Sara take to ensure she had enough postage?**

Kara Karla,

Mi tre kontentas, ke mi decidis veni al la UK! Bratislavo estas multe pli bela ol mi pensis! Ĝi estas eble la plej bela urbo, kiun mi iam ajn vizitis, kvankam multe malpli granda ol mi atendis. Kaj la UK mem estas bonega; certe multe pli amuza ol resti en Britio! Kaj estas multe pli varme ol en Britio, kompreneble.

Mi esperas, ke vi ricevos ĉi tiun poŝtkarton. La afranko por sendi alilanden kostas pli ol sendi ene de Slovakio, sed ĉar mi ne parolis la slovakan, mi ne povis peti ĝustan poŝtmarkon. Tial mi aĉetis du normalajn! Du estos pli bonaj ol unu, ĉu ne?

Amike,

Sara

AL:

ADRESO:

Ĉi tiu UK estas multe pli bona ol la antaŭa, kiun vi partoprenis kaj ne ŝatis. Mi opinias, ke ĝi eĉ estas la plej amuza. Aparte plaĉas al mi, ke biero en Slovakio estas multe malpli kosta ol kutime, ja la malplej kosta biero, kiun mi iam ajn aĉetis. Tial mi bierumas multe pli ol kiam ni estis en Norvegio!

Mi aĉetis malpli da libroj ol kiam ni estis ĉe la UK en Francio, ĉar mi havas malpli da mono ol tiam. Sed ĉiaokaze, mi jam havas la librojn, kiujn mi plej volas legi. Same kiel en Francio, mi renkontis plurajn novajn amikojn tre interesajn kaj revidis Erikan; ŝi nun estas multe pli bela eĉ ol antaŭe, certe la plej bela kaj ĉarma el ĉiuj virinoj ĉi tie.

Amikajn salutojn – fartu bone!

2 **Match the English and Esperanto.**

a Is much cheaper than usual

b Just like in the UK

c Three are better than two

d This is much better than I expected

e The postage for sending abroad

f Indeed the least expensive

g I bought less chocolate

h Much smaller than I expected

i I have less money than then

j Which I most want to eat

1 Tri estas pli bonaj ol du

2 Kiujn mi plej volas manĝi

3 Mi havas malpli da mono ol tiam

4 Multe malpli granda ol mi atendis

5 Same kiel en Britio

6 Tio estas multe pli bona ol mi atendis

7 Estas multe malpli kosta ol kutime

8 La afranko por sendi alilanden

9 Mi aĉetis malpli da ĉokolado

10 Ja la malplej kosta

3 **Select the correct option to reflect what was written on the postcards.**

a Biero ne kostas multe da mono en (Norvegio / Slovakio).

b Erika estas (bela / malbela).

c Sara (bedaŭras / estas feliĉa), ke ŝi ĉeestas la Universalan Kongreson.

d La vetero en Bratislavo kaj Britio (estas / ne estas) la sama.

e Sara pensis antaŭe, ke Bratislavo estas (granda / malgranda) urbo.

f Roberto (aĉetis / ne aĉetis) librojn en Francio.

g Roberto (drinkas / ne drinkas) dum la Universala Kongreso.

h Sara (bedaŭras / kontentas), ke ŝi ne plu estas en Britio.

4 **13.04 Listen again to Karla and Stefano reading out loud their messages and repeat.**

> **LANGUAGE TIP**
>
> Sara says that Bratislava is **malpli granda ol mi atendis** *smaller than I expected.* Note that **atendi** translates as both *to wait* and *to expect.*

Language discovery 1

1. **Find the words for *more beautiful* and *most beautiful* in the messages sent by Sara and Roberto.**
2. **Note all the times when a word with an a-ending follows pli and malpli. How would you translate them into English?**
3. **When you make a comparison in Esperanto, what's the equivalent to *than*?**

1 COMPARATIVE

When comparing two or more things or people, the most important phrases are **tiel … kiel** (*as … as*) and **pli … ol** (*more … than*). For example, you might say:

Li estas tiel mallaŭta, kiel muso.   *He is as quiet as a mouse.*

Mia frato estas pli inteligenta ol li.   *My brother is more intelligent than him.*

Mal- is added to **pli** to make comparisons with *less* rather than with *more*.

Mia frato estas alta, sed malpli alta ol Jakobo.   *My brother is tall, but less tall than Jacob.*

Note that while English makes comparisons using a suffix (*bigger, stronger, easier*), an adverb (*more beautiful, more expensive*), or uses other irregular forms (*better* from *good, worse* from *bad*), Esperanto is totally regular, building with **pli**: **pli granda**, **pli forta**, **pli facila**, **pli bona**, **pli malbona**.

> **LANGUAGE TIP**
>
> Don't forget to think about the **n**-ending after **ol**; its presence or absence can change what's being expressed: **Mi amas vin pli ol li** *I love you more than he does* is not the same as **Mi amas vin pli ol lin** *I love you more than I love him.*

2 SUPERLATIVE

To compare one person or thing with every other member of the group, indicating that it's at the upper or lower limit compared with everything else, use **la plej** *the most*:

Ĉi tiu estas la plej grava el ĉiuj miaj projektoj.   *This is the most important out of all my projects.*

Nia filo estas la plej rapida.   *Our son is the fastest.*

The prefix **mal-** is used to express the lower extreme:

Nia hundo estas la plej afabla / la malplej mordema.   *Our dog is the friendliest / the least likely to bite.*

Practice 1

1 Match the adjectives (comparative and superlative) with their translation.

> pli bela   pli granda
> malpli malgranda
> la plej malfrua
> la malplej malĝentila
> la plej rapida

a the latest
b less small
c the fastest
d the least impolite
e more beautiful
f bigger

2 Use pli, malpli, la plej or la malplej to complete the following sentences.

a Rusio estas _____ granda lando en la mondo.
b La Suno estas _____ longe for ol la Luno.
c _____ da homoj loĝas en Ĉinio ol en Luksemburgo.
d _____ frua esperantisto estis Ludoviko Zamenhof.
e La avo estas _____ juna ol la nepo.
f Kanado estas _____ granda ol Rusio, sed _____ granda ol Britio.
g La Luno estas _____ longe for ol la Suno.
h Mia edzino estas _____ bela kaj afabla virino en la tuta mondo, tial mi amas ŝin tiom multe.
i _____ maljuna el la kvin infanoj Jackson estis Michael.
j La oka vespere estas _____ frua horo ol la oka matene, sed _____ frua ol la naŭa vespere.

3 Look back at Vocabulary builder 1 in Unit 12 on books and create three sentences using pli, malpli, plej or malplej to describe a book. For example, La dua libro en tiu serio estas malpli bona ol la unua, sed ĝi estas pli bona ol la tria.

Vocabulary builder 2

 13.05 Look at the words and complete the missing English words. Then listen and try to imitate the pronunciation of the speakers.

LOKOJ EN LA URBO *PLACES IN TOWN*

urbo	*town, city*
loko	*place, location*
parko	_____
vendejo, butiko	_____
bakejo	*bakery*
trinkejo	*bar, pub*
bazaro	*market*
superbazaro	_____
kinejo	*cinema*
(nacia) muzeo	*(national) museum*
preĝejo (preĝi)	*church (to pray)*
lernejo	_____
banko	_____
policejo	*police station*
urbodomo	*town hall*

Conversation 2

NEW EXPRESSIONS

 13.06 Look at and listen to the words and expressions that are used in the following conversation. Note their meanings.

Ĉu ĉio estas en ordo?	*Is everything OK?*
mi forgesis kunporti miajn sun-okulvitrojn	*I forgot to bring my sunglasses*
mi iris tra la parko …	*I went through the park …*
por ĝui verdaĵojn kaj ripozi	*… in order to enjoy the greenery and to relax*
biletvendilo apud la turist-informejo	*the ticket machine next to tourist information*
baldaŭ estos nokto	*it will be night soon*
mi estas sur trotuaro, sed mi ne scias ĝuste kie	*I'm on a pavement but I don't know exactly where*
ejo, kie eblas spekti filmojn	*a place where it's possible to watch films*
mi prenis urbomapon	*I took a map of the city*
faru tion tuj	*do that immediately*

13.07 *Sara goes to town to buy a pair of sunglasses, but by evening she still hasn't returned.*

1 Has something happened to her? Why does Sara tell Roberto she can't meet up with him in 20 minutes?

Roberto	Kie vi estas, Sara? Mi pensis, ke okazis io al vi! Ĉu ĉio estas en ordo?
Sara	Mi estas en la urbo. Mi ja diris al vi pli frue, ke mi iros en la urbon, Roberto. Mi diris, ke mi forgesis kunporti miajn sunokulvitrojn, kaj do mi iros en la urbon por aĉeti novajn.
Roberto	Jes, sed tio estis antaŭ pluraj horoj. Jam estas vespero.
Sara	Nu, jes, mi komprenas. Mi iris al aliaj lokoj sen pensi pri la horo.
Roberto	Vi iris aliloken senpense? Ĉu vi scias nun, kie vi estas?
Sara	Nu … mi ne tute certas. Mi hazarde vidis kelkajn amikojn, kiuj invitis min trinki kun ili en kafejo. Poste mi vidis la enirpordon de la parko, decidis iri tien por ĝui verdaĵojn kaj iom ripozi. Ho, kaj mi pensis, ke estos utile aĉeti trajnbiletojn por morgaŭ, do aĉetis per biletvendilo apud la turistinformejo.
Roberto	Sed kie vi estas nun? Baldaŭ estos nokto. Ĉu mi venu serĉi vin?
Sara	Mi estas sur trotuaro, sed mi ne scias ĝuste kie. Kion mi vidas? Estas … kiel diri? … filmspektejo ĉe la fino de la strato.
Roberto	'Filmspektejo'? Ho, mi komprenas; ejo, kie eblas spekti filmojn. Bone, mi scias, kie troviĝas la kinejo. Iru ĝis ĝi kaj turniĝu dekstren. Ĉu vi vidas la grandan preĝejon?
Sara	Jes, apud la nacia muzeo.
Roberto	Nu, malantaŭ ĝi troviĝas la policejo. Iru tien kaj petu helpon de policano!
Sara	Roberto, mi ne povas fari tion! Sed mi ekhavis ideon. Kiam mi aĉetis la biletojn pli frue, mi ankaŭ eniris la apudan turistinformejon kaj prenis urbomapon. Do mi devas nun nur trovi la preĝejon sur la mapo, kaj poste mi scios kiel atingi la kongresejon.
Roberto	Bone, jen solvo. Faru tion tuj kaj mi vidos vin post 20 minutoj.
Sara	Ne, mi ne povas tuj fari tion; unue mi aĉetos la sunokulvitrojn!

2 Match the English and Esperanto.

a I thought it would be useful to buy tickets   **1** Do decidis iri tien por ĝui verdaĵojn

b I've just had an idea   **2** Mi iris al aliaj lokoj sen pensi pri la horo

c I know where the cinema is   **3** Mi jam diris, ke mi iros en la urbon

d I went to other places without thinking about the time   **4** Mi ekhavis ideon

e So decided to go there to enjoy some greenery   **5** Mi hazarde vidis kelkajn amikojn

f I already said I'd go into town   **6** Iru tien kaj petu helpon de policano

g I thought that something had happened to you   **7** Iru ĝis ĝi kaj turniĝu dekstren

h Go there and ask a policeman for help

i Go as far as it and turn right

j I bumped into some friends

8 Mi pensis, ke okazis io al vi

9 Mi pensis, ke estos utile aĉeti biletojn

10 Mi scias, kie troviĝas la kinejo

💡 Language discovery 2

1 Roberto tells Sara to ask *a police officer* **policano**. What is the word for *the police*?

2 There are several words ending in **-ejo** in the conversation. What does **-ej-** show?

3 How does Sara describe the word for cinema?

4 How does Roberto express that Sara went somewhere else without thinking about it?

1 INVENT PLACE NAMES WITH -EJ-

Names for places can be created by using the **-ej-** suffix. It can be attached to a word to indicate a place where that activity occurs or a place for that thing:

lernejo	*school*	**policejo**	*police station*
trinkejo	*a place for drinking*	**bakejo**	*bakery*

There might happen to be more specific words to hand too: for example **restoracio** is an example of a **manĝejo** and a **kafejo** is a type of **trinkejo**. The **-ej-** suffix allows you to express yourself when you're not sure what the proper word is. If you didn't know the word **hospitalo**, you could use **malsanulejo** (**mal-san-ul-ej-o**); both are valid Esperanto words.

-ej- makes it possible to be creative (describing a place full of gamers as a **ludemulejo**) or to indicate the purpose of a location, such as when you're at a conference. You might not actually have a cinema or restaurant on site but labelling rooms as **kinejo** and **manĝejo** will make it clear to people what their purposes are.

The word **ejo** is often used on its own to mean *the place* or *venue* when there's no doubt what it is you're talking about, for example when you're walking in town and want to get back to the place where the centre of activity occurs, such as the **kongresejo**:

Ni iru al la ejo.   *Let's go to the venue.*

> **LANGUAGE TIP**
>
> Some words for places are established without **-ej-**. Some words with **ĉambro** *room* appended (**dormoĉambro** *bedroom*) are the established forms, while others might make use of **loko** *place* or specific words (**restoracio** rather than **manĝejo**). Some place words are actually the basic name of the concept (**teatro** *theatre*, **teatraĵo** *a play*) and so can't be built using a word with **-ej-**.

---

2 INDIRECT SPEECH

Indirect speech is a means of expressing the content of things that have been said without directly quoting them. In some languages, including English, the tense of verbs is shifted in indirect speech. This doesn't happen in Esperanto. When Sara spoke to Roberto in the morning, she said:

Mi forgesis kunporti miajn sunokulvitrojn, kaj do mi iros en la urbon por aĉeti novajn.

I forgot to bring my sunglasses so I'll go into town to buy some new ones.

When she spoke to Roberto on the phone later she reminded him what she'd said that morning:

Mi diris, ke mi forgesis kunporti miajn sunokulvitrojn, kaj do mi iros en la urbon por aĉeti novajn.

I said I'd forgotten to bring my sunglasses so I'd go into town to buy some new ones.

Whereas in English *I forgot* became *I'd forgotten* and *I'll go* became *I'd go*, in Esperanto, the content doesn't change: **mi forgesis** and **mi iros** stay as they were.

Practice 2

1 Choose the appropriate word from the box and insert it into the gap so that each sentence makes sense.

> dušejo (duši = to shower)
> malagrablulejo   kuirejo
> dormejo   kunvenejo
> plendejo   manĝejo   legejo

a Vi ŝajnas al mi treege laca, Andreo. Ĉu vi volas iri al la _____?

b Pardonu, sed ni estas nekredeble malsataj. Ĉu vi scias, kie troviĝas la _____?

c Resti en kvieta loko kun libroj plaĉas al vi, ĉu ne? Mi rekomendas, ke vi vizitu la _____n.

d Estas multe tro varme, ĉu ne? Mi iros al la _____ por meti min sub malvarman akvon.

e Anna ĵus aĉetis pastaĵojn kaj saŭcon. Ŝi estas nun en la _____ por prepari la manĝaĵon. Poste ni povos ĉiuj kune manĝi ĝin.

f En ĉi tiun ĉambron homoj venas por diskuti kune pri aferoj, ekzemple por plani tion, kio okazos morgaŭ. Ni nomas ĝin la _____.

g Ĉiam ĉiuj tie diras, ke ĉio estis pli bona antaŭe, ke la manĝaĵo ne estas sufiĉe bongusta, ke la vetero ne plaĉas, kaj tiel plu. Ĝi vere estas _____.

h Neniu tie estas amikema. Mi ne plu volas iri al ĉi tiu _____.

2 Transform the following sentences following the same model as in the example.

Example: Mi kredas, ke morgaŭ estos jaŭdo.   *Mi kredis, ke morgaŭ estos jaŭdo.*

a Mi legas en la ĵurnalo, ke pluvos posttagmeze.

b Mi opinias, ke la vetero estos pli bona morgaŭ.

c Mi intencas aĉeti sandviĉon por tagmanĝo.

d Mi kredas, ke Sara estos la unua, kiu revenos hejmen.

e Mi scias, ke vi faros vian laboron.

f Mi promesas, ke mi ne tro drinkis.

g Mi esperas, ke mia frato ne forgesos viziti nian patrinon.

h Mi supozas, ke homoj en Afriko estas malpli riĉaj ol en Usono.

Reading

Read the following conversation between Petro and Tomaso.

Petro	Mi ne konsentas. Estas fakto, ke fiziko (*physics*) estas tre grava, ke ĝi estas la plej grava scienco el ĉiuj. Sed ankaŭ kemio (*chemistry*) estas grava. Iom malpli grava, sed tamen grava. Ĉu vi konsentas?
Tomaso	Tute ne. Por vi, eble. Sed por mi ne. Por mi, la plej grava scienco estas biologio (*biology*).
Petro	Ĉu vi volas diri, ke por vi biologio estas pli grava ol fiziko?
Tomaso	Jes. Por mi, fiziko ne estas tiel grava kiel biologio. Ĝi estas malpli grava ol kemio, kaj kemio estas malpli grava ol biologio. Biologio estas ne nur pli grava ol fiziko, sed la plej grava el ĉiuj sciencoj.

1 **What does Petro consider the most important of the sciences?**
2 **Does Tomaso think that physics and biology are equally important?**
3 **What does Tomaso think about physics?**

Writing

Write a postcard to your friend from holiday, giving details about what you're doing, the people and location. Use an appropriate greeting and sign-off.

Listening

 13.08 **Listen to this recording from an Esperanto podcast. What is the speaker's favourite way to make new Esperanto contacts?**

Listening and speaking

 13.09 Take part in the following conversation about a recent holiday. Then record yourself describing a holiday of your own.

Amiko: Ni tre bone manĝis dum la tuta semajno. La mangâĵoj estis ege bongustaj, ĉu ne?

You: (Say 'The food was even better than in Paris.')

Amiko: Prave, ja la plej bongustaj, kiujn mi iam ajn manĝis. Kaj ankaŭ la homoj estis treege afablaj, ĉu ne?

You: (Say 'The people there were the nicest people in the world.')

Amiko: Kaj la vetero! Ĉi tie ĉiam pluvas, sed tie la suno ĉiam brilis, ĉe ne?

You: (Say 'It was much hotter there than here.')

Amiko: Ni ne povis kredi, kiom ni kapablas aĉeti, ĉar la prezoj estas malaltaj, ĉu ne?

You: (Say 'It was possible to buy more beer and wine than we could drink.')

Amiko: Ni ne volis reveni hejmen, ĉu ne?

You: (Say 'We wanted to stay much longer.')

Test yourself

1 Add the missing words.

Nigra estas _____ hela (*light*) ol blanka. Blanka estas _____ malhela (*dark*) koloro el ĉiuj.

2 Create words describing the locations where the activities occur.

Junuloj iras al _____ por lerni. Dum la lunĉpaŭzo ili iras al la _____ por manĝi. Posttagmeze ili rajtas ludi tablotenison en la _____ aŭ fari sporton en la _____.

3 Add the correct endings.

Kiam mi est_____ juna, mi kred_____, ke mi est_____ riĉa, kiam mi est_____ pli maljuna. Sed mi est_____ maljuna nun kaj est_____ pli malriĉa ol mi kred_____, ke mi est_____, kiam mi est_____ juna.

SELF-CHECK	
I CAN ...	
⚪	… make comparisons.
⚪	… use superlatives.
⚪	… talk about incidents.
⚪	… use indirect speech.
⚪	… create names for the place where an activity takes place.

14 Amo kaj amikeco
Love and friendship

In this unit, you will learn how to:
▶ *talk about possibilities and conditional events.*
▶ *express moods.*
▶ *say what's worth doing.*
▶ *express contempt and dislike.*

CEFR: (B1) *Can describe experiences and events, dreams, hopes and ambitions and briefly give reasons and explanations for opinions and plans.* **(B1)** *Can express and respond to feelings such as surprise, happiness, sadness, interest and indifference.*

⭐ Lingvo por ĉion esprimi *A language to express everything*

Like all living languages, Esperanto can be used in a range of everyday fields. People can argue and reconcile in it, tell jokes and be creative and witty with it.

English has lots of words which sound identical to others with different meanings, which makes it **taŭga** (*fit, appropriate*) for **kalemburado** (*making puns*). Since Esperanto doesn't have this feature, you might think there's no punning. That's not the case, as the French banker Raymond Schwartz abundantly demonstrated in his **poemoj** (*poems*) and **romanoj** (*novels*). You might even understand the best-known Esperanto **kalemburo** (*pun*): **Kial ĝirafo neniam estas sola? Ĉar ĝi ĉiam havas kolegon!** (*Why is a giraffe never alone? Because it always has a big neck / colleague!*)

Because of word building, you can **efektive** (*actually*) create homonyms in Esperanto! You can probably **jam** (*already*) work out for **vi mem** (*yourself*) that **kukurbo** means *cake town*; but it's also the word for a *pumpkin*! Adding a **supersigno** (*accent*) to a word can humorously change the meaning. These features mean that you can not only devise side-splitting **limerikoj** (*limericks*) but also create cryptic crosswords, especially given that words can also be anagrams of others, such as **lampoj** (*lamps*) and **palmoj** (*palm trees*).

And with Esperanto all things are possible in poetry, **ĉu** (*whether*) expressions of love delivered with great pathos, **ĉu** (*or*) a witty delivery of complaints, such as Julio Baghy's classic summary of the **memkontenta** (*self-satisfied*) critic in his **Estas mi esperantisto** (*I'm an Esperantist*).

Two of Esperanto's greatest exponents of the art of poetry were nominated for the Nobel Prize for Literature for their work. In 1953 and 1954 they even had a friendly duel **rondele** (*in rondel*), a 14th century French verse form. Over the course of those years, William Auld and Marjorie Boulton exchanged 84 postcards, which were compiled and published in 1976 as **Rimleteroj** (*rhyme letters*).

The word **aktuala** means *current, at this time*. How do you say *actually* in Esperanto to mean *in fact*? The text contains the expression **vi mem** *yourself* and **memkontenta** *self-satisfied*. What is the Esperanto word for *self*?

Vocabulary builder 1

14.01 Look at the words and phrases and complete the missing English words and expressions. Then listen and try to imitate the pronunciation of the speakers.

SENTOJ KAJ EMOCIOJ *FEELINGS AND EMOTIONS*

etoso	*atmosphere, mood*
humoro	*mood*
Pozivitaj	*Positive*
enamiĝinta	*in love*
memfida	*confident*
kuraĝa	*brave*
festema	*in the mood for partying*
Neŭtralaj	*Neutral*
scivolema	*curious*
Negativaj	*Negative*
sola	*alone, lonely*
konfuzita	_____
ĉagrenita	*annoyed*
streĉita	*stressed*
embarasita	*embarrassed*
trista / malfeliĉa	*sad*
ĵaluza	_____
envia	*envious*
kulpa	*guilty*

Conversation 1

NEW EXPRESSIONS

14.02 Look at and listen to the words and expressions that are used in the following conversation. Note their meanings.

ĉe koncerto	*at a concert*
mi ja staras sole, sed …	*I am standing on my own but …*
mi miskomprenis tion	*I misunderstood that*
kulpas mi	*it's my fault, mea culpa*
bruo / brue	*noise / noisy*
mi ne vere volas festumi	*I don't really want to party*
malstreĉita	*relaxed*
okazas karaokeo en la drinkejo	*there is karaoke at the bar*
mankas al mi kuraĝo	*I'm lacking courage*
kvieta loko	*a quiet place*
se mi scius, mi dirus tion tuj!	*if I had known, I would have said so immediately!*

14.03 *Sara is at a concert when a man comes up to talk to her.*

1 Why doesn't Sara feel much like partying?

Leonardo	Saluton! Mi rimarkis vin ĉi tie tute sola. Kiel vi fartas?
Sara	Ne, mi ne estas sola.
Leonardo	Nu, mi estas konfuzita, ĉar mi ne vidas iun alian kun vi, tial mi decidis veni paroli kun vi.
Sara	Mi ne komprenas, kiel mi konfuzis vin. Ho, jes, pardonu! Mi sentas min iom embarasita. Nu, mi ja staras sole, sed mi ne sentas min sola. Mi miskomprenis tion, kion vi celis.
Leonardo	Nu, kulpas mi. Mi devus demandi malpli konfuze. Estas bona la etoso ĉi tie, ĉu ne? Ĉu vi festemas?
Sara	Mi estus pli kontenta, se ne estus tiom da bruo. Sed la muzikon mi tre ŝatas. Festumi mi ne vere volas fari, tamen; mi sentas min iom streĉita lastatempe, do mi preferus ripozi iom kaj aŭskulti la muzikon.
Leonardo	Ĉu plaĉus al vi iri aliloken? Vi sentus vin malpli streĉita, se ni irus al loko pli kvieta, ĉu ne?
Sara	Nu, iom ĝenas la bruo. Eble estus bona ideo iri aliloken. Okazas karakeo en la drinkejo.
Leonardo	Ho … nu, mankas al mi kuraĝo por fari tion. Mi ne estas tre memfida pri tiaĵoj. Krome, daŭre estus tro brue, ĉu ne? Ĉu ne estus pli bone iri al kvieta loko? Loko, kie estus malpli da homoj, ekzemple?
Sara	Ho … ĉu vi celas, kion mi pensas, ke vi celas? Vi devus diri antaŭe!
Leonardo	Ĉu vere? Se mi scius, mi dirus tion tuj!
Sara	Ek al la gufujo!

> ### LANGUAGE TIP
> The verb **manki** conveys that something is missing or lacking: **Mankas libroj!** *We're missing some books!* Notice that *I'm missing something* is **io mankas al mi** in Esperanto: the subject is the thing that's missing, unlike in English.

2 Match the English and the Esperanto.

a Maybe it would be a good idea

b A place where there would be fewer people

c I'm not very confident about that sort of thing

d Would you like to go somewhere else?

e You should've said before

f If I'd known I'd have said before

g Do you mean what I think you mean?

h I wonder

i I'd prefer to relax a bit

j I misunderstood what you meant

1 Ĉu plaĉus al vi iri aliloken?

2 Mi demandas min

3 Vi devus diri antaŭe

4 Loko, kie estus malpli da homoj

5 Mi preferus ripozi iom

6 Mi ne estas tre memfida pri tiaĵoj

7 Mi miskomprenis tion, kion vi celis

8 Eble estus bona ideo

9 Ĉu vi celas, kion mi pensas, ke vi celas?

10 Se mi scius, mi dirus antaŭe

3 Complete the sentences with appropriate words from the box so that they reflect what was said in the conversation.

> kvieta   muzikon   memfidon
> bruon   miskomprenis
> loko   neniun

   a Leonardo decidis paroli kun Sara, ĉar li vidis _____ kun ŝi.
   b Leonardo ne havas sufiĉan _____ por fari karaokeon.
   c Leonardo proponis, ke ili iru al _____ loko.
   d Sara konsentas, ke estus bona ideo iri al _____ malpli brua.
   e Sara _____, kion celis Leonardo.
   f Sara ŝatas la _____, sed ne la _____.

4 14.04 **Now listen to the conversation line by line and repeat.**

> **LANGUAGE TIP**
>
> The prefix **mis-** implies something being done wrongly: **mi miskomprenis** *I misunderstood* and **mi misaŭdis** *I misheard*.

Language discovery 1

1 **How does Leonardo say *to another place* in one word?**

2 **What do you notice about words ending in –us in the conversation?**

3 **Why is there some confusion about whether Sara is sola?**

1 THE CONDITIONAL

The conditional is used to describe something hypothetical and is indicated by the verb ending **-us** in Esperanto:

se mi estus vi	*if I were you*
Daŭre estus tro brue, ĉu ne?	*It would still be too noisy, wouldn't it?*

There is no time associated with **us**-forms. They can relate to something in the future or in the past:

Mi devus peti vin veni.	*I should ask you to come.*
Mi devus peti vin veni (pli frue).	*I should've asked you to come (earlier).*

> **LANGUAGE TIP**
>
> As happens in English with *would*, people often use the **us**-form in Esperanto as a way of speaking politely:
>
> | | |
> |---|---|
> | **mi volas / deziras du biletojn** | *I want two tickets* |
> | **mi volus / dezirus du biletojn** | *I would like two tickets* |

2 CONDITIONAL SENTENCES

Conditional sentences using **se** *if* are used to speak about something that happens or could happen dependent on something else. What form the verbs take depends on whether you're talking about a statement of fact or a hypothetical event that is likely, unlikely, or impossible. If something is a statement of fact, the following construction with **se** is used:

Se vi varmigas akvon ĝis cent gradoj, ĝi bolas.   *If you heat water to 100 degrees, it boils.*

In the case of something which is likely to happen, the following construction is used:

Se ne pluvos posttagmeze, ni ludos futbalon kune.   *If it doesn't rain in the afternoon, we'll play football together.*

Sometimes the situation is unlikely and becomes a little more hypothetical. This is shown with **-us** in Esperanto and *would* in English:

Se mi gajnus la loterion, mi aĉetus grandan domon.   *If I won the lottery, I'd buy a big house.*

Se mi scius, ke ŝi respondos jese, mi petus ŝin manĝi kun mi.   *If I knew that she'd say yes, I'd ask her to eat with me.*

The **us**-ending is also used in impossible situations.

Se mi aĉetus la bileton, mi gajnus la loterion.   *If I had bought a ticket, I would have won the lottery.*

Se mi scius, ke ŝi respondos jese, mi petus ŝin manĝi kun mi.   *If I had known she'd say yes, I would have asked her to eat with me.*

Notice that the structure is identical in Esperanto in both the unlikely and impossible scenarios.

Practice 1

1 Match the sentence parts to make complete sentences.

   a Se mi havus sufiĉe da mono,

   b Se mi scius, ke pluvos,

   c Se la vetero estos pli bona posttagmeze,

   d Se mi ne forgesus mian libron,

   e Se mi povus elekti, ĉu havi monon, ĉu esti bonsana,

   f Se mi povus paroli kun pli juna mi, mi dirus al li,

   1 mi preferus esti ne malsana ol riĉa.

   2 ke mi scias, kiuj estas la ĝustaj numeroj por gajni la loterion tiun tagon.

   3 mi aĉetus novan aŭton kaj vojaĝus per ĝi tra la tuta lando.

   4 mi restus hejme kaj ne estus nun tute malseka.

   5 ni povos ludi futbalon aŭ promeni en la urbon.

   6 mi povus ĝin legi, dum mi havas nenion alian por fari.

Remember there's no time shift with indirect speech, including with conditional structures: **Se mi scius, ke la koncerto estos tiel laŭta, mi venus ĉi tien tuj.** That's **estos** because back when Sara might have had the thought, the concert would've been in the future: **La koncerto estos brua. Mi iros aliloken.**

2 **Fill in the correct word endings in these conditional sentences.**

a Mi dubas, ĉu ŝi venos, sed se ŝi ja ven_____, mi est_____ la plej feliĉa viro en la mondo.

b Mi ne scias, ĉu estas bona tiu nova filmo. Mi legos iom pri ĝi, kaj se la raportoj est_____ bonaj, ni ir_____ spekti ĝin.

c Se mi sci_____, ke Esperanto est_____ tiel amuza, mi eklern_____ ĝin multe pli frue!

d Mi diris, ke se ne pluv_____ posttagmeze, mi kaj la knaboj lud_____ futbalon ekstere.

e Ne, kompreneble ŝi ne kantos. Ĉu vi pov_____ imagi, kio okaz_____? Se ŝi kant_____, ĉiuj forir_____ kaj neniam plu reven_____.

f Se mi pov_____ helpi lin, mi ja far_____, sed mi ne povis, do ne faris.

3 **Which moods or emotions do these images express?**

scivolema	ĉagrenita	ĵaluza
enamiĝinta	konfuzita	embarasita
malfeliĉa / trista	kulpa	

a) _____
b) _____
c) _____
d) _____

e) _____
f) _____
g) _____
h) _____

Vocabulary builder 2

14.05 Look at the words and complete the missing English words. Then listen and try to imitate the pronunciation of the speakers.

ROMANTIKAJ VORTOJ KAJ ESPRIMOJ *ROMANTIC WORDS AND EXPRESSIONS*

ami	_____
amata	*loved, beloved*
aminda	*lovable*
amindumi	*to try to appeal to somebody*
koramiko / koramikino	*boyfriend / _____*
koketi	*to flirt*
amrendevui	*to date*
fianĉo	*fiancé (male)*
fianĉino	_____
fianĉ(in)iĝi	*to get engaged*
nupto	*wedding*
korrompulo	*heartbreaker*

Conversation 2

NEW EXPRESSIONS

14.06 Look at and listen to the words and expressions that are used in the following conversation. Note their meanings.

ĉesis la bruo	*the noise stopped*
malgranda/eta glaso da ruĝa vino	*a small glass of red wine*
alkoholaĵo	*an alcoholic drink*
jen nia teo, po unu	*here's our tea, one each*
kvazaŭ ni estus duopo	*as though we were a couple*
Mi honeste opinias, ke …	*I honestly believe that …*
eviti / evitendaĵo	*to avoid / something to be avoided*
Mi ne intencis diri ion fian.	*I didn't intend to say anything awful.*

14.07 *Sara and Leonardo have left the concert and are now in a bar.*

1 What is Leonardo going to try drinking for the first time?

Sara	Jam estas multe pli bone ĉi tie, ĉu ne? Estas bone, ke ĉesis la bruo. Se mi scius, ke la koncerto estos tiel laŭta, mi venus ĉi tien tuj.
Leonardo	Sed se vi farus tion, vi ne renkontus min, ĉu ne? Kion vi dezirus trinki? Mi ŝatus malgrandan glason da ruĝa vino.
Sara	Trinki alkoholaĵojn ĉi tie? Tio estas via unua fojo en la gufujo, ĉu ne? Ĉi tie trinkendas teo. Do, al mi plaĉus teo. Kaj ankaŭ al vi.
Leonardo	Mi ne scias, ĉar mi neniam antaŭe trinkis teon, nur kafon. Se mi jam provus trinki teon, mi scius, ĉu plaĉos al mi, sed nun estos la unua fojo.
Sara	Estu kuraĝa. La teo ĉi tie estas vere trinkinda, laŭ mi.
Leonardo	Ho, permesu, ke mi pagu! Estus por mi granda plezuro aĉeti por vi trinkaĵon.

Sara	Nu, dankon, sed la teo ne estas pagenda.
Leonardo	Do, jen nia teo, po unu. Prenu vian.
Sara	Dankon, Leĉjo.
Leonardo	Ne dankinde. Eble ni povus veni denove morgaŭ.
Sara	Estas iom frue por paroli kvazaŭ ni estus duopo, ĉu ne? Ni apenaŭ konas nin.
Leonardo	Pardonu, Sanjo. Mi ne intencis diri ion fian.
Sara	Mi ne celis, ke vi parolis fie aŭ aĉe, pardonu, ne miskomprenu min, Leĉjo. Fakte, plaĉus al mi veni ĉi tien denove kun vi.
Leonardo	Ankaŭ mi ŝatus reveni ĉi tien kun vi, Sanjo.
Sara	Do, ĉu via unua taso da teo estas atendinda? Kion vi opinias pri ĝi?
Leonardo	Honeste? Ne multon. Nu, ĝi estas aĉa. Fakte, mi ne plu povas trinki ĝin. Ĉu eblas trinki kafon? Ĉi tiun teaĉon mi volas forgesi. Se mi scius antaŭe, kiel aĉa estas teo, mi ne petus tason. Kia evitendaĵo! Ho, mi celas la teon, ne vin!

> **LANGUAGE TIP**
>
> **Halti**, which you've met in **haltejo**, only means *stop* as in *no longer be in motion, come to a stop*. The conversation between Sara and Leonardo introduced another word for *stop*, **ĉesi** *to cease*: **ĉesis la bruo** *the noise has stopped*. If you mean *stop doing something* use **ĉesi**: **Bonvolu ĉesi paroli tiel** *Please stop speaking like that*.

2 **Match the English and Esperanto.**

a I mean the tea, not you!

b Well, it's horrible

c I want to forget this awful tea

d Here's our tea; one each

e The tea's well worth drinking

f Actually, I'd like to come here again

g You've got to drink tea here

h I didn't mean to say anything shameful

i It's good that the noise has stopped

j I would've come straight here

k As though we were a couple

1 Ĉi tiun teaĉon mi volas forgesi

2 Fakte, plaĉus al mi reveni ĉi tien denove

3 Ĉi tie teo trinkendas

4 Mi ne intencis diri ion fian

5 Nu, ĝi estas aĉa

6 Estas bone, ke ĉesis la bruo

7 Kvazaŭ ni estus duopo

8 La teo estas vere trinkinda

9 Mi venus ĉi tien tuj

10 Mi celas la teon, ne vin!

11 Jen nia teo, po unu

> **LANGUAGE TIP**
>
> **Kvazaŭ** *as though, as if* introduces something that isn't real. If it's followed by a subclause, then the verb uses the **us**-ending: **Vi agas, kvazaŭ tio estus via propra domo** *You act as though this were your own home*.

Language discovery 2

1 How does Sara change words like **trinki** and **pagi** to give the idea of *must be drunk* and *must be paid for*?

2 How does Sara convey the idea of *worth waiting for* in one word?

MORE WORD BUILDING WITH -IND- AND -END-

The suffix **-ind-** means that something is worth doing. You can say that Rome is **vizitinda** *worth visiting*, a person you like is **aminda** *loveable*, and a castle somewhere is **vidinda** *worth looking at*. It also occurs in the expressions **ne dankinde** *you're welcome* and **bedaŭrinde** *unfortunately*.

-ind- can be combined with other suffixes as required:

amindulo   *a loveable person*   **vidindaĵoj**   *the sights*

Its lookalike **-end-** is used to indicate that something must be done. Leonardo thought that the tea was **pagenda** *had to be paid for*. It was actually provided free but, as Sara pointed out, it was **trinkenda** *necessary to drink* in the **gufujo**.

The suffix **-aĉ-** can be used to say that something is bad in quality:

domo   *a house*   **domaĉo**   *a shack*

skribo   *writing*   **skribaĉo**   *a scrawl*

It sometimes crosses over a little with the exclamation **Fi!** *Shame!* The nuance is that **-aĉ-** is poor in quality, while **fi-** is poor in morality:

aĉulo   *a bad person*   **fiulo**   *a disgraceful person*

domaĉo   *a shack*   **fidomo**   *a house of ill repute*

Practice 2

1 Insert **-ind-**, **-end-**, **-aĉ-** and **fi-** into the following words to create Esperanto words with the requested meanings. Where required, use **-ul-** to create a person and **-aĵ-** to create a thing from an adjective.

Example: aĉeti (*something worth buying*)   *aĉetindaĵo*

   a ĵurnalo (*a rag*)
   b pagi (*payable, due, has to be paid*)
   c fari (*worth doing*)
   d fari (*something worth doing*)
   e fama (*notorious, infamous*)
   f ridi (*laughable, mockworthy*)
   g ridi (*a mockworthy thing*)
   h ridi (*somebody mockworthy*)
   i infano (*an unpleasant child*)

j solvi (*has to be solved*)

k solvi (*something which has to be solved*)

l vorto (*a swear word*)

m viziti (*something worth visiting*)

n viziti (*a person worth visiting*)

o pagi (*something which has to be paid*)

2 **Each of these sentences contains an error. Underline the errors and write the correct versions.**

    a Se mi gajnis la loterion, mi vojaĝus ĉirkaŭ la mondon.

    b Se telefonas morgaŭ mia patrino, mi scios, ĉu mia patro estas ankoraŭ malsana.

    c Mi studos la japanan, se mi povus loĝi en Japanio.

    d Se mi scius, ke ŝi ne venus, ankaŭ mi ne venus.

> **CULTURE TIP**
>
> Some people jokingly refer to the Esperanto language as **Edzperanto**, which translates loosely as *the means to get / become a husband*.

Reading

Read these two adverts from *La Esperantisto*, the first Esperanto magazine, and *Lingvo Internacia*, the second, and answer the questions. (These men were beginner learners so there are some mistakes.)

1 **What nationalities are the two men?**

2 **What age range is the first man looking for?**

La Esperantisto (1889–1895), May 1892.

JUNA HOMO

(22 jaroj), polo, deziras korespondadi kun ia esperantistino, en celo konatiĝi kun ŝi kaj edziniĝi; plena garantio de silentado; seriozajn ofertojn esperantistinoj povos sendadi laŭ la sekvanta adreso:

Arĥangelsk (Russie), al sinjoro A. Zakrĵevski, por sinjoro .*.

Lingvo Internacia (1895–1914), March 1900.

Writing

Explain what you would do in the following situations, giving as much detail as possible.

    a Se mi havus milionon, …

    b Se ŝtormo detruus mian domon, …

    c Se mi devus loĝi en alia lando, …

Listening

14.08 **Listen to the four extracts from an Esperanto radio station. What is the mood of each speaker? What's causing them to feel as they do?**

    1 _____

    2 _____

    3 _____

    4 _____

Speaking

How would you feel in each of the following situations? Record yourself saying how you feel and add a short sentence or two to explain why.

Example: Your neighbour buys a beautiful new car and it's much better than yours.
Mi estas envia, ĉar mi ĉiam volis havi tian aŭton, sed neniam havis sufiĉe da mono.

a You've got an exam today. You know it's your strongest subject and you've worked hard all year, so you have the feeling that you're going to do very well.

b You don't understand why you've received a salad. That's not what you ordered.

c You've just heard some bad news about a friend.

Test yourself

1 Add the correct endings to these sentences:

Mi estas konfuzita. Mia patro promesis al mi, ke se mi est_____ bonkonduta kaj labor_____ diligente, li don_____ al mi bileton por spekti la futbalon. Mi ne komprenas, ĉar mi ja est_____ bonkonduta kaj labor_____ diligente, sed patro ne don_____ al mi bileton. Se mi sci_____, ke li romp_____ la promeson, mi nek est_____ bonkonduta nek labor_____ diligente!

2 Which of these words are positive attributes?

aminda, ĵaluza, honesta, aĉa, fidinda, afabla, senkuraĝa

3 Which suffix do you see in the Esperanto equivalent to *you're welcome*?

SELF-CHECK	
I CAN ...	
○	… talk about possibilities and conditional events.
○	… express moods.
○	… say what's worth doing.
○	… express contempt and dislike.

15 Kulturaj diferencoj
Cultural differences

In this unit, you will learn how to:
▶ *talk about cultures, traditions and differences.*
▶ *resolve problems.*
▶ *speak impersonally.*
▶ *use reflexive pronouns and reciprocal forms.*

CEFR: (B1) *Can develop an argument well enough to be followed without difficulty most of the time. Can explain why something is a problem.* **(B1)** *Can fluently sustain a straightforward description of one of a variety of subjects of interest, presenting in a linear sequence of points.*

 Esperantaj kulturaj diferencoj *Esperanto cultural differences*

Perhaps the biggest surprise newcomers will find at an Esperanto event is that they can't use English when they need to explain something. Truly international events bring in people from all over the world, many of whom have never had **aliro** (*access*) to English. Esperanto really **uziĝas** (*gets used*) for everything.

Esperantujo has often been considered a natural home for idealistic people. As far back as 1893, articles about **vegetaranismo** (*vegetarianism*) featured in the first Esperanto magazine, **La Esperantisto**, and were adopted by Ludoviko Zamenhof into his **Fundamenta Krestomatio**, a 461-page book **eldonita** (*released*) in 1903 containing articles in model Esperanto.

Indeed, Esperanto events were early leaders in making sure that **vegetaranoj** (*vegetarians*) and **veganoj** (*vegans*) were catered for. You will usually find an option to indicate your **prefero** (*preference*) when you sign up to an event. Some will even **antaŭsupozi** (*assume*) that you're vegetarian by default unless you indicate that you're a **ĉionmanĝanto** (*omnivore*). You may find that the food costs for the event are **iom pli altaj** (*a little higher*) if you're a meat eater. Lots of people deliberately sign up as vegetarians, even though they're not; they **taksas la vegetaran manĝon pli bona** (*rate the vegetarian food as better*).

Ne surpriziĝu (*don't be surprised*) if people seem very friendly; many people at these events have been friends for years and don't see each other very often, so there might be more **kisoj** (*kisses*) and **brakumoj** (*hugs*) than you would expect.

 What do you notice about the word for *to assume*? What about *hugs*?

Vocabulary builder 1

15.01 Look at the words and phrases and complete the missing English words and expressions. Then listen and try to imitate the pronunciation of the speakers.

KORPAJ AGOJ *GESTURES*

kisi unu la alian	to _____ *each other*
tuŝi	*to touch*
manpremi unu la alian	*to shake one another's hands*
teni la manojn	*to hold _____*
klini sin	*to bow*
gesto	*a gesture*
brakumi	*to hug*
tusi	*to cough*
terni	*to sneeze*
kapjesi	*to nod*
kapskui	*to shake one's head*
levi la brakon	*to raise/lift one's arm*

Conversation 1

NEW EXPRESSIONS

15.02 Look at and listen to the words and expressions that are used in the following conversation. Note their meanings.

estas maniero saluti inter proksimaj amikoj	*it's a way of greeting between close friends*
mi devus diri voĉe	*I should say 'verbally'*
ni tute maltuŝemas	*we really don't touch at all*
Kiaj aliaj kulturaj diferencoj ekzistas?	*What other cultural differences exist?*
Kiel alie oni povus senintence ofendi homojn?	*How else could you accidentally offend people?*
Vi konas la internacian pacgeston, ĉu ne?	*You know the international peace gesture, don't you?*
ne estus dece diri	*it wouldn't be proper to say*
oni fakte skuas sian kapon	*you actually shake your head*
oni riskus gajni por si reputacion	*you'd risk getting yourself a reputation*
dankmono estas maniero esprimi, ke oni kontentas pri la servo	*a tip is a way to show that you're satisfied with the service*

1 How do American tourists in Japan inadvertently risk offending some people through their kindness?

Sara	Ho, Lena, nekredeble! Rigardu ilin, tie! Mi ĵus vidis Jevgenijn kaj alian viron kisi unu la alian! Tiuj du, ili ĵus salutis unu la alian per kiso. Se mi estus Natalja, mi volus scii, ke mia edzo faris tion.
Lena	Ha! Ne, tio ne signifas tion, kion vi pensas. Estas simple maniero saluti inter proksimaj amikoj en Rusio. Ĝi signifas neniom pli ol tion. Evidente oni ne faras tiel en Britio, ĉu?
Sara	Ne ĉe viroj, ne. Oni simple salutas unu la alian buŝe. Ho, fakte mi devus diri voĉe! Foje viroj manpremas unu la alian, eble eĉ brakumas inter si. Sed kutime oni simple demandas 'Kiel vi fartas?'.
Himeko	Oni faras eĉ tiom? En Japanio oni tute ne tuŝas unu la alian. Ni tute maltuŝemas. Oni klinas sin tre ofte en Japanio, kiel ĉiuj scias, sed oni ne emas tuŝi.
Sara	Ĉu? Mi aŭdis, ke en Svedio kaj Norvegio oni ne staras tiel proksime al aliaj homoj, sed mi ne sciis, ke ekzistas landoj, kie oni tute evitas tuŝi unu la alian.
Himeko	Jen interesa temo, ĉu ne? Mi demandas min, kiaj aliaj kulturaj diferencoj ekzistas. Kiel alie oni povus senintence ofendi homojn pro nescio?
Sara	Ho, jen bona ekzemplo! Nebritoj povus facile krei problemojn por si en Britio. Vi konas la internacian pacgeston, ĉu ne? Oni faras 'v' per siaj unua kaj dua fingroj, ĉu ne? Nu, internacie ne gravas, ĉu estas la supro aŭ malsupro de la mano, kiun oni montras. Sed tio ja gravas en Britio, ĉar estas tre ofende fari la 'v' se oni vidas la supran parton de la mano! Ĝi signifas … nu, ne estus dece diri.
Himeko	Mi aŭdis, ke la vorton 'kapjesi' povus miskompreni homoj en Grekio kaj Bulgario, ĉar en ĉi tiuj landoj oni kapjesas por indiki 'ne'. Por 'jesgesti' tie oni fakte skuas sian kapon, kiel por diri 'ne' en la plimulto de kulturoj. Aŭ eble ili levetas la kapon. Mi ne plu bone memoras.
Lena	Mi havas similan rakonton. En Germanio oni nepre devas alveni ĝustahore; malfrui estas tre insulte. Sed mi havis du amikinojn, argentinanon kaj ĉilianon. Kaj ili ĉiam malfruis, minimume kvaronhore. Kial? Ĉar ĉe ili fakte estas malafable alveni ĝustahore; oni riskus gajni por si reputacion esti ege manĝema.
Himeko	Usonanoj ĉiam tute senintence ofendas en Japanio. En ilia lando oni ĉiam donas dankmonon al kelneroj kaj kelnerinoj, ĉu ne? Ne fari tion estas maniero esprimi, ke oni ne kontentas pri la servo. Sed en Japanio kaj Ĉinio, proponi dankmonon estas insulte; oni ne bezonas plian monon por fari sian laboron bone. Oni do facile miskomprenas tiajn aferojn, ĉar la usonanoj sentus sin malĝentilaj, se ili ne proponus la monon.

2 Match the English and Esperanto.

a Sometimes men shake each other's hands

b Could create problems for themselves

c Even hug among themselves

d People actually shake their head

e I just saw them kissing each other

f People totally avoid touching each other

g That doesn't mean what you think

h People bow very often in Japan

1 Eĉ brakumi inter si

2 Mi ĵus vidis ilin kisi unu la alian

3 Oni tute evitas tuŝi unu la alian

4 Foje viroj manpremas unu la alian

5 Oni klinas sin tre ofte en Japanio

6 Tio ne signifas, kion vi pensas

7 Oni fakte skuas sian kapon

8 Povus krei problemojn por si

3 Fill in the gaps in the sentences with a word from the box to reflect what was said in the conversation.

> dankmonon   malafable
> kapjesas   maldeca   klinas sin
> ĝustahore   kapskuas   malfrue
> proksime   pacgesto   tuŝas

a En Grekio oni _____ por indiki 'ne'.

b Nepras alveni _____ en Germanio.

c Estas malafable en Usono, se oni ne donas _____.

d En Bulgario oni _____ por indiki 'jes'.

e Oni _____ en Japanio, sed ne _____ aliulojn.

f En Ĉilio oni ĉiam alvenas _____. Fari alie estus _____.

g Oni ne staras _____ al aliuloj en Norvegio.

h Oni devas atenti pri la _____ en Britio, ĉar ĝi similas al _____ gesto.

 4 15.04 Now listen to the conversation again line by line and repeat.

> **LANGUAGE TIP**
>
> Where English often uses *they* or *people* to speak generally, Esperanto tends to use the pronoun **oni** *one*: **Oni parolas la francan en Francio** *people speak French in France.*

Language discovery 1

1 Find the occasions where oni is used in the conversation.

2 What was unclear when Sara said *They greet each other verbally* given the context? How did she clarify what she meant by changing a word?

3 Which preposition does Sara use to say that kissing each other in greeting isn't something you find among men back home?

1 THE REFLEXIVE PRONOUN SI

When the subject of a sentence is one of the third-person pronouns (**li**, **ŝi**, **ĝi**, **oni**, **ili**), Esperanto uses a special pronoun, **si**, when that subject appears again in the sentence in another role.

When the subject is **mi**, **vi** or **ni**, the pronouns referring back to it look the same:

Mi vizitas mian patrinon, kaj vi vizitas vian.   *I visit my mother and you visit yours.*

If the subject is in the third person, the pronoun referring back to it switches to a form of **si**:

Li vizitas sian patrinon.   *He visits his mother.* (his own mother)

If the pronoun doesn't change, then it doesn't refer back to the subject but refers to somebody or something else:

Li vizitas lian patrinon.   *He visits his mother.* (some other male's mother)

Si has to reflect back on the subject; it can never be a subject itself. It is therefore not correct to say **Li kaj 'sia' frato iris en la urbon**. The sentence **Li kaj lia frato iris en la urbon** could mean either 'and his own brother' or 'and another male's brother'.

Si may appear as a complement of the subject:

Li iris en la urbon kun sia frato.   *He went into town with his brother.*

When a sentence involves several clauses, **si** represents the implied subject of its sub-clause and not the subject of the main clause:

La patrino ordonis al la knabo vesti sin.   *The mother ordered the boy to dress himself.*

The implied subject of **vesti** is **la knabo** and so **sin** represents *the boy*. If the mother wanted the boy to dress her rather than himself, then **vesti ŝin** would be used instead.

2 RECIPROCALS: DOING SOMETHING TO 'EACH OTHER'

To give the idea of reciprocity, the construction **unu la alian** can be used, with various prepositions as required:

Ili kisas unu la alian.   *They're kissing each other.*

Ili donis pomojn unu al la alia.   *They gave apples to each other.*

Practice 1

1 **Choose which of the pronouns is correct in each sentence.**
   a La knabo ludas kun (lia / sia) frato. (*his own brother*)
   b La knabo ludas kun (lia / sia) frato. (*some other boy's brother*)
   c La knabino ludas kun (lia / sia) frato.
   d Sara kaj (ŝia / sia) amikino iras al loka restoracio.
   e Roberto manĝas picon kun (lia / sia) amiko. (*Roberto's friend*)
   f Ŝi ŝatas la viron, kiun ŝi vidis paroli hieraŭ kun (liaj / ŝiaj / siaj) infanoj. (*the woman's children*)
   g Ŝi ŝatas la viron, kiun ŝi vidis paroli hieraŭ kun (liaj / ŝiaj / siaj) infanoj. (*the man's own children*)

h La reĝo ordonis al la reĝino vesti (lin / ŝin / sin). (*the king*)

i La reĝo ordonis al la reĝino vesti (lin / ŝin / sin). (*the queen*)

j Oni devas labori por subteni (onian / sian) familion.

2 **Fill in the gaps in the sentences with oni or a version of si as required.**

   a En Italio _____ manĝas spagetojn tre ofte por _____ vespermanĝo.

   b _____ povas aĉeti ĉokoladon, sed ne tro ofte, se _____ volas resti maldika.

   c Estas malfacile scii, ĉu _____ respondis ĝuste al la demando, ĝis _____ ricevas _____ rezultojn.

   d La knaboj bele ludis inter _____.

   e Se _____ faras malbonon, _____ devus pardonpeti.

   f Se _____ faras malbonon, _____ devus peti pardonon pro _____ kulpoj.

3 **Match the sentence beginnings with their endings.**

   a Ili kisas unu   **1** post la alia

   b La infanoj kuris en la ĝardenon unu   **2** la alian

   c Ili disputis kaj kuris for unu   **3** al la alia

   d La geedzoj donis unu … la manon   **4** pri la alia

   e Ili volis lerni pli unu   **5** de la alia

Vocabulary builder 2

 15.05 **Look at the words and complete the missing English words. Then listen and try to imitate the pronunciation of the speakers.**

BESTOJ *ANIMALS*

besto	*animal*
hejmbesto	*pet*
ido	*offspring*
hundo	*dog*
kato	_____
leono	*lion*
tigro	_____
lupo	*wolf*
porko	_____
bovo	*cow*
ŝafo	*sheep*
ĉevalo	*horse*
urso	*bear*
simio	*monkey*
kuniklo	*rabbit*
muso	*mouse*

rato	_____
birdo	_____
koko	*chicken*
fiŝo	_____
serpento	_____

Conversation 2

NEW EXPRESSIONS

 15.06 Look at and listen to the words and expressions that are used in the following conversation. Note their meanings.

Eĉ rilate bestojn …	*Even regarding animals …*
opinias siajn hejmbestojn familianoj	*think of their pets as family members*
sed porkaĵo kaj bovaĵo manĝeblas	*but pork and beef are edible*
ne ekzistas virkokoj por manĝi	*there aren't any male chickens to eat*
ne inaj kokoj, sed malinaj	*not female chickens but males*
Imagu, se oni farus tiel al katidoj aŭ al hundidoj!	*Imagine if it were like that with kittens and puppies!*
kio laŭ mi estas tute aĉa afero	*which, in my view, is a totally disgusting thing*
al mi ne gravas, ĉu oni manĝas ŝafidaĵon	*I don't mind if people eat lamb*
same kiel multaj baratanoj ĝenerale ne manĝas bovaĵon ĉe si	*just like many people living in India generally don't like eating beef in their country*
sed laŭ tiu pensmaniero	*but with that way of thinking*
mi havas la plej facilan problem-evitilon	*I have the easiest thing for avoiding the problem*

 15.07 *Sara and her friends are now discussing eating customs around the world.*

1 Why does Sara think eating lamb is fine?

Sara	Eĉ rilate bestojn kaj manĝaĵojn oni riskas ofendi inter diversaj landoj kaj kulturoj. Vi ĉiuj scias, ke britoj ofte opinias siajn hejmbestojn familianoj, ĉu ne? Estas neeble por ili pensi, ke oni povus manĝi ĉi tiujn bestojn.
Himeko	Ĉu? Eĉ fiŝojn?
Sara	Nu, ne fiŝojn. Fiŝaĵon oni povas manĝi. Ne siajn hejmfiŝojn, komprenble, sed ĝenerale. Mi parolas pri katoj kaj hundoj. En Britio oni ne komprenas, kiel oni povas, en sud-orienta Azio, ekzemple, manĝi kataĵon kaj hundaĵon.
Himeko	Sed porkaĵo kaj bovaĵo manĝeblas ĉe vi, ĉu ne?
Sara	Certe. Kaj oni ankaŭ manĝas multe da kokaĵo. Nu, 'kokinaĵo' estas eble pli ĝusta esprimo. Ne ekzistas virkokoj por manĝi.
Himeko	Virkokoj?! Ho, mi ekkomprenas. Ne inaj kokoj, sed malinaj. Ne kokino, sed vira koko.
Sara	Ĝuste. Ne kokinoj sed viraj kokoj. Mi kredas, ke ilin oni mortigas kiam ili estas kokidoj, ĉar virkokojn oni ĝenerale ne bezonas.

Lena	Tio laŭ mi estas tute aĉa afero. Imagu, se oni farus tiel al katidoj aŭ al hundidoj! Kiel oni dirus en Britio pri tio, Sara? Ĉu oni kontentus? Tute ne.
Sara	Sed estas diferenco inter hejmbestoj kaj aliaj bestoj, ĉu ne? Eblas manĝi bestojn, sed ne hejmbestojn. Al mi ne gravas, ĉu oni manĝas ŝafidaĵon, ekzemple, ĉar ŝafoj ne estas hejmbestoj. Ili loĝas kune en ŝafaro, kaj unu tagon oni manĝas ilin.
Lena	Do, ĉevalaĵon vi manĝus, ĉu ne, ĉar ĉevaloj ne estas hejmbestoj? Kompreneble ne. Same kiel multaj baratanoj ĝenerale ne manĝas bovaĵon ĉe si.
Himeko	Sed laŭ tiu pensmaniero, oni povus manĝi nenian viandon, ĉu ne? Kiel vi faras por eviti senintence ofendi, kiam vi estas en alia lando, Lena? Ĉu vi scias, kian beston en ĉiu lando oni povas manĝi? Kiel vi scius ne peti ĉevalaĵon aŭ hundaĵon en Britio, ekzemple?
Lena	Mi havas la plej facilan problem-evitilon: mi estas veganino.

2 Match the English and Esperanto.

a With that way of thinking

1 Al mi ne gravas, ĉu oni manĝas ŝafidaĵon

b How would you know not to ask for horsemeat?

2 Rilate bestojn

c What would people in Britain say about that?

3 Estas neeble por ili pensi

d Not female chickens but male

4 Ne ekzistas virkokoj por manĝi

e I don't mind if people eat lamb

5 Eviti senintence ofendi

f Regarding animals

6 Kiel vi scius ne peti ĉevalaĵon?

g There are no cockerels to eat

7 Imagu, se oni farus tion al katidoj

h Imagine doing that to kittens

8 Kion oni dirus en Britio pri tio?

i Avoid accidentally offending

9 Ne inaj kokoj sed malinaj

j It's impossible for them to think

10 Laŭ tiu pensmaniero

Language discovery 2

1 Note the instances where **-aĵ-** is being used with an animal name. What is it conveying?

2 Why does Himeko get confused when Sara mentions cockerels?

3 What expression does Sara use to convey that she doesn't mind people eating sheep?

DESCRIBING ANIMALS

Esperanto's affix system means that words to describe animals and associated vocabulary can be formed regularly using a range of suffixes:

bovo	*cow*	**bovaĵo**	*beef*
fiŝo	*fish*	**fiŝaĵo**	*fish* (to eat)
leono	*lion*	**leonaro**	*pride of lions*
baleno	*whale*	**balenaro**	*pod of whales*
ĉevalo	*horse*	**ĉevalejo**	*stable*
hundo	*dog*	**hundejo**	*kennel*

The suffix **-id-** gives the name of the offspring:

kato	*cat*	**katido**	*kitten*
anaso	*duck*	**anasido**	*duckling*

Animal names are generally considered to be neuter and can apply to both males and females of the species. To specify a female, you can make use of the **-in-** suffix:

koko	*chicken*	**kokino**	*hen*
vulpo	*fox*	**vulpino**	*vixen*

The traditional solution for specifying the male of the species is to add **vir-** in front of the name or as an adjective:

ansero	*goose*	**viransero**	*gander*
erinaco	*hedgehog*	**vira erinaco**	*boar*

Practice 2

1 Use the suffixes you've learned so far to create the following words from porko *pig*.

    a a sow

    b a piglet

    c a female piglet

    d boars and sows

    e a group of pigs

    f pork

    g a pigsty

    h a little pig

    i a dirty pig, low-quality pig

    j a group of piglets

    k a huge pig

    l a huge sow

    m a group of sows

    n a little piglet

    o a place for piglets

    p piglet meat

2 Decide whether the following words need **-aĵ-** or **-ad-** to convey the meanings in parentheses.

a dir_____o (*a saying*)

b leg_____o (*reading*)

c honest_____o (*an honest thing or act*)

d plor_____o (*crying*)

e skrib_____o (*writing, handwriting*)

f vest_____oj (*clothes*)

g havebl_____o (*something available*)

h vest_____o (*getting dressed*)

i plend_____o (*complaining*)

j pork_____o (*pork*)

k konstru_____o (*building*)

l mirind_____o (*a wonder*)

m kuir_____o (*cooking*)

n leg_____o (*something read*)

o demand_____o (*questioning*)

p nov_____o (*piece of news*)

q fiŝkapt_____o (*fishing*)

CULTURE TIP

The oldest active international vegetarian organization uses Esperanto as its working language. The **Tutmonda Esperantista Vegetarana Asocio** was founded in 1908. Its slogan is **vivu kaj lasu vivi** (*live and let live*).

Reading

Read the following summary about Novaj sep mirindaĵoj de la mondo *Seven new wonders of the world* **and answer the questions.**

Vi sendube jam aŭdis pri la *Sep mirindaĵoj de la antikva mondo*. Sed ĉu vi sciis, ke en 2007 okazis publika voĉdonado (*voting*) por elekti *Novajn sep mirindaĵojn*? La homoj, kiuj voĉdonis, elektis la sep sekvaĵojn:

Chichén Itzá, ruinejon en Meksiko; Statuon de Kristo, kiu aperis publike en la brazila urbo Rio-de-Ĵanejro en la jaro 1931; la Grandan Ĉinan Muron; Maĉupikĉuon, la plej gravan arkeologian lokon, kiu restas en Peruo; la urbon Petra, la plej popularan vidindaĵon en Jordanio; la Taĝ-Mahalon, monumenton en Barato.

1 Which one was built in the 20th century?

2 Which one could be described as a **murego**?

Writing

Imagine that there's an Esperanto event in your country and you're part of the organizing team.

Write between 100 and 200 words about some of the cultural norms in your country to help vistors prepare for their trip.

Speaking

Practise speaking the text from the writing exercise, paying particular attention to your pronunciation.

Listening

 15.08 Listen to the conversation. What was the problem? How did it get resolved?

Test yourself

1 Insert the correct pronoun into the following sentence so that it reads as the natural Esperanto way to say *English is spoken in England / in England people speak English.*

   En Anglio, _____ parolas la anglan.

2 Add the missing words so that the Esperanto sentence is a direct translation of *a man and a woman are talking to each other*:

   Viro kaj virino parolas _____.

3 Insert the correct pronoun into this sentence to give the meaning *the boy is eating with his (the boy's) father*:

   La knabo manĝas kun _____ patro.

SELF-CHECK	
I CAN ...	
⬤	... talk about cultures, traditions and differences.
⬤	... resolve problems.
⬤	... speak impersonally.
⬤	... use reflexive pronouns and reciprocal forms.

16 Muzika prezento
A musical performance

In this unit, you will learn how to:
▶ *talk about music.*
▶ *indicate a change in state.*
▶ *persuade somebody to do something.*
▶ *change a verb type.*

CEFR: (B1) *Can give detailed instructions.* **(B1)** *Can write a description of an event – real or imaginary.* **(B1)** *Can understand texts that consist mainly of high-frequency everyday or job-related language.* **(B1)** *Can give detailed instructions.* **(B1)** *Can write a description of an event – real or imaginary.* **(B1)** *Can understand texts that consist mainly of high-frequency everyday or job-related language.*

 ## Esperanta muziko *Esperanto music*

Esperanto isn't just a **parolata lingvo** (*spoken language*); it's **kantata** (*sung*) too. The **Esperanto-movado** (*Esperanto movement*) has a hymn, **la Espero** (*the Hope*), which was a poem Ludoviko Zamenhof wrote in Russian and then translated. It has been set to music on several occasions, the **plej konata se ne la plej bona** (*most known if not the best*) being marching music by the French **komponisto** (*composer*) Félicien Menu de Ménil.

But Esperanto music isn't limited to **malnov-stila** (*old-style*) marching music. There are bands which play **rok-muziko** (*rock*) and pop songs, and which are often on the programme at some of the larger international events. There's JoMo, a Frenchman who has held world records for performing concerts using the most languages, as well as reggae singers, a gangsta rap group and a death metal band!

There's even an Esperanto record company, Vinilkosmo, founded in 1990, which helped professionalize standards when **alie** (*otherwise*) bands wouldn't have been able to record. Without the efforts of the firm and its founder, Flo Martorell, there wouldn't be so much music and **neniam estus eble** (*it would never have been possible*) to launch the 24-hour online **muzik-kanalo** (*music channel*) Muzaiko in 2011.

 How could you reduce **neniam estus eble** to two words and still keep the same meaning? If **parolata lingvo** is *a spoken language* and **kantata lingvo** is *a language which is sung*, what's **legata lingvo**?

Vocabulary builder 1

16.01 Look at the words and phrases and complete the missing English words and expressions. Then listen and try to imitate the pronunciation of the speakers.

MUZIKO *MUSIC*

sono	*sound*
kanzono / kanto	*a song*
strofo	*a verse*
refreno	*a chorus*
ĥoro / koruso	*a choir*
komponi	*to compose*
akordi	*to tune, be in tune*
tono	*tone*
melodio	_____
harmonio	_____
ritmo	*rhythm*
instrumento / muzikilo	_____

> **LANGUAGE TIP**
>
> Owing to its guttural pronunciation, the sound **ĥ** has been unpopular in Esperanto since the language's early days and replacing it with other letters, usually **k**, has been common for over a century. This is why both **ĥoro** and **koruso** mean *choir*. (**Koro** wasn't possible as an alternative because it already has a meaning: *heart*.) Even Ludoviko Zamenhof used both **teĥnika** and **teknika** in his answers to requests for language advice. All of the older words with **ĥ** are still official and you can use them if you want to.

Conversation 1

NEW EXPRESSIONS

16.02 Look at and listen to the words and expressions that are used in the following conversation. Note their meanings.

Mi avertas vin, ke …	*I'm warning you that …*
Ni esperu, ke ŝi pliboniĝis.	*Let's hope she has improved.*
Ni esperu, ke la fenestroj ne rompiĝos!	*Let's hope the windows won't break!*
ŝi kliniĝas anstataŭ ruĝiĝi	*she bows instead of blushes*
li estas bonega komediisto	*he is a great comedian*
tiel nomis lin liaj gepatroj	*that's what his parents named him*
li naskiĝis la 14-an de februaro	*he was born on February 14*
surscenejiĝas nun	*coming on stage now (stage = **scenejo**)*
Esperantujo havas talentulojn / lertulojn	*Esperantoland has talented / skilled people*
mi vere interesiĝas pri li	*I'm really interested in him*
li opinias sin granda ŝercisto	*he thinks himself a great joker*
se vi ne endormiĝos / ekdormos	*if you don't fall asleep*
Mi duonpensas enlitiĝi por eviti lin!	*I'm half-thinking about getting into bed to avoid him!*
Memoru vekiĝi poste.	*Remember to wake up afterwards.*

16.03 *Sara, Roberto and Lena are watching the acts performing at the event's* **Internacia Vespero.**

1 What does Lena hope won't break?

Sara	Mi pardonpetas, ke mi alvenis malfrue! Ĉu la Internacia Vespero jam komenciĝis, Roberto?
Roberto	Ankoraŭ ne. Tiu virino estas la unua, sed ŝi ankoraŭ ne komencis kanti. Mi avertas vin, ke mi aŭskultis ŝin lastan jaron, kaj ŝi ne bele kantis. Ni esperu, ke ŝi pliboniĝis.
Lena	Ni esperu, ke la fenestroj ne rompiĝos! Mi duoncertas, ke lastan jaron ŝia voĉo rompis ilin ĉiujn!
Sara	Mi estis trankvila antaŭ du minutoj; nun mi maltrankviliĝas!
Lena	Ne nervoziĝu, Sara; ŝi baldaŭ ĉesos kanti! Ho, jen la momento por feliĉiĝi. Ne rompiĝis la fenestroj!
Roberto	Ŝi tamen ŝajnas esti tre kontenta; rigardu, kiel ŝi klinas sin por gratuliĝi!
Lena	Nekredeble, ke ŝi kliniĝas anstataŭ ruĝiĝi, ĉu ne?
Sara	Mi esperas, ke la sekva estos pli bona. Ĉu vi konas lin?
Lena	Jes, li estas bonega komediisto. Li nomiĝas Valentino. Li amuzos vin.
Sara	Valentino? Ĉu lia komedio temas pri amo?
Roberto	Ne, ne, tio estas lia vera nomo. Tiel nomis lin liaj gepatroj. Li naskiĝis la 14-an de februaro, do tiun nomon ricevis.
Sara	Ho, vi pravis, Lena! Li estis tre bona, haha! Mi bele amuziĝis! Kiu sekvos?
Roberto	Surscenejiĝas nun … fakte, mi ne scias. Iuj muzikistoj. Ni vidu, kiaj ili estas.
Lena	Ili ludas kaj kantas belege, ĉu ne? Mi tre ŝatis tiujn harmoniojn, kiujn ili faras. Ĉio akordas perfekte. Esperantujo havas talentulojn!
Roberto	Ho, ĝuu la senton, dum ĝi daŭros! Mi ĵus vidis Ĉun. Li estos la sekva.
Sara	Kiu estas Ĉun? Nun ke vi avertis min tiel, mi vere interesiĝas pri li!
Roberto	Vi estos la sola, do. Ĉun interesas neniun. Li opinias sin granda ŝercisto, sed fakte li estas nekredeble teda. Vi faros bone, se vi ne endormiĝos!
Lena	Ho, vi pravas. Mi duonpensas enlitiĝi por eviti lin!
Roberto	Memoru vekiĝi poste. Se ne, mi petos, ke veku vin la unua kantistino!

2 Match the English and the Esperanto.

a	That's how his parents named him	**1**	Ni esperu, ke ŝi pliboniĝis
b	She hasn't started singing yet	**2**	Ne rompiĝis la fenestroj!
c	I'm really interested in that	**3**	Ĉu ĝi jam komenciĝis?
d	Now I'm getting worried	**4**	Rigardu, kiel ŝi klinas sin
e	Let's hope that she's improved	**5**	Ŝi ne ruĝiĝas, sed kliniĝas
f	Look how she's bowing	**6**	Enlitiĝi
g	Has it already started?	**7**	Ŝi ankoraŭ ne komencis kanti
h	She's not blushing, she's bowing	**8**	Endormiĝi
i	To fall asleep	**9**	Tio interesas neniun

j The windows didn't break!

k That doesn't interest anyone

l To get into bed

10 Tiel nomis lin liaj gepatroj

11 Mi vere interesiĝas pri tio

12 Nun mi maltrankviliĝas

3 Based on the conversation, fill the gaps in the sentences using the words in the box.

> kliniĝas   interesiĝis   amuzis   alvenis
> Esperantujo   naskiĝtago   lito   ruĝiĝis

a Pro la belega ludado de la muzikistoj, Lena anoncas, ke _____ havas talentulojn.

b Lena pensas iri al sia _____ por eviti Ĉun.

c Valentino estis bona komediisto kaj _____ Saran.

d Roberto ne povas kredi, ke la malbona kantistino _____ poste.

e Lena ne povas kredi, ke la malbona kantistino ne _____ poste.

f Sara timis, ke ŝi _____ tro malfrue.

g Valentino ricevis sian nomon pro sia _____.

h Post kiam ŝi ekaŭdis pri li, Sara vere _____ pri Ĉun.

4 **16.04 Now listen to the conversation line by line and repeat.**

Language discovery 1

1 There are several examples of pairs of verbs in the conversation. They feature in their normal forms and also with the suffix **-iĝ-**. Which ones in the pairs have objects taking the **n**-ending?

2 How does Lena form *don't get nervous* from the adjective **nervoza**? How does Roberto create *to get congratulated* from **gratuli** *to congratulate*?

3 How does Lena say *to get into bed* in one word? How about Roberto saying *to fall asleep*?

1 THE SUFFIX -IĜ-

The suffix **-iĝ-** has two main roles. The first is that it indicates a change of state.

La knabino ruĝiĝis.	*The girl blushed (became red).*
Via Esperanto pliboniĝis (pli + bon).	*Your Esperanto has improved (has become better).*

-iĝ- can combine with prepositions and **o**-words to create new words indicating a change:

Mi enlitiĝos (en + lito *bed***) post la koncerto.**	*I'll get into bed after the concert.*
Mi elaviadiliĝis (el + aviadilo *aeroplane***) kaj baldaŭ poste entrajniĝis (en + trajno** *train***).**	*I got off the aeroplane and soon afterwards got on the train.*

-iĝ- can also be turned into a verb **iĝi** *to become*:

Ŝi iĝis fama. = Ŝi famiĝis.	*She became famous.*
Ŝi iĝis maltrankvila. = Ŝi maltrankviliĝis.	*She became anxious.*

2 CHANGING VERB TYPES WITH -IĜ-

Many Esperanto verbs must have an object. For example, **rompi** *to break* and **trovi** *to find* have to relate to something which will take the **n**-ending:

Li rompis la fenestron.	*He broke the window.*
Li trovis la ĝustan trajnon.	*He found the correct train.*

In some instances the object might actually be an infinitive rather than an **n**-ending. Both may be implied rather than stated:

Ĉu ni komencu (la kunmanĝadon, manĝi, kuiri, danci, la konkurson)?	*Shall we start (feasting, eating, cooking, dancing, the contest)?*
Ĉu vi finis (manĝi, vian konversacion, plendi)?	*Have you finished (eating, your conversation, complaining)?*

The suffix **-iĝ-** allows you to change the verb type, so that you can use these verbs without objects. The meanings of these verbs change when you do this:

Ni komencu la konkurson.	*Let's start the competition.*
La konkurso komenciĝis.	*The competition started.*
Mi vendas librojn.	*I sell books.*
Lia libro bone vendiĝas.	*His book is selling very well.*

When you do this, **-iĝ-** often has a similar effect to the passive:

La kongresejo troviĝas en tiu strato.	*The congress venue is found in that street.*
Ilia bela kato nomiĝas Heidi.	*Their beautiful cat is named Heidi.*

Sometimes **-iĝ-** may be used with verbs which don't require an object, in which case they indicate a transition to that action, mirroring **ek-**:

ili sidiĝis = ili eksidis	*they sat down*

Practice 1

1 Match the words in the box with their translations.

> ruĝiĝi   interesiĝi   laciĝi   malboniĝi
> moviĝi   fariĝi   ellitiĝi   troviĝi
> blankiĝi   naskiĝi   malsaniĝi   enaviadiliĝi

a to become ill

b to worsen (become worse *not* make worse)

c to get tired

d to whiten, become pale

e to become (alternative to **iĝi**)

f to be interested

g to get out of bed

h to blush

i to be born

j to move (but *not* to move something)

k to board an aeroplane

l to be located, found

2 Insert -iĝ- in these sentences where it's required.

a Mi komenc_____is kanti kiam mi estis nur trijara, do ne estas surprizo, ke mi far_____is kantisto

b La kurso komen_____is frue kaj tial mi devis vek_____ frue. Mi ne sukcesis (tre malfacile mi vek_____as), sed mia patrino enĉambr_____is por vek_____i min, do mi finfine alvenis ĝustahore.

c Mi perd_____is mian hundon. Ĝi perd_____is, dum ni promenad_____is en la arbaro. Mi provis trov_____i ĝin sed ne sukcesis. Mi havas nenian ideon, kie ĝi nun trov_____as.

d Mia fratino ne povas ven_____ i por manĝ_____i kun ni ĉi-vespere, ĉar ŝi baldaŭ nask_____os infanon. Evidente ŝi preferas, ke la infano nask_____u en hospitalo kaj ne en restoracio.

e Mi enamiĝis al ŝi, kiam mi la unuan fojon ekvid_____is ŝin. Mi tute ne povas kred_____i, ke tia belulino konsent_____is edzin_____i al mi!

f Ni ne scias ĝuste kiel la mondo komenc_____is aŭ kiel ĝi fin_____os. Sed evident_____is, ke la arbaregoj malaperad_____as tro rapide, ĉar la homaro detru_____as ilin. Ni esperu, ke la tuta mondo ankaŭ ne detru_____u!

Vocabulary builder 2

 16.05 Look at the words and complete the missing English words. Then listen and try to imitate the pronunciation of the speakers.

MUZIKSTILOJ *MUSIC STYLES*

ĝenro	*genre*
bluso	*blues*
elektronika muziko	*electronic music*
hiphopo	_____
ĵazo	*jazz*
novepoka muziko	*new-age music*
pop-muziko	*pop music*
rok-muziko	_____
punko	_____
regeo	*reggae*
repo	*rap*
sambo	*samba*
klasika muziko	_____

 # Conversation 2

 16.06 Look at and listen to the words and expressions that are used in the following conversation. Note their meanings.

vi kritikis la unuan kantistinon	*you criticized the first singer*
Ĉu la penso timigas vin?	*Does the thought scare you?*
vi forkurigus la tutan ĉambron	*you'd make the whole room run away*
kiajn mensogojn vi elbuŝigas	*what lies you're coming out with*
vi sukcese kantigis min	*you've managed to make me sing / you've got me singing*
ĝojigas min, ke mi kuraĝigis vin	*it makes me happy that I encouraged you*
li anoncas, ke …	*he announces that …*
li devigis min kanti!	*he's made me have to sing!*
li ruĝigis vin kaj ridigis ĉiun alian	*he has made you blush and everybody else laugh*
li malebligis al mi eviti	*he has made it impossible for me to avoid*
Fakte vi plibonigis la kvaliton.	*You improved the quality, actually.*
mirigis min, kiel bele vi kantas	*it has amazed me how beautifully you sing*
kanto via povus esti en la furorlisto	*a song of yours could be in the charts*
Kial vi antaŭe ne sciigis nin?	*Why didn't you make us aware before?*

16.07 *The presenters in the programme ask audience members whether they want to perform.*

1 Why didn't Lena tell the others that she was a really good singer?

Sara	Nu, vi kritikis la unuan kantistinon, Roberto. Kial vi ne kantos? Ĉu la penso timigas vin?
Roberto	Ne, mi ne timas, tute ne. Estas nur tio, ke mi ne volas. Se mi volus, mi farus.
Lena	Mi ne kredas vin, Roberto! Se vi kantus, vi forkurigus la tutan ĉambron, ĉu ne?
Roberto	Ho, kiajn mensogojn vi elbuŝigas, Lena! Bone, vi sukcese kantigis min. Mi iros tien nun. Vi aŭdos; mi povus esti rok-kantisto.
Lena	Ĝojigas min, ke mi kuraĝigis vin, Roberto.
But instead of singing, Roberto announces that Lena is coming up to sing!	
Lena	Ho mia dio, kion mi povas fari? Nun li devigis min kanti!
Sara	Li ankaŭ ruĝigis vin kaj ridigis ĉiun alian! Do, kion vi atendas?
Lena	Nu, li malebligis al mi eviti, do mi iros. Sed poste mi mortigos lin!
Lena returns after singing.	
Roberto	Gratulon, Lena! Vi surprize bele kantas. Fakte vi plibonigis la kvaliton. Mirigis min, kiel bele vi kantas.
Sara	Li pravas, Lena. Kanto via povus esti en la furorlisto. Kial vi antaŭe ne sciigis nin, ke vi tiel bone kantas?
Lena	Ĉar mi mem ne sciis; neniu antaŭe en mia tuta vivo sukcese kantigis min!

2 Match the English and the Esperanto.

a You improved the quality	**1** Mirigis min, kiel bele vi kantas
b Why didn't you let us know?	**2** Li ankaŭ ruĝigis vin
c Does it frighten you?	**3** Kiajn mensogojn vi elbuŝigas!
d After singing	**4** Vi plibonigis la kvaliton
e He's made it impossible for me to avoid	**5** Vi sukcese kantigis min
f What lies you're coming out with!	**6** Li devigis min kanti
g You've managed to make me sing	**7** Kial vi ne sciigis nin?
h It amazed me how well you sing	**8** Mi kuraĝigis vin
i He has made me have to sing	**9** Postkante
j You'll make the whole room run away	**10** Li malebligis al mi eviti
k He also made you blush	**11** Ĉu ĝi timigas vin?
l I encouraged you	**12** Vi forkurigus la tutan ĉambron

> **CULTURE TIP**
>
> The **Internacia Vespero** is something of an international talent show held at several Esperanto events, where people sing songs and read poetry from their native countries. It has expanded to include other forms of art, culture and entertainment, including comedy and even belly dancing.

Language discovery 2

1. How does Sara change the conventional word order to come up with something meaning *a song of yours* rather than *your song*?

2. How did Sara and Lena create words to mean *to make somebody blush* and *to encourage* from the adjectives **ruĝa** and **kuraĝa**?

3. There are several examples of pairs of verbs in the conversation. They feature in their normal forms and also with the suffix **-ig-**. Can you work out from the context what the difference between the pairs is?

4. How does Roberto create an expression as an equivalent to *to come out with* as a slang way of saying *to say*? How does Lena create *to make run away* in one word?

1 CAUSING THINGS TO HAPPEN USING -IG-

The suffix **-ig-** has an effect of causing something to happen, of making somebody do or be something.

La komplimento ruĝigis min.	*The compliment made me blush (made me red).*
Ŝi plibonigis sian scion pri Esperanto.	*She improved her knowledge about Esperanto (made better).*

You can insert it into adjectives to indicate this causative effect:

pensiga artikolo	*a thought-provoking article*
kuraĝigaj vortoj	*encouraging words*

You can also use it with verbs to show that you made somebody else do it, which changes the meaning slightly:

La knabo daŭre timas min, ĉar mi iam timigis lin.	*The boy is still scared of me because I frightened him once.*

(**timi** *to be afraid, to fear*, **timigi** *to scare, to frighten*)

Kiam mi scios, mi sciigos vin.	*When I know I'll let you know.*

(**scii** *to know*, **sciigi** *to make known, to inform*)

As you might expect, you can also combine other types of words with it to create new ones:

Mi elbuŝigis (el + buŝo) la veron.	*I made the truth come out (of x's mouth).*

And **igi** can be used as a verb in its own right:

Mi igis lin kompreni la teorion.	*I made him understand the theory.*

> **LANGUAGE TIP**
>
> Switching to **igi** + **-i** is a handy way of working around the problem caused by having more than one object. You wouldn't be able to say '**Mi komprenigis lin la teorion**' because a single verb cannot take two objects (**lin** and **la teorion**) like that. **Mi igis lin kompreni la teorion** provides a verb for each object.

2 CHANGING VERB TYPES WITH -IG-

As there are verbs which must have an object, whether it's implied or stated, there are also verbs which cannot take one. Think of **mi iras** *I go* or **ŝi mortis** *she died*. You can't ask *What did he go?* or *What did he die?* English and Esperanto are the same in not allowing objects for these verbs.

It's possible in Esperanto to change this verb type, though, so that these objectless verbs can take them. It's one of the uses of **-ig-**.

Kial li ridis? Ĉar mi ridigis lin.	*Why did he laugh? Because I made him laugh / caused him to laugh.*
Mi silentigis la infanojn per glaciaĵo.	*I made the children be quiet with ice cream.*

Practice 2

1 Match the words in the box with their translations.

> devigi   bruligi   klarigi   ruĝigi   paroligi   nuligi
> mortigi   plibonigi   neniigi   konstruigi   timigi   ĉesigi

a   to cause to blush
b   to explain, clarify
c   to cause to speak, talk
d   to kill
e   to get something built
f   to make someone have to (do something)
g   to improve, cause something to be better
h   to frighten, scare
i   to cancel (= to nullify)
j   to burn (something *not* to be burning)
k   to stop, to bring to a stop
l   to annihilate

2 Select the word that matches the definition.

Example: to get something built:	konstrui	konstruiĝi	<u>konstruigi</u>
a to feed:	manĝi	manĝiĝi	manĝigi
b to make somebody come:	veni	venigi	veniĝi
c to upset somebody:	malfeliĉi	malfeliĉa	malfeliĉigi
d to become upset:	malfeliĉa	malfeliĉiĝi	malfeliĉigi
e to be found, located:	troviĝi	trovi	trovigi
f to get someone out of bed:	ellitigi	ellitiĝi	enlitigi
g to get married (male):	edzi	edziĝi	edzigi
h an explanation:	klara	klarigo	klaro

i	pleasing:	kontenta	kontenti	kontentiga
j	mandatory:	deviga	devo	deviĝo
k	to name:	nomi	nomiĝi	nomigi
l	to remind:	memori	memoriĝi	memorigi

Reading

Read the excerpt from the website of Somera Esperanto-Studado and answer the questions.

1 In what part of the day can people watch films?

2 In what part of the day will people be learning about Esperanto?

3 When will there be excursions and sport?

Writing

Imagine that you have just attended an evening of concerts at an Esperanto event. Some performances you enjoyed, others less so. You know that your friends are interested in what you're doing while you're away, so write a short status update for your social media account, around 300 words.

Listening

16.08 Listen to the announcement and answer the questions.

1 What are the three concerts tonight?

2 What kind of music are they?

3 Where can people go after the concert?

Speaking

Record yourself speaking about music. What types do you like listening to? Who is your favourite band and how long have you liked them? Which songs do you particularly like?

Test yourself

1 Change these adjectives into verbs, indicating that somebody is becoming one of these adjectives.
   a ruĝa
   b maljuna
   c maltrankvila
   d feliĉa

2 Change the meaning of these verbs from *to x* to *to make somebody x*. Are there alternative English verbs for the ones you've created?
   a paroli
   b veni
   c devi
   d manĝi

3 Which of these verbs would need to have **-ig-** added in order to be followed by objects with the **n**-ending?
   a manĝi
   b dormi
   c morti
   d havi

SELF-CHECK

I CAN ...
… talk about music.
… indicate a change in state.
… persuade somebody to do something.
… change a verb type.

17 La malaperinto
The missing person

In this unit, you will learn how to:
▶ *describe what people were doing when something happened.*
▶ *express 'might-have-beens'.*
▶ *use active participles.*
▶ *create abstractions, such as friendship from friend.*

CEFR: (B1) *Can narrate a story.* **(B2)** *Can pass on detailed information reliably.* **(B2)** *Can write a review of a film, book or play.* **(B2)** *Can synthesize information and arguments from a number of sources (e.g. can watch a TV show and read an article about it and write a review).*

⭐ La utopia motivo malantaŭ Esperanto *The utopian motivation behind Esperanto*

Esperanto started with the work of one man. **Estas malfacile bildigi al si** (*it's difficult to get a picture*) of how much dedication must have been required to initiate a project like this. **Sennombraj** (*countless*) hours were spent crafting away, revising, translating and starting again. And remember that there was nobody else to speak with.

Ludoviko Zamenhof explained that his motivation lay in his upbringing, particularly that he was, in his words, a **hebreo el la ghetto** (**judo el la geto** in modern Esperanto, *a Jew from the ghetto*). In his **infanaĝo** (*childhood*) he had witnessed ethnic separation in his hometown, with people mixing only with their own ethnic groups. The most visible **identigilo** (*identifier*) or **disigilo** (*separator*) was the languages spoken by the people.

It was during his early years that the idea formed in his head that if people **kunhavis** (*shared*) a common language, then they would be able to speak to each other and not see each other as different. He soon realized that this shared language would have to be neutral, a language not belonging to one of the groups who would speak it. He initially toyed with the idea of bringing back a **mortinta** (*dead*) language but that proved to be unfeasible so, while he was still at school, he began to create a language.

Over 30 years after he started out on the project, he stood on stage in front of the 688 people **partoprenantaj** (*participating in*) the first **Universala Kongreso**. Using the language that he'd begun work on as a child, he **klarigis** (*made clear, explained*) the **pensmaniero** (*way of thinking*) which had pushed him through those **lacigaj** (*tiring*) decades: **hodiaŭ inter la gastamaj muroj de Bulonjo-sur-Maro kunvenis ne francoj kun angloj, ne rusoj kun poloj, sed homoj kun homoj** (*today between the welcoming walls of Boulogne-sur-Mer are gathered not Frenchmen with Englishmen, not Russians with Poles, but people with people*).

 What word did Ludoviko Zamenhof use to mean *a Jew*? What word is used in modern Esperanto?

Vocabulary builder 1

17.01 Look at the words and phrases and complete the missing English words and expressions. Then listen and try to imitate the pronunciation of the speakers.

FILMOJ *FILMS*

filmo	_____
aktoro, aktorino	_____
ĉefrolanto	*lead actor*
stelulo, stelulino	*a star*
reĝisoro	*a director*
produktisto	*a producer*
kreinto	*a creator*
ekrano	*a screen*
fono	*background*
malfono	_____
enhavo	*content*

Conversation 1

NEW EXPRESSIONS

17.02 Look at and listen to the words and expressions that are used in the following conversation. Note their meanings.

mi klarigos la kialon, ke ĉi tiu ŝerco ne funkciis	*I will explain the reason this joke didn't work*
Ne spektinte la filmojn kaj sciante nenion pri la fono	*Not having watched the films and knowing nothing about the background*
estas facile imiti lin	*it's easy to imitate him*
oni havas liberecon ŝanĝi la vortordon	*you have the freedom to change the word order*
neniu estus povinta rekoni	*nobody could have recognized*
fermiĝas la koncertejo	*the concert hall is closing*
restas ŝia monujo kuŝanta sur la tablo	*her wallet remains lying on the table*
ŝi foriris por necesejumi	*she left in order to use the bathroom*
mia amikino estas malaperinta	*my friend has disappeared*
Forirante ŝi diris, ke …	*Upon leaving she said that …*
Se ni estus sidantaj aliloke, eble ni estus vidintaj ŝin	*If we were sitting someplace else, we might have seen her*
paroli pri la estonteco ne helpas	*talking about the future doesn't help*

17.03 *The* Internacia Vespero *has finished and the group is chatting, without Sara.*

1 One of the new people spotted Sara leave. How long ago was it?

Roberto:	Nu, mi klarigos la kialon, ke ĉi tiu ŝerco ne funkcis. Ne spektinte la filmojn kaj sciante nenion pri la fono, vi ne povus rekoni tiun etan verdulon. Li havas tre malkutiman manieron paroli en la angla, do estas facile imiti lin. Ekaŭdante unu frazon, oni tuj rekonas lin. Sed en Esperanto ne estas strange paroli tiel, ĉar oni havas liberecon ŝanĝi la vortordon. 'Paroli tiel oni povas.' Do, la ŝerco ne funkcis, ĉar neniu estus povinta rekoni, pri kiu temas; nek la jamaj spektintoj, nek la steluloj, nek eĉ la reĝisoro kaj film-kreinto!
…	
Roberto	Momenton, Lena. Nun fermiĝas la koncertejo, ĉiuj enlitiĝas, kaj daŭre ne revenis Sara. Ŝi diris, ke ŝi revenos, ĉu ne? Kaj restas ŝia monujo kuŝanta sur la tablo, do ŝajnas, ke ŝi ja intencis reveni.
Lena	Mi konsentas. Ni demandu al homoj, ĉu ili vidis ŝin. Mi iros al ĉi tiuj novuloj; vi demandu la komencintojn tie …
Lena	Pardonu, ĉu vi vidis nian amikinon, Saran? Ŝi estis sidanta apud ni kaj foriris por necesejumi.
Novulo	Mi vidis ŝin foriranta antaŭ eble duonhoro. Mi restos ĉi tie dum la venonta horo, do se ŝi revenos, mi diros al ŝi, ke vi estis serĉanta ŝin.
Roberto	Mia amikino estas malaperinta. Ŝi nomiĝas Sara, el Britio. Forirante ŝi diris, ke ŝi baldaŭ revenos. Sed nun oni fermas ĉion. Ĉu vi vidis ŝin?
Komencinto	Mi bedaŭras, sed ni rimarkis nenion. Mi ne povis vidi vian tablon. Se ni estus sidantaj aliloke, eble ni estus vidintaj ŝin.
Lena	Kion diris la komencintaro, Roberto? Ion utilan?
Roberto	Tute ne. Demandinte ilin, mi daŭre scias nenion. Ili ne estas helpaj, dirante, ke eblis vidi nenion. Kion pri la novularo?
Lena	Fakte, ili vidis Saran foriranta kaj diris, ke ili restos dum iom pli da tempo. Se Sara revenos post nia foriro, ili diros al ŝi, ke ni estis serĉantaj ŝin. Sed paroli pri la estonteco ne helpas; ni devas serĉi la malaperinton.

2 Match the English and the Esperanto.

a	To go to the toilet	**1**	Neniam spektinte la filmon
b	Upon hearing one sentence	**2**	Ili vidis ŝin foriranta / foriri
c	My friend is missing	**3**	Ŝi ne estas reaperinta
d	Nobody could've recognized who it was about	**4**	Necesejumi
e	We would've seen her	**5**	Demandinte ilin mi daŭre scias nenion
f	She hasn't returned	**6**	Mia amikino estas malaperinta
g	If we were sitting somewhere else	**7**	Neniu povus rekoni pri kiu temas
h	They saw her leaving	**8**	Ekaŭdante unu frazon
i	Never having watched the film	**9**	Ni estus vidintaj ŝin
j	Having asked them, I still don't know anything	**10**	Se ni estus sidantaj aliloke

3 **Decide whether these statements are true vera (V) or false malvera (M). If false, rewrite it so that it's true.**

   a La ŝerco estis sukcesa, ĉar estis facile rekoni, pri kiu temas.
   b La koncertejo komencis fermiĝi antaŭ ol Sara revenis.
   c Roberto kaj Lena kredis, ke Sara intencas reveni.
   d Roberto opinias, ke paroli kun la komencintoj estis utile.
   e Novulo diris, ke se Sara revenos poste, li nenion diros al ŝi.
   f La komencinto diris, ke se ili sidus en alia loko, ili vidus Saran, sed ne eblis en la loko, kie ili fakte sidis.

4 **17.04 Now listen to the conversation again line by line and repeat.**

Language discovery 1

1 **What do you think Lena might mean when she speaks of komencintoj?**
2 **How would you translate the words ending in -ante in forirante ŝi diris and dirante, ke eblis vidi nenion?**
3 **From the context, what do you think ŝi estis sidanta means? How would you normally express this more simply?**

1 THE PRESENT ACTIVE PARTICIPLE

The present active participle **-ant-** demonstrates that an action is currently ongoing:

parolanta birdo (= **birdo, kiu parolas**)   *a talking bird*

spektantaj homoj (= **homoj, kiuj spektas**)   *people watching, spectating*

You can combine it with different tenses of **esti** to give information about when the action was ongoing:

La viro estas / estis / estos fermanta la pordon.   *The man is / was / will be closing the door.*

It's rare that you'll need to use these compound tenses because the standard **as**-ending already indicates an ongoing or habitual activity.

By changing the last letter you can give the participle various roles. When it takes the **a**-ending it's an adjective, but you can switch it to the **e**-ending to create an adverb:

Gustumante la ĉokoladon, mi tuj komprenis, kial vi rekomendas ĝin tiom multe.   *Tasting the chocolate, I immediately understood why you recommend it so much.*

If you apply the **o**-ending you create the person who is engaged in the activity:

Mi komencas lerni Esperanton; mi estas komencanto.   *I'm starting to learn Esperanto; I'm a beginner.*

This example shows how the word *beginner* is created. It's built on **komenci** – **komencanta** – **komencanto**.

2 OTHER ACTIVE PARTICIPLES

Just as verbs come in past, present and future forms, so do Esperanto's participles.

The participle **-int-** indicates that the action was already over:

falinta muro (= **muro, kiu falis**)	*a wall which has fallen down*
Ricevinte malbonan novaĵon, mi estis	*Having received bad news, I was anxious all day.*
maltrankvila dum la tuta tago.	

-int- can be combined with the different versions of **esti** to give some real detail about when
something had or will have happened:

Mi estis / estas / estos leginta la libron.   *I had / have / will have read the book.*

As with **-ant**, you can create a person by adding an **o**-ending: **parolinto** *a person who has
spoken*.

You use **-ont-** when the action will happen but hasn't started yet. Imagine that your roof is
giving way and at some point the water is going to leak in. Because the roof is just about
holding it's not yet **falanta akvo**; it's **falonta akvo** *water that will be falling*:

La akvo ankoraŭ ne estas falanta; ĝi   *The water isn't yet falling; it will be falling tomorrow.*
estos falanta morgaŭ.

or

La akvo estas falonta; morgaŭ ĝi estos   *The water is about to fall; tomorrow it will be*
falanta kaj postmorgaŭ ĝi estos falinta.   *falling and after tomorrow will have fallen.*

As with the other participles, you can add the **o**-ending to create a person. Think of the
gladiators addressing Caesar in English: *We who are about to die salute you*. In Esperanto, as in
the original Latin, a single word can be used to express the concept: **Ni mortontoj salutas vin**.

Practice 1

1 Insert -int-, -ant- or -ont- to give the correct meaning.

a Fal_____a arbo blokas la vojon. (*A tree which has fallen is blocking the way.*)

b La pas_____an semajnon mi vojaĝis al kaj Londono, kaj Parizo, kaj Romo! (*Last week I travelled to London. Paris and Rome!*)

c La rapide kur_____a hundo atingis la pordon. (*The dog, running quickly, reached the door.*)

d Li aŭskultis la radion, trink_____e teon. (*He listened to the radio while drinking tea.*)

e Vid_____e lin promeni kun alia virino, ŝi malfeliĉiĝis. (*Having seen him walking with another woman, she became unhappy.*)

f Mi telefonis vin, aĉet_____e bileton. (*I phoned you when I was about to buy a ticket.*)

2 Match the English and the Esperanto.

a I was watching a film (when …)	**1**	Mi estis spektonta filmon
b I had watched a film (when …)	**2**	Mi estis spektanta filmon
c I was about to watch a film (when …)	**3**	Mi estis spektinta filmon
d I was about to play tennis (but then it started to rain)	**4**	Mi estis ludinta tenison
e I was playing tennis (when I heard the bang)	**5**	Mi estis ludonta tenison
f I had played tennis (already in the morning, that's why I didn't go in the afternoon)	**6**	Mi estis ludanta tenison
g I've been eating (chocolate all day and now I feel sick)	**7**	Mi estis manĝonta
h I was about to eat (some more chocolate and then remembered that I'd already eaten too much)	**8**	Mi estis manĝanta
i I'd been eating too much (chocolate, and that's why I was sick)	**9**	Mi estas manĝanta
j I was about to tell her the truth (but then the telephone rang)	**10**	Mi estas dirinta
k I will have told her the truth tomorrow	**11**	Mi estis dironta
l I've told (her the truth and now she won't talk to me)	**12**	Mi estos dirinta

> **LANGUAGE TIP**
>
> People often use **-unt-** in a similar way, such as **prezidunto** *a would-be president* (maybe he would've won but withdrew).

Vocabulary builder 2

17.05 Look at the words and complete the missing English words. Then listen and try to imitate the pronunciation of the speakers.

FILMGENROJ *FILM GENRES*

sciencfikcio	*science fiction*
fantasto	*fantasy*
hororo	_____
dramo	*drama*
komedio	_____
tragedio	_____
krimo	*crime, thriller*
vakero, vakera filmo	*cowboy, a western*
romantika filmo	*romantic film*
porinfana filmo	*children's film*
dokumentfilmo	*documentary*
vivrakonto	*biography, biopic*

Conversation 2

NEW EXPRESSIONS

17.06 Look at and listen to the words and expressions that are used in the following conversation. Note their meanings.

Kurante nun, ni alvenos antaŭ ol ŝi foriros.	*By running now, we'll arrive before she leaves.*
ni diskuris por serĉi vin	*we ran off in all directions to look for you*
ni devis dissendi ĉien la mesaĝon	*we had to send the message out everywhere*
en la pasinteco mi estis tre forgesema	*in the past, I was very forgetful*
Ĉu vi ne devas forpreni ion?	*Don't you have to take something away?*
estus utile aĉeti grandan ujon	*it would be useful to buy a big container*

17.07 *Lena has some good news: Sara has been spotted nearby.*

1 What does Roberto say Sara should buy to stop her losing her purse?

Lena	Novulo raportas esti vidanta Saran en la gufujo antaŭ ne longe. Kurante nun, ni alvenos antaŭ ol ŝi foriros.
...	
Roberto	Ho, jen la malaperinto! Kio okazis, Sara? Dum dudek minutoj ni diskuris por serĉi vin. Ni devis dissendi ĉien la mesaĝon, ke ni estas serĉantaj vin.
Sara	Ĉu? Kial? Mi nur sidis ĉi tie kun Natalja kaj Jevgenij, trinkante teon. Mi ne estis malaperinta.
Roberto	Nu, ni ne estus serĉintaj vin, se vi ne dirus al ni, ke vi revenos poste.
Lena	Kaj se vi ne estus forgesinta vian monujon. Jen ĝi.
Sara	Ho, mi eĉ ne sciis! En la pasinteco mi estis tre forgesema, sed mi opiniis min esti pliboniĝinta. Ŝajne ne!
Natalja	Nu, ne plu restas teo. Dankon pro via amikeco, sed alvenas la horo por enlitiĝi. Bonan nokton al vi, la tetrinkintoj kaj Sara-serĉintoj!
Lena	Atendu, Sara. Ĉu vi ne devas forpreni ion? La denove malaperintan monujon?
Sara	Ho, kio okazis al ĝi? Ĉie estas tasoj, kandeloj, kaj libroj, sed ne mia monujo. Kien ĝi malaperis?
Lena	Ĝi ne estas malaperinta; ĝi estas kuŝanta malantaŭ la kafujo. Tien vi metis ĝin. Jen - apud la kandelingo.
Roberto	Ha! Vi estis forironta sen ĝi denove! Eble estus utile aĉeti grandan ujon, en kiun vi povus meti ĝin. Oni povus nomi ĝin monujujo!

2 Match the English and the Esperanto.

a	Where has it disappeared to?	**1**	Estontece
b	Running now	**2**	Mi opiniis min esti pliboniĝinta
c	In the future	**3**	Jen la malaperinto
d	In which I could put it	**4**	Kurante nun
e	I thought I'd improved	**5**	Ni devis dissendi ĉien la mesaĝon
f	People who drank tea and looked for Sara	**6**	Se vi ne estus forgesinta
g	There's the missing person	**7**	Te-trinkintoj kaj Sara-serĉintoj
h	We had to spread the message everywhere	**8**	Kien ĝi malaperis?
i	If you hadn't forgotten	**9**	En kiun mi povus meti ĝin

Language discovery 2

1 Given that in the first conversation **estonteco** was used to mean *the future*, can you think of an alternative word to **pasinteco** for *the past*?

2 If **amikeco** is *friendship* and **libereco** is *freedom*, what do **stulteco** (from **stulta** *stupid*) and **justeco** (from **justa** *fair*) mean?

AFFIXES

The prefix **dis-** gives the idea of separation or spreading out:

Diskuru kaj trovu ŝin!	*Run off in different directions and find her!*
Ni sukcese disigis la batalantojn.	*We successfully separated the fighters.*

-uj- can be used to indicate a container for a certain thing:

monujo	*a purse*	**kafujo**	*a cafetière*

When **-uj-** is applied to names of countries, it means where people of certain nationalities are found. Since English people are not found uniquely in England (or solely English people there), for example, the use of **-uj-** for country names was already challenged in Esperanto's early years. **Britio, Francio, Italio**, etc. became much more popular than **Brituujo, Francujo** and **Italujo**.

-uj- is also used in older texts to name the tree that a fruit comes from:

pomujo	*apple tree*	**ĉerizujo**	*cherry tree*

This usage of **-uj-** has largely fallen out of use, since it's much more straightforward simply to add the word **arbo** *tree*: **pomarbo, ĉerizarbo**, etc.

A similar concept to **-uj-** is the suffix **-ing-**. The difference is that an **ingo** holds only one of something, which is typically only partially covered; an **ujo** can be *a box, a container, a storage room*, etc:

glavo	*a sword*	**glavujo**	*a container for swords*	**glavingo**	*a sheath*
kandelo	*a candle*	**kandelujo**	*a container for candles*	**kandelingo**	*a candlestick*

The suffix **-ec-** allows you to form an abstraction or a noun expressing a quality:

amiko	*a friend*	**amikeco**	*friendship*
frato	*brother*	**frateco**	*brotherhood*
unu	*one*	**unueco**	*oneness, unity*
infano	*child*	**infaneco**	*childhood, childishness*

Words for past and future can be built with active participles and **-ec-**:

la pasinteco, estinteco   *the past*   **la estonteco**   *the future*

If you're using an **a-** or **e**-ending, you don't need to include **-ec-**:

Pasintaj problemoj solviĝis kaj estonte ni estos amikoj.   *Past problems got solved and we're going to be friends in future.*

Practice 2

1   **Insert dis-, -uj-, -ing- or -ec- into the Esperanto words on the left to create the given English words.**

   a amiko (*friendship*)
   b rompi (*to smash, to break apart*)
   c floro (*a vase*)
   d infano (*childhood, childishness*)
   e kandelo (*candlestick*)
   f blovi (*to blow everywhere*)
   g lavi (*a sink, a basin*)
   h glavo (*a sheath for a sword*)
   i viro (*manliness, virility*)
   j akvo (*a cistern*)
   k sendi (*to distribute*)
   l salo (*a salt cellar*)
   m ofta (*frequency, regularity*)
   n glavo (*a container for sheaths*)

Reading

Read the following short film reviews and answer the questions.

  www.filmoj.com

a Atendinte la novan en la serio dum tiom da jaroj, mi kun ĝojo decidis spekti la filmon la unuan tagon, anstataŭ iri al la laborejo. La atendita filmo tamen ne estis tiel bona, kiel mi esperis. La ĉefrolanto tute ne konas la rakonton, kaj tio tuj vidiĝis, kiam li aperis unue sur la ekrano. Sciencfikcio estas facila ĝenro, sed ĉi tiu filmo estis por mi hororo.

b 100 jaroj post la pasintaĵoj, la nuna estas ja la ĝusta jaro por fari dokumentfilmon pri la okazintaĵoj. Nek la reĝisoro, nek la kreinto malsukcesis, malgraŭ tio, ke ili estis timintaj, ke ĝi ne finfine aperos. Kaj mi ĝojas povi raporti, ke ĝi tute taŭgas por infanoj!

1 What kind of film was the first one? Was the viewer impressed?

2 What kind of film was the second? Did the viewer think it was appropriate for children?

Writing

Write two short film reviews for your blog, between 50 and 100 words each.

What kind of films were they? Did you enjoy them? Did anything notable happen?

Listening

 17.08 Listen to the recording and answer the questions.

1 Did the first speaker enjoy the film?

2 What did the first person think is the reason that the second didn't understand it?

3 What does the first person propose that they do in the evening?

Speaking

Take the text from your writing exercise and record yourself saying it. Pay attention to your accent and try to speak fluently, without unnatural pauses.

Test yourself

1 You were watching a film when something suddenly happened. Rewrite **mi spektis filmon, kiam ...** using an active participle so that you get across the idea of an ongoing activity taking place when another one suddenly happened:

Mi _____ _____ filmon, kiam ...

2 You **komencis lerni Esperanton** *started learning Esperanto* 17 units ago, so you could call yourself a **komencinto** rather than **komencanto** now. Imagine that you've just ordered a copy of *Complete Esperanto* for your friend. It hasn't arrived yet but when it does, **li/ŝi komencos lerni Esperanton** *he/she will start to learn Esperanto*. Insert one letter into the following sentence so that it means *my friend is about to be a beginner*:

Mia amiko estas komenc_____nto.

3 Insert an appropriate active participle into the gaps so that the sentence means *having read and enjoyed the book so much, I decided to watch the film*:

Leg_____e kaj ĝu_____e tiom multe la libron, mi decidis spekti la filmon.

18 Vidindaĵumado
Sightseeing

In this unit, you will learn how to:

▶ *use passive constructions.*
▶ *talk about the distant past.*
▶ *express measurements.*

CEFR: (B1) *Can understand main point of many radio or TV programmes on current affairs or topics of personal or professional interest when the delivery is relatively slow and clear and in a standard dialect (could give personal opinion on programme).* **(B2)** *Can scan quickly through long and complex texts, locating relevant details (scan a long travel itinerary or hotel registration info sheet for information).* **(B2)** *Can understand in detail a wide range of lengthy, complex texts likely to be encountered in social, professional or academic life, identifying finer points of detail including attitudes and implied as well as stated opinions (i.e. understand a 300–500-word article about family life).*

★ Esperanto: estinteco kaj estonteco *Esperanto: past and future*

Esperanto was **pli-malpli** (*more or less*) limited to the Russian Empire in its first few years. Although copies of the **Unua Libro** were written in Polish, German and French (all in 1887) and English (**origine** (*originally*)) in 1888, **reverkita** (*reworked*) in 1889), the language hadn't really taken off elsewhere. When Zamenhof published the names in 1889 of the first 1000 people who had pledged to learn the language, 919 of them came from the Russian Empire, his **patrujo** (*homeland*).

Esperanto **fariĝis pli internacia** (*became more international*) when the first magazine, **La Esperantisto, eldoniĝis** (*was published*) in Germany from 1889 to 1895, followed by the second, **Lingvo Internacia**, from Sweden in 1895. But it was in France in the late 1890s that there was really impetus.

The question of what should be the **mondlingvo** (*world language*) was a legitimate one of the time; this was the age of steamships and wireless telegraphy, and Paris **gastigis** (*hosted*) the World Fair in 1900. Ludoviko Zamenhof even received the medal of the French **Honora Legio** (*Légion d'honneur*) in 1905 and was made **Komandanto de la Ordeno de Izabela la Katolikino** (*Commander of the Order of Isabella the Catholic*) in 1909 by King Alfonso XIII of Spain. It seemed that the **Fina Venko** (*final victory*), the universal adoption of Esperanto as an international language, was only a matter of time.

The First World War, during which Zamenhof died, was the first **bremso** (*brake*). The **nove fondita** (*newly founded*) League of Nations discussed several times whether to introduce Esperanto into schools but the pre-war French endorsement was no more and the country's representative was instructed to **dronigi** (*drown*) Esperanto. **Baldaŭ poste** (*soon afterwards*), Hitler and Stalin persecuted Esperantists, before the world was again plunged into total war.

Esperanto has a history, but it isn't history. **Male** (*on the contrary*), it's flourishing more than it ever did in the past. The internet makes Esperanto accessible in a way that was beyond the wildest dreams of the pioneers. The language is now used every day for the purpose for which it was designed: as a bridge between people from different language backgrounds. Esperanto will continue to **kreski** (*grow*) and have a **brila estonteco** (*bright future*).

What verbs mean *to drown (something)* and *to grow* in the text? How would you say something *drowned* and *to grow (something)*?

Vocabulary builder 1

18.01 **Look at the words and phrases and complete the missing English words and expressions. Then listen and try to imitate the pronunciation of the speakers.**

VIDINDAĴUMADO *SIGHTSEEING*

vidindaĵo	*sight*
konstruaĵo	*building, construction*
palaco	_____
kastelo	*castle*
katedralo	*cathedral*
klasika	_____
monumento	_____
pordego	*gate*
turo	*tower*
ĉefplaco	*main square*
statuo	_____
galerio	*gallery*
foiro	*market, fair*
rivero	_____
ponto	*bridge*
ĉiĉeronado	*guided tour*
promenado laŭ la rivero	*walk along the river*

Conversation 1

NEW EXPRESSIONS

 18.02 Look at and listen to the words and expressions that are used in the following conversation. Note their meanings.

la prezidanta palaco estis konstruita en 1760	*the presidential palace was built in 1760*
dum pluraj jarcentoj / en la deknaŭa jarcento	*for several centuries / in the 19th century*
ĝi estis detruita de fajro en 1811	*it was destroyed by a fire in 1811*
ĉio estis bruligita	*everything was burned*
ĝi estos renovigita	*it will be renovated*
dum proksimume 20 jaroj	*for approximately 20 years*
konstruita por honori sovetajn soldatojn	*built to honour Soviet soldiers*
statuo de drako estis metita sur la supron	*a statue of a dragon was put on its top*
Nifo estas Neldentigita Fluganta Objekto (fluganta subtaso)	*a UFO is an Unidentified Flying Object (flying saucer)*
Sendube!	*Without a doubt! Definitely!*

18.03 *Sara and Roberto are being shown around Bratislava by Miro, the man who met them at the airport.*

1 Why did the UFO Bridge get its name?

Miro	Ĉi tiu blanka konstruaĵo estas la prezidanta palaco, kiu estis konstruita en 1760. Ne eblas viziti ĝin hodiaŭ, ĉar ĝi estas fermita. Ĝi estos malfermita morgaŭ, se vi deziros viziti ĝin. Baldaŭ eblos vidi … jes … la kastelon. Jen ĝi!
Roberto	Bele! Kiam ĝi estis konstruita?
Miro	Dum pluraj jarcentoj. Fakte ĝi estis rekonstruita en la 19-a jarcento, ĉar ĝi estis detruita de fajro en 1811. Ĉio estis bruligita. Estis decidite en la 1930-aj jaroj, ke ĝi estos renovigata post kelkaj jaroj. Ĝi finfine restis renovigota dum proksimume 20 jaroj, ĝis la laboro estis komencita en 1956. Ĉu vi vidas tiun grandan monumenton apud ĝi? Ĝi estas la Monumento Slavín, konstruita por honori sovetajn soldatojn, kiuj estis mortigitaj en 1945. Ĝi altas 37 metrojn.
Sara	Kion ni vidos poste, Miro?
Miro	Ni trairos la Pordegon de Mikaelo, kiu estis unue starigita en proksimume la jaro 1300 kaj rekonstruigita kvincent jarojn poste, kiam statuo de drako estis metita sur la supron. Tiel ni baldaŭ vidos la malnovan urbon, la naciajn muzeon kaj galerion, kaj atingos la riveron.
After a few minutes …	
Miro	Do jen la rivero Danubo. Ĉu vi vidas la pontojn? La unua, nomata nun la Malnova Ponto, estis konstruita en 1891. La plej konata, tamen, estas la tiel nomata Nifo-ponto. Mi ne certas, ĉu nifo estas konata esprimo en Esperanto. Ĉu vi scias ĝian signifon?

Roberto	Tute ne. Pri kio temas?
Miro	Nifo estas Neldentigita Fluganta Objekto. La ponto estas nomata tiel, ĉar ĝia kafejo pensigas onin pri kosmoŝipo. Ho, atentu la tramon! La unua estis konstruita en 1895. Domaĝe, ke oni ne povas vojaĝi per tramo al nia celita loko, la Blua Preĝejo. Eble kiam estos konstruita la nova metrostacio, ni ne devos iri piede. Ĝi estas konstruata nun kaj estos finita post eble tri jaroj.

After a pleasant walk along the river ...

Miro	Kaj jen la plej vizitata preĝejo en Bratislavo. Estas malpermesate eniri ĝin nun, sed ĝi povas esti admirata de la ekstero, ĉu ne? Ĝi estas nomata la Blua Preĝejo, kvankam la vera nomo estas la Preĝejo de Sankta Elizabeta. Iam estis decidite, ke estos konstruita belega konstruaĵo por honori ŝin. La celito kontentus, se ŝi scius, ĉu ne?
Roberto	Sendube! Kia belo urbo estas Bratislavo. Mi tute ne komprenas, kial ĝi ne estas pli bone konata.
Miro	Atentu, ke ankoraŭ ne estas finiĝinta la tago, kaj restas aliaj aferoj por vidi. Sed mi malsatas post tiom da gvidado. Indas viziti la katedralon; sed endas antaŭe tagmanĝi!

2 **Match the English and the Esperanto.**

a	Here's the most visited church	**1**	Ĝi estos malfermita morgaŭ
b	So-called	**2**	Ĝi estis rekonstruita
c	It will be open tomorrow	**3**	Iam estis decidite
d	It's being built now	**4**	Statuo de drako estis metita sur la supron
e	It was rebuilt	**5**	La celito estus kontenta, se ŝi scius
f	Everything was burned	**6**	Jen la plej vizitata preĝejo
g	It was decided at some point	**7**	Ĝi estis detruita de fajro
h	The person in mind would be pleased if she knew	**8**	Ĉio estis bruligita
i	When the new one is (will be) built	**9**	Ĝi estas konstruata nun
j	A statue of a dragon was put on the top	**10**	Tiel nomata
k	It was destroyed by fire	**11**	Estas malpermesate eniri
l	It's forbidden to go in	**12**	Kiam estos konstruita la nova

3 **Decide whether these statements are true or false and mark them vera (V) or malvera (M). If false, rewrite it, attempting the style used in the conversation.**

a Oni nomas la riveron en Bratislavo Danubo.

b Oni finis la rekonstruon de la prezidanta palaco en 1956.

c Oni konstruis la prezidantan palacon antaŭ du jarcentoj.

d Oni ne povas vojaĝi al la Blua Preĝejo per tramo.

e Ili vidas la Maljunan Ponton, kiun oni konstruis en 1981.

f Oni povas viziti la prezidantan palacon hodiaŭ.

g Oni starigis la Pordegon de Mikaelo en la 14a jarcento.

h Ili havis permeson eniri la Bluan Preĝejon.

4 18.04 **Now listen to the conversation line by line and repeat.**

Language discovery 1

1 The presidential palace is **fermita** today and will be **malfermita** tomorrow. What is the difference?

2 If the first bridge **estis konstruita** was built in 1891, what does **estos konstruita** mean?

3 The text says that the most visited church **estas nomata** *is named* the **Blua Preĝejo**. How could you rewrite that using **-iĝ-**? How about with **oni**?

1 THE PAST PASSIVE PARTICIPLE

The past passive participle **-it-** indicates that an action is completed:

legita libro (= **libro, kiun oni legis**) *a read book*

fermitaj pordoj (= **pordoj, kiujn oni fermis**) *closed doors*

Where active participles describe something carrying out the activity, passive participles are the result of something acting upon the thing described:

la caŝinta kato	*the cat that was hunting*	**la kato ĉasis**	*the cat hunted*
la ĉasita muso	*the hunted mouse*	**iu ĉasis la muson**	*somebody hunted the mouse*

You can combine the past passive participle with different tenses of **esti** to give information about when the action was completed:

La pordo estis / estas / estos fermita. *The door was / is being / will be closed.*

As with active participles, you can change the role of passive participles by amending the last letter. An **e**-ending creates an adverb:

Demandite tro rapide, ŝi ne kapablis *Asked too quickly, she wasn't able to think how*
pensi kiel respondi ĝuste en Esperanto. *to answer correctly in Esperanto.*

Adding an **o**-ending presents a person:

kaptito (= **iu kaptita**) *a prisoner* (somebody who has been captured)

atakito (= **iu atakita**) *an assaulted person* (somebody who was attacked)

2 MORE PASSIVE PARTICIPLES -AT- AND -OT-

The participle **-at-** is used to indicate that an action is currently being done or gets done regularly:

La viro estas mordata ĝuste nun! *The man is being bitten right now!*

Tiu muziko estas ludata ĉiam, kiam *This music is always played when the king or*
envenas la reĝo aŭ reĝino. *queen enters.*

The participle **-ot-** shows that an action isn't being done yet but will be:

Tiu viro estas mordota! *That man's about to get bitten!*

Atentu la rompotan fenestron! *Be careful of the window that's about to get broken!*

You can combine the passive participles with the different tenses of **esti** to give more detail about when something is being done or will be done:

La pordo estis / estas / estos fermata. *The door was / is being / will be closed.*

La bileto estis / estas / estos aĉetota. *The ticket was / is about to be / will be bought.*

You can add **e-** and **o**-endings to create adverbs and people:

Estas sciate, ke la plej inteligentaj homoj *It's known that the most intelligent people speak*
parolas Esperanton. *Esperanto.*

la kritikato	*the person being criticized*	**la demandato**	*the person being asked*
la venkoto	*the person about to be defeated*	**la vidoto**	*the person about to be seen*

> **LANGUAGE TIP**
>
> You can only use passive participles with a verb which can take an object because something is being done to it by something else, so you will never see **-iĝ-** used with one. You change a verb into one which can take an object using **-ig-** and then use that in the passive: **bruli** *to burn (be on fire)* > **bruligi** *to burn (cause to burn)* > **bruligita** *burnt*.

Practice 1

1 Insert -it-, -at- or -ot- to give the correct meaning.

a La send_____a letero finfine alvenis hodiaŭ. (*The letter which was sent finally arrived today.*)

b La laboro estas far_____a, sed mi ne scias, kiam mi havos tempon. (*The work is still to be done but I don't know when I'll have time.*)

c Mia am_____a kato ne povas eniri. (*My beloved cat can't come in.*)

d Estas sci_____e, ke la plej bonaj pastaĵoj estas trov_____aj en Italio. (*It's known that the best pasta is found in Italy.*)

e Estis decid_____e konstrui la ponton nur en 1980. (*It was decided to build the bridge only in 1980.*)

f Estas konfirm_____e, ĉu la Universala Kongreso okazos en Stokholmo aŭ en Novjorko. (*It's to be confirmed whether the UK will be held in Stockholm or New York.*)

2 Match the English and the Esperanto.

a	He was about to be attacked.	**1**	Li estas atakota.
b	He's about to be attacked.	**2**	Li estis atakita.
c	He was attacked.	**3**	Li estis atakota.
d	The mystery will be solved.	**4**	La mistero estis solvita.
e	The mystery was being solved.	**5**	La mistero estos solvita.
f	The mystery had been solved.	**6**	La mistero estis solvata.
g	The victim was killed.	**7**	La viktimo estos mortigita.
h	The victim will have been killed.	**8**	La viktimo estis mortigota.
i	The victim was about to be killed.	**9**	La viktimo estis mortigita.
j	The coffee will be being drunk.	**10**	La kafo estas trinkata.
k	The coffee will have been drunk.	**11**	La kafo estos trinkita.
l	The coffee is being drunk.	**12**	La kafo estos trinkata.

3 Here is an excerpt from a tourism brochure. Add the missing passive participles to the gaps, using the words in parentheses to guide you.

_____ (viziti) de milionoj da turistoj ĉiun jaron kaj trifoje _____ (elekti) la plej bela loko en la tuta mondo, Esperantujo atendas vin! _____ (koni) pro sia ĉiama bela vetero, la lando estas _____ (trovi) sub la plej blua ĉielo iam ajn _____ (vidi). Vi kaj via familio estos _____ (bonvenigi) de la ridantaj Esperantujanoj. Venu baldaŭ – vi estas ĉiuj _____ (atendi)!

Vocabulary builder 2

 18.05 Look at the words and complete the missing English words. Then listen and try to imitate the pronunciation of the speakers.

HISTORIO   *HISTORY*

revolucio	_____
sendependa / sendependeco	*independent / _____*
unuiĝo / disiĝo	*unification, separation*
Antikva Grekio	*Ancient Greece*
bronza epoko / fera epoko	*Bronze Age / Iron Age*
keltaj triboj	*Celtic tribes*
imperio / imperiestro	*empire / emperor*
dua mondmilito	*WWII*
fondi	*to found, set up, establish*
kristana, katolika, islama	*Christian, Catholic, Islamic*
ĉefurbo (de Hungario)	*capital (of Hungary)*
krono de sankta Stefano	*crown of Saint Stephen*
reĝo, reĝino	*king, queen*
eksa komunista lando	*former Communist country*
monunuo	*currency, monetary unit*

Conversation 2

NEW EXPRESSIONS

 18.06 Look at and listen to the words and expressions that are used in the following conversation. Note their meanings.

ekscii pli pri ĝia praa historio	*to get to know more about its early history*
verdire, mi apenaŭ aŭdis pri Slovakio mem	*to be honest, I'd barely heard of Slovakia itself*
estis konstruitaj domoj kaj muroj	*houses and walls were built*
laŭ ordonoj de la tiamaj ĉefoj	*on the orders of the chiefs of the time*
la slavaj triboj, niaj praavoj	*the Slavic tribes, our ancestors*
Slovakio estis aldonita al la Granda Moravia Imperio	*Slovakia was added to the Great Moravian Empire*
la urbo estis ĉirkaŭata de muroj	*the city was surrounded by walls*
por montri dankemon	*to show gratitude*
estis agnoskite en 1993, ke …	*It was acknowledged in 1993 that …*

 18.07 *Miro leads Sara and Roberto to St Martin's Cathedral and tells them about the history of Bratislava*

1 Why does the main square contain a statue of a French soldier?

Miro	Kiom vi scias pri la historio de Bratislavo? Ĉu vi interesiĝus ekscii pli pri ĝia praa historio?
Sara	Verdire, antaŭ ol estis decidite veni ĉi tien, mi apenaŭ aŭdis pri Slovakio mem, kaj pri Bratislavo tute neniom sciis.
Roberto	Ankaŭ mi interesiĝus, Miro. Estas sciata en nia lando nenio pri via.
Miro	Nu, la loko, kiu nun estas nomata Bratislavo, estis unue loĝita de homoj antaŭ sep mil jaroj. Multe da bronzo estis produktata ĉi tie. Poste venis kelkaj keltaj triboj kaj estis konstruitaj domoj kaj muroj apud la rivero Danubo, laŭ ordonoj de la tiamaj ĉefoj. La domoj de la unuaj slavaj triboj, do niaj praavoj, estis kreitaj ĉi tie en la kvina jarcento. Du jarcentojn poste estis starigita la imperio de Samo, trib-ĉefulo kaj militisto.
Roberto	Mi neniam aŭdis pri nek tiu imperio, nek tiu imperiestro!
Miro	Nu, ĝi ne daŭris longe, ĉar en la jaro 833 estis fondita la Granda Moravia Imperio, al kiu estis aldonitaj Slovakio, Moravio, kaj partoj de Hungario, suda Pollando, kaj Aŭstrio. La unua kristana preĝejo en Mezeŭropo estis konstruita tiam.
Sara	Ĉio, kion vi diras estas al mi tute nova, Miro! Bonvolu rakonti plu!
Miro	Nu, ĉu vi sciis, ke Bratislavo iam estis la ĉefurbo de Hungario? Ne? Ĝi estis elektita la nova ĉefurbo en 1536, ĉar la antaŭa, Buda, estis invadita de la turkoj. Ĉiuj hungaraj soldatoj estis mortigitaj en unu tago. Ho, jen la katedralo de sankta Marteno. Ĝi estis konstruita de la 13-a ĝis la 15-a jarcentoj. Ĝia turo estas 85 metrojn alta. Ĉu vi vidas la kronon ĉe la supro? Ĝi estas modelo de la krono de sankta Stefano kaj pezas 300 kilogramojn.
Sara	Ĝi ŝajnas grava preĝejo.

Miro	Nu, jes ja. En ĝi estis kronitaj 11 reĝoj kaj 8 reĝinoj inter 1563 kaj 1830, inkluzive de Maria Tereza en 1741. Ŝi estis tre grava reĝino, ĉar la urbo estis pligrandigita de ŝi.
Sara	Ĉu? Kiel ŝi faris?
Miro	Nu, antaŭe la urbo estis ĉirkaŭata de muroj. Sed ili estis malkonstruigitaj de ŝi. Kaj antaŭe la Pordego de Mikaelo estis ne la sola, sed unu el kvar. Sed la aliaj tri estis detruitaj laŭ ŝiaj ordonoj. Estis bezonataj tiuj muroj en 1809, kiam Bratislavo estis vizitata de Imperiestro Napoleono kaj liaj soldatoj!
Roberto	Ho, nun mi ekkomprenas, kial statuo de franca soldato estis starigita en la ĉefplaco!
Miro	Ĝuste, tial. Ho, ĉu vi sciis, ke en 1918 Bratislavo estis renomita 'Urbo Wilson', por montri dankemon al la prezidanto de Usono? Feliĉe la nomo estis baldaŭ poste ŝanĝita denove al Bratislavo. Post la Dua Mondmilito Slovakio estis komunista lando dum preskaŭ duon-jarcenton, ĝis estis detruita la Berlina Muro en 1989 kaj disiĝis poste Sovetio. Estis agnoskite en 1993, ke eksa komunista lando Slovakio nun estos libera, sendependa lando. Kaj en 2004 ĝi estis akceptita kiel nova membro de la Eŭropa Unio. Baldaŭ poste estis decidite, ke la eŭro estos akceptita kiel nia nacia monunuo. Kaj jen pli-malpli ĉio.
Roberto	Dankegon, Miro – mi tiom lernis de vi!
Sara	Vi estas tre informita, Miro, kaj la plej bona gvidanto!
Miro	Kaj vi du estas la plej bonaj gviditoj!

2 Match the Esperanto and the English.

a	Soon afterwards it was decided	**1**	Antaŭ ol estis decidite veni ĉi tien
b	People who were guided	**2**	La aliaj estis detruitaj laŭ ŝiaj ordonoj
c	Before it was decided to come here	**3**	Estis bezonataj tiuj turoj, kiam
d	Until the wall was destroyed	**4**	Baldaŭ poste estis decidite
e	The others were destroyed on her orders	**5**	Estas sciata nenio en mia lando pri via
f	Its door was 50 metres tall	**6**	Poste estis starigita la imperio
g	Afterwards the empire was established	**7**	Gviditoj
h	In my country nothing is known about yours	**8**	Ĝis estis detruita la muro
i	These walls were needed when	**9**	Disiĝis Sovetio
j	The Soviet Union split up	**10**	Ĝia pordo estis 50 metrojn alta

💡 Language discovery 2

1 How does Miro ask *Would you be interested in finding out about its ancient history*?

2 Miro says that the walls estis malkonstruigitaj de ŝi. How would this change if we were trying to say that the queen actually knocked down the walls with her own hands?

3 How could you rewrite la nomo estis nelonge poste ŝanĝita denove al Bratislavo without using the passive?

1 AFFIXES

Pra- has the meaning of long ago in time:

prahistorio *ancient history* **praavoj** *ancestors*

ĉef- means that something is the most important or highest in rank:

ĉefo *chief* **ĉefurbo** *capital city* **ĉefplaco** *main square*

ĉef- can often overlap with **-estr-**, which denotes the person who makes the decisions:

estro *leader* **imperiestro** *emperor*

urbestro *mayor* **lernejestro** *headteacher*

eks- works the same as English *ex*, indicating a former status:

eksedzo ex-husband **eksinstruisto** a former / retired teacher

> **LANGUAGE TIP**
>
> One way of applying an honorific title in Esperanto is to use the word **moŝto**. You could address a **reĝo** *king* or **urbestro** *mayor* as **via reĝa / urbestra moŝto** *Your Royal Highness, Your Worshipfulness the Mayor.*

2 MEASUREMENTS

The conversation shows an additional use of the **n**-ending, which is to relay measurement:

Ĝia turo estas 85 metrojn alta. *Its tower is 85 metres high.*

Giving measurements can also be made with the preposition **je**:

Ĝia turo estas alta je 85 metroj.

The norm is very much to use the **n**-ending, although it is useful to know that you can remove the **n**-ending and use **je** instead.

Practice 2

1 Fill in the blanks using the words from the box.

> eksiĝis   estris   eksigi
> estrigis   eksigita   estrata
> ĉefan   praa   ĉef   estro

a 'Roma' estas la _____ _____ urbo de la romanoj. ('Roma' is the ancient capital city of the Romans.)

b Gordiano I kaj Gordiano II _____ la roman imperion. Tamen ĝi estis _____ de ili dum nur mallonga tempo. (*Gordian I and Gordian II led the Roman Empire. It was led by them only for a short time, however.*)

c Oni ĵus _____ mian _____ malamikon kaj mi certas, ke mi estos _____ de li baldaŭ. (*They just promoted my worst enemy and I'm sure that I'm going to be fired by him soon.*)

d Mi _____ de mia laborposteno, antaŭ ol mia nova _____ povos _____ min! (*I quit my job before my new boss could fire me!*)

2 Insert **pra-**, **ĉef-**, **-estr-** or **eks-** into the Esperanto words to create the given English words.

   a artikolo (*an editorial, a leader (article)*)

   b urbo (*a mayor*)

   c patroj (*forefathers*)

   d ministro (*prime minister*)

   e amiko (*a former friend*)

   f strato (*main street*)

   g arbaro (*a primeval forest*)

3 Complete the blanks in the following sentences to show the measurements given in English.

   a La monto Everesto estas _____ (*8848 metres*) alta.

   b La kongresejo estas _____ (*300 metres*) for.

   c La nova restoracio troviĝas _____ (*1 kilometre*) distanca de la malnova.

   d Mia eta frato estas preskaŭ _____ (*2 metres*) alta.

Reading

Read the following short article about Harold Bolingbroke Mudie, the first president of the Universala Esperanto-Asocio.

Harold Bolingbroke Mudie naskiĝis en 1880, la sola infano de Alfred kaj Ann Mudie. Edukiĝis la juna Harry unue en privata lernejo en Handsworth, kaj poste plurajn pliajn jarojn en Folkestone.

Mudie jam sufiĉe bone kapablis legi plurajn lingvojn, kiam li unue eksciis pri Esperanto en Oktobro 1902, leginte artikolon de W.T. Stead en la fama *Review of Reviews*. Iam en tiuj tagoj Stead petis al Mudie, ke li publikigu novan gazeton en Esperanto. Tiel en Novembro 1903 naskiĝis *The Esperantist*, 16-paĝa monata gazeto. Konsiderindas, ke Mudie estis nur 23-jara tiam kaj Esperanton lernadis nur dum unu jaro!

En 1907 okazis la tria Universala Kongreso, tiun jaron en Kembriĝo, Britio. Mudie, kune kun D-ro George Cunningham, dentisto, kaj Kolonelo John Pollen, prezidanto de la Brita Esperanto-Asocio, estis unu el la organizantoj, nomitaj 'la Trio por la Tria'. Mudie trovis loĝadon kun esperantistaj familioj por vizitantoj alilandaj, kaj aranĝis tabloj n tiel, ke neniu sidis apud samlingvanoj, tiel devigante la kongresanojn uzi Esperanton.

En 1908, sub la gvidado de la juna sviso Hector Hodler, aro da esperantistoj fondis la Universalan Esperanto-Asocion. Ili invitis al Mudie esti ĝia unua prezidanto, posteno, kiun li havis ĝis sia frua morto en akcidento en 1916. Li havis samtempe la prezidantecon de la Brita Esperanto-Asocio, kiam li mortis en norda Francio.

1 How many brothers and sisters did he have?

2 How often did Mudie's magazine, *The Esperantist*, appear?

3 Who is the person who led the discussions which led to the creation of the **Universala Esperanto-Asocio?**

Writing

Write at least two paragraphs about a historical person you admire. Include information about when and where they were born and something about an achievement for which the person became famous. Aim to write 100–200 words.

Listening

 18.08 Listen to a new learner ask an experienced speaker about the first Universala Kongreso, which took place in Bulonjo-ĉe-Maro in France. Then answer the questions.

1 How many people participated in it?

2 How many countries did they come from?

3 What was the only language spoken there?

> **CULTURE TIP**
> The Esperanto flag was originally the flag of the local group in Bulonjo-ĉe-Maro.

Speaking

Imagine that your city is going to host an international Esperanto event. You've been tasked by the organizers with putting together a short guide for the visitors. Record yourself suggesting a nice place to eat and some sights to see.

Test yourself

1 If a **kaptita homo** is *somebody who was captured*, then how would you form the word for *a prisoner* with a participle?

2 If the passive construction **konfirmote** is *to be confirmed*, then how could you create *to be decided* from **decidi**?

3 Esperanto isn't just a **skribata lingvo** (*written language*) but one which people speak too. How do you get *spoken language* from **paroli** *to speak*?

Review for Units 13–18

Grammar

Here is a summary of the grammar covered in Units 13–18.

Basic endings	
-us	Conditional, e.g. **mi irus, mi manĝus**
-anta	Present active participle (e.g. **ĉasanta** – *who is chasing*)
-ata	Present passive participle (e.g. **ĉasata** – *who is chased*)
-inta	Past active participle (e.g. **ĉasinta** – *who was chasing*)
-ita	Past passive participle (e.g. **ĉasita** – *who was chased*)
-onta	Future active participle (e.g. **ĉasonta** – *who will be chasing*)
-ota	Future passive participle (e.g. **ĉasota** – *who will be chased*)

Creating new words	
dis-	Spreading out, e.g. **diskuri, disvastigi**
eks-	*ex-*, e.g. **eksministro, eksedzo**
fi-	Bad morals, e.g. **fiulo, fivorto**
pra-	Long ago, e.g. **prahomo, prahistorio**
vir-	Male, e.g. **virkoko**
-aĉ-	Bad quality, e.g. **domaĉo, hundaĉo**
-ec-	Abstract quality, e.g. **amikeco, boneco**
-ej-	Place, e.g. **trinkejo, lernejo**
-estr-	Decision maker, e.g. **urbestro, imperiestro**
-id-	Offspring, e.g. **hundido, katido**
-ig-	Cause something, e.g. **ruĝigi, manĝigi**
-iĝ-	Become, change state, e.g. **ruĝiĝi, rompiĝi**
-ind-	Worthy, e.g. **vizitinda, aminda**
-ing-	Holder, e.g. **kandelingo, glavingo**

COMPARISONS

When comparing two or more items or people, the key patterns are **tiel … kiel**, **(mal)pli … ol** and **la (mal)plej …** . Examples:

Ŝi estas tiel bela kiel somera tago.

Mia frato estas pli inteligenta ol li. Li estas malpli inteligenta ol mia frato.

Ŝi estas la plej inteligenta virino (en la tuta mondo).

INDIRECT SPEECH

Unlike in English, there is no shift in tenses in Esperanto when reporting speech. If someone said **'Ili ludos en la parko'** (*They will play in the park*), the indirect form is **Li diris, ke ili ludos en la parko** (*He said that they would play in the park*).

REFLEXIVE

When the subject of a sentence is not **mi**, **vi** or **ni**, and later comes up in the same phrase, **si**, **sin** or **sia** are used as pronouns. Sentences are therefore less ambiguous than in English.

Li lavas sian aŭton. vs. **Li lavas lian aŭton.**

RECIPROCALS

The basic equivalent of *each other* is **unu la alian**. This can change to **unu de la alia**, **unu kun la alia**, **unu por la alia**, etc. depending on which preposition is required.

Practice

1 Write a postcard in Esperanto, imagining you're still on your last holiday.

AL :

ADRESO :

2 **The following are major events in 20th century history. Put them in chronological order.**

kreiĝo de la eŭro, dua mondmilito, ĉefministriĝo de Margaret Thatcher, unua mondmilito, rusa revolucio, morto de Hitler, sendependiĝo de Barato

3 **Here's the description of an actual Esperanto music album. Fill in the right endings (-ig-, -iĝ-, participles and others).**

Jen nova albumo de la fama rege-kant_____ Jonny M. Post lia paŭzo por veki kre_____on kaj kolekti kantojn, nun publik_____ Kreaktiva. 14 freŝnovaj kantoj, inter alie kunlaboroj kun La Perdita Generacio, Dolchamar kaj JoMo, danc_____ ritmoj kaj bone pripens_____ tekstoj atendas vin.

Aldon_____ estas kaptipovaj, kunkant_____ melodioj, kiuj sen via volo ekdanc_____ viajn piedojn.

La plej vigla kanto 'Ni estas fortaj' jam havis sukceson en indonezia kongreso. Pliaj verkoj estas ekzemple la kanto 'Por mia patro', kiun Jonny M verkis por sia mort_____ patro, la socio-kritika 'Ribeluloj' kun Dolchamar, aŭ la kanto 'Bam bam', kiu temas pri la konserv_____ de la medio kaj vegana manĝaĵo.

4 **Translate this book review.**

 www.legado.com

The book 'Fajron sentas mi interne' is my favourite Esperanto book! It is less easy than 'Gerda Malaperis', but still easy, and the story is much more interesting. I read it very quickly and then I re-read it in order to improve my Esperanto vocabulary. While reading it the second time, I found new things that I had not noticed the first time. I really like it a lot. If I had known it would be so good, I would have read it before.

5 **Using the affixes listed at the beginning of this review section, create Esperanto words that mean the following:**

   a a tomcat

   b a person to be ignored

   c things to be done

   d a former headteacher

   e to give out

   f to make someone nervous

   g to become bigger

   h beauty

   i the quality of being danceable

   j to rip to pieces and spread out

6 **An Iranian friend is asking you how people greet each other in your country, e.g. through hugs, handshakes, bows and so on. Answer in Esperanto, describing both greetings between strangers and greetings between friends.**

7 **What words have you learned for places in a city? Find 19 of them in this wordsearch. Note that it uses the h-method (ch = ĉ, gh = ĝ …) rather than Esperanto letters.**

H	Y	T	F	O	I	R	O	O	P	Y	O	K
N	A	S	B	L	T	D	K	O	H	P	E	F
Q	K	A	M	A	Z	R	L	U	T	R	Z	D
T	I	P	M	R	K	I	I	X	F	E	U	I
P	N	O	Z	D	C	E	X	N	O	G	M	P
A	E	N	I	E	C	S	J	C	K	H	M	E
O	J	T	J	T	T	O	A	O	W	E	U	P
L	O	O	U	A	M	L	J	H	W	J	J	W
E	K	R	T	K	P	F	B	E	P	O	P	O
T	O	U	Y	F	O	J	E	D	N	E	V	I
S	O	M	E	T	R	O	T	U	A	R	O	C
A	G	H	O	K	R	A	P	H	F	F	E	I
K	C	P	O	R	D	E	G	O	B	C	G	L

8 **Finally, note a few phrases that might come in handy at your next Esperanto Congress: Complete the blanks with sentences in Esperanto.**

   a I don't like the rhythm and melody of this song.   _____

   b It's too loud.   _____

   c The guitarist is awful.   _____

   d I would prefer to listen to the other singer.   _____

   e It would be quieter somewhere else.   _____

   f I'd avoid this concert; he sings terribly.   _____

   g Sorry, I misheard because of the noise.   _____

   h I'm having a great time.   _____

Grammar reference

TABLE WORDS

All 45 of Esperanto's table words are presented below. There are five beginnings and nine endings. The meaning of each table word is entirely predictable based on what beginning and ending it is built from.

	i- Indefinite *some*	**ki-** Interrogative or relative *which, what*	**ti-** Demonstrative *that*	**ĉi-** Universal *every, each, all*	**neni-** Negative *no*
-a Quality *kind, sort*	**ia** of some kind, of any kind	**kia** of what kind, what kind of, what a __!	**tia** of that kind, of that kind, such a __	**ĉia** of every kind, every kind of	**nenia** of no kind, no kind of
-al Cause *reason*	**ial** for some reason	**kial** why	**tial** that's why, for that reason, therefore	**ĉial** for every reason	**nenial** for no reason
-am Time	**iam** at some time, ever	**kiam** when	**tiam** at that time, then	**ĉiam** always	**neniam** never
-e Place	**ie** in some place, somewhere	**kie** where	**tie** there	**ĉie** everywhere	**nenie** nowhere
-el Manner *way*	**iel** in some way, somehow	**kiel** how, like	**tiel** in that way, like that, so, thus	**ĉiel** in every way	**neniel** in no way
-es Association, possession	**ies** someone's, somebody's	**kies** whose	**ties** that one's	**ĉies** everyone's, everybody's	**nenies** no one's, nobody's
-o Thing	**io** something	**kio** what thing, what	**tio** that thing, that	**ĉio** everything, all	**nenio** nothing
-om Quantity	**iom** some quantity, somewhat	**kiom** how much, how many	**tiom** that quantity, so much, so many	**ĉiom** the whole quantity, all of it	**neniom** no quantity, not a bit, none
-u Individuality *person, a particular x*	**iu** someone, some (person or thing)	**kiu** which (one), who	**tiu** that (one)	**ĉiu** everybody, everyone, every, each	**neniu** nobody, no, no one

The table words ending with **-a**, **-e**, **-o**, and **-u** can take the **n**-ending. The **j**-ending can be applied to the table words which end with **-a** and **-u**.

You may hear people refer to these words as *correlatives* (**korelativoj** in Esperanto), which is the traditional label. There are many online resources for helping you practise them.

TRANSITIVITY

Nearly all Esperanto verbs take subjects but many verbs cannot take an object. These are called intransitive verbs. Examples include **veni** (*to come*), **esti** (*to be*), **sidi** (*to sit*). Other verbs, called transitive verbs, do take objects, which will be shown with the **n**-ending. Among these are **havi** (*to have*), **preni** (*to take*), **vendi** (*to sell*).

The transitivity of verbs is fixed in Esperanto. It's important to know what the transitivity is so that you don't give objects to verbs which cannot accept them. On many occasions, this will be obvious; you'll be so familiar with, say, **esti** and **havi** that you automatically know which you can't use with an object. In other situations, you'll have to discover what the transitivity is.

One method is to look up the word in a dictionary. Good ones mark the transitivity for you. You might see **ntr** (*netransitiva*) or **tr** (*transitiva*) by the entry in monolingual dictionaries, for example. Another way of working out the transitivity is to see how the verb is used in example sentences. If it takes an object, you know it's a transitive verb.

Because a verb's transitivity is such an important thing to know, it is recommended that when you learn a new verb, you also make a point of remembering its transitivity. You'll find that committing an example sentence to memory helps.

Another tip is to learn the definition of a verb rather than its translation. Knowing that **boli** is *to boil* doesn't indicate to you how to use it, especially because *to boil* can be used transitively and intransitively in English. (*The water is boiling* is intransitive whereas *I am boiling the water* is transitive because *the water* is the direct object.) Once you learn that the definition of **boli** is '*to become hot until giving off bubbles, which burst at the surface*', then you know that it's an intransitive verb in Esperanto and can't take an object. This is a lot more work than simply learning the translation with an example sentence, but if you're capable of thinking this way, you'll find it comes in very handy for you.

Changing a verb's transitivity

Fortunately, Esperanto provides tools for changing a verb's transitivity, using the suffixes **-iĝ-** and **-ig-**. Use **-iĝ-** with a transitive verb to create an intransitive one:

Naturally transitive	Intransitive after adding -iĝ-
vendi (*to sell*)	**vendiĝi** (*to sell*)
Mi vendis multajn novajn aŭtojn.	**La nova aŭto bonege vendiĝas.**
I've sold lots of new cars.	*The new car is selling really well.*
solvi (*to solve*)	**solviĝi** (*to get solved*)
Mi provas rapide solvi la misteron.	**La mistero rapide solviĝis.**
I'm trying to solve the mystery quickly.	*The mystery got solved quickly.*

Similarly, adding **-ig-** to an intransitive verb will create a transitive verb:

Naturally intransitive	Transitive after adding -ig-
morti (*to die*)	**mortigi** (*to kill*)
La maljunulo mortis en decembro.	**La kato rapide mortigis la muson.**
The old man died in December.	*The cat quickly killed the mouse.*
ĝoji (*to be happy*)	**ĝojigi** (*to make happy*)
Mi ĝojas, ke ŝi foriros morgaŭ.	**Ŝia foriro multe ĝojigis min.**
I'm happy that she's going away tomorrow.	*Her departure made me really happy.*

USES OF THE N-ENDING

The **n**-ending plays several roles in Esperanto.

Marking the direct object

Esperanto differentiates the subject from the direct object by applying the **n**-ending to the latter: **La viro mordis la etan hundon** (*The man bit the little dog*). Here, **la viro** is the subject and **la etan hundon** is the direct object. Both the **o**-word and its **a**-word take the **n**-ending.

You may often hear people refer to this use as 'the accusative', which is the shorthand for 'the accusative case', the conventional grammatical label for the situation where the direct object is marked with the **n**-ending.

Showing motion towards

In Esperanto grammar the **n**-ending doesn't usually follow a preposition. If it does, then it's indicating motion towards: **La infanoj kuras en la ĝardeno** (*The children are running in the garden*) – **La infanoj kuras en la ĝardenon** (*The children are running into the garden*).

Measurement

The **n**-ending can be used to indicate measurement, such as distance, weight and duration. It may be thought of as replacing a preposition: **La urbo troviĝas tri kilometrojn for [je tri kilometroj for]** (*The town is found three kilometres away*) – **La granda pomo pezas 300 gramojn** (*The large apple weighs 300 grams*) – **Mi laboris la tutan tagon [dum la tuta tago]** (*I worked the whole day*).

Points in time, including dates

When a time phrase is neither a subject nor an object, the **n**-ending can be applied to show that you're referring to some point in time: **Unu tagon mi vizitos vin** (*I'll visit you one day*). It is frequently used with dates, replacing a construction with **je: Li naskiĝis la 17-an de decembro [je la 17-a de decembro]** (*He was born on the 17th of December*) – **Mi vidos vin sabaton! [je sabato!]** (*I'll see you on Saturday!*).

In set expressions

You greet people in Esperanto with **Bonan matenon!** (*Good morning!*) or **Saluton!** (*Hello!*), and thank them with **Dankon!** (*Thank you!*). People often clarify that these are short for **Mi deziras al vi bonan tagon** (*I wish you a good day*), which helps explain many instances of its use. Sometimes, though, it can be hard to imagine what the implied part of the sentence might be, so it can be handy to consider these expressions as another use of the **n**-ending.

AFFIXES

Esperanto's affix system makes it exceptionally easy to build new words. You've encountered nearly all of the 41 official affixes in this course.

Prefixes

The 10 official prefixes in Esperanto are:

BO-: related by marriage, an in-law.

patrino (*mother*)   **bopatrino** (*mother-in-law*)

(*See Unit 3*)

ĈEF-: the most important, the main something.

strato (*street*)   **ĉefstrato** (*High Street, Main Street*)

(*See Unit 18*)

DIS-: spreading, going out in multiple directions, scattering.

doni (*to give*)   **disdoni** (*to distribute*)

(*See Unit 18*)

EK-: start of an action, sudden action.

sidi (*to sit*)   **eksidi** (*to start sitting down*)

flamo (*a flame*)   **ekflami** (*a flash*)

(*See Unit 10*)

EKS-: corresponds with English's ex, denoting a former state.

edzino (*wife*)   **eksedzino** (*ex-wife*)

(*See Unit 18*)

GE-: both sexes, used either to mean one of each or several together.

patro (*father*)   **gepatroj** (*parents*)

knabo (*boy*)   **geknaboj** (*boys and girls*)

(*See Unit 3*)

MAL-: the opposite.

bela (*beautiful*)   **malbela** (*ugly*)

bona (*good*)   **malbona** (*bad*)

(See Unit 2)

MIS-: equivalent to mis- in English, showing that something is wrong, bad or erroneous.

kompreni (*to understand*)   **miskompreni** (*to misunderstand*)

(*See Unit 14*)

PRA-: a very long time ago, ancient, primitive; in family relationships it shows a generation further away from the word it's attached to

historio (history)   **prahistorio** (*ancient history*)

avo (*grandfather*)   **praavo** (*great-grandfather*)

nepo (grandson)   **pranepo** (*great-grandson*)

(*See Units 3 & 18*)

RE-: the same as English's re-, indicating meaning to happen or do something again or to make as it was before.

veni (*to come*)   **reveni** (*to come back, to return*)

(*See Unit 6*)

Suffixes

The 31 official suffixes in Esperanto are:

-AĈ-: bad in quality

domo (*a house*)   **domaĉo** (*a shack, a hovel*)

(See Unit 14)

-AD-: continuing action, repetition, duration

bato (*a strike, a hit*)   **batado** (*striking, hitting*)

(*See Unit 10*)

-AĴ-: something, often physical, associated with an action; something characterised by an adjective; the flesh of an animal

trinki (*to drink*)   **trinkaĵo** (*a drink*)

pensi (*to think*)   **pensaĵo** (*a thought*)

nova (*new*)   **novaĵo** (*something new, news*)

bovo (*a cow*)   **bovaĵo** (*beef*)

(*See Units 4 & 15*)

-AN-: shows a person's association to something, maybe as a member, as an adherent to an idea or doctrine, or as a resident or citizen.

klubo (*a club*)   **klubano** (*a member of a club*)

Jesuo Kristo (*Jesus Christ*)   **kristano** (*a Christian*)

vilaĝo (*a village*)   **vilaĝano** (*a villager*)

Usono (*the USA*)   **usonano** (*an American*)

(*See Unit 9*)

-AR-: expresses a group or collection of something, whether it consists of lots of the same thing, something chiefly composed of that thing, or all of the same thing in a general sense.

haro (*a hair*)   **hararo** ((*a head of*) *hair*)

arbo (*tree*)   **arbaro** (*a forest*)

vorto (*a word*)   **vortaro** (*a dictionary*)

homo (*a person*)   **homaro** (*mankind*)

(*See Unit 9*)

-ĈJ-: creates familiar names for men. Usually the name is reduced by removing some letters, unless it's already very short.

patro (*a father*)   **paĉjo** (*Dad*)

Vilhelmo (*William*)   **Vilĉjo, Viĉjo** (*Bill, Will, Billy*)

(*See Unit 3*)

-EBL-: works the same as *-able* and *-ible* in English, expressing what's possible.

kompreni (*to understand*)   **komprenebla** (*understandable*)

(*See Unit 3*)

-EC-: allows you to form an abstraction or a noun expressing a quality.

amiko (*friend*)   **amikeco** (*friendship*)

frato (*brother*)   **frateco** (*brotherhood*)

(*See Unit 18*)

-EG-: intensifies something, makes it larger or more important.

domo (*a house*)   **domego** (*a mansion*)

grava (*important*)   **gravega** (*extremely important*)

(*See Unit 2*)

-EJ-: a place where an activity occurs or a place for that thing.

lerni (*to learn*)   **lernejo** (*a school, a place intended for learning*)

baki (*to bake*)   **bakejo** (*a bakery*)

(*See Unit 13*)

-EM-: a characteristic tendency or inclination.

paroli (*to speak*)   **parolema** (*talkative*)

studi (*to study*)   **studema** (*studious*)

(*See Unit 5*)

-END-: something which must be done.

pagi (*to pay*)   **pagenda** (*payable, must be paid*)

(*See Unit 14*)

-ER-: a very small part of something which consists wholly of lots of these things.

salo (*salt*)   **salero** (*a grain of salt*)

sablo (*sand*)   **sablero** (*a grain of sand*)

(*See Unit 12*)

-ESTR-: the decision maker, the leader.

urbo (*city*)   **urbestro** (*mayor*)

lernejo (*school*)   **lernejestro** (*schoolmaster, headteacher*)

(*See Unit 18*)

-ET-: reduces something in size or intensity.

knabino (*a girl*)   **knabineto** (*a little girl, a small girl*)

dormi (*to sleep*)   **dormeti** (*to nap, to doze*)

(*See Unit 2*)

-ID-: denotes the offspring.

ŝafo (*a sheep*)   **ŝafido** (*a lamb*)

(*See Unit 15*)

-IG-: to cause to happen:

ruĝa (*red*)   **ruĝigi** (*to make red, to make blush*)

paroli (*to speak*)   **paroligi** (*to make speak*)

pli bona (*better*)   **plibonigi** (*to improve*)

(*See Unit 17*)

-IĜ-: to change state, to become.

ruĝa (*red*)   **ruĝiĝi** (*to blush*)

en lito (*in bed*)   **enlitiĝi** (*to get into bed*)

(*See Unit 16*)

-IL-: the instrument, the means for doing something.

skribi (*to write*)   **skribilo** (*a pen*)

(*See Unit 11*)

-IN-: specifies a female.

patro (*father*)   **patrino** (*mother*)

(*See Unit 1*)

-IND-: worth doing.

viziti (*to visit*)   **vizitinda** (*worth visiting*)

ami (*to love*)   **aminda** (*lovable*)

(*See Unit 14*)

-ING-: a container for one of something, into which it is usually partially placed.

glavo (*a sword*)   **glavingo** (*a sheath*)

(*See Unit 18*)

-ISM-: behaves like *-ism* in English.

marksismo (*Marxism*)   **alkoholismo** (*alcoholism*)

(*See Unit 9*)

-IST-: somebody occupied with something, often professionally, though not necessarily.

instrui (*to teach*)   **instruisto** (*a teacher*)

kanti (*to sing*)   **kantisto** (*a singer*)

(*See Unit 1*)

-NJ-: creates familiar names for women. Usually the name is reduced by removing some letters, unless it's already very short.

patrino (*a mother*)   **panjo** (*Mum, Mom, Mummy, Mommy*)

Anabela (*Annabella*)   **Anja/Anjo** (*Anna, Bella*)

(*See Unit 3*)

-OBL-: multiplication.

du (*two*)   **duobla** (*double*)

(*See Unit 7*)

-ON-: division.

tri (*three*)   **triono** (*a third*)

(*See Unit 7*)

-OP-: a group comprising a certain number.

kvar (*four*)   **kvaropo** (*a quartet*)

(*See Unit 7*)

-UJ-: a container for something, the meaning of which can be used to name the plant which produces a certain fruit and the country from where a certain ethnic group comes from.

mono (*money*)   **monujo** (*a purse*)

pomo (*an apple*)   **pomujo/pomarbo** (*an apple tree*)

brito (*a British person*)   **Britujo/Britio** (*Great Britain*)

(*See Units 9 & 18*)

-UL-: a person with a certain kind of characteristic.

juna (*young*)   **junulo** (*a young person, a youth*)

(*See Unit 5*)

-UM-: doesn't have a particular meaning and is used to build words which have some type of relationship but which can't be expressed clearly with another affix.

suno (*sun*)   **sunumi** (*to tan*)

akvo (*water*)   **akvumi** (*to water* (*plants etc*))

(*See Unit 12*)

Answer key

Unit 1

Interreto: Singular nouns in Esperanto end with the letter o. If they're pluraj, a j is added. The word for the is la. There isn't a word for a.

Vocabulary builder 1: Greetings and farewells: Good, Good

Conversation 1: 1: Davido lives in Australia and so said good morning. Sara didn't realize that he lives there, so it surprised her to read good morning when it's evening in London. The Esperanto word for I is mi and you is vi. **2: a** - 7; **b** - 5; **c** - 1; **d** - 8; **e** - 6; **f** - 2; **g** - 3; **h** - 4. **3: a** V; **b** V; **c** M; **d** M; **e** M; **f** M; **g** V; **h** V; **i** M; **j** V

Language discovery 1: 1: The conversation contains mi pardonpetas I apologize, mi estas I am, mi loĝas I live, mi komprenas I understand and mi nomiĝas I am called. **2:** The conversation contains Skotlando Scotland, Italio Italy, Britio the United Kingdom, Aŭstralio Australia, Brazilo Brazil and Japanio Japan. **3:** To tell somebody that you're a beginner you say mi estas komencanto.

Practice 1: 1: a Mi trinkas, I drink (/am drinking) **b** Vi ludas, You play (/are playing) **c** Li havas, He has **d** studi, Ŝi studas, She studies (/is studying) **e** ni, Ni aĉetas, We buy (/are buying) **f** saluti, Ili salutas, They greet (/are greeting) **g** dormi, Ĝi dormas, It sleeps (/is sleeping) **h** Ŝi nomiĝas, She is called **2: a** to accept **b** to dance **c** to have **d** to help **e** to start **f** to learn **g** to move **h** to prefer **i** to recommend **j** to answer, to respond **k** to study **l** to suppose **m** to visit

Vocabulary builder 2: Words for professions: Programisto (neutral or male) and programistino (female) both mean programmer. Laboristo (neutral or male) and laboristino (female) both mean worker. Vendistino is a female shop assistant or saleswoman.

Conversation 2: 1: Roberto is a teacher. Sara wants to be a scientist. **2: a** - 4; **b** - 5; **c** - 2; **d** - 1; **e** - 6; **f** - 3

Language discovery 2: 1: Mi estas instruisto means I am a teacher while mi laboras kiel instruisto is I work as a teacher. **2:** Aktoro actor, futbalisto footballer, studento student, politikisto politician, advokato barrister, solicitor, attorney, muzikisto musician, profesoro professor **3:** Sara uses the suffix -in- to indicate that she's a female.

Practice 2: 1: a Ĉu vi komprenas? **b** Ĉu ŝi estas instruistino? **c** Ĉu ŝi studas en Londono? **d** Ĉu ili kantas bele? **e** Ĉu li laboras multe? **f** Ĉu mi parolas bone? **g** Ĉu vi volas esti kantisto? **h** Ĉu li laboras kiel kelnero? **2: a** Ĉu vi loĝas en (anywhere other than Paris)? **b** Ĉu vi volas esti instruisto? **c** Ĉu vi laboras kiel (anything other than a waitress)? **d** Ĉu li parolas bone kaj kantas bele? **e** Kiu vi estas? (Also accepted: Kiel vi nomiĝas?) **f** Kie vi studas? **g** Kio estas tio? **h** Kial vi studas sciencon? **3: a** - 5: Ne, ĝi ne estas en Italio **b** - 2: Jes, ŝi estas aktorino **c** - 6: Ne, ĝi ne estas lando **d** - 4: Jes, ŝi estas verkistino **e** - 3: Jes, ĝi estas en Usono **f** - 1: Ne, li ne venas el Britio

Reading: Marko: Saluton! Mi estas Marko el Italio! Mi loĝas en Romo. Kiu vi estas?

Isabel: Saluton, Marko! Mi nomiĝas Isabel.

Stefano: Saluton, Marko kaj Isabel. Mi nomiĝas Stefano kaj ankaŭ mi venas el Italio!

Writing: Bonan vesperon, Marko, Isabel kaj Stefano! Mi nomiĝas Laura. Mi estas komencanto. Mi studas en Londono. Mi volas esti aktorino.

Listening: 1: Paola and Marko **2:** He comes from Italy but lives in Britain **3:** She lives in Toulouse, France, and studies at the university there **4:** He is a doctor

Test yourself: 1: a Mi ne loĝas en Usono **b** Mi ne nomiĝas Alfredo **c** Mi ne laboras kiel instruisto **d** Mi ne volas esti sciencistino **e** Mi ne ŝatas studi **2: a** Ĉu vi estas Mikaelo? **b** Ĉu ŝi loĝas en Germanio? **c** Ĉu ili nomiĝas sinjoro Smith kaj sinjorino Jones? **d** Ĉu Parizo estas en Francio? **e** Ĉu li volas esti programisto? **3: a** Kie vi loĝas? **b** Kiu ŝi estas? (It could also be Kio ŝi estas? for What is she?) **c** Kiel li nomiĝas? **d** Kio estas tio? **e** Kial vi volas esti futbalisto kaj ne instruisto?

Unit 2

Esprimoj en Esperanto: Aligatori to alligator is the verb for when you speak a language other than your own in an Esperanto environment.

Vocabulary builder 1: Malsani is to be unwell, to be ill; dormi is to sleep.

Conversation 1: 1: Emiljo lacegas is extremely tired because he's been studying a lot. **2: a** - 11; **b** - 4; **c** - 2; **d** - 12; **e** - 8; **f** - 1; **g** - 9; **h** - 5; **i** - 7; **j** - 10; **k** - 3; **l** - 6. **3: a** Malvera **b** Vera **c** Malvera **d** Malvera

Language discovery 1: 1: feliĉa happy, malfeliĉa sad, mi ĝojas I am glad and mi fartas malbone I'm doing badly. **2:** Mijoŝi says malsanega and Emiljo uses studegas. They've taken the usual words and added -eg- to intensify them. **3:** The words are pli more and malpli less.

Practice 1: 1: a Ŝi estas malsana **b** Mi studas kaj laboras tro multe **c** Mi estas laca, ĉar mi ne bone dormas **d** Mia instruisto estas maljuna, sed li instruas tre bone **e** La malsana studento ne fartas bone **f** Mi dancas bone, sed ne estas bona kantisto **g** Ŝi estas feliĉa, ĉar hodiaŭ ŝi bone fartas **2: a** kanto **b** danki **c** vida **d** laboro **e** lernas **f** kosti **g** bele **h** mojosa **i** nomiĝas **j** bone **3: a** laboro **b** helpo **c** helpa **d** bele **e** problema **f** mana **g** fino **h** fina **i** fakto **4: a** Li estas malfeliĉa **b** Mi fartas bonege **c** La kato dormetas **d** Mi komprenetas **e** malgranda **f** grandega **g** malbonega **h** Li nur manĝetas **i** Mi lacegas

Conversation 2: 1: Roberto names all the months except the summer ones! **2:** januaro, februaro, marto, aprilo, majo, junio, julio, aŭgusto, septembro, oktobro, novembro, decembro (which can all be written with capitals and originally were); printempo, somero, aŭtuno, vintro (which have never been written with capitals)

Language discovery 2: 1: Pluvegas gives the idea of something more intensive than normal raining, such as a downpour. Briletas is a less intensive version of brilas, so shining a little bit. **2:** Mijoŝi adds ĉu ne? to the end of his statement, which works like English's question tag isn't it? **3:** Anna gives the weather by saying tondras and fulmas.

Practice 2: 1: a Jes, estas varme en Hispanio. **b** Jes, la suno estas varma. **c** Ne, ne pluvas en la dezerto. **d** Jes, estas varmege en la dezerto. **e** Ne, ne neĝas en Brazilo. **f** Ne, la suno ne brilas en vintro en Skotlando.

2: a Estas malvarme **b** Bonege! Mi ĝojas, ke vi konsentas! **c** Bona instruisto instruas bone. **d** Ho, ĉu vi venas el Francio? Mojose! Francio estas mojosa lando! **e** Ĉu vi scias, ke paroli en Esperanto estas amuze? **f** Loĝi en Italio estas bonege!

Reading: 1: He says that the weather in Scotland is malvarmega very cold. **2:** He says that it's warm in the south of England but that the weather is bad in the north. **3:** He doesn't like the weather in Wales. He says it's malbona bad.

Writing: En Kimrio estas varmega tago kaj la suno brilas. En Skotlando la suno briletas. En la nordo de Anglio estas ventego kaj en la oriento pluvas. Fulmas kaj tondras en la sudo.

Listening: 1: Winter is in December, January and February. **2:** Ramona says it ofte neĝas snows often. **3:** Even though it's the start of spring, it's still cold in April. **4:** Ramona is tre feliĉa very happy in summer.

Listening and speaking: Jes, en aprilo. Pluvetas. / Ne, ne neĝas. Estas malvarme, sed ne neĝas. Kutime pluvas. / Jes, estas varme. Ne estas varmege, sed varme. Kutime la suno brilas. Mi estas feliĉa en somero. / Ankaŭ mi estas feliĉa en aŭtuno. Estas bela sezono.

Test yourself 1: a malbona (bad, evil) **b** maljuna (old) **c** malfeliĉa (unhappy) **d** malbela (ugly) **e** malmojosa (uncool) **2: a** neĝego **b** pluveto **c** ventego

3:

				M	A	R	D							
				E										
S	O	M	E	R		V			S	A	B	A	T	
				K		I		V				Ŭ		
			P	R	I	N	T	E	M	P		T		
				E		T		N				U		
		L	U	N	D		R		D	I	M	A	N	Ĉ
							R							
							E							
				Ĵ	A	Ŭ	D							

Unit 3

Esperantaj familioj: Just like nouns add a j if they're plural, so do adjectives, as though in English we'd say reds cars. You might have spotted patr from patro father within gepatroj. The prefix ge- is added to patro to create parents from it. Removing this prefix from gefiloj sons and daughters will give you filo son.

Vocabulary builder 1: to dance, to visit

Conversation 1: 1: Lan wants to sing with her friend. **2: a** - 7; **b** - 6; **c** - 10; d - 9; **e** - 1; **f** - 12; **g** - 4; **h** - 11; **i** - 2; **j** - 5; **k** - 8; **l** - 3 **3: a** Malvera **b** Malvera **c** Vera **d** Vera

Language discovery 1: 1: The conversation contains vespero evening, hodiaŭ today, kanti to sing, manĝi to eat, dormi to sleep and iri to go to the theatre. **2:** Amiko has been modified to amikino to get female friend and ŝatas has been changed to ŝategas to mean really like. **3:** You can express I've got to go now as mi devas foriri nun.

Practice 1: 1: a Mi ŝatas lerni Esperanton **b** Mi kredas, ke lerni Esperanton estas amuze **c** Mi pensas, ke la viro ŝatas bicikli **d** Mi devas sendi leteron al mia patrino **e** Laŭ mi li ne volas vojaĝi al Britio **f** Mi scias, ke vi ne volas helpi **g** Mi ne povas movi la tablon **h** Mi devas komenci studi **i** Mi pensas, ke li volas uzi forkon por manĝi la spagetojn **2: a** Mi volas iri al la teatro. **b** Ŝi kredas, ke mi volas esti instruisto. **c** Kion vi volas fari poste? **d** Anna devas studi morgaŭ. **e** Roberto loĝas en Skotlando, sed li volas loĝi en Francio. **f** Mijoŝi pensas, ke lerni Esperanton estas malfacile. **g** Davido kantas, dancas kaj manĝas tre bone. **h** Ili devas iri al la universitato por studi kaj poste labori.

Vocabulary builder 2: frato / fratino / gefratoj brother / sister / siblings; filo / filino / gefiloj son / daughter / children; avo / avino / geavoj grandfather / grandmother / grandparents; onklo / onklino / geonkloj uncle / aunt / uncles and aunts; kuzo / kuzino / gekuzoj cousin / cousin / cousins; nepo / nepino / genepoj grandson / granddaughter / grandchildren; edzo / edzino / geedzoj husband / wife / spouses; knabo / knabino / geknaboj boy / girl / boys and girls

Conversation 2: 1: Sara can't decide whether to go to the restaurant or to the park. Lan suggests she solve her dilemma by doing both. **2: a** - 5; **b** - 6; **c** - 1; **d** - 2; **e** - 4; **f** - 3

Language discovery 2: 1: A kuzino is a female cousin, whereas a kuzo is a male one. **2:** 'My praavo is the father of my grandfather.' He's your great-grandfather. **3:** Sara says fari ambaŭ ne estas eble, ĉu ne?

Practice 2: 1: a Olivia estas la fratino de Samĉjo kaj la kuzino de Lunjo. **b** La geavoj de Anjo nomiĝas Karlo kaj Sofia. **c** Andreo kaj Paŭlo estas bofratoj. Paŭlo estas la frato de Sali. Ŝia edzo nomiĝas Andreo. **d** La filino de Sofia estas Sali. Ŝia nevino nomiĝas Lunjo. **e** Paŭlo estas la onklo de Samĉjo, la patro de Bo, kaj la filo de Karlo. **f** Maria estas la edzino de Paŭlo. Ili estas geedzoj. Iliaj gefiloj/infanoj estas Lunjo, Bo kaj Anjo **g** La onklino de Olivia nomiĝas Maria. **h** La geavoj de Lunjo nomiĝas Karlo kaj Sofia. Ili estas la gepatroj de Sali kaj Paŭlo kaj la bogepatroj de Andreo kaj Maria. **2: a** Mi estas brito. Mia nomo estas [a name]. **b** Ĉu vi pensas, ke lia patro dormas nun? **c** Laura estas bona kuiristino. Ŝia kuko gustas tre bone! **d** Davido kaj lia edzino dancas tre ofte. **e** Nia domo estas granda. Ankaŭ via domo estas granda.

Reading: 1: La kuzo de Olivia nomiĝas Bo. **2:** La avo nomiĝas Karlo. **3:** La bofilo de Karlo estas Andreo. **4:** Paŭlo estas la frato de Sali. **5:** Sali kaj Maria estas bofratinoj.

Listening: 1: To the pub after work **2:** Bill can't make it because he and his wife are going to a restaurant **3:** Petro can't make it the next day because his daughter's visiting from Liverpool. **4:** Bill points out that students like pubs, so he thinks Petro could come after all.

Speaking:

Harry:	Saluton! Ĉu vi iras al la teatro?
You:	Mi ne iras al la teatro, mi iras al la restoracio.
Harry:	Ho, kun kiu? Kun via edzino, ĉu ne?
You:	Ne, ne kun mia edzino, mi iras kun miaj gepatroj.
Harry:	Ĉu vi ofte iras al la restoracio kun viaj gepatroj?
You:	Ne, mi ne ofte iras al la restoracio kun miaj gepatroj, ĉar ili loĝas en Francio.

Harry: Ĉu vi planas iri al Francio?

You: Ne, mi ne planas iri al Francio … mi planas iri al la restoracio! Ĝis!

Test yourself: 1: a fratego **b** frateto **c** infaneto **d** knabineto **2: a** patrino **b** genepoj **c** bopatro **d** geavoj **e** paĉjo **f** kuzo **g** infano **h** gefratoj **i** panjo **j** nevino

Unit 4

Kluboj por Esperantistoj: The expression danke al thanks to has long been abbreviated to dank' al.

Vocabulary builder 1: butero butter; malsata / malsati hungry / to be hungry; koktelo cocktail

Conversation 1: 1: Sara likes milk with her tea but no sugar; she's sweet enough! **2: a** - 3; **b** - 5; **c** - 6; **d** - 1; **e** - 4; **f** - 2. **3: a** Vera **b** Vera **c** Malvera. It means the first time. **d** Malvera. Olivia is young **e** Vera **f** Malvera. It's asking do you want something to drink?

Language discovery 1: 1: Alkoholaĵoj alcoholic drinks, biero beer, teo tea, kafo coffee, koktelo cocktail **2:** Kun lakto, sen sukero **3:** He could use the -et- suffix to create kuketo biscuit, cookie from kuko cake.

Practice 1: 1: a Mi estas Alano. Mi ne trinkas akvon. **b** Mi preferas teon kun lakto. **c** Mi ŝatas legi mian gazeton. Ĝia nomo estas The Esperanto Times. **d** Kion vi volas fari hodiaŭ? **e** Mi havas fraton kaj fratinon. Mia fratino estas studento. Ŝi studas biologion kaj fizikon en universitato. **f** Ĉu vi konas la viron? Mi ŝatas lin, sed ne scias lian nomon. Ĉu vi kredas, ke li ŝatas min? **g** Ili ne volas iri al la muzeo kun mi, do mi devas iri sen ili. **h** Mi ne memoras ŝian nomon, sed mi renkontis ŝin en la loka klubo. Ŝi ne volis paroli kun mi. Mi pensas, ke ŝi estas malafabla kaj mi ne ŝatas ŝin. **2: a** Mi estas knabo kaj ŝi estas knabino **b** Mi studas sciencon **c** Mi loĝas en Skotlando kaj li loĝas en Francio **d** Mi ŝatas trinki teon, sed mi ne ŝatas trinki kafon **e** Li estas mia amiko. Li havas fratinon. Ŝia nomo estas Matilda. **f** Mi tre ŝatas (/ŝategas) Davidon. Estas amuze paroli kun li. **g** Mia patrino estas tre bona kuiristino. Ŝi tre ŝatas baki kukojn … kaj mi tre ŝatas manĝi ilin! **h** Kion vi volas manĝi hodiaŭ? Ĉu vi volas [manĝi] kukon? **i** Kion vi ŝatas trinki? Ĉu bieron? **j** Ĉu vi kredas/opinias, ke li preferas kafon aŭ kukon? Kun aŭ sen lakto?

Vocabulary builder 2: sandviĉo a sandwich; burgero a burger; banano a banana; oranĝo an orange; karoto a carrot; pizoj peas; tomato tomato; brokolo broccoli

Conversation 2: 1: Olivia suggests going out to find something to eat. **2: a** - 5; **b** - 4; **c** - 1; **d** - 2; **e** - 6; **f** - 3

Language discovery 2: 1: Just like vin, Alano and Klara's names are the objects in the sentence estas plezuro renkonti vin, Alanon kaj Klaron it's a pleasure to meet you, Alano and Klara. Since their names readily accept the n-ending (and especially because they appear to use Esperanto forms rather than their real names), it's applied, as it would be to any other noun. **2:** Sara says Mi ne plu vidas Alanon I can't see Alan any more, because ne plu has the effect of meaning no longer, not any more.

Practice 2: 1: a Something funny or amusing **b** A possession, something which you have or own **c** Something useful **d** A stupid or silly thing **e** Something childish **f** Something baked **g** Writing, something written **h** Something which is growing or has grown, a plant

Practice 2: 2: a Mi ne kredas, ke mi volas la brunaĵon **b** Esti malfeliĉa estas teruraĵo **c** Mi kredas, ke ĝi estas segaĵo **d** Mi ne scias la nomon, sed ĝi estas bruaĵo

Reading: 1: Alice could eat the sandwich but only if she orders the cheese one. The other is a chicken salad. **2:** The sandwich option comes with apple juice or orange juice. **3:** The pizza option isn't available for children because it comes with beer or wine.

Listening: 1: The man asked for rice with chicken. **2:** The man asked for vegetables but was hoping the waiter would say that he didn't have any, so he could order some junk food with a clear conscience. **3:** The man had to be on his best behaviour because his doctor would have found out … she was sitting at the table with him!

Listening and speaking:

Phillip:	Saluton kaj bonvenon al la klubo! Mi ne konas vin. Kiel vi nomiĝas?
You:	Ĝuste, mi estas [name]. Mi estas komencanto.
Phillip:	Nu, estas plezuro por mi renkonti vin. Ĉu vi volas ion por trinki? Ni havas kafon.
You:	Mi pardonpetas, sed mi ne ŝatas kafon. Ĉu eble vi havas teon?
Phillip:	Ho, jes, kompreneble. Teon ni havas. Ĉu kun sukero?
You:	Dankon, sed sen sukero. Ĉu vi havas lakton?
Phillip:	Mi kredas, ke jes.
You:	Dankon. Teon kun lakto, sed sen sukero, se tio ne ĝenas vin.
Phillip:	Tio tute ne ĝenas min. Mi iras nun serĉi por vi vian teon.

Test yourself: 1: a butero **b** manĝaĵo **c** pastaĵoj **d** sandviĉo **e** pico **f** ĉokolado **g** suko **h** frukto **i** trinkaĵo **j** rizo **k** pano **l** viando **m** kokaĵo **n** legomo

2:

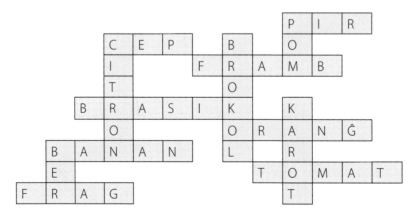

3: a Mi konas Andreon. Li scias kiel fari belegan kukon tre dolĉan. **b** Ĉu vi scias, ĉu la ĉokolado estas bona? **c** Mi ne scias, ĉu mi konas ŝin. Ĉu vi scias, kiel ŝi nomiĝas? **d** Ŝi volas scias, ĉu mi preferas mian teon kun aŭ sen sukero. Vi konas min, do jam scias la ĝustan respondon, ĉu ne?

Unit 5

Libroj en Esperanto: The expression kaj tiel plu and so on is usually cut down to ktp etc. and pronounced like the names of the letters: ko to po.

Vocabulary builder 1: studi literaturon study literature; aŭskulti muzikon listen to music; kulturo culture; interesiĝi pri arto to be interested in art

Conversation 1: 1: Alano has the spare time on his hands to teach Esperanto because he's retired. **2: a** - 2; **b** - 6; **c** - 1; **d** - 5; **e** - 4; **f** - 3

Language discovery 1: 1: The conversation contains liberan tempon free time, legi ne plu estas plezuro por mi reading is no longer a pleasure for me and kion vi studas? what do you study? **2:** Novajn and malnovajn are agreeing with nouns which take the n-ending so they take it too. Afablaj and bonaj aren't tied to anything taking the n-ending. **3:** Sara uses the preposition ĉe to mean at university and at your house. Until now we've deliberately said en in but ĉe is the usual way. You can think of it like French chez; that's where it comes from.

Practice 1: 1: kion alian / bonajn filmojn / miaj amikoj / malbona dancistino / bonajn filmojn / multajn librojn / mia hejmo / mia loka universitato / multan liberan tempon / miajn proprajn studentojn / mia domo / novajn gazetojn, ĵurnalojn / malnovajn librojn / bonaj studentoj / bonajn studentojn **2: a** - 4: bela kato; **b** - 3: maljunaj familianoj; **c** - 1: grandan viron; **d** - 2: afablajn virinojn **3: a** Ŝi havas belan katon **b** La infanoj estas tre junaj **c** Estas bone, spekti novan filmon **d** Mi ŝatas drinki bonan bieron kun mia patro **e** Mia fratino kaj ŝia amikino estas inteligentaj kaj ĉarmaj **f** Mi estas feliĉa kiam mi aĉetas novajn librojn kaj havas liberan tempon por legi ilin **4: a** Mia patrino estas bona kuiristino **b** Ŝi ŝatas legi amuzajn librojn kaj legas ilin ofte **c** Mi kaj mia fratino havas multajn afablajn geamikojn **d** Ĉu vi kredas, ke mi estas bela?

Vocabulary builder 2: baki belajn kukojn to bake beautiful cakes; programi to program; kolekti malnovajn fotojn collect old photos; fari sporton to do sport; bicikli to cycle, ride a bike

Conversation 2: 1: Ĝejmzo refers to Olivia as la ĉarmulino the charming woman.
2: a malvera, **b** malvera, **c** malvera, **d** vera

Language discovery 2: 1: Sara adds the -in- suffix to underline that she's female. In modern Esperanto people do this less and less often, either because the sex is obvious, or because they consider it irrelevant. **2:** Studema studious, parolema talkative, belulo a handsome person, novulo a newcomer **3:** Ĝejmzo calls him a laboregemulo, from labori + -eg- + -em- + -ul- + o, so somebody who works very hard. **4:** Alano speaks about a plia another new friend. He could have used alia another, too, because there's no scope for misunderstanding. If he's asked for another beer, though, he might have got one more of the same or another type, depending on which word he used.

Practice 2: 1: 1 – l; 2 - e; 3 - h; 4 - a; 5 - g; 6 - d; 7 – b; 8 - f; 9 - c; **2: a** forgesema **b** laborema **c** ridema **d** parolema **3: a** belulo **b** inteligentulino (also inteligentulo; you don't necessarily need to force -in- in) **c** bonkorulino (also belulo; you don't necessarily need to force -in- in) **d** Malsanulo

Reading:1: John indicates that he watches a lot of sport rather than plays it, so changes his description of himself to sportspektema instead. **2:** John says he's a master at burger and chips. **3:** John refers to himself as a joker. **4:** He describes himself as vojaĝema; he likes travelling.

Listening: 1: Bob claims he's been studying a lot. He's not even a student! **2:** Bob claims that he's become a reader. Geoff knows him better than that! **3:** Bob has recently become a grandfather and loves spending time with his grandson, so he hasn't been going to the club so often.

Speaking:

You: Bonan matenon, Geoff. Mi volas/deziras paroli kun vi, se ne ĝenas vin.

You: Mi konas virinon. Ŝia nomo estas Elaine kaj ŝi volas lerni Esperanton. Sed ŝi estas tre timema.

You: Tre bonkora kaj inteligenta. Vi estas helpemulo, Geoff. Ĉu vi povas helpi ŝin?

You: Ŝi ne planas veni, ĉar ŝi ne parolas Esperanton bone. Nu, ŝi ne pensas/kredas, ke ŝi parolas Esperanton bone.

You: Ne, sed mi povas doni al ŝi vian.

Test yourself: 1: a ludi tenison plaĉas al mi (al mi plaĉas ludi tenison, etc.) **b** tre plaĉas al mi aŭskulti la radion (aŭskulti la radion tre plaĉas al mi, etc.) **c** kolekti artaĵojn plaĉegas al ŝi (plaĉegas al ŝin kolekti artaĵojn, etc.) **2: a** sportemulo **b** futbalemulo (or piedpilkemulo) **c** legemulo **3: a** legi librojn **b** ludi futbalon **c** naĝi **d** spekti televidon **e** aŭskulti muzikon **f** spekti filmojn

Unit 6

Esperanto en nombroj: The ordinal numbers end with a because they're adjectives describing o-words. They're formed by adding the a-ending to the ordinary numbers.

Vocabulary builder 1: blanka white; blua blue; koloro colour

Conversation 1: 1: Sara paid £10 for her red phone case. **2: a** 6 **b** 3 **c** 2 **d** 5 **e** 1 **f** 4

Language discovery 1: 1: Olivia asks Kiu estas via telefon-numero? **2:** The numbers are nul, unu, du, tri, kvar, kvin, ses, sep, ok, naŭ. **3:** Using the verb kosti and the question word kiom? how much?, how many? you can ask Kiom (ĝi) kostas?

Practice 1: 1: a 1969 (mil naŭcent sesdek naŭ) **b** 1600 aK (mil sescent antaŭ Kristo) **c** 1776 (mil sepcent sepdek ses) **d** 1066 (mil sesdek ses) **e** 29 (dudek naŭ) **f** 476 (kvarcent sepdek ses) **g** 1492 (mil kvarcent naŭdek du) **h** 1990 (mil naŭcent naŭdek) **i** 753 aK (sepcent kvindek tri antaŭ Kristo) **j** 1789 (mil sepcent okdek naŭ) **k** 1887 (mil okcent okdek ok) **2: a** (De) naŭ al kvin **b** Dek tri tagoj **c** La somero de (mil naŭcent) sepdek naŭ **d** Dek kvar jaroj **e** Dudek kvar horoj **f** Kiam mi estos (will be) sesdek kvar **g** Naŭdek naŭ ruĝaj balonoj **h** Ŝi estas nur deknaŭ-jar(aĝ)a/ŝi havas nur dek naŭ jarojn **3:** The number is 0737 714 0840.

Vocabulary builder 2: salato salad; supo soup; saŭco sauce; deserto dessert; botelo da ruĝa vino a bottle of red wine; glaso da biero a glass of beer; taso da teo a cup of tea

Conversation 2: 1: Olivia doesn't think she'd be good for recommending food because she's a vegetarian. **2: a** Mi konsentas **b** Jes, kompreneble **c** Mi ne certas **d** Mi ne kredas tion **e** Ĝi ne ŝajnas al mi bona **f** Mi ne rekomendas ĝin!

Language discovery 2: 1: Vegetarano a vegetarian, manĝi vegetare to eat vegetarian food **2:** Sara says that her meal is senvianda meatless, doesn't contain meat combining sen and viando **3:** It's the difference between this restaurant ĉi tiu restoracio and that restaurant tiu restoracio.

Practice 2: 1: a Tio estas kafo **b** Mi loĝas tie **c** Tiu virino estas mia patrino **d** Tial mi demandas vin **e** Mi preferas tiun sandviĉon **2: a** Mi loĝas tie, en la granda domo **b** Mi ne scias kiel paroli la francan **c** Mi ne komprenas, kial ŝi estas tiel malbona **d** Mi volas fari tion, sed ne havas la tempon **e** Kiu scias fari tion? **f** Ŝi loĝas tie, kie estas la restoracio **g** Kion vi volas fari morgaŭ? **h** Mi ne ŝatas tiun bieron. Mi preferas ĉi tiun

Reading: 1: It's too late for lunch and too early for dinner, so Alice sticks with drinks. **2:** Alice orders three large glasses of red wine and some bread. **3:** The wine costs £5 each and the bread £2, so Alice's bill is £17.

Writing: Example: "Bob ne povas veni al la restoracio, ĉar li estas malsana. Lia manĝaĵo estas supo, kokaĵo kun pastaĵoj, kaj glaciaĵo. Ho, kaj ankaŭ fromaĝo por deserto, kun taso da kafo. Ĝis poste."

Listening: 1: The winning prize was £1.3 million. **2:** You had four correct numbers so win £150.

Listening and speaking:

Ĵenja:	Do, kion manĝi? Mi estas malsatega. Kion pri vi?
You:	Jes, ankaŭ mi malsategas. Mi volas manĝi multe da manĝaĵo.
Ĵenja:	Por komenci mi pensas pri salato. Ĉu estas same por vi.
You:	Mi estas tro malsata por manĝi nur salaton. Mi preferas panon kaj supon.
Ĵenja:	Bona ideo. Kaj poste? Ĉu rizo kun karea saŭco kaj kokaĵo, eble?
You:	Prefere viando kun terpomoj kaj legomoj.
Ĵenja:	Kaj por deserto? Ĉu frukto? Eble fromaĝo?
You:	La torto ŝajnas bongusta. Eble kun taso da kafo.
Ĵenja:	Kaj litro da vino, ĉu ne?
You:	Mi ŝatas vinon, sed litro estas tro!

Test yourself:

1: Kiom jara (/jaraĝa) vi estas? Kiom da jaroj vi havas?

2: a du **b** dudek **c** dek kvar **d** dudek ok **e** cent naŭdek ok **f** dudek du

3: a glaso da biero **b** du boteloj da biero **c** multe da kuko **d** pli da teo

Review for Units 1-6

1: Example for Lingling: Saluton! Mi estas / nomiĝas Lingling Wang. Mi loĝas en Ŝanhajo, Ĉinio, kie mi ankaŭ iras al la universitato. Mi havas du gepatrojn kaj unu frateton. Mi tre ŝatas legi librojn, kaj mi estas tre dancema, vera dancemulino! **Example for François:** Saluton! Mi estas / nomiĝas François Dufour. Mi loĝas en Parizo, Francio. Mi laboras por Volkswagen en Parizo. Mi havas edzinon kaj unu filon. Miaj hobioj estas kuiri, manĝi bone, kaj trinki vinon.

2: fratino, gefratoj/gepatroj, ĝojas, kuiristino, restoracio, manĝaĵoj, ŝatas, aĉetas, fritojn, facila

3: a Potato soup with fish **b** Yellow Thai curry with beef, Asian vegetables and rice. **c** Pasta with red sauce made from tomatoes and cheese. Only **c** is vegetarian.

4: a malrapida, **b** bierego, **c** pens(em)ulo, **d** malfrui, **e** malfru(em)ulo, **f** malfru(em)ulino, **g** bieremulo, **h** malnecesa, **i** malnecesaĵo, **j** malbelaĵo, **k** geonkloj

5: a dek sep, **b** dudek tri, **c** naŭdek naŭ, **d** cent sesdek kvar, **e** ducent kvindek ses, **f** mil unu, **g** mil naŭcent okdek kvar **h** dumil kvardek, **i** kvardek kvin mil

6: Tom is the only one who isn't happy. He said 'I don't like newbies. They always crocodile.' 'to crocodile' is to speak your native language when Esperanto would be more appropriate, for example at an Esperanto event.

7: a La koktelo havas interesan koloron **b** Estas malfrue nun **c** La infanoj jam dormas **d** Forta vento blovas kaj pluvas **e** Mi restas hejme kaj manĝas

8: a correct **b** correct **c** instruistoN **d** viN **e** correct **f** ĝiN **g** correct **h** matematikoN

9: a Mi komprenas **b** Mi ne komprenas **c** Bonega ideo! **d** Mi havas problemon **e** Mi estas komencanto **f** Mi ne komprenas vin **g** Jes / Ne / Eble **h** Ĉu vere? **i** Ĉu vi povas helpi min? **j** Vi parolas tro rapide **k** Ĉu vi povas paroli pli malrapide? **l** Ĉu vi povas ripeti tion? **m** Ĉu vi scias? **n** Mi scias **o** Poste **p** Mi ne havas tempon nun **q** Ĝis poste!

Unit 7

Esperanto ĉirkaŭ la mondo: We wrote por la unua fojo as unuafoje.

Vocabulary builder 1: merkredo Wednesday, sabato Saturday

Conversation 1: 1: Anna said je la deka without any other context, because she didn't anticipate any confusion. Olivia, however, doesn't use the 24-hour clock and so assumed the wrong 10 o'clock. **2: a** - 2; **b** - 4; **c** - 11; **d** - 7; **e** - 1; **f** - 12; **g** - 10; **h** - 9; **i** - 6; **j** - 3; **k** - 8; **l** - 5. **3: a** Anna havas fratinon, kiu ne lernas Esperanton **b** La geonkloj vizitos Annan posttagmeze **c** Olivia havos libertempon en la semajno **d** Olivia volas scii kion Anna faros vendredon **e** La geamikoj de Olivia manĝos kun ŝi en la vespero

Language discovery 1: 1: The os-ending on verbs indicates that we're talking about the future. **2:** Anna and Olivia take the usual nouns mateno and vespero and give them e-endings: matene, vespere. **3:** En la semajno (in the week); morgaŭ (tomorrow); postmorgaŭ (the day after tomorrow); merkredo (Wednesday); en la mateno (in the morning); en la vespero (in the evening); vespere (in the evening); matene (in the morning); unu tagon (one day); vendredon (on Friday); dum la tago (during the day); dum la tuta tago (all day long); semajnfine (at the weekend); sabaton (on Saturday); tagmezo (noon, lit. day-middle); posttagmeze (in the afternoon); dimanĉe (on Sunday, on Sundays); dimanĉon (on Sunday); sabaton vespere (on Saturday evening)

Vocabulary builder 2: mi vestas min, to brush teeth / hair, to prepare lunch

Practice 1: 1: a Mi estas kontenta, ke mi fratino vizitos min merkredon. **b** Ŝi volas scii, ĉu mi venos lundon aŭ mardon. **c** Mi estas studento nun sed unu tagon mi estos fama kantisto. **d** Se ne pluvos morgaŭ, ni povos ludi tenison. **e** Kiam li scios la respondon, li diros al mi, tiam mi ripetos ĝin al vi. **f** Se vi ne manĝos vian kokaĵon, vi malsatos vespere! **g** Kutime mi preferas manĝi picon, sed ili ne plu havas, do mi manĝos spagetojn, kiam mi iros al la restoracio ĵaŭdon vespere. **2:** lundo, mardo, merkredo, ĵaŭdo, vendredo, sabato, dimanĉo **3: a** Sabaton Sara manĝos kun Olivia en restoracio je la 19:00 **b** Je dimanĉo Sara laboros de la 10:00 ĝis la 16:00 kaj poste studos Esperanton je la 18:00 **c** Lundon Sara iros al universtitato de la 08:00 ĝis la 14:00 kaj poste parolos kun Roberto en la vespero **d** Je mardon Sara iros al la universitato inter la 08:00 kaj la 12:00. Poste ŝi laboros de la 14:00 ĝis la 22:00 **e** Merkredon Sara studos Esperanton kun Roberto vespere

Conversation 2: 1: Mijoŝi needs to catch a bus to get to work. There's one at 06:52 and if he misses it, he'll be late. **2: a** - 4; **b** - 5; **c** - 2; **d** - 1; **e** - 6; **f** - 3 **3: a** - 4; **b** - 6; **c** - 1; **d** - 3; **e** - 2; **f** - 5

Language discovery 2: 1: estas ĉi tie nur la dudeka kvardek kvin (20:45), mi ĉiam enlitiĝas je la dudekunua (21:00), Kial ne enlitiĝi je la dudekunua kaj duono (21:30)?, mi vekiĝas je la kvina ĉiutage (05:00), Kial ne enlitiĝi je la dudekunua kaj duono (21:30), je la dudekunua kaj tri kvaronoj (21:45), aŭ io tia?, ellitiĝas je la kvina kaj kvin (05:05), Je la kvina kaj dek mi (05:10) kaj la hundo ludas dum kvin minutoj, kaj je la kvarono (05:15) mi donas al ĝi ĝian matenmanĝon, ĉar je la duono (05:30) mi ekzercas min dum kvarona horo (kvaronhoro), je la kvina kvardek kvin (05:45) mi duŝas min, Je la sesa (06:00) mi vestas min, je la sesa kaj dek (06:10) mi matenmanĝas, kiam ĝi alvenas je la sesa kaj kvindek du (06:52), La sekva ne venas ĝis la sepa kaj dudek du (07:22) **2:** A half is duono (du-on-o); a quarter is kvarono (kvar-on-o). **3:** Mijoŝi says mi ekzercas min dum kvarona horo.

Practice 2: 1: a Mi vidos vin je sabato, Charlie! **b** Sabato estas la plej bona tago en la semajno, ĉar mi ne devas labori **c** Mi ne povas vidi vin nun, sed mi ja povos veni sabaton **d** Unu tagon mi tute bone povos paroli Esperanton senprobleme **e** Mi preferas vojaĝi en somero kaj ne dum la vintro **f** Mi lacegas, ĉar mi devis studi la tutan tagon **g** Estas ja malplaĉe studi dum la tuta tago, ĉu ne? **h** Mi renkontis ŝin por la unua fojo unu tagon antaŭ ol mi renkontis lin **2: a** la deka (/dekdua) **b** la dudeka kaj duono **c** la dua (/dekkvara) kaj tri kvaronoj (/kaj kvardek kvin) **d** la sesa (/dekoka) kaj kvarono (/kaj dek kvin) **e** la oka (/dudeka) kaj dudek **f** la dekunua (dudektria) kaj tridek kvin

Reading: 1: La Universala Kongreso okazos inter la 22a kaj la 29a de julio **2:** La Internacia Junulara Kongreso okazos de la 30a de julio ĝis la 6a de aŭgusto **3:** La Internacia Junulara Semajno komenciĝos je la 12a de aŭgusto **4:** Somera Esperanto-Studado finiĝos je la 15a de julio **5:** La Junulara E-Semajno komenciĝos je la 27a de decembro kaj finiĝos je la 3a de januaro

Listening: They're going to meet on Saturday evening at 9.

Listening and speaking:

Amiko: Saluton! Kiel vi fartas?

You: Bone dankon. Kaj vi?

Amiko: Mi fartas tre bone, dankon! Ĉu vi havas libertempon? Mi deziras paroli kun vi.

You: Jes, mi havas libertempon. Kion ni faros?

Amiko: Manĝi kune? Ĉu vi estos libera lundon vespere?

You:	Ne, sed mi estos libera mardon vespere.
Amiko:	Ankaŭ mi! Bonege! Ni manĝos kune tiam.
You:	Je kioma horo?
Amiko:	Ĉu estos bone por vi je la oka?
You:	Jes, je la dudekdua estas bone por mi. Mi vidos vin tiam!
Amiko:	Ĝis tiam!

Test yourself: 1: a 9:00am la naŭa (matene) **b** 10:15am la deka kaj kvarono/la deka (kaj) dekkvin **c** 1:55pm la unua (kaj) kvindek-kvin (posttagmeze)/la dektria (kaj) kvindek-kvin **d** 6:03pm la sesa (kaj) tri [vespere]/la dekoka (kaj) tri **e** 11:30pm la sesa (kaj) tri (vespere)/la dekoka (kaj) tri, la dekunua kaj duono/la dekunua (kaj) tridek (vespere/nokte)/la dektria kaj duono/la dektria (kaj) tridek **2: a** vespere **b** lundo **c** semajnfino **d** libertempo **e** posttagmeze **3:** b a d h c e g f

Unit 8

PIV kaj PMEG: We wrote published in two ways. The first was with publikigi (publik + ig + i), which literally means to make public. We also used eldoni (el + doni), to give out. The conventional word for a publisher is eldonisto and the publishing house eldonejo.

Vocabulary builder 1: inteligenta intelligent; modesta modest; nervoza nervous; trankvila calm

Conversation 1: 1: Sara thinks that there were maybe 20 people at the club. **2: a** - 7; **b** - 4; **c** - 1; **d** - 2; **e** - 6; **f** - 8; **g** - 3; **h** - 5. **3: a** - 3; **b** - 1; **c** - 2

Language discovery 1: 1: The is-ending indicates the past. It's Esperanto's ending to make verbs express the past tense. **2:** The three words have the e-ending because they're adverbs. They translate as secretly, obviously and perfectly. **3:** It's not possible to apply the endings to the start of the other sentence because the first sentence requires something plural and which will take an n-ending, whereas the second cannot have an n-ending because it follows the preposition kun.

Practice 1: 1: a George Washington estis prezidento de Usono **b** Mi vizitis mian patrinon antaŭhieraŭ, sed ŝi jam foriris do mi ne vidis ŝin **c** Mi ne memoras kiam mi unue aŭdis pri Esperanto, sed mi komencis lerni ĝin antaŭ ses monatoj **d** Kiam mi estis juna mi loĝis en Italio. Mi esperas viziti Italion en la somero **e** Nelson Mandela estis bonega homo. Mi esperas, ke kiam mi estos pli maljuna ankaŭ mi estos bona homo kiel li. **2: a** - 2: Mi loĝas en Londono nun, sed kiam mi estis infano mi loĝis en Germanio. **b** - 4: Hodiaŭ estas mardo. Antaŭhieraŭ estis dimanĉo. **c** - 6: Antaŭ du mil jaroj vivis Jesuo Kristo. **d** - 1: Antaŭ ol komenci lerni Esperanton mi sensukcese provis lerni la francan. **e** - 8: Mi volis legi mian novan libron, sed mi ne povis, ĉar miaj gepatroj venis viziti min. **f** - 7: Mi antaŭe ne sciis kion diri, sed mia amikino donis al mi bonan ideon ĝustatempe. **g** - 3: Mi unue demandis ŝin kaj poste ŝi diris al mi la veron. **h** - 5: Post kiam mi parolis al li, li petis mian telefon-numeron.

3: a Kiam mi estis infano mi estis aktor(in)o **b** Mia patro estis instruisto sed nun li estas sciencisto **c** Mi konis lin antaŭ ol li estis muzikisto **d** Post manĝi (/Post kiam ni manĝis) en la restoracio ni vizitis miajn gepatrojn **e** Mi adiaŭis lin sed poste mi revidis lin **f** Mi ludis futbalon kaj tenison **g** Kiam ni estis infanoj ni manĝis ĉokoladon la tutan tagon **h** Antaŭ matenmanĝi (/antaŭ ol mi matenmanĝis) mi legis mian gazeton

Vocabulary builder 2: nazo nose; lipoj lips; dentoj teeth; fingro finger

Conversation 2 1: Poor Emiljo fell the day before and now his arm's hurting. Fortunately, he doesn't think he's broken it. **2: a** Neither write nor play. **b** Tomorrow or after tomorrow, so in one or two days' time. **c** The day before yesterday. **d** Sara lives with a student studying dentistry.

Language discovery 2: 1: The day before yesterday. **2:** Because in Esperanto we have to make adjectives agree with their nouns. **3:** Sara says Baldaŭ mi scios, ĉu ŝi kredas mian doloran denton rompita. There's no n-ending on rompita because this is a special case called predicate agreement, which is explained in the grammar section.

Practice 2: 1: a La plej bona biero estas senpaga biero! **b** Mi memoras, ke la maljuna virino preferas trinki varman teon kun bongusta kuko. **c** Mi rompis miajn fingrojn kiam mi estis juna knabo. **d** Mia brako kaj mia piedo estas doloraj. **e** Miaj brako kaj piedo estas rompitaj. **f** Doloras miaj eta piedfingro kaj nazo. **g** Liaj okuloj estas strangaj; unu estas blua kaj la alia verda. **h** Mi vidis liajn strangajn okulojn; mi preferas la bluan. **i** Mia pli juna frato demandis mian etan fratinon. **j** La nova ideo estas bona, sed mi preferas la antaŭan. **2: a** Mia piedo treege doloras ekde hieraŭ **b** Vi konas mian fratinon jam dum sep jaroj, ĉu ne? **c** Mia brako doloris dum la tuta semajno, sed nun ĉio estas en ordo **d** Mi apenaŭ povas paroli, ĉar mi jam parolas dum preskaŭ du horoj sen trinki akvon! **e** Mi atendis vin dum longa tempo, sed decidis iri sen vi, ĉar vi ne venis **f** Ŝi loĝis en Italio, kiam ŝi estis juna, sed nun ŝi loĝas en Londono dum ses jaroj **g** Li komencis studi la latinan, kiam li estis 18-jara, do li studas ĝin jam dum dek jaroj

Reading: 1: Sara thinks she's making progress at Esperanto **2:** Sara doesn't find pronouncing the letter r easy. **3:** Sara says that her favourite part of the meeting was being offered cake all the time by a man.

Listening and speaking:

Amiko:	Ĉu via kafo estas bongusta?
You:	Jes, dankon, ĝi ja estas bongusta.
Amiko:	Do, vi iris al Esperanto-klubo, ĉu ne?
You:	Ĝuste. Mi tre ĝuis esti tie.
Amiko:	Bone. Do, kiaj estis la homoj?
You:	Ili estis afablaj kaj amikaj.
Amiko:	Kion vi faris?
You:	Ni parolis en Esperanto!
Amiko:	Ĉu vere? Ĉu tio estis malfacila por vi?
You:	Jes, antaŭe tio estis malfacila, sed poste tio estis pli facila.
Amiko:	Do, ĉu vi iros denove?
You:	Jes, mi iros la sekvan fojon ĉar mi ĝuis esti tie kaj la homoj estis afablaj.

Test yourself: 1: a - 4; **b** - 8; **c** - 6; **d** - 2; **e** - 10; **f** - 1; **g** - 13; **h** - 7; **i** - 14; **j** - 12; **k** - 9; **l** - 5; **m** - 11; **n** - 3 **2: a** Hodiaŭ mia kapo ege doloras. **b** Ĝi jam doloris hieraŭ, do mi ne povas labori dum du tagoj. **c** Tamen hieraŭ vespere mi sentis min pli bone, do mi iris al festo. **d** Ĉe la festo mi drinkis multe. **e** Mi estas malsana ekde hieraŭ. **f** Mi esperas ke morgaŭ mi sentos min pli bone, ĉar morgaŭ estos sabato. **3: a** Honesta (+), **b** avara (-), **c** fidela (+), **d** brila (+), **e** freneza (-), **f** amuza (+), **g** malmodesta (-)

Unit 9

Aligatorejo: We created lingvemulo language enthusiast from lingvo + -em- + -ul- + o, lokulo a native/local from loko + -ul- + o, and plurlingvuloj someone who speaks several languages from plur- + lingvo + -ul- + oj.

Vocabulary builder 1: la japana Japanese, la araba Arabic, mi iam lernis la germanan I once learned German, mi parolas la italan iomete I speak a little Italian

Conversation 1: 1: Sara says that she's never heard a **fremda akĉento** *foreign accent* in Esperanto before. Although she has friends from other countries, their 'talking' online has always been the typed variety. **2: a** - 4; **b** - 5; **c** - 9; **d** - 2; **e** - 7; **f** - 10; **g** - 1; **h** - 6; **i** - 3; **j** - 8 **3: a** - 4; **b** - 1; **c** - 6; **d** - 2; **e** - 3; **f** - 5

Language discovery 1: 1: Fremda akĉento foreign accent, samlandano a person from the same country, alilandano someone from another country. **2:** Sara says Dankon, ke vi akceptis helpi min lerni Esperanton. This is a neater form than the alternative with pro, which would look something like Dankon pro via akcepto helpi min lerni Esperanton, which is fine grammatically but rather heavy. **3:** Sara combines tuta and sola into tutsole to make all by myself in one word. **4:** Sara could've said Ĉu vi povas paroli pli malrapide?

Practice 1: 1: There were some very obvious countries in the text: Alĝerio, Tunisio, Maroko, Senegalo, Malio, Togolando, Niĝero, Egiptio, Niĝerio, Svazilando, Zanzibaro. Well done if you got Sud-Afriko (South Africa) and Malavio (Malawi). And we take our hats off if you managed to get Eburbordo; that's Ivory Coast. **2:** The compass points are nordo north, sudo south, oriento east, and okcidento west. **3: a** ruso, rusa **b** dano, dana **c** meksikano, meksika **d** islandano, islanda **e** kroato, kroata **f** aŭstraliano, aŭstralia **g** japano, japana **h** gvatemalano, gvatemala **i** skoto, skota **j** kanadano, kanada **k** novzelandano, novzelanda **l** polo, pola

Conversation 2: 1: Kimiko's colleagues always needlessly use the lift when it's working. If they're making use of it all the time to go up a single flight, it won't necessarily be there for her when she needs it! **2: a** - 3; **b** - 8; **c** - 1; **d** - 6; **e** - 4; **f** - 5; **g** - 2; **h** - 7

Vocabulary builder 2: partatempa part-time, oficejo office

Language discovery 2: 1: We use work to mean different things in English. There's the sense which first comes to mind of working at a job. But don't forget that we use the word to mean operating successfully, such as those infuriating moments when your car won't start, even when the key's in. Esperanto uses labori for the first meaning, and funkcii for the second. **2:** Kimiko's expression for not far away from looks very much like the English one: ne longe for de. For is away, and you've seen it in foriri to go away. **3:** A set of hours, or a timetable as we would call it, is simply horaro, horo + ar + o. By reversing that process you can easily work out that a ŝtupo is a step.

Practice 2: 1: a amikaro **b** dentaro **c** kukaro **d** klubano **e** hararo (We can't use haro because that's only one hair. We could use haroj but hararo is preferred.) **f** familiano **g** familianaro **h** kongresano **i** kongresanaro **j** alilandano **2: a** - 4; **b** - 3; **c** - 8; **d** - 7; **e** - 2; **f** - 1; **g** - 6; **h** - 5; **i** - 10; **j** - 6; **k** - 8; **l** - 11

Reading:

Woke up early	✗
Had a shower	✗
Bought some fruit on the way to university	✓
Had to answer questions from her tutor	✓
Gave a presentation	✗
Had to study	✓
Had to go back home	✓
Worked a shift at her job	✗
Went back to university to study	✓

Listening: 1: Spanish; Spanish **2:** French; French and English **3:** Welsh; English and Welsh **4:** Chinese. He doesn't say which language he speaks. In Esperanto you'd expect him to say la ĉina Chinese. He could specify which variety of Chinese (Mandarin, Cantonese, etc.) if required **5:** American; (American) English **6:** Italian (but lives in the UK); Italian and French (and you would expect English because of where he lives, though he doesn't state it)

Test yourself: 1: We give the male inhabitants, since this would be the customary way of answering the question in Esperanto. You already know how to specify females or both sexes together if necessary. Irlando = irlandano, Francio = franco, Germanio = germano, Japanio = japano, Meksiko = meksikano, Togolando = togolandano, Usono = usonano, Ĉinio = ĉino, Rusio = ruso, Brazilo = brazilano, Nov-Zelando = novzelandano, Aŭstralio = aŭstraliano, Kanado = kanadano **2: a** Bonvolu paroli malrapide! **b** Ĉu vi povas ripeti tion? **c** Ĉu vi povas skribi tion? **d** Kiel diri X en via lingvo? **e** Mi ne komprenas. Ĉu vi parolas Esperanton? **3:** avo grandfather, kareo curry, dentobroso toothbrush

Unit 10

Ĉiujaraj Esperanto-eventoj: Something which takes place every year is a ĉiujara event. If it lasts a week, then its unusemajna.

Conversation 1: 1: Being of the internet generation, Sara comes out with **ho mia dio!** *Oh my god!* **2: a** - 5; **b** - 4; **c** - 12; **d** - 2; **e** - 1; **f** - 9; **g** - 3; **h** - 7; **i** - 10; **j** - 6; **k** - 8; **l** - 11 **3: a** Sara neniam komencis lerni la slovakan **b** Roberto intencas multon (ĉiom) manĝi **c** Sara havas nenion por fari **d** Ĉiuj parolos Esperanton tie **e** Sara havis nenian ideon pri kio okazos **f** Ĉiuj estas bonvenaj ĉe la UK

Language discovery 1: 1: Sara presents the first side of her argument with unuflanke on the one hand and the other with aliflanke on the other. Flanko is a side, both physical and metaphorical. **2:** A reason is kialo or, in other words, the tabelvorto kial made into a noun. **3:** Saluti is to greet and a saluto is a greeting. When you say 'Saluton!' to somebody, you're really wishing or giving them a saluto, which is why there's an n-ending. The same is true with the other exclamations, like dankon (expressing a danko) or bonan matenon (wishing somebody a bona mateno). **4:** Lurking in the conversation are neniu nobody, ĉies everybody's, neniam never, iel somehow, nenies nobody's, and ial for some reason.

Practice 1: 1: a (in no way) eblas, ke mi estos lia edzino. Estas (no kind of) kialo fari tion **b** Mi manĝas (so much) da kuko, ke restis preskaŭ (none) por la aliaj **c** (all kinds of) homoj estas fratoj, eĉ (those), (who) mi ne ŝatas **d** (no matter how) mi provis fari ĝin, mi ne sukcesis **e** Mia mano estas rompita, (that's why / therefore) mi (so) malbone skribas **f** (every) virino estas (somebody's) filino **2: a** Kiam vi pensas vojaĝi al Usono? – Mi ne certas. Iam baldaŭ, eble en somero. **b** Ĉu vi parolas la portugalan? – Mi parolas ĝin iom sed ne multe. **c** Kial via frato ne parolas kun mi? – Ial sed mi ne certas, fakte. **d** Ĉu vi ŝatis la koncerton? – Jes! Ĝi estis tiel bona, ke mi volas iri denove! **e** Kiom da kuko restis? – Ĉiom! Ĝi estis tro malbongusta por manĝi! **f** Kiel vi faros ĝin? – Mi ne scias, sed iel mi sukcesos fari ĝin. **3:** Estis grava tasko por fari. Ĉiu certis, ke faros ĝin Iu. Povus fari ĝin Iu Ajn, sed Neniu faris ĝin. Iu koleris pri tio, ĉar estis la devo de Ĉiu. Ĉiu kredis, ke Iu Ajn povus fari ĝin, sed Neniu eksciis, ke faros ĝin Neniu. Rezulte, Ĉiu plendis pri Iu, kiam Neniu faris tion, kion povus fari Iu Ajn.

Vocabulary builder 2: esti kontenta to be content, malcerta uncertain, ekscitita excited

Conversation 2: 1: Roberto's not stressed because he knows there'll be somebody meeting them at the airport who will point out what they need to do next. **2: a** - 5; **b** - 6; **c** - 1; **d** - 7; **e** - 9; **f** - 2; **g** - 3; **h** - 4; **i** - 10; **j** - 8

Language discovery 2: 1: Kunlabori is to work together; think of collaborate and you'll see that the Esperanto approach isn't a new invention. Kunloĝi kun iu alia means living with somebody else. You could use a simple loĝi but the kun at the beginning gives an idea of it being a bit more of a unit than two people individually going about their lives. Kuntrinki is, to no surprise, a way of specifying that you're not alone in the activity. **2:** Roberto seems a sociable sort, the type of person who prefers eating in company than on his own. **3:** The restaurant which is there could be la restoracio kiu estas tie, but it seems much quicker just to say la tiea restoracio. Barack Obama isn't the president now but he was at the time being discussed; he was the then president in English and la tiama prezidento in Esperanto. And you already know what kioma horo estas? means. If there's an English equivalent for kioma, we don't know what it is. The how-many-th? Not everything has to be translatable. That's the power of Esperanto; you can create and use words for which you don't even seem to have an equivalent in your own language.

Practice 2: 1: a ekmanĝi **b** amikaro **c** dormado **d** ekdormeti **e** paperaro **f** ekplui **g** ekscii **h** manĝado **i** Esperantistaro **j** hararo **2: a** Mi aĉetis tiom, kiom eblis aĉeti, ĉar mi treege ŝatas ĝin **b** Ŝi ne estas tia, kia vi imagas ŝin. Ŝi fakte estas tre afabla **c** Mi faris ĝin tiel, kiel vi diris, sed ĝi ne funkcias **d** Mi ĝis nun ne komprenas tion, kion vi celas. Bonvolu diri alivorte **e** Jen iu, kiu alvenas ĝuste nun **f** Jen iu, kiun mi konas

Reading: b (best) - c - d - a (worst)

Listening: Georgo is horrified at the thought of going to Japan because he doesn't like fish at all but believes that that's all that will be on offer in Japan. It must be a severe dislike because as soon as the reality is pointed out, Georgo immediately decides to sign up.

Listening and speaking:

Amiko: Kaj post tiam ni iris al alia hotelo. Sed ankaŭ ĉi tiun ni ne ŝatis. Ĝi estis longe for de la urbo kaj ni ne povis bone vidi dum la vespero kiam ni revenis. Mi vere timis.

You: Kiel timige!

Amiko: Ĝuste! Do ni decidis resti en la hotelo kaj ne iri al aliaj lokoj. Ĉio estis do tre teda.

You: Terure! Kiom tede! (/kiel tede!)

Amiko: Sed ne ĉiam teda, tamen. Ĉu vi scias, kiu ni vidis en la hotelo unu tagon? Tiu kantisto, kiun vi amas!

You: Ho mia dio! Mojose!

Amiko: Kaj ĉu vi vidas? Li skribis mesaĝon por vi en mia libro.

You: Nekredeble!

Test yourself: 1: a thinking, contemplation **b** playing **c** dancing **d** studying **e** to start working **f** to start sleeping, fall asleep **g** to flash, start shining **2: a** koleri **b** kulpa **c** trista **d** streĉita **e** amata **f** konfuzita **g** kontenta **h** memfida **i** superŝutita **j** embarasita **3: a** organizantoj (organizantaro) **b** aliĝilo **c** akceptejo **d** aligatorejo

Unit 11

Pasaporta servo: Instructions, requests, orders and wishes are shown in Esperanto by using the u-ending with verbs, as in serĉu look for, kontaktu contact, and mendu book in the final sentence.

Vocabulary builder 1: taksio taxi, buso bus

Conversation 1: 1: Miro is carrying an Esperanto flag with him, which is how they recognize him. He tells them that the walk to the bus stop won't even take two minutes. **2: a** - 9; **b** - 8; **c** - 7; **d** - 1; **e** - 10; **f** - 5; **g** - 2; **h** - 4; **i** - 3; **j** - 6 **3: a** malĝuste **b** malĝuste **c** ĝuste **d** malĝuste **e** malĝuste **f** ĝuste

Language discovery 1: 1 Sara says rigardu! look! and venu! come on! Note how her instructions take a u-ending. **2** Roberto says ni ne faru tion for we shouldn't do that / let's not do that. **3** The preposition per shows the means by which something is done, equivalent to by / with / using / from in different situations in English.

Practice 1: 1: a - 8; **b** - 5; **c** - 9; **d** - 1; **e** - 7; **f** - 3; **g** - 2; **h** - 10; **i** - 4; **j** - 6 **2: a** Bonvolu veni viziti min, bonvole venu viziti min **b** Bonvolu aĉeti du biletojn, bonvole aĉetu du biletojn! **c** Bonvolu renkonti min ĉe la flughaveno, bonvole renkontu min ĉe la flughaveno **d** Bonvolu ne forgesi vian flugon, bonvole ne forgesu vian flugon! **e** Bonvolu vojaĝi per buso ĝis la stacidomo, bonvole vojaĝu per buso ĝis la stacidomo **f** Bonvolu veturi al la stacidomo por trovi min, bonvole veturu al la stacidomo por trovi min **3: a** doni **b** parolu **c** respondi **d** Bonvolu **e** Bonvole

Vocabulary builder 2: antaŭ / malantaŭ la domo in front of / behind the house; dekstre / maldekstre on the right / on the left; sub la akvo under the water; inter vi kaj mi between you and me

Conversation 2: 1: They need to head to the last bus stop. **2: a** - 11; **b** - 6; **c** - 8; **d** - 12; **e** - 9; **f** - 2; **g** - 1; **h** - 3; **i** - 5; **j** - 4; **k** - 13; **l** - 7; **m** - 10

Language discovery 2: 1: Katarina uses the e-ending to show how she travelled: aviadile (by plane) and trajne (by train). **2:** Esperanto's n-ending can be added to words to indicate motion from one location to another. **3:** You would translate Esperanto's preposition ĉe using several different prepositions in English. It broadly shows that something is in general proximity or located close by something.

Practice 2: 1: a La infanoj kuras en la ĉambro, **b** La infanoj kuras en la ĉambron, **c** La knabino parolas kun la virino en la trajno, **d** La knabo devas iri en la trajnon, **e** Ni iros en la urbon por manĝi morgaŭ, **f** Iru al la vendejo kaj aĉetu fromaĝon, **g** La viro staras tie, apud la monumento, **h** Bonvolu iri tien kaj aĉeti ion por manĝi, **i** En la mondon venis nova sento, **j** La knabino devas meti la ludilon en la skatolon, **k** Revenu hejmen antaŭ la oka!, **l** La viro eniras la ĉambron, **m** Mi vidas la viron tra la pordo **2: a** La knabino eliras el la ĉambro, **b** La trajno foriris, **c** La knabo hejmeniros sabaton, **d** La bona knabo supreniris, **e** Preteriru tiun arbon kaj vi vidos lin, **f** La Luno ĉirkaŭiras la Teron, **g** Atentu, kiam vi transiros la straton, **h** La Tero iras ĉirkaŭ la Suno **3: a** Mi aĉetis ĝin per mono/monbiletoj, **b** Mi veturos tien per buso, **c** Li lernis Esperanton per bonega libro, **d** veturilo, **e** komputilo, **f** flugilo

Reading: 1: Left **2:** Down - he has to go down some stairs **3:** His bus stop

Writing: Mi kaj Roberto sukcese flugis al la flughaveno, kie nin renkontis loka viro, Miroslav. Li rekomendis veturi per taksio, sed ni preferis iri buse. Li do montris al ni la bushaltejon. Ne gravis, ke mi ne parolas la slovakan, ĉar eblis aĉeti bileton per maŝino. Alia homo renkontis nin, post kiam ni eliris el la buso, kaj baldaŭ ni sukcese atingis la kongresejon.

Listening: You end up at the castle.

Speaking: 1: Example answers: Por atingi la cirkon, iru preter la picejon ĝis vi atingos la bushaltejon. Promenu inter la domoj. Kiam vi atingos la monumenton, trairu ĝin kaj vi vidos la cirkon. **2:** Por atingi la artmuzeon, transiru la riveron kaj piediru al la bushaltejo. Iru maldekstren. La artmuzeo estas preter la picejo kaj apud la monumento. Aŭ eblas iri maldekstren preter la lernejon, se vi volas. Marŝu dekstren inter la domoj kaj iru trans la riveron. Vi vidos la artmuzeon maldekstre de la monumento. **3:** Por atingi la restoracion, trairu la monumenton kaj poste iru dekstren. Ĉe la bushaltejo iru maldekstren kaj marŝu preter la kafejon. Transiru la riveron kaj vi vidos la restoracion je via maldekstra flanko.

Test yourself: 1: a Iru! **b** Venu ĉi tien! **c** Ne faru tion! **d** Ne manĝu tion! **e** Estu bona knabo! **2:** Ni vojaĝis al Bratislavo por partopreni la Universalan Kongreson. Kiam ni alvenis al la kongresejo, ni trairis grandan pordon kaj trovis la akceptejon. Ni iris en ĝin kaj ricevis niajn manĝkuponojn ĝustatempe por iri al la manĝejo. Do, ni tuj iris manĝejen! **3: a** ekster **b** sur **c** malantaŭ/post

Unit 12

Literaturo en Esperanto: English uses the word old as opposite of young and new. In Esperanto, of course, these are juna and nova, so their opposites are maljuna and malnova. The New Testament is the Nova Testamento, so the Old Testament has to be the Malnova Testamento.

Vocabulary builder 1: poezio poetry, komikso comic

Conversation 1: 1: Sara wants to get her sister learning Esperanto too, so she's going to buy a beginners' book to try to encourage her. **2: a** - 5; **b** - 3; **c** - 8; **d** - 1; **e** - 7; **f** - 4; **g** - 6; **h** - 2. **3: a** vera **b** malvera – he writes about modern Russia **c** vera **d** vera **e** vera **f** malvera – it's based in the first century

Language discovery 1: 1 Did you find tieaj (adjective), ĉieas (verb) and tien (motion)? **2:** There's no n-ending. Think of the example from Unit 8 about farbi la bluan pordon blanka painting the blue door white. Mi opiniis ĝin (esti) ekscita. **3:** In all three cases the missing verb ending is u because the sentence constructions express a wished-for state.

Practice 1: 1: a Yes **b** Yes **c** No **d** Yes **e** Yes - note that the English could also be They prefer me not to go there **f** No **g** Yes **h** Yes **2: a** Kiam mi estos pli maljuna, mi estos futbalisto **b** La eta knabino volis manĝi ĉokoladon hieraŭ, sed ŝia frato jam ĉiom manĝis, tial ŝi devis manĝi frukton **c** La knabineto koleras nun, ĉar hieraŭ ŝi devis manĝi frukton anstataŭ ĉokolado **d** Ŝi ne volis, ke li manĝu la ĉokladon, sed tion li faris (Could be -as -u -as if you're not following from b and c) **e** Krom futbalo li ankaŭ ŝatas ludi tenison (Accept -is -i if you thought we're talking about the past) **f** Nepras manĝi bone kaj necesas trinki multe da akvo ĉiutage **g** Nepras, ke vi manĝu frukton hodiaŭ anstataŭ ĉokolado. **h** Unu tagon mi iros al la Universala Kongreso, kredu min! **i** Mi ne scias, kiam li revenos. Ciuokaze, mi ne volas, ke li revenu, do ne estas grave, ke li ankoraŭ ne estas ĉi tie **3: a** Mi rekomendas aĉeti novan libron de tiu fama aŭtoro **b** Necesas legi kaj fikcion kaj komiksojn **c** Mi konsilas, ke vi ne legu ĉi tiun libron. La traduko estas malbona **d** Ĉu vi deziras, ke la aŭtoro verku plian en la serio? **e** Diru al li, ke vi preferas, ke li traduku ĝin en Esperanton **f** Ŝi petis, ke mi aĉetu por ŝi la novan poezion, kiun verkis la konata kroata poeto **g** Li proponis, ke mi legu ĉi tiun libron, antaŭ ol spekti la filmon

Vocabulary builder 2: kreditkarto credit card, multekosta expensive

Conversation 2: 1: Members get a discount, so Roberto could have saved some money. **2: a** - 10; **b** - 5; **c** - 1; **d** - 9; **e** - 2; **f** - 3; **g** - 4; **h** - 6; **i** - 7; **j** - 8

Language discovery 2: 1: Johano uses the word po to indicate he's talking about an individual unit and sume for all of them together. **2:** The -er- suffix indicates a small part of a whole made up of the same thing. You can use it to make a neĝero snowflake from neĝo snow, monero coin from mono money, fajrero flame from fajro fire, and so on.

Practice 2: 1: a Krom la manĝaĵo, ĉio estis bonega **b** Mi volis manĝi kokaĵon, sed ili ne havis. Do, anstataŭ kokaĵo mi manĝis porkaĵon **c** Krom The Beatles mi ŝatas ankaŭ The Rolling Stones, The Who … ĉion! **d** Anstataŭ la verdaj ŝi aĉetis la bluajn, ĉar ili kostis nur po £5 **e** Post la rabato la vino kostis po £3 por glaso anstataŭ £5. Bonega rabato! **f** Mi ŝatas ĉiajn legomojn krom pizoj. Ilin mi tute ne ŝatas **g** Mi dankis ilin ĉiujn krom mia frato, ĉar li faris nenion por helpi **h** Krom facila Esperanto estas bela. Mi ĝojas, ke mi decidis lerni ĝin anstataŭ lerni latinon

2:

		Necessary	Normal	Possible
a	Mi kaj mia frato ricevis po dek pundoj_____		✓	
b	Ŝi ŝatas ĉian ĉinan manĝaĵon, krom ĉi tiu_____			✓
c	Ŝi ricevis promeson anstataŭ mono_____!			✓
d	Anstataŭ ricevi mono_____ ŝi ricevis promeson!	✓		
e	Krom mi_____, ŝi ŝatas mian tutan familion			✓
f	Ili kostas po kvin pundoj_____		✓	
g	Krom kisi mi_____, li ankaŭ kisis ĉiun alian virinon en la urbo!	✓		

Reading: 1: The blurb is full of relative clauses, used to connect two shorter sentences into a longer one. There are instances of kiu and kiun throughout. **2:** We added -um- to Esperanto to create a verb esperantumi, which we've given the u-ending to. **3:** In this case, we'd interpret the word esperantumu to mean something like do stuff with Esperanto.

Listening: 1: The hungry man buys cheese sandwiches. **2:** They cost two euros each. **3:** He buys three. **4:** Because he gets a discount, he only pays five euros.

Listening and speaking:

Librovendisto: Bonan vesperon, sinjoro. Kion mi povas fari por helpi vin?

You: Bonan vesperon. Mi estas legemulo, do mi volas aĉeti novan libron.

Librovendisto: Ho, vi estas legema? Do, vi estas en la ĝusta loko. Kiajn librojn vi preferas legi.

You: Kutime mi legas fikciajn librojn sed hodiaŭ mia patrino petis, ke mi aĉetu por ŝi poezion.

Librovendisto: Do mi rekomendas, ke vi aĉetu por ŝi ĉi tiun. Ĝi estas tute nova kaj la aŭtoro tre bona. Ĉiuj aĉetas ĝin lastatempe kaj ne restas multaj.

You: Bone, mi aĉetos ĝin. Ĉu vi povas rekomendi al mi bonan misteran romanon?

Librovendisto: Misteran romanon ne, sed mi konsilas ĉi tiun krimromanon.

You: Kiom (ĝi) kostas?

Librovendisto: Por vi nur 8 pundojn. Kaj la poezia libro por via patrino kostas 10 pundojn, do 18 pundojn sume. Mi preferas, ke vi pagu per monbiletoj, se vi havas.

You: Mi bedaŭras, mi havas nur kreditkarton.

Librovendisto: Dankon. Jen viaj libroj. Agrablan tagon!

Test yourself:

1: Antaŭhieraŭ mi vizitis Petron. Li ne estis hejme, sed lia edzino diris, ke mi atendu, ĉar li nur iris ekzerci sin. Mi ne sciis kion mi faru dum atendado, do mi proponis, ke ni babilu iomete. Feliĉe Petro revenis antaŭ ol ni ne plu havis temojn. **2: a** - 4; **b** - 1; **c** - 7; **d** - 2; **e** - 6; **f** - 3; **g** - 8; **h** - 5 **3: a** Mi proponas, ke vi provu ĉi tiun ĉokoladon **b** Mi tiom deziras, ke li estu mia edzo! **c** Mi opinias, ke vi vojaĝu al Francio unue **d** Mi konsilas, ke vi respondu poste, sed ne nun **e** Mi vere rekomendas, ke vi aĉetu lian novan libron

Review for Units 7–12

1: 'Mi estis la cent-tridek-unua el pli ol dudek mil partoprenantoj!' - 'Mojose! Gratulon, Sara!'

2: Check Unit 7 for vocabulary and an example text.

3: kredos, parolis, estis, ekaŭdis, diris, partoprenos, demandis, okazos, sciis, povas, diris

4: Double-check whether you added the -j endings everywhere. **a** La verdaj bananoj **b** La misteraj rusoj **c** La danĝera somero **d** La frenezaj kuracistoj (doktoroj)

5: a amikaro, **b** amikarano, **c** kuntrinki, **d** Italujo, **e** kvinonoj, **f** manĝiloj / manĝilaro, **g** skribadi, **h** ekaŭdi

6: ien ajn, al iu ajn, iam ajn

7:

Lando	Loĝantoj	Adjektivo	Lingvo
Francio (Francujo)	francoj	franca	la franca
Germanio (Germanujo)	germanoj	germana	la germana
Anglio (Anglujo)	angloj	angla	la angla
Italio (Italujo)	italoj	itala	la itala
Hispanio (Hispanujo)	hispanoj	hispana	la hispana
Ĉinio (Ĉinujo)	ĉinoj	ĉina	la ĉina
Japanio (Japanujo)	japanoj	japana	la japana
Kanado	kanadanoj	kanada	la (kanada) angla/franca
Usono	usonanoj	usona	la (usona) angla
Irlando	irlandanoj	irlanda	la irlanda, la (irlanda) angla

8: Across: 4 ekzemplo, **7** traduko, **8** doloras **Down: 1** posteno, **2** mensogas, **3** denaska, **5** prelego, **6** pagis, **8** dubu

9: a Mojose! **b** Ĉi tio bongustas. **c** Aĉe! **d** Helpu min! **e** Bonvolu montri al mi. **f** Po 10€, sume 50€. **g** Ĉu vere? Tio estis antaŭ kvin jaroj! **h** Nekredeble! **i** Eblas. **j** Vi pravas.

Unit 13

Internaciaj kontaktoj per Esperanto: A century is a jarcento, the words jaro year and cent one hundred put together. A decade follows this same pattern; it's a jardeko. We expressed people with other languages in one word as alilingvuloj.

Vocabulary builder 1: estimataj gesinjoroj Dear ladies and gentlemen

Conversation 1: 1: Sara bought two normal stamps, hoping that they would be enough to get the postcard abroad. **2: a** - 7; **b** - 5; **c** - 1; **d** - 6; **e** - 8; **f** - 10; **g** - 9; **h** - 4; **i** - 3; **j** - 2 **3: a** Biero ne kostas multe da mono en Slovakio **b** Erika estas bela **c** Sara estas feliĉa, ke ŝi ĉeestas la Universalan Kongreson **d** La vetero en Bratislavo kaj Britio ne estas la sama **e** Sara pensis antaŭe, ke Bratislavo estas granda urbo **f** Roberto aĉetis librojn en Francio **g** Roberto drinkas dum la Universala Kongreso **h** Sara kontentas, ke ŝi ne plu estas en Britio

Language discovery 1: 1: Sara writes 'Bratislava estas multe pli bela ol mi pensis! Ĝi estas eble la plej bela urbo, kiun mi iam ajn vizitis.' The first means more beautiful; the second is the most beautiful. **2:** pli bela: more beautiful; malpli granda: less big, smaller; pli amuza: more fun; pli varme: warmer; kostas pli: costs more; pli bonaj: better; malpli kosta: less expensive; mi aĉetis malpli da libroj: I bought fewer books; mi havas malpli da mono: I have less money. **3:** The Esperanto equivalent to English's than in comparisons is ol.

Practice 1: 1: a la plej malfrua **b** malpli malgranda **c** la plej rapida **d** la malplej malĝentila **e** pli bela **f** pli granda **2: a** Rusio estas la plej granda lando en la mondo **b** La Suno estas pli longe for ol la Luno **c** Pli da homoj loĝas en Ĉinio ol en Luksemburgo **d** La plej frua esperantisto estis Ludoviko Zamenhof **e** La avo estas malpli juna ol la nepo **f** Kanado estas malpli granda ol Rusio, sed pli granda ol Britio **g** La Luno estas malpli longe for ol la Suno **h** Mia edzino estas la plej bela kaj afabla virino en la tuta mondo, tial mi amas ŝin tiom multe **i** La malplej maljuna el la kvin infanoj Jackson estis Michael **j** La oka vespere estas malpli frua horo ol la oka matene, sed pli frua ol la naŭa vespere **3:** You'll have to grade this for yourselves. By this stage, we're confident you'll get the answers correct.

Vocabulary builder 2: parko park, vendejo / butiko shop, superbazaro supermarket, lernejo school, banko bank

Conversation 2: 1: Sara went out to buy sunglasses. She never got round to getting them, so she's going to make sure she does before heading back. **2: a** - 9; **b** - 4; **c** - 10; **d** - 2; **e** - 1; **f** - 3; **g** - 8; **h** - 6; **i** - 7; **j** - 5

Language discovery 2: 1: The word for police officer policano is -an- added to polico (the police). **2:** The places are built by taking the word which indicates the activity and adding -ej- to it. -ej- indicates the purpose of a place or where an action occurs. **3:** Even though Sara doesn't know the word for cinema, she can describe it in one word, thanks to the -ej- suffix: filmspektejo (= loko por spekti filmojn). **4:** Roberto uses the formulation Vi iris aliloken senpense?! Notice how he's used the n-ending to indicate motion.

Practice 2: 1: a dormejo **b** manĝejo **c** legejo **d** duŝejo **e** kuirejo **f** kunvenejo **g** plendejo **h** malagrablulejo **2: a** Mi legis en la ĵurnalo, ke pluvos posttagmeze **b** Mi opiniis, ke la vetero estos pli bona morgaŭ **c** Mi intencis aĉeti sandviĉon por tagmanĝo **d** Mi kredis, ke Sara estos la unua, kiu revenos hejmen **e** Mi sciis, ke vi faros vian laboron **f** Mi promesis, ke mi ne tro drinkis **g** Mi esperis, ke mia frato ne forgesos viziti nian patrinon **h** Mi supozis, ke homoj en Afriko estas malpli riĉaj ol en Usono

Reading: 1: 1: Petro thinks that physics is the most important science. **2:** Tomaso says that physics isn't as important as biology. **3:** Tomaso thinks that physics is less important than chemistry.

Listening: The speaker is very shy and doesn't like making the first move in person, so prefers to use the internet to meet people.

Listening and speaking:

You: La manĝaĵoj estis ankoraŭ pli bonaj ol en Parizo.

You: La homoj tie estas/estis la plej afablaj en la mondo.

You: Estis multe pli varme tie ol ĉi tie.

You: Eblis aĉeti pli da biero kaj vino ol ni kapablis drinki/trinki.

You: Ni volis resti multe pli longe.

Test yourself:

1: Nigra estas malpli hela ol blanka. Blanka estas la malplej malhela koloro el ĉiuj. **2:** Junuloj iras al lernejo por lerni. Dum la lunĉpaŭzo ili iras al la manĝejo por manĝi. Posttagmeze ili rajtas ludi tablotenison en la ludejo aŭ fari sporton en la sportejo. **3:** Kiam mi estis juna, mi kredis, ke mi estos riĉa, kiam mi estos pli maljuna. Sed mi estas maljuna nun kaj estas pli malriĉa ol mi kredis, ke mi estos, kiam mi estis juna.

Unit 14

Lingvo por ĉion esprimi: The Esperanto word for actually as in in fact, in reality is efektive. The word mem means self: mi faris mem la laboron I did the work myself.

Vocabulary builder 1: konfuzita confused, ĵaluza jealous

Conversation 1: 1: Sara has been stressed recently so came to relax rather than party. **2: a** - 8; **b** - 4; **c** - 6; **d** - 1; **e** - 5; **f** - 10; **g** - 9; **h** - 2; **i** - 3; **j** - 7 **3: a** Leonardo decidis paroli kun Sara, ĉar li vidis neniun kun ŝi **b** Leonardo ne havas sufiĉan memfidon por fari karaokeon **c** Leonardo proponis, ke ili iru al kvieta loko **d** Sara konsentas, ke estus bona ideo iri al loko malpli brua **e** Sara miskomprenis, kion celis Leonardo **f** Sara ŝatas la muzikon, sed ne la bruon

Language discovery 1: 1: Leonardo invites Sara to go aliloken to another place with him. **2:** The us-ending is something called a conditional and is for imagined situations which might be the consequence of some course of action: If I had enough money, I would give up work, for example. **3:** Sola means alone, lonely, on one's own. Leonardo meant that Sara was alone, feeling lonely. Sara interpreted it as being on her own. She agreed that she was sola because nobody else was there; but it wasn't a confession that she was feeling lonely.

Practice 1: 1: a - 3; **b** - 4; **c** - 5; **d** - 6; **e** - 1; **f** - 2

2: a Mi dubas, ĉu ŝi venos, sed se ŝi ja venus, mi estus la plej feliĉa viro en la mondo **b** Mi ne scias, ĉu estas bona tiu nova filmo. Mi legos iom pri ĝi kaj se la raportoj estas bonaj, ni iros spekti ĝin. (It's not unlikely for a film to have good reviews, so he's not talking particularly hypothetically. He's just going to check to confirm.) **c** Se mi scius, ke Esperanto estas tiel amuza, mi eklernus ĝin multe pli frue! **d** Mi diris, ke se ne pluvos posttagmeze, mi kaj la knaboj ludos futbalon ekstere **e** Ne, kompreneble ŝi ne kantos. Ĉu vi povus imagi, kio okazus? Se ŝi kantus, ĉiuj forirus kaj neniam plu revenus **f** Se mi povus helpi lin, mi ja farus, sed mi ne povis, do ne faris.

3: a ĉagrenita **b** ĵaluza **c** malfeliĉa / trista **d** enamiĝinta **e** konfuzita **f** kulpa **g** embarasita **h** scivolema

Vocabulary builder 2: ami to love, fianĉino fiancée (female), koramikino girlfriend

Conversation 2: 1: This will be the first time that Leonardo tries drinking tea. **2: a** - 10; **b** - 5; **c** - 1; **d** - 11; **e** - 8; **f** - 2; **g** - 3; **h** - 4; **i** - 6; **j** - 9; **k** - 7

Language discovery 2: 1: Sara uses -end- and applies it to trinki and pagi with an a-ending to describe the thing being talked about: trinkenda must be drunk and pagenda must be paid for. **2:** Sara uses -ind- with atendi to ask whether the tea was atendinda worth waiting for.

Practice 2: 1: a ĵurnalaĉo **b** pagenda **c** farinda **d** farindaĵo **e** fifama **f** ridinda **g** ridindaĵo **h** ridindulo **i** infanaĉo **j** solvenda **k** solvendaĵo **l** fivorto **m** vizitindaĵo **n** vizitindulo **o** pagendaĵo **2: a** gajnus not gajnis. It's an easy mistake to make because in English we use past forms. **b** telefonos not telefonas. If you're talking about the future in Esperanto, use OS. English is unusual in these constructions in that it uses the present in the first part but a future in the second. **c** studus not studos. This is a hypothetical situation. You're not talking about it being likely that you'll go to Japan but what you would do if you did. **d** ŝi ne venos not ŝi ne venus. Remember that there's no time shift in indirect speech. If this hypothesis were feasible, then at the time you'd have known that ŝi ne venos.

Reading: 1: The first man is from Finland (Finlandano, although it should be finnlandano) and the second says that he's a Pole (polo). **2:** The first man says that he wants somebody who is no older than 25 (ne pli maljuna ol 25 jaroj).

Listening: 1: konfuzita; the woman he likes sometimes responds to his messages and sometimes doesn't. He doesn't know whether it's worth contacting her again and thinks she might want him to stop. **2:** scivolema; the speaker is desperate to know what her brother gets up to when he's out and about with his friends. **3:** streĉita; she has far too much to do. She works in the day and studies in the evening, has been sick all week, and has a book due in two days' time. **4:** kuraĝa; the speaker is terrified of mice but can see that one is going to be in trouble if the cat gets it, so is going to try to pick up the mouse to save it.

Test yourself: 1: Mi estas konfuzita. Mia patro promesis min, ke se mi estos bonkonduta kaj laboros diligente, li donos al mi bileton por spekti la futbalon. Mi ne komprenas, ĉar mi ja estis bonkonduta kaj laboris diligente, sed patro ne donis al mi bileton. Se mi scius, ke li rompus la promeson, mi nek estus bonkonduta nek laborus diligente! **2:** Aminda, honesta, fidinda (= trustworthy) and afabla are all positive attributes compared to ĵaluza, aĉa and senkuraĝa (= cowardly) **3:** When somebody says dankon! in Esperanto, the customary response is ne dankinde, which contains -ind-.

Unit 15

Esperantaj kulturaj diferencoj: We created to assume by combining antaŭ and supozi. The Esperanto word for a hug, brakumo, is formed from brako arm and the suffix -um-, which has no defined meaning and is used when no other affix is logical.

Vocabulary builder 1: kisi unu la alian to kiss each other, teni la manojn to hold hands

Conversation 1: 1: Americans tip serving staff as a matter of course; it would be rude in their country if they didn't. However, this can be interpreted in Japan as a pay-off to the waiter for having done his job properly, as though he wouldn't have otherwise. **2: a** - 4; **b** - 8; **c** - 1; **d** - 7; **e** - 2; **f** - 3; **g** - 6; **h** - 5 **3: a** En Grekio oni kapjesas por signifi 'ne' **b** Nepras alveni ĝustahore en Germanio **c** Estas malafable en Usono se oni ne donas dankmonon **d** En Bulgario oni kapskuas por signifi 'jes' **e** Oni klinas sin en Japanio, sed ne tuŝas aliulojn **f** En Ĉilio oni ĉiam alvenas malfrue. Fari alie estus malafable **g** Oni ne staras proksime al aliuloj en Norvegio **h** Oni devas atenti pri la pacgesto en Britio, ĉar ĝi similas al maldeca gesto

Language discovery 1: 1: There are lots of easy-to-find examples in the dialogue. In English we'd tend to say things like 'in Japan people bow a lot', 'they speak French in France' or 'you have to leave a tip in the USA'. Although these structures are all possible in Esperanto, using oni is the most common way to express these things. **2:** Given that Sara was explaining that men in England don't greet each other with a kiss, her explanation that they greet each other buŝe with the mouth to mean verbally was unclear. She corrected it by saying voĉe with the voice. **3:** Sara uses ĉe when expressing 'you don't find that with / among men'.

Practice 1: 1: a sia **b** lia **c** sia - no hint offered because you didn't have ŝia as an option **d** ŝia - remember, you can't use si or sia in the subject **e** sia - you could also rewrite this as Roberto kun sia amiko manĝas picon **f** ŝiaj - kiun is the object of vidis but also the implied subject of paroli **g** siaj - kiun is the implied subject of paroli **h** lin - la reĝino is the implied subject of vesti, so sin would reflect back on her **i** sin - la reĝino is the implied subject of vesti **j** sian - there is a form onia but since oni is a third-person subject, you need to use si here **2: a** En Italio oni manĝas spagetojn tre ofte por sia vespermanĝo **b** Oni povas aĉeti ĉokoladon, sed ne tro ofte, se oni volas resti maldika **c** Estas malfacile scii, ĉu oni respondis ĝuste al la demando, ĝis oni ricevis siajn rezultojn **d** La knaboj bele ludis inter si **e** Se oni faras malbonon, oni devus pardonpeti **f** Se oni faras malbonon, oni devus peti pardonon pro siaj kulpoj **3: a** - 2; **b** - 1; **c** - 5; **d** - 3; **e** - 4

Vocabulary builder 2: kato cat, tigro tiger, porko pig, rato rat, birdo bird, fiŝo fish, serpento snake

Conversation 2: 1: Since people don't keep sheep as pets, Sara thinks they're fine to eat. **2: a** - 10; **b** - 6; **c** - 8; **d** - 9; **e** - 1; **f** - 2; **g** - 4; **h** - 7; **i** - 5; **j** - 3

Language discovery 2: 1: When used with an animal name, -aĵ- indicates the name of the meat. **2:** Sara refers to male chickens as virkokoj, which is the usual way of establishing you mean a male of the species. Because viro means man, Himeko temporarily visualized some sort of half-man, half-chicken creature. 3: Sara gets across that 'I don't mind' by saying al mi ne gravas.

Practice 2: 1: a porkino **b** porkido **c** porkidino **d** geporkoj **e** porkaro **f** porkaĵo **g** porkejo **h** porketo **i** porkaĉo **j** porkidaro **k** porkego **l** porkinego **m** porkinaro **n** porkideto **o** porkidejo **p** porkidaĵo **2: a** diraĵo (a saying) **b** legado (reading) **c** honestaĵo (an honest thing or act) **d** plorado (crying) **e** skribaĵo (writing, handwriting) **f** vestaĵoj (clothes) **g** haveblaĵo (something available) **h** vestado (getting dressed) **i** plendado (complaining) **j** porkaĵo (pork)

k konstruado (building) **l** mirindaĵo (a wonder) **m** kuirado (cooking) **n** legaĵo (something read) **o** demandado (questioning) **p** novaĵo (piece of news) **q** fiŝkaptado (fishing)

Reading: 1: The Statue of Christ the Redeemer in Brazil was built in the 20th century. **2:** The Great Wall of China could be described as a murego.

Listening: One of the friends has just seen the menu and it contains only the one thing that his religion forbids him from eating: pork! It's not the end of the world, though: his friend informs him that the restaurant is famous for its pork products and so has a special menu, which is what they're looking at. But there's a general menu too, which contains chicken, pasta and even salad.

Test yourself: 1: En Anglio, oni parolas la anglan **2:** Viro kaj virino parolas unu al la alia **3:** La knabo manĝas kun sia patro

Unit 16

Esperanta muziko: It would never have been possible is neniam estus eble. Six words required in English, three in Esperanto. We could even have said neniam eblus to bring it down to two. A legata lingvo is a language which is read.

Vocabulary builder 1: melodio melody, harmonio harmony, instrumento instrument

Conversation 1: 1: Lena's hoping that the windows won't get broken. She really doesn't rate this woman's singing highly! **2: a** - 10; **b** - 7; **c** - 11; **d** - 12; **e** - 1; **f** - 4; **g** - 3; **h** - 5; **i** - 8; **j** - 2; **k** - 9; **l** - 6. **3: a** Pro la belega ludado de la muzikistoj, Lena anoncas, ke Esperantujo havas talentulojn **b** Lena pensas iri al sia lito por eviti Ĉun **c** Valentino estis bona komediisto kaj amuzis Saran **d** Roberto ne povas kredi, ke la malbona kantistino kliniĝis poste **e** Lena ne povas kredi, ke la malbona kantistino ne ruĝiĝis poste **f** Sara timis, ke ŝi alvenis tro malfrue **g** Valentino ricevis sian nomon pro sia naskiĝtago **h** Post kiam ŝi ekaŭdis pri li, Sara vere interesiĝis pri Ĉun

Language discovery 1: 1: The following pairs appear in the conversation: komenci / komenciĝi, rompi / rompiĝi, klini / kliniĝi, nomi / nomiĝi, amuzi, amuziĝi, interesi / interesiĝi. No verb containing the -iĝ- suffix can take an object. Only the original forms can. **2:** Lena uses the suffix -iĝ- to turn nervoza into nervoziĝi to get nervous. Roberto uses the same suffix to create gratuliĝi from gratuli. **3:** Lena combines en and lito and adds -iĝ- to create enlitiĝi. Roberto takes the same approach with en and dormo to get endormiĝi.

Practice 1: 1: a malsaniĝi **b** malboniĝi **c** laciĝi **d** blankiĝi **e** fariĝi **f** interesiĝi **g** ellitiĝi **h** ruĝiĝi **i** naskiĝi **j** moviĝi **k** enaviadiliĝi **l** troviĝi **2: a** Mi komencis kanti kiam mi estis nur trijara, do ne estas surprizo, ke mi fariĝis kantisto **b** La kurso komeniĝis frue kaj tial mi devis vekiĝi frue. Mi ne sukcesis (tre malfacile mi vekiĝas), sed mia patrino enĉambriĝis por veki min, do mi finfine alvenis ĝustahore. **c** Mi perdis mian hundon. Ĝi perdiĝis dum ni promenadis en la arbaro. Mi provis trovi ĝin, sed ne sukcesis. Mi havas nenian ideon, kie ĝi nun troviĝas. **d** Mia fratino ne povas veni por manĝi kun ni ĉi-vespere, ĉar ŝi baldaŭ naskos infanon. Evidente ŝi preferas, ke la infano naskiĝu en hospitalo kaj ne en restoracio. **e** Mi enamiĝis al ŝi, kiam mi la unuan fojon ekvidis ŝin. Mi tute ne povas kredi, ke tia belulino konsentis edziniĝi al mi! **f** Ni ne scias ĝuste kiel la mondo komenciĝis aŭ kiel ĝi finiĝos. Sed evidentiĝis, ke la arbaregoj malaperadas tro rapide, ĉar la homaro detruas ilin. Ni esperu, ke la tuta mondo ankaŭ ne detruiĝu!

Vocabulary builder 2: Hiphopo hip hop, rok-muziko rock music, punko punk, klasika muziko classical music

Conversation 2: 1: It wasn't until she was made to sing that Lena had ever tried to before. She had no idea that she could do it! **2: a** - 4; **b** - 7; **c** - 11; **d** - 9; **e** - 10; **f** - 3; **g** - 5; **h** - 1; **i** - 6; **j** - 12; **k** - 2; **l** - 8

Language discovery 2: 1: Via kanto would mean your song. Of course, Sara's talking about a hypothetical song, not one which really exists. In English, we show this with a song of yours. By inverting the word order to kanto via, Sara gave the same nuance. **2:** They both use the suffix -ig- to create ruĝigi to cause to blush and kuraĝigi to encourage. **3:** You'll find the following pairs of verbs in the conversation: timi / timigi, kanti / kantigi, scii / sciigi. The difference between the pairs is that somebody does the first; somebody makes somebody else do the second. **4:** Roberto's slang version of diri is formed from el and buŝo combined with -ig- to create elbuŝigi. Lena takes a similar approach with for and kuri.

Practice 2: 1: a ruĝigi **b** klarigi (from klara clear) **c** paroligi **d** mortigi **e** konstruigi (konstrui is to build, adding -ig- means getting somebody else to konstrui) **f** devigi **g** plibonigi **h** timigi **i** nuligi **j** bruligi **k** ĉesigi **l** neniigi (from nenio nothing) **2: a** manĝigi **b** venigi **c** malfeliĉigi **d** malfeliĉiĝi **e** troviĝi **f** ellitigi **g** edziĝi **h** klarigo **i** kontentiga **j** deviga **k** nomi **l** memorigi

Reading: 1: People can watch films in the evening **2:** People will be learning about Esperanto in the morning **3:** Sport and excursions are part of the afternoon programme

Listening: There's a pop group called La Skaraboj (the Beetles), followed by a rock group called Reĝino (Queen). Last but not least, people can enjoy the MC Martelo's (MC Hammer's) rap. Once the concerts are over, everybody is welcome to the Esperanto Nightclub.

Test yourself:

1: a ruĝiĝi, **b** maljuniĝi, **c** maltrankviliĝi, **d** feliĉiĝi **2: a** paroligi, **b** venigi (to summon in some circumstances), **c** devigi (to obligate, oblige), **d** manĝigi (to feed) **3:** You've used manĝi and havi enough to know that they're followed by n-endings. Dormi and morti don't take objects, so to make this possible you'd need to add -ig- creating dormigi to cause to sleep and mortigi to cause to die, to kill.

Unit 17

La utopia motivo malantaŭ: Ludoviko Zamenhof always used the word hebreo to mean a Jew. Given that judo was in use at the time and reflects the modern Jew rather than the Hebrew from biblical times, some people speculate that this was an unconscious reaction to the times he grew up in, when Jews were victims of pogroms, including some which happened in Warsaw when he lived there and caused him to participate in the early Zionist movement, which he left around the time he published the Unua Libro.

Vocabulary builder 1: filmo film, aktoro, aktorino actor, actress, malfono foreground

Conversation 1: 1: The new person who Lena speaks to thinks he saw her leave around half an hour before. **2: a** - 4; **b** - 8; **c** - 6; **d** - 7; **e** - 9; **f** - 3; **g** - 10; **h** - 2; **i** - 1; **j** - 5 **3: a** M - La ŝerco ne estis sukcesa, ĉar ne estis facile rekoni, pri kiu temis **b** V **c** V **d** M - Roberto ne opinias, ke paroli kun la komencintoj estis utile - demandinte ilin, li daŭre scias nenion **e** M - Novulo diris, ke se Sara revenos poste, li diros al ŝi, ke ŝiaj amikoj serĉas ŝin **f** V

Language discovery 1: 1: Lena means somebody who's a little bit more experienced than a komencanto; she means somebody who komencis lerni Esperanton. **2:** In English these would be adverbs ending in -ing: going away, she said; saying that it wasn't possible to see anything. **3:** It means *she was sitting*. Normally you'd use the simple forms that you already know: *ŝi sidis*.

Practice 1: 1: a Falinta arbo blokas la vojon **b** La pasintan semajnon mi vojaĝis al kaj Londono, kaj Parizo, kaj Romo! **c** La rapide kuranta hundo atingis la pordon **d** Li aŭskultis la radion, trinkante teon **e** Vidinte lin promeni kun alia virino, ŝi malfeliĉiĝis **f** Mi telefonis vin, aĉetonte bileton

2: a - 2; **b** - 3; **c** - 1; **d** - 5; **e** - 6; **f** - 4; **g** - 9; **h** - 7; **i** - 8; **j** - 11; **k** - 12; **l** - 10

Vocabulary builder 2: hororo horror, komedio comedy, tragedio tragedy

Conversation 2: 1: Roberto jokes that Sara should buy some sort of container to keep her purse in. In Esperanto this means creating a word meaning money-container-container. **2: a** - 8; **b** - 4; **c** - 1; **d** - 9; **e** - 2; **f** - 7; **g** - 3; **h** - 5; **i** - 6

Language discovery 2: 1: Lots of people use the word estinteco to mean the past. **2:** The suffix -ec- creates an abstraction, such as the relationship between friend and friendship. Stulteco is stupidity and justeco would be fairness.

Practice 2: 1: a amikeco **b** disrompi **c** florujo **d** infaneco **e** kandelingo **f** disblovi **g** lavujo **h** glavingo **i** vireco **j** akvujo **k** dissendi **l** salujo **m** ofteco **n** glavingujo

Reading: 1: The first film was science fiction. The viewer had been looking forward to it but doesn't seem to have been impressed, commenting that it wasn't as good as hoped for and that the lead actor clearly wasn't familiar with the story. **2:** The second film was a documentary. The viewer is happy to report that it's absolutely appropriate for children.

Listening: 1: The first person really enjoyed the film and wants to watch it a second time. **2:** The second person didn't understand the film and the first realises it's because he hasn't seen the first two in the series. **3:** He suggests that they watch the first two films at his house in the evening.

Test yourself:

1: Mi estis spektinta filmon, kiam … **2:** Mia amiko estas komenconto (komencos lerni Esperanton) **3:** Leginte kaj ĝuinte tiom multe la libron, mi decidis spekti la filmon

Unit 18

Esperanto: estinteco kaj estonteco: We wrote dronigi Esperanton, which should tell you that the verb droni to drown can't take an object and so requires -ig-. So, to say something drowned, you simply use the verb droni: io dronis. We wrote Esperanto kreskos, meaning Esperanto will grow. Since kreski can't take an object, to say to grow something, you'll have to use the suffix -ig-: kreskigi.

Vocabulary builder 1: palaco palace, klasika classical, monumento monument, statuo statue, rivero river

Conversation 1: 1: The UFO Bridge in Bratislava got its name because the café at the top looks like a flying saucer. **2: a** - 6; **b** - 10; **c** - 1; **d** - 9; **e** - 2; **f** - 8; **g** - 3; **h** - 5; **i** - 12; **j** - 4; **k** - 7; **l** - 11. **3: a** V **b** M - La laboro renovigi la prezidantan palacon estis komencigita en 1956 **c** M - La prezidanta palaco estis konstruita en 1760 **d** V **e** La ponto ne estas nomata la Maljuna Ponto. La Malnova Ponto estis konstruita en 1891 **f** M - La prezidanta palaco estas fermita hodiaŭ **g** V **h** Estas malpermesate eniri la Bluan Preĝejon

Language discovery 1: 1: The presidential palace is fermita closed today. Tomorrow it will be malfermita open. **2:** Estos konstruita means will be built. In the text, Miro is talking about a prospective metro station. **3:** One of the first sentences you learned was mi nomiĝas. You could use that here: ĝi nomiĝas la Blua Preĝejo. (You could technically do the opposite for your name: mi estas nomata X. Nobody does, but it's possible.) You could also say oni nomas ĝin la Blue Preĝejo.

Practice 1: 1: a La sendita letero finfine alvenis hodiaŭ **b** La laboro estas farota, sed mi ne scias, kiam mi havos tempon **c** Mia amata kato ne povas eniri **d** Estas sciate, ke la plej bonaj pastaĵoj estas trovataj en Italio **e** Estis decidite konstrui la ponton nur en 1980 **f** Estas konfirmote, ĉu la Universala Kongreso okazos en Stokholmo aŭ en Novjorko **2: a** - 3; **b** - 1; **c** - 2; **d** - 5; **e** - 6; **f** - 4; **g** - 9; **h** - 7; **i** - 8; **j** - 12; **k** - 11; **l** - 10 **3:** Vizitata de milionoj da turistoj ĉiun jaron kaj trifoje elektita la plej bela loko en la tuta mondo, Esperantujo atendas vin! Konata pro sia ĉiama bela vetero, la lando estas trovata sub la plej blua ĉielo iam ajn vidita. Vi kaj via familio estos bonvenigataj de la ridantaj Esperantujanoj. Venu baldaŭ – vi estas ĉiuj atendataj!

Vocabulary builder 2: Revolucio revolution, sendependeco independence

Conversation 2: 1: There's a statue of a French soldier in the main square to acknowledge Napoleon's paying a visit with his soldiers in 1809. **2: a** - 4; **b** - 7; **c** - 1; **d** - 8; **e** - 2; **f** - 10; **g** - 6; **h** - 5; **i** - 3; **j** - 9

Language discovery 2: 1: Miro asks Ĉu vi interesiĝus ekscii pli pri ĝia praa historio? There are lots of nice things to note in there; he uses the us-ending to be polite, correctly inserts -iĝ- into interesi, avoids the mistake that English speakers often make of using en (because we say 'interested in something'), and uses the pra- prefix as an adjective to denote a long time ago. **2:** Recall that oni konstruas ion but if we don't actually mean that the person did the work but simply got somebody else to do it, then we can use the -ig- suffix to relay that. We've got the same thing here, so if you remove the -ig-, you indicate that the person actually did the job of pulling down the walls instead of having somebody else do it: la muroj estis malkonstruitaj de ŝi. **3:** The passive is perfectly reasonable here but if you wanted to express the sentence without using it, you could say oni baldaŭ poste ŝanĝis la nomon denove al Bratislavo or even la nomo baldaŭ poste ŝanĝiĝis denove al Bratislavo.

Practice 2: 1: a 'Roma' estas la praa nomo de la ĉefurbo de la romanoj **b** Gordiano I kaj Gordiano II estris la roman imperion. Tamen ĝi estis estrata de ili dum nur mallonga tempo **c** Oni ĵus estrigis mian ĉefan malamikon kaj mi certas, ke mi estos eksigata de li baldaŭ **d** Mi eksiĝis de mia laborposteno, antaŭ ol mia nova estro povos eksigi min! **2: a** ĉefartikolo

b urbestro **c** prapatroj **d** ĉefministro **e** eksamiko / eks-amiko **f** ĉefstrato **g** praarabaro **3: a** La monto Everesto estas 8848 metrojn alta (je 8848 metroj) **b** La kongresejo estas 300 metrojn for (/ je 300 metroj) **c** La nova restoracio troviĝas 1 kilometron (/ je unu kilometro) distanca de la malnova **d** Mia eta frato estas preskaŭ 2 metrojn alta (/ je du metroj)

Reading: 1: Mudie was an only child (solinfano). **2:** He published The Esperantist monthly (monate). **3:** The person leading the discussions which created the Universala Esperanto-Asocio was a young Swiss man called Hector Hodler, after whom UEA's library is named. As with Mudie, who died aged only 36, Hodler's life was also cut short, by tuberculosis at the age of 32.

Listening: 1: 688 people **2:** 20 different countries. **3:** The only language spoken was Esperanto, of course. One of the postcards at the time bore the message 'interpreters not needed'.

Teach yourself: 1: The regular Esperanto word for a prisoner is kaptito, from kapti to capture **2:** Decidote **3:** Esperanto estas parolata lingvo

Review for Units 13–18

1: Find examples in Unit 13.

2: unua mondmilito, rusa revolucio, dua mondmilito, morto de Hitler, sendependeco de Barato, ĉefministriĝo de Margaret Thatcher, kreiĝo de la eŭro

3: rege-kantisto, kreemon, publikiĝis, dancigaj, pripensitaj, aldonite, kunkantindaj, ekdancigos, mortinta, konservado

4: La libro 'Fajron sentas mi interne' estas mia plej ŝatata Esperanto-libro! Ĝi estas malpli facila ol 'Gerda Malaperis', sed tamen facila, kaj la rakonto estas multe pli interesa. Mi legis ĝin tre rapide kaj poste re-legis ĝin por plibonigi mian vortprovizon en Esperanto. Legante ĝin la duan fojon, mi trovis novajn aferojn, kiujn mi ne estis rimarkinta la unuan fojon. Mi vere ŝatas ĝin multe. Se mi scius (estus scianta) ke ĝi estus tiom bona, mi legus (estus leginta) ĝin antaŭe.

5: a virkato, **b** ignorendulo, **c** farendaĵoj, **d** ekslernejestro, **e** disdoni, **f** nervozigi, **g** pligrandiĝi, **h** beleco, **i** dancebleco / dancigeco, **j** dispecigi

6: Example solution: Homoj, kiuj ne konas unu la alian, kutime nur manpremas, ili ne alie tuŝas unu la alian. Geamikoj tamen povas brakumi unu la alian aŭ interŝanĝi kisetojn.

7: Words in the wordsearch: bakejo, kastelo, lernejo, policejo, preghejo, trotuaro, chefplaco, katedralo, muzeo, ponto, statuo, turo, foiro, kinejo, parko, pordego, trinkejo, vendejo, muro

8: a Mi ne ŝatas la ritmon kaj melodion de ĉi tiu kanto. **b** Ĝi (= la kanto) estas tro laŭta. / Estas tro laŭte. (la etoso) **c** La gitaristo estas aĉega. **d** Mi preferus aŭskulti la alian kantiston. **e** Estus pli kviete aliloke. **f** Mi evitus ĉi tiun koncerton; li kantas aĉe. **g** Pardonu, mi misaŭdis pro la bruo. **h** Mi bele amuziĝas!

Esperanto–English glossary

aĉe *awfully, wretchedly*

aĉeti *to buy, purchase*

aĉetumi *to shop*

aĉulo *bad person*

adiaŭ *goodbye*

adiaŭi *to say goodbye*

afabla *nice, pleasant, affable*

afero *thing*

afiŝo *poster, post*

afranko *postage*

Afriko *Africa*

agi *to act*

agado *activity*

agnoski *to acknowledge, recognize*

aĝo *age*

ajlo *garlic*

ajn *-ever, -soever, any, at all*

ajna *any, any kind of*

aĵo *thing*

akceptejo *reception*

akcepti *to accept*

akcidento *accident*

akĉento *accent (way of speaking)*

akordi *be in agreement, be in tune*

aktorino *actress*

aktoro *actor*

akuzativo *accusative*

akuzi *to accuse*

akvo *water*

al *to*

aldoni *to add*

Alĝerio *Algeria*

alia *other*

alie *otherwise, else*

aligatori *to speak a language which isn't your own in an Esperanto environment*

aligatoro *alligator*

aliĝi *to join*

aliĝilo *registration form*

alilandano *foreigner*

alilanden *to another country*

alirebla *accessible*

aliri *to approach*

alkoholaĵo *alcoholic drink*

almenaŭ *at least*

alta *high, tall*

alveni *to arrive*

alveno *arrival*

amata *loved, beloved*

ambaŭ *both*

amema *loving*

ami *to love*

amike *as a friend (also letter ending)*

amikeco *friendship*

amikino *female friend*

amiko *friend (male)*

aminda *lovable*

amindumi *to court*

amo *love*

amrendevui *to date*

amuza *amusing*

amuzado *fun*

amuze *amusingly, entertainingly*

anasido *duckling*

anaso duck

angla English

Anglio England

ankaŭ also, too

ankoraŭ still, yet

anonci to announce

ansero goose

anstataŭ instead of

antaŭ before, in front of

antaŭbrako forearm

antaŭe previously

antaŭen forwards, onwards

antaŭĝui to look forward to

antaŭhieraŭ day before yesterday

antaŭmendi to pre-order

antaŭmendo pre-order

antaŭpagi to prepay

antaŭtagmeze a.m. (before noon)

anticipe in advance

antikva ancient

antologio anthology

aparta separate, particular

aparte particularly

apenaŭ barely, hardly

aperi to appear

apo app

aprilo April

apud beside, next to

araba Arab, Arabic

araneo spider

aranĝi to arrange

arbaro forest, wood

arbo tree

arkeologio archaeology

armeo army

aro set, pile, heap, group

artaĵo artwork

arto art

asocio association

aspekti to seem, to look, look like

aspekto appearance

atendi to wait, await, expect

atenti to pay attention (to)

atingi to reach

aŭ or

aŭ … aŭ either … or

aŭdi to hear

aŭgusto August

aŭskulti to listen

Aŭstralio Australia

aŭto car

aŭtuno autumn

avara miserly, mean, greedy

avĉjo grandad, grandpa

averti to warn

aviadilo aircraft

avinjo granny

avino grandmother

avo grandfather

azeno donkey

babili to chat

bakejo bakery

baki to bake

baldaŭ soon

baleno whale

banano banana

banko bank

baratano Indian

Barato India

bazaro *market*

bazo *base*

bedaŭri *to be sorry, regret*

bedaŭrinde *unfortunately*

bela *beautiful, pretty*

bele *beautifully*

beleco *beauty*

belega *gorgeous, extremely beautiful*

beleta *cute, pretty*

belulino *beautiful woman*

belulo *handsome man*

bero *berry*

besto *animal*

bezoni *to need*

bicikli *to bicycle, bike*

biciklo *bicycle, bike*

biero *beer*

bildstrio *comic strip*

bileto *ticket*

biletvendilo *ticket machine*

biologio *biology*

birdo *bird*

blanka *white*

blankiĝi *to become pale, whiten*

blovi *to blow*

blua *blue*

bluso *blues*

bofrato *brother-in-law*

bogepatroj *in-laws*

boli *to boil*

Bonan matenon *Good morning*

Bonan nokton *Good night*

Bonan tagon *Good morning/afternoon*

Bonan vesperon *Good evening*

bondeziroj *well wishes*

bondezirojn *best wishes (letter ending)*

bone *well*

bonege *great*

bongusta *tasty, delicious*

bonkonduta *well-behaved*

bonkora *kind, good-hearted*

bonŝanca *lucky*

bonveniga *welcoming*

Bonvenon *Welcome*

bonvolu *please*

bopatrino *mother-in-law*

bopatro *father-in-law*

botelo *bottle*

bovaĵo *beef*

bovo *cow*

brako *arm*

brakumi *to hug*

brakumo *hug*

brasiko *cabbage*

Brazilo *Brazil*

brila *bright, shiny*

brili *to shine*

Britio *Britain*

brito *Brit, Briton*

brokolo *broccoli*

bronzo *bronze*

brosi *to brush*

broso *brush*

brue *noisily*

bruli *to burn (be on fire)*

bruligi *to burn (cause something to burn)*

bruligita *burned*

bruna *brown*

bruo *noise*

brusto *chest*

burgero *burger*

buso *bus*

buŝo *mouth*

butero *butter*

butiko *shop*

butikumi *to go shopping, shop*

celi *to aim*

celo *goal, target*

cent *hundred*

centra *central*

centro *centre*

cepo *onion*

certa *certain, sure*

certe *certainly, surely*

certi *to be sure*

citrono *lemon*

ĉagreno *annoyance*

ĉagrenita *upset*

ĉambro *room*

ĉar *because*

ĉarma *charming*

ĉasi *to hunt*

ĉe *at, in the vicinity, at a person's house*

ĉeesti *to be present*

ĉefa *main, principal*

ĉefministro *prime minister*

ĉefo *chief, boss*

ĉefplaco *main square*

ĉefrolanto *main character*

ĉefurbo *capital city*

ĉemizo *shirt*

ĉerizarbo *cherry tree*

ĉesi *to cease, stop*

ĉesigi *to stop, bring to a stop*

ĉevalejo *stables*

ĉevalo *horse*

ĉi tie *here*

ĉi tiu *this*

ĉi-jare *this year*

ĉi-monate *this month*

ĉi-semajne *this week*

ĉi-vespere *tonight, this evening*

ĉiam *always*

ĉiaokaze *in any case*

ĉiĉeronado *guided tour*

ĉiĉerono *tour guide*

ĉie *everywhere*

ĉies *everyone's*

Ĉilio *Chile*

ĉina *Chinese*

ĉio *everything*

ĉionmanĝanto *omnivore*

ĉipsoj *crisps, chips*

ĉirkaŭ *around*

ĉirkaŭi *to surround*

ĉiu *each, every*

ĉiuj *all*

ĉiujara *annual*

ĉiujare *every year*

ĉiuokaze *in any case*

ĉiutage *every day*

ĉiuvespere *every evening*

ĉokolado *chocolate*

ĉu *(word for making a statement into a question), whether*

ĉu … ĉu *whether … or*

da *of (quantity)*

damne *damn*

damo lady

danci to dance

danĝera dangerous

danĝere dangerously

Danio Denmark

dank' al thanks to

dankemo gratitude

dankinde worthy of thanks

dankmono tip

dankon thank you, thanks

dato date

daŭre continually

daŭri to continue, last

de from, of

dece properly

decembro December

decidi to decide

dek ten

dek du twelve

dek kvar fourteen

dek kvin fifteen

dek mil ten thousand

dek naŭ nineteen

dek ok eighteen

dek sep seventeen

dek ses sixteen

dek tri thirteen

dek unu eleven

deka tenth

dekstra right

dekstre on the right

dekstren to the right, rightwards

delegito delegate

delfeno dolphin

demandaro questionnaire

demandi to ask (a question)

demando question

denaska native

denove again

dentdoloro toothache

dentisto dentist

dento tooth

deprimita depressed

deprimo depression

deserto dessert

detalo detail

detrui to destroy

devi must, to have to

deviga compulsory, obligatory

devigi to compel, to oblige

devo duty, obligation

dezerto desert

deziri to desire

deziro wish

diferenco difference

difino definition

dika thick, fat

diligente diligently

dimanĉo Sunday

dio god

diraĵo saying

diri to say

dise spread about, here and there

disigi to disband, disconnect, separate

disiĝo break-up

diskuri to run about

disrompi to smash

dissendi to send out, broadcast

distanco distance

do so

dokumentfilmo *documentary (film)*

dokumento *document*

dolaroj *dollars*

dolĉaĵo *sweet*

dolori *to ache, hurt*

doloro *ache, pain*

domaĉo *shack, hovel*

domaĝe *regrettably*

Domaĝe *What a pity, What a shame*

domo *house*

doni *to give*

dormĉambro *bedroom*

dormi *to sleep*

dorso *back*

drako *dragon*

dramo *drama*

drinkejo *pub*

droni *to drown*

du *two*

du mil *two thousand*

dua *second*

dubi *to doubt*

dubo *doubt*

ducent *two hundred*

dudek *twenty*

dudek du *twenty-two*

dudek unu *twenty-one*

dufoje *twice*

dum *during, while*

dume *in the meantime, meanwhile*

duobla *double*

duonfrato *half brother*

duono *half*

duopo *pair, couple*

duŝi sin *to take a shower*

ebla *possible*

eblas *it is possible*

eble *maybe, perhaps*

ebli *to be possible*

eblo *possibility*

Eburbordo *Ivory Coast, Côte d'Ivoire*

eĉ *even*

eduki *to educate*

edziĝi *to get married*

edzino *wife*

edzo *husband*

efektive *actually, in fact*

ege *extremely*

Egiptio *Egypt*

ejo *place*

ekbrili *to flash*

ekde *from, since*

ekdormi *to fall asleep*

ekkoleri *to get angry*

ekkoni *to get to know*

ekkrii *to cry out, shout out*

eklerni *to begin learning*

ekrano *screen*

eksa *former, ex-*

ekscii *to learn, realize*

ekscita *exciting*

ekscitita *excited*

ekscito *excitement*

eksedzo *ex-husband*

eksigi *to fire, dismiss*

ekster *outside*

eksterlande *abroad*

ektimi *to begin to fear*

ekvidi *to catch sight of, glimpse*

ekzemple *for example*

ekzemplo *example*

ekzerci sin *to practise*

ekzisti *to exist*

el *from, out of*

elbuŝigi *to come out with (to say something)*

eldoni *to publish*

elefanto *elephant*

elekti *to choose*

elektronika *electronic*

eliri *to go out, exit*

elirejo *exit*

ellitiĝi *to get out of bed*

embarasi *to embarrass*

embarasita *embarrassed*

embaraso *embarrassment*

en *in, into*

en ordo *OK*

ena *inner, inside*

enamiĝi *to fall in love*

enamiĝinta *in love*

endormiĝi *to fall asleep*

ene *inside, internally*

ene de *within*

enhavo *content*

enirejo *entrance*

eniri *to enter, go in*

enirpordo *entrance*

enlitiĝi *to go to bed*

enua *boring*

enui *to be bored*

enuiĝi *to get bored*

enveni *to come in, enter*

envia *envious*

epoko *epoch, period*

eraro *error, mistake*

erinaco *hedgehog*

Esperantujo *Esperantoland*

espereble *hopefully*

esperi *to hope*

espero *hope*

esprimi *to express*

estas *is, am, are*

esti *to be*

estimata *esteemed*

estonteco *future*

estri *to govern, lead*

eta *small, tiny*

etoso *atmosphere*

etulo *little one*

eŭroj *Euros*

Eŭropo *Europe*

evento *event*

evidente *obviously*

eviti *to avoid*

facila *easy*

fajro *fire*

fako *area of expertise, specialty, field*

fakte *actually, in fact*

fakto *fact*

fali *to fall*

faligi *to drop, knock down*

fama *famous, notable*

familiano *family member*

familio *family*

fantasto *fantasy*

farbi *to paint (apply paint to wall, etc.)*

fari *to do, make*

fariĝi *to become*

farti *to fare*

februaro *February*

feliĉa *happy*

fenestro *window*

fermi *to shut*

fero *iron*

festema *in a mood to party*

festi *to celebrate*

festo *celebration, party*

festumi *to party*

Fi! *Shame!*

fia *disgusting, shameful*

fianĉiĝi *to become engaged, get engaged (as a man)*

fianĉiniĝi *to become engaged, get engaged (as a woman)*

fianĉino *fiancée (female)*

fianĉo *fiancé (male)*

fidela *faithful, trusty*

fidinda *trustworthy*

fidomo *house of ill repute*

fifama *infamous, notorious*

fikcia *fictional, fictitious*

fikcio *fiction*

filino *daughter*

filmo *film, movie*

filo *son*

fina *final*

finaĵo *ending, suffix*

financa *financial*

financo *finance*

finfine *finally, at last*

fingro *finger*

fini *to finish*

finiĝi *to finish, come to an end*

finita *finished, completed*

Finnlando *Finland*

finno *Finn*

fino *end*

fiŝaĵo *fish meat*

fiŝkapti *to fish, go fishing*

fiŝo *fish*

fiulo *immoral person*

fivorto *swear word*

fiziko *physics*

flago *flag*

flanko *side*

flava *yellow*

floringo *vase*

flue *fluently*

flughaveno *airport*

flugi *to fly*

flugilo *wing*

flugo *flight*

foiro *fair*

foje *sometimes, on occasion*

fojo *occasion*

folio *leaf, sheet*

fondi *to found, establish*

fondiĝi *to be founded*

fondiĝo *foundation*

fono *background*

fonto *source*

for *away*

foresti *to be absent, be away*

forgesema *forgetful*

forgesi *to forget*

foriri *to go away, leave*

forko *fork*

forkuri *to run away*

forkurigi *to make someone run away*

formiko *ant*

forpreni *to take away, remove*

forta *strong*

foto *photo*

fotokopiilo *photocopier*

fotokopio *copy*

frago *strawberry*

frambo *raspberry*

franca *French*

Francio *France*

franco *French person*

frateco *brotherhood*

fratino *sister*

frato *brother*

frazo *sentence*

fremda *foreign*

fremdulo *foreigner*

freneza *crazy*

fritoj *French fries, chips*

fromaĝo *cheese*

frosti *to freeze*

frue *early*

frukto *fruit*

fulmo *lightning*

fumanto *smoker*

fumi *to smoke*

funkcii *to work (function)*

furora *hit, best-selling*

furorlisto *charts, bestseller list*

futbalisto *football player*

futbalo *football*

galerio *gallery*

gasa akvo *fizzy water, sparkling water*

gaso *gas*

gastiganto *host*

gastigi *to host, accommodate*

gasto *guest*

gazetaro *press, newspapers*

gazeto *magazine, newspaper*

geamikoj *friends*

geavoj *grandparents*

geedzoj *husband and wife, couple*

gefratoj *siblings*

genepoj *grandchildren*

geografio *geography*

gepatroj *parents*

germana *German*

Germanio *Germany*

gesinjoroj *ladies and gentlemen, Mr and Mrs*

gesto *gesture*

geto *ghetto*

glaciaĵo *ice cream*

glaso *glass*

glavingo *sheath, scabbard*

glavo *sword*

gradoj *degrees*

granda *big, large*

grandega *enormous, huge*

gratuli *to congratulate*

gratuliĝi *to receive congratulations*

Gratulon! *Congratulations!*

grava *important*

gravas *it is important*

Grekio *Greece*

gripo *the flu, influenza*

griza *grey*

grupo *group*

gufo *eagle-owl*

gufujo *tea lounge, owlery*

gusto *taste*

Gvatemalo *Guatemala*

gvidi *to guide*

ĝangalo *jungle*

ĝardeno *garden*

ĝenerala *general*

ĝeni *to bother, to irritate*

ĝenro *genre*

ĝentila *polite*

ĝenulo *nuisance, pest*

ĝi *it*

ĝia *its*

ĝirafo *giraffe*

ĝis *until*

Ĝis poste! *See you later!*

Ĝis revido! *See you!*

Ĝis! *Bye!*

ĝoji *to be glad*

ĝojigi *to make glad*

ĝojo *joy*

ĝui *to enjoy*

ĝusta *correct, right*

ĝustatempe *on time, timely, punctually*

ĝuste *correctly, precisely*

hajli *to hail*

hajlo *hail*

haltejo *stop (bus stop, taxi stop)*

halti *to halt (come to a stop)*

hararo *hair (collection, e.g. on the head)*

harmonio *harmony*

haro *hair (one hair)*

havaĵo *property*

havebla *available*

haveno *harbour*

havi *to have*

hazarde *by accident, by chance, at random*

hejma *domestic*

hejmbesto *pet*

hejme *at home*

hejmen *home(wards)*

hejmo *home*

hela *bright*

helpa *helpful*

helpema *helpful*

helpi *to help*

heroino *heroine*

heroo *hero*

hieraŭ *yesterday*

hiphopo *hip-hop*

hispana *Spanish*

Hispanio *Spain*

historio *history, story*

ho *oh*

Ho ve! *Oh no!*

hobio *hobby*

hodiaŭ *today*

homaro *humanity, mankind*

homo *human*

honeste *honestly*

honori *to honour*

honoro *honour*

honti *to be ashamed*

horaro *schedule, timetable*

horo *hour*

hororo *horror*

hospitalo *hospital*

hotelo *hotel*

humoro *humour, mood*

hundejo *kennel*

hundido *puppy*

hundo *dog*

ĥoro *choir*

iam *some time, ever*

iam ajn *any time*

idealisto *idealist*

idealo *ideal*

identigi *to identify*

identigilo *identifier*

idento *identity*

ideo *idea*

idiotismo *idiom*

ie *somewhere*

iel *somehow*

igi *to cause, make*

iĝi *to become*

ili *they*

ilia *their*

ilo *tool*

imagi *to imagine*

imiti *to imitate*

imperiestro *emperor*

imperio *empire*

inda *deserving, worthy*

indiki *to indicate*

indikilo *indicator, marker*

infanaĉo *unpleasant child*

infanaĝo *childhood, infancy*

infaneco *childhood, infancy, childishness*

infano *child*

informejo *inquiry office*

informilo *brochure*

informo *information*

ingo *holder, socket, sheath*

inkluzive de *including*

instrui *to teach*

instruisto *teacher*

instrumento *instrument*

insulto *insult*

inteligenta *intelligent*

intenci *to intend*

intenco *intention*

inter *between, among*

interesa *interesting*

interesiĝi *to be interested in*

intereso *interest*

internacia *international*

interpreti *to interpret*

interpretisto *interpreter*

Interreto *internet*

intertempe *meanwhile*

invadi *to invade*

inviti *to invite*

io *something*

io ajn *anything*

io tia *something like that*

iomete *a little*

Irako *Iraq*

iri *to go*

irlanda *Irish*

irlandano *Irish person*

Irlando *Ireland*

ironia *ironic*

ironie *ironically*

ironio *irony*

islamano *Muslim*

Islando *Iceland*

itala *Italian*

Italio *Italy*

iu *somebody, someone*

iu ajn *anybody, anyone (at all)*

ja *after all, indeed*

jaguaro *jaguar*

jam *already, yet*

jam temp' está *it's already the time*

januaro *January*

japana *Japanese*

Japanio *Japan*

jarcento *century*

jarlibro *yearbook*

jaro *year*

jen *here is / are, look*

jes *yes*

ju pli … des pli *the more … the more*

jubileo *jubilee, anniversary*

judo *Jew*

julio *July*

juna *young*

junio *June*

junularo *youth*

junulo *youth*

justa *just*

ĵaluza *jealous*

ĵaŭdo *Thursday*

ĵazo *jazz*

ĵurnalo *newspaper, journal*

ĵus *just (a moment ago)*

kabei *to leave the Esperanto movement*

kafejo *café*

kafo *coffee*

kaftaso *coffee cup*

kafujo *coffee pot*

kaj *and*

kaj tiel plu (ktp) *and so on, et cetera (etc.)*

kaj … kaj *both … and*

Kalifornio *California*

kanadano *Canadian*

Kanado *Canada*

kanalo *canal, channel*

kandelingo *candle stick*

kandelo *candle*

kanti *to sing*

kantisto *singer*

kanzono *song, ballad, chanson*

kapabla *capable*

kapabli *to be able*

kapdoloro *headache*

kapjesi *to nod (in agreement)*

kapo *head*

kapsiko *pepper*

kapskui *to shake one's head*

kapti *to catch*

kaptito *prisoner, captive*

kara *dear*

karaokeo *karaoke*

kareo *curry*

karoto *carrot*

karto *card*

Kartvelio *Georgia*

kastelo *castle*

katedralo *cathedral*

kategorio *category*

katido *kitten*

kato *cat*

katoliko *Catholic*

ke *that*

kekso *biscuit, cookie*

kelkaj *several*

kelnero *waiter*

kelta *celtic*

Kembriĝo *Cambridge*

kia *what kind of*

kial *why*

kialo *reason*

kiam *when*

kie *where*

kiel *how, as*

kien *where, whither*

kies *whose*

kilogramo *kilo, kilogramme*

kimra *Welsh*

Kimrio *Wales*

kinejo *cinema, movie theatre*

kio *what*

kio alia *what else*

kiom *how many, how much*

kioma horo *what time*

kisi *to kiss*

kiso *kiss*

kiu *who, which*

klarigi *to clarify, explain*

klarigo *explanation*

klasika *classic, classical*

klini sin *to bow*

klubano *club member*

klubo *club*

knabino *girl*

knabo *boy*

koketado *flirting*

koketi *to flirt*

kokaĵo *chicken (meat)*

kokino *hen*

koko *chicken*

koktelo *cocktail*

kolegaro *group of colleagues*

kolego *co-worker, colleague*

kolekti *to collect*

kolekto *collection*

kolera *angry*

koleri *to be angry*

kolo *neck*

kolombo *pigeon, dove*

koloro *colour*

komandanto *commander*

komediisto *comedian*

komedio *comedy*

komencanto *beginner*

komence *at first, in the beginning*

komenci *to begin something, start*

komenciĝi *to begin, start (it is starting)*

komenco *beginning*

komento *comment*

komikso *comic strip, graphic novel*

komo *comma*

kompare *comparatively*

komplika *complex, complicated*

komponi *to compose*

komponisto *composer*

kompreneble *of course*

kompreni *to understand*

komputi *to compute*

komputilo *computer*

komuna *common*

komunista *communist*

konata *known, well-known*

koncerto *concert*

konduti *to behave*

konfirmi *to confirm*

konfirmilo *confirmation letter*

konfirmo *confirmation*

konfuza *confuing*

konfuzita *confused, perplexed*

kongresejo *convention centre*

kongreso *conference*

koni *to know*

konkurso *competition, contest*

konsenti *to agree to, consent*

konsideri *to consider, regard*

konsili *to advise*

konstati *to notice*

konstruaĵo *building*

konstrui *to build*

kontakti *to contact*

kontenta *satisfied*

kontentiga *satisfactory, pleasing*

kontisto *accountant*

kontraŭ *against, in exchange for*

kontribui *to contribute*

kontribuo *contribution*

konversacio *conversation*

kopii *to copy*

koramikino *girlfriend*

koramiko *boyfriend*

kore *cordially, heartily*

Koreio *Korea*

korespondado *correspondence*

korespondi *to correspond*

koro *heart*

korpo *body*

korrompulo *heart breaker*

koruso *choir*

kosmoŝipo *spaceship*

kosti *to cost*

kosto *price, cost*

kotizo *fee*

kredi *to believe*

kreditkarto *credit card*

kredo *belief, faith*

krei *to create*

kreinto *creator*

kreski *to grow, increase*

krii *to shout*

krima *criminal*

krimo *crime*

kristana *Christian*

Kristano *Christian (person)*

kritiki *to criticize*

Kroatio *Croatia*

krokodili *to speak a language besides Esperanto with Esperantists*

krokodilo *crocodile*

krom *apart from, except*

krono *crown*

kruro *leg*

ktp *etc.*

Kubo *Cuba*

kuirejo *kitchen*

kuiri *to cook*

kuiristo *cook, chef*

kuketo *cookie, cupcake*

kuko *cake*

kukurbo *pumpkin, squash*

kulpa *guilty*

kulpas mi *it's my fault*

kulpo *guilt*

kulturo *culture*

kun *with*

kune *together*

kunhavi *to share*

kuniklo *rabbit*

kunkanti *to sing along*

kunlabori *to collaborate*

kunlaboro *collaboration*

kunmanĝema *to enjoy eating in company*

kunporti *to bring along, take along*

kunveni *to gather, congregate*

kunveno *gathering, meeting, assembly*

kuraci *to treat (medically)*

kuracilo *remedy*

kuracisto *doctor, physician*

kuraĝa *brave, courageous*

kuraĝigi *to encourage*

kuraĝo *courage*

kuri *to run*

kurso *course*

kuŝi *to recline*

kutime *usually*

kuzino *(female) cousin*

kuzo *(male) cousin*

kvalito *quality*

kvankam *although*

kvar *four*

kvara *fourth*

kvardek *forty*

kvarobla *quadruple*

kvarono *quarter*

kvaropo *quartet*

kvazaŭ *as if, as though*

kvieta *quiet, calm*

kvin *five*

kvina *fifth*

kvindek *fifty*

kvinono *fifth*

la *the*

laboregi *to work hard*

labori *to work*

laboristo *worker*

laboro *work*

laborposteno *job*

labortablo *desk, desktop, workspace*

laca *tired*

lacegi *to be exhausted*

laci *to be tired*

laciga *tiring*

laciĝi *to become tired*

lakto *milk*

lampo *lamp*

lando *country, land*

lango *tongue*

lasi *to let, allow, leave*

lasta *last*

lastatempe *recently*

laŭ *according to, along*

laŭ la rivero *along the river*

laŭte *loudly, aloud*

lavi *to wash*

lavujo *basin, sink*

legebla *legible*

legemulo *avid reader*

legi *to read*

legio *legion*

legomo *vegetable*

leono *lion*

leporo *hare*

lernanto *learner*

lernejestro *headmaster*

lernejo *school*

lerni *to learn*

lernolibro *textbook*

letero *letter (written by someone; not a letter of the alphabet)*

leviĝi *to rise, get up*

li *he*

lia *his*

libera *free*

libereco *freedom, liberty*

liberigi *to liberate*

libertempo *free time*

libreto *booklet*

libro *book*

libroservo *book service*

lifto *lift, elevator*

limeriko *limerick*

limo *limit*

lingvo *language*

lingvoscio *language knowledge*

lipo *lip*

listigi *to list*

listo *list*

literaturo *literature*

litero *letter (of the alphabet)*

lito *bed*

litro *litre*

loĝado *accommodation*

loĝi *to live, reside*

loka *local*

loko *place*

lokulo *a local (person)*

Londono *London*

longa *long*

longe *a long time, lengthy*

longo *length*

loterio *lottery*

ludi *to play*

ludilo *toy*

lukto *fight, wrestling*

lumo *light*

lunĉo *lunch, snack*

lundo *Monday*

luno *moon*

majo *May*

majstro *maestro, master*

majstroverko *masterpiece, masterwork*

malafabla *unpleasant*

malalta *short, low*

malamiko *enemy*

malantaŭ *behind*

malaperi *to disappear*

malbela *ugly*

malbona *bad, evil*

malbone *badly*

malbongusta *bad-tasting*

malcerta *uncertain, unsure, doubtful*

maldekstra *left*

maldekstre *on the left*

maldekstren *to the left, leftwards*

maldika *thin*

male *on the contrary*

malebla *impossible*

malfacila *difficult, hard*

malfeliĉa *sad, unhappy*

malfermi *to open*

malfono *foreground*

malforta *weak*

malfrua *late*

malfrue *late*

malgranda *little, small*

malgrava *unimportant*

malĝentila *impolite, rude*

malĝuste *incorrectly*

malhela *dark*

malhelpi *to hinder, impede*

Malio *Mali*

maljuna *old (not young)*

maljusta *unjust, unfair*

malkuraĝigi *to dishearten, discourage*

mallibera *captive*

mallonga *short*

mallumo *darkness*

malmultaj *few*

malmultekosta *cheap, inexpensive*

malnecesa *unnecessary*

malnova *old (not new)*

malo *opposite*

malpermesi *to forbid, prohibit*

malplej *least*

malplena *empty*

malpli *less*

malpravi *to be wrong*

malrapida *slow*

malrapide *slowly*

malriĉa *poor*

malsama *different*

malsana *ill, sick, unhealthy*

malsani *to be ill, to be sick, to be unwell*

malsaniĝi *to fall ill, become sick*

malsanulejo *hospital*

malsata *hungry*

malsati *to be hungry*

malsato *hunger*

malseka *wet*

malsimpla *complex, difficult*

malstreĉita *relaxed*

maltrankvila *agitated, anxious, restless*

malutila *useless*

malvarma *cold*

malvarmumo *cold*

malvera *false, untrue*

malvero *untruth*

mana *manual*

manĝado *eating*

manĝaĵo *food*

manĝebla *edible*

manĝejo *dining room*

manĝemulo *a gourmand*

manĝi *to eat*

manĝigi *to feed*

manĝilaro *cutlery, eating utensils*

manĝilo *an eating utensil, item of cutlery*

manĝkupono *food coupon*

maniero *manner*

manki *to be lacking*

mano *hand*

manpremi *to shake hands*

mapo *map*

mardo *Tuesday*

Maroko *Morocco*

marŝi *to walk, march, stride*

martelo *hammer*

marto *March*

maŝino *machine*

matene *in the morning, in mornings*

matenmanĝo *breakfast*

mateno *morning*

Meksiko *Mexico*

melodio *melody, tune*

mem *self*

membro *member*

memfida *confident, self-assured*

memkontenta *self-content, self-satisfied*

memori *to remember*

memorigi *to remind*

mendi *to order*

mendo *order (for goods)*

mensogi *to lie*

mensogo *lie, falsehood*

menuo *menu*

merkredo *Wednesday*

mesaĝejo *messenger, chat room*

mesaĝo *message*

meti *to put*

metro *metre*

metroo *metro, subway, underground*

meza *middle*

mi *I*

Mi pardonpetas *I apologize*

mia *my*

mil *thousand*

miliono *million*

militisto *warrior*

milito *war*

ministro *minister*

minuto *minute*

miri *to be amazed, be astonished*

mirigi *to amaze, astonish*

mirindaĵo *wonder, marvel*

misaŭdi *to mishear*

miskompreni *to misunderstand*

misparoli *to speak inaccurately, wrongly*

mistera *mysterious*

modesta *modest*

mojosa *cool*

mojose *cool*

momento *moment*

momenton *a moment, a few minutes*

monato *month*

monbileto *bank note*

mondlingvo *world language*

mondmilito *world war*

mondo *world*

monero *coin*

mono *money*

monto *mountain*

montri *to show*

monujo *purse, wallet*

monumento *monument*

monunuo *currency unit, monetary unit*

mordi *to bite*

morgaŭ *tomorrow*

morti *to die*

mortigi *to kill*

mortinta *dead*

morto *death*

moŝto *Majesty, Highness, Eminence, Excellency, etc. (respectful form of address)*

movi *to move*

multa *many, much, lots*

multaj *many, several, lots*

multe *a lot*

multekosta *expensive, dear, costly*

murdi *to murder*

muro *wall*

muso *mouse*

muŝo *fly*

muzeo *museum*

muziko *music*

nacia *national*

nacilingva *national language*

nacio *nation*

naĝejo *swimming pool*

naĝi *to swim*

naski *to give birth*

naskiĝi *to be born*

naskiĝtago *birthday*

naŭ *nine*

naŭdek *ninety*

nazo *nose*

ne *no*

ne dankinde *you're welcome, don't mention it*

ne plu *no longer, no more*

necesa *necessary*

necesejo *toilet, restroom*

Nederlando *The Netherlands*

neĝas *it's snowing*

neĝero *snowflake*

neĝi *to snow*

nek … nek *neither … nor*

nekredeble *incredibly, unbelievably*

neniam *never, at no time*

nenie *nowhere*

nenies *no one's*

neniigi *to annihilate*

nenio *nothing*

neniu *nobody*

Nepalo *Nepal*

nepino *granddaughter*

nepo *grandson*

nepras, ke vi aĉetu *you absolutely have to buy*

nepre *absolutely, definitely*

nervoza *nervous*

nescio *ignorance*

nevino *niece*

nevo *nephew*

ni *we*

nia *our*

nifo *UFO*

nigra *black*

Niĝerio *Nigeria*

Niĝero *Niger*

nokto *night*

nombro *number*

nomi *to name*

nomiĝas *is called*

nomo *name*

nomŝildo *name badge*

nordo *north*

nova *new*

novaĵo *news, novelty, something new*

novembro *November*

novepoka *new age*

novepoka muziko *new-age music*

Novjorko *New York*

novulo *new person*

nu *well, um*

nul *zero*

nuligi *to cancel, nullify*

numero *number*

nun *now*

nuntempa *current, present*

nuntempe *at present, currently, nowadays, these days*

nupto *wedding*

nur *only*

objekto object

odori to smell (give off a smell, have an odour)

odoro smell

ofendi to offend

oferti to offer

oferto offer

oficejo office

oficiala official

ofte often

ofteco frequency

ok eight

okazi to happen, occur

okazo event

okcidento west

okdek eighty

oktobro October

okulo eye

ol than

oni one (they, people)

onklino aunt

onklo uncle

opinii think, have an opinion

opinio opinion

oranĝo orange

oranĝsuko orange juice

ordeno order, fraternity

ordo order

ordoni to command, to order

ordono order, command

orelo ear

organizanto organizer

organizi to organize

organizo organization

oriento east

origine originally

paciento patient

paco peace

paĉjo daddy, dad

pagi to pay

pago payment

paĝo page

palaco palace

palmo palm tree

pando panda

panjo mum, mom, mummy, mommy

pano bread

pantero panther

papero paper

pardonon sorry, excuse me

pardonpeti to apologize

parenco relation, relative

parko park

parolado speech

parolanto speaker

parolata spoken

parolema talkative

paroli to speak, talk

parto part

partopreni to participate

partatempa part-time

pasia passionate

pasinteco past

pastaĵoj pasta

patrino mother

patro father

patrujo fatherland, motherland

paŭzo pause

penso thought

pensi think

pensiga thought-provoking

pensmaniero *way of thinking*

pentri *to paint (a picture, portrait, etc.)*

pentristo *painter (artist)*

perfekte *perfectly*

permesi *to allow, permit*

permeso *permission*

persono *person*

Peruo *Peru*

peti *to ask for, request*

pezi *to weigh*

pico *pizza*

piediri *to walk, go on foot*

piedo *foot*

piedpilko *football*

pilko *ball*

pingveno *penguin*

pioniro *pioneer*

piro *pear*

pizoj *peas*

plaĉas al mi *I like, pleases me*

plaĉi *to please*

plani *to plan, schedule*

plasto *plastic*

plej *-est, most*

plej fora *furthest, farthest*

plej granda *biggest, largest*

plej rapide *fastest, quickest*

pleje *at most, most*

plena *full*

plendemulo *moaner, complainer*

plendi *to complain*

plenigi *to fill, to carry out, to fulfil*

plentempa *full-time*

plezure *with pleasure*

plezuro *pleasure*

pli *more*

pli bone *better*

pli longe *longer*

pli malmultekosta *cheaper*

pli-malpli *more or less*

plia *extra*

pliboniĝi *to improve, become better, get better*

pligrandigi *to enlarge, increase*

plorado *crying, weeping*

plori *to cry, to weep*

plu *even longer, ever more, more*

plumamiko *pen pal*

plumo *feather, pen*

pluraj *several, multiple*

plurlingva *multilingual*

pluvas *it's raining*

pluvero *raindrop*

po *@, apiece, at the rate of*

poemo *poem*

poeto *poet*

poezio *poetry*

pola *Polish*

policano *police officer*

policejo *police station*

polico *police*

Pollando *Poland*

pomarbo *apple tree*

pomo *apple*

pomsuko *apple juice*

pontlingvo *bridge language*

ponto *bridge*

pop-muziko *pop music*

populara *popular*

pordego *gate*

pordo *door, gate*

porinfana filmo *children's film*

porkaĵo *pork*

porko *pig*

porkomencanta *for beginners*

porti *to carry*

portugala *Portuguese*

posedanto *owner, proprietor*

posedi *to own, possess*

post *after, behind*

poste *after, afterwards*

posteno *post (job)*

postmorgaŭ *day after tomorrow*

posttagmeze *in the afternoon*

posttagmezo *afternoon*

postuli *to demand, require*

postvivi *to survive, outlive*

poŝtelefono *mobile phone*

poŝtkarto *postcard*

poŝtmarko *postage stamp*

poŝto *post, mail*

praa *ancient, primal, primeval, primitive, primordial*

praarbaro *primeval forest*

praavino *great-grandmother*

praavo *great-grandfather*

praavoj *ancestors*

prahistorio *ancient history*

pravi *to be right*

precipe *chiefly, mainly, principally*

prefere *preferably, rather*

preferi *to prefer*

prefero *preference*

preĝejo *church (building)*

preĝi *to pray*

prelego *lecture*

premi *to press, squeeze*

premio *prize*

prepari *to prepare*

preskaŭ *almost*

preta *ready*

preter *beyond, past*

prezidanto *president*

prezidento *president (of a republic)*

pri *about*

printempo *spring*

pripensi *to think about, ponder*

priskribi *to describe*

pro *because of, on account of, owing to*

problema *problematic*

problemo *problem*

produkti *to produce*

produktisto *producer*

programi *to program*

programisto *programmer*

progresi *to progress, make progress*

progreso *progress*

proksima *close, near*

proksimume *approximately*

promenado *stroll, walk*

promeni *to walk, stroll*

promesi *to promise*

promeso *promise*

prononci *to pronounce*

prononco *pronunciation*

proponi *to propose, suggest*

propra *one's own*

proverbo *proverb*

provi *to try, attempt*

prozo *prose*

publika *public*

publikigi *to publish*

pumo *puma, cougar, mountain lion*

pundo *pound (unit of currency)*

punko *punk*

punkto *spot, point*

rabato *discount*

rajti *to have the right to, be entitled to*

rakonti *to tell*

rakonto *story*

rano *frog*

rapida *fast, quick*

rapide *fast, quickly*

raporto *report*

raso *race*

re- *re-*

refreno *chorus*

regeo *reggae*

reĝino *queen*

reĝisoro *director*

reĝo *king*

reiri *to go back, return*

rekomendi *to recommend*

rekomendo *recommendation*

rekoni *to recognize*

rekte *straight ahead, directly*

religio *religion*

renkonti *to meet*

renovigi *to renew, renovate*

repo *rap (music)*

reprezenti *to represent*

reputacio *reputation*

respondi *to answer*

respondo *answer*

resti *to stay, to remain*

restoracio *restaurant*

retpoŝtadreso *email address*

retejo *website*

reto *net, internet*

retadreso *email address*

retpoŝto *email*

retumi *to surf the web*

retumilo *browser*

reveni *to come back*

revidi *to see again*

revolucio *revolution*

rezulto *result*

ricevi *to receive*

riĉa *rich*

ridi *to laugh*

ridinda *laughable*

rifuzi *to refuse*

rilate *as to, as regards, concerning, with respect to*

rilato *relation*

rimarki *to notice*

rimo *rhyme*

ripeti *to repeat*

ripeto *repeat, repetition*

ripozi *to rest*

riski *to risk*

ritmo *rhythm*

rivero *river*

rizo *rice*

Rok-muziko *rock music*

romano *novel*

romantika *romantic*

Romo *Rome*

rompi *to break*

rompita *broken*

rugbeo *rugby*

ruĝa *red*

ruĝiĝi *to blush, redden*

ruino *ruin*

rusa *Russian*

Rusio *Russia*

rutino *habit, routine*

sabato *Saturday*

salato *salad*

salo *salt*

salti *to jump*

saluti *to greet*

saluto *greeting*

saluton *hi, hello*

sambo *samba*

same *equally*

same por mi *same for me*

samlandano *compatriot*

samtempe *at the same time*

sana *healthy*

sandviĉo *sandwich*

sankta *sacred, holy*

sano *health*

sata *full (not hungry), sated*

saŭco *sauce*

scenejo *stage*

sceno *scene*

sciencfikcio *science fiction*

sciencisto *scientist*

scii *to know*

sciigi *to inform*

scio *knowledge*

scivolema *curious*

se *if*

sed *but*

segaĵo *sawdust*

segi *to saw*

seka *dry*

sekrete *secretly*

sekva *next, following*

sekvi *to follow*

semajnfino *weekend*

semajno *week*

sen *without*

senamika *friendless*

senbezone *needlessly, unnecessarily*

senco *meaning, sense*

sendependa *independent*

sendependeco *independence*

sendi *to send*

sendube *no doubt, undoubtedly*

Senegalo *Senegal*

senespera *hopeless*

sengasa akvo *still water*

senintence *unintentionally, by accident*

sennombra *countless*

senpaga *free, free of cost*

senpage *for nothing, free*

senprobleme *without a problem*

sensenca *nonsensical, senseless*

sensencaĵo *nonsense*

sensukcese *unsuccessfully*

sensurprize *unsurprisingly*

senti *to feel*

senti sin *to feel*

sento *feeling, sensation, sense*

sep *seven*

sepdek *seventy*

septembro *September*

serĉi *to search*

serio *series*

serioza *serious*

servistino *maid, servant*

servisto *servant*

servo *service*

ses *six*

sesdek *sixty*

sezono *season*

si *oneself (reflexive pronoun for **li**, **ŝi**, **ĝi**, **oni**, **ili**)*

sidi *to sit*

sidiĝi *to sit down, become seated*

signifi *to mean*

simila *similar*

simile *likewise, similarly*

simio *monkey*

simpla *simple*

sincere *sincerely*

sinjorino *Mrs, Madam*

sinjoro *Mr, Sir*

sinsekva *consecutive*

sistemo *system*

skatolo *box*

Skotlando *Scotland*

skoto *Scot*

skribaĉo *scrawl, scribble*

skribi *to write*

skribilo *pen*

skribo *writing*

skui *to shake*

slava *Slav*

slovaka *Slovak*

Slovakio *Slovakia*

sociema *sociable*

socio *society*

soifi *to thirst to be thirsty*

soifo *thirst*

sola *alone, lonely, only*

soldato *soldier*

sole *alone, only, solely*

solvo *solution*

somero *summer*

sono *sound*

soveta *Soviet*

spagetoj *spaghetti*

speciala *special*

spekti *to watch, spectate*

sperta *experienced*

sperto *experience*

spertulo *expert*

sporto *sport*

stacidomo *station*

stari *to stand*

starigi *to set up*

statuo *statue*

stelo *star*

stelulo *star (of a film, etc.)*

stilo *style*

stomako *stomach, belly*

stranga *strange*

strato *street*

streĉita *stressed, under pressure*

streĉo *stress*

strigo *owl*

strofo *verse*

studema *studious*

studento *student*

studeti *to study a little*

studi *to study*

stulta *stupid*

sub *below, beneath, under, underneath*

Sud-Afriko *South Africa*

Sud-Koreio *South Korea*

sudo *south*

suferi *to suffer*

sufiĉe *enough, sufficiently*

sukcesi *to succeed, to manage*

sukceso *success*

sukera *sugary*

sukero *sugar*

suko *juice*

sume *in total, all together*

suno *sun*

sunokulvitroj *sunglasses*

sunumi *to sunbathe*

super *above, over*

superbazaro *supermarket*

supersigno *accent (on letter)*

superŝutita *overwhelmed*

supo *soup*

supozeble *supposably, presumably*

supozi *to suppose*

supraĵo *surface*

supro *top*

sur *on, onto*

surhavi *to have on, wear*

surpapere *on paper*

surpriziga *surprising*

surpriziĝi *to be surprised*

surprizita *surprised*

surprizo *surprise*

surscenejiĝi *to go on stage*

sviso *Swiss person*

ŝafido *lamb*

ŝafo *sheep*

ŝajni *to seem*

ŝanco *chance, luck*

ŝanĝi *to change*

ŝanĝiĝi *to change, be changed*

ŝanĝo *change*

ŝati *to like*

ŝercemulo *joker*

ŝerci *to joke*

ŝercisto *joker*

ŝerco *joke*

ŝi *she*

ŝia *her*

ŝinko *ham*

ŝipo *ship*

ŝtormo *storm*

ŝtuparo *staircase*

ŝtupo *step*

ŝuldi *to owe*

ŝuldo *debt*

ŝultro *shoulder*

ŝuti *to load, to dump*

tablo *table*

tabloteniso *table tennis, ping pong*

taglibro *diary, journal*

tagmanĝo *midday meal*

tagmezo *noon*

tago *day*

tajpi *to type*

taksi *to rate*

taksio *taxi*

talento *talent*

tamen *however*

tasko task

taso cup

taŭga suitable, appropriate

teatro theatre

teda boring, tedious

teĥnika technical

teknika technical

telefoni to call, phone, telephone

telefono phone, telephone

telefonvoko telephone call

televido television

temas pri it's about, it's a matter/question of

temo theme

tempo time

teni to hold

teniso tennis

teo tea

teorio theory

terni to sneeze

tero earth

terpomo potato

terura terrible

terure terribly

testamento testament, will

tiaĵoj such things

tial so, for this reason

tiam then

tiama of that time

tie there

tiel in that way, so, thus

tigro tiger

timema afraid, timid

timi to fear, be scared

timida shy

timige frightfully, scarily

timigi to frighten, scare

timo fear, fright

tio that (thing)

tiu that

Togolando Togo

tomato tomato

tondro thunder

tono tone

torento torrent

torto pie, tart

tra through

traduki translate

traduko translation

trafoliumi to leaf through

tragedio tragedy

trairi to go through

trajno train

trankvila quiet, calm

tranokti to spend the night

trans across

transiri to cross

travivi to experience, live through, survive

tre very

tri three

tria third

tribo tribe

tricent three hundred

tridek thirty

trinkaĵo drink

trinkejo pub, bar

trinki to drink

triobla triple

triono third

triopo trio

trista sad

tristeco *sadness*

tro *too*

trotuaro *pavement, sidewalk*

trovi *to find*

troviĝi *to be found, be located*

tuj *immediately*

Tuluzo *Toulouse*

Tunizio *Tunisia*

turismo *tourism*

turismado *tourism*

turistinformejo *tourist information*

turisto *tourist*

turo *tower*

tusi *to cough*

tuŝi *touch*

tuta *complete, entire, total, whole*

tute *completely, entirely, fully, totally*

tute ne *not at all*

tutmonda *global, worldwide*

tutsole *all alone, completely alone*

ujo *container*

universitato *university*

unu *one*

unu al la alia *one to the other*

unu la alian *each other, one another*

unu post la alia *one after the other*

unua *first*

unuafoje *for the first time*

unueco *unity*

unuflanke … aliflanke … *on one hand … on the other …*

unuiĝo *unification*

unulingva *monolingual*

unusemajna *weeklong*

urbestro *mayor*

urbo *city*

urbodomo *town hall*

urso *bear*

usonano *American, US citizen*

Usono *USA*

utila *useful*

utile *usefully*

uzi *to use*

vakero *cowboy*

varma *warm*

varme *warmly*

varmega *hot*

varmigi *to warm, to heat*

ve *alas, woe*

vegano *vegan*

vegetarano *vegetarian*

veki *to awaken*

vekiĝi *to wake up*

venas *come*

vendejo *market, shop, store*

vendi *to sell*

vendistino *saleswoman*

vendisto *salesman, vendor*

vendredo *Friday*

venonta *coming, next*

vento *wind*

ventro *belly, stomach*

ventrodoloro *stomach ache*

vera *true*

verda *green*

verdaĵoj *green things*

verdire *to tell the truth, in all honesty*

vere *really, truly*

verkaro *works (collected)*

verki *to compose*

verkisto *author, writer, composer*

verko *work (literary or artistic)*

vero *reality, truth*

verŝajne *apparently*

vespere *in the evening*

vespermanĝo *evening meal, supper*

vespero *evening*

vestaĵo *item of clothing*

vesti *to dress*

vesti sin *to dress (oneself)*

vetero *weather*

veturi *to ride*

vi *you*

via *your*

viando *meat*

vida *visual*

vide *visually*

vidi *to see*

vidinda *worth seeing*

vidindaĵo *sight, sight worth seeing*

vido *sight, vision, view*

vilaĝano *villager*

vinberoj *grapes*

vino *wine*

vintro *winter*

vira erinaco *male hedgehog*

viransero *gander*

virina *female, feminine, womanly*

virino *woman*

virkoko *cock, cockerel, rooster*

viro *man*

vivi *to be alive, live*

vivo *life*

vivrakonto *life story*

vizaĝo *face*

viziti *to visit*

Vjetnamio *Vietnam*

voĉe *vocally, verbally*

voĉo *voice, vote*

vojaĝi *travel*

vojo *path, way*

voli *to want*

vortaro *dictionary*

vorto *word*

vortolisto *word list*

vortordo *word order*

vulpino *vixen*

vulpo *fox*

zebro *zebra*

English–Esperanto glossary

-est **plej**

-ever **ajn**

-soever **ajn**

@ **po**

a little **iomete**

a long time **longe**

a lot **multe**

a moment! **Momenton!**

a.m. **antaŭtagmeze**

about **pri**

above **super**

abroad **eksterlande**

absolutely **nepre, tute**

accent **akĉento, supersigno**

accept **akcepti**

accessible **alirebla**

accident **akcidento**

accommodate **gastigi**

accommodation **loĝado**

according to **laŭ**

accountant **kontisto**

accusative **akuzativo**

accuse **akuzi**

ache **dolori, doloro**

acknowledge **agnoski**

across **trans**

act **agi, aktori**

actor **aktoro**

actress **aktorino**

actually **efektive, fakte**

add **aldoni**

advise **konsili**

aeroplane **aviadilo**

affable **afabla**

affront **insulto**

afraid **timema**

Africa **Afriko**

after **post, poste**

afternoon **posttagmezo**

afterwards **poste**

again **denove**

against **kontraŭ**

age **aĝo**

agitated **maltrankvila**

agree **konsenti**

aim **celi**

airport **flughaveno**

alas **ve**

alcoholic drink **alkoholaĵo**

Algeria **Alĝerio**

all **ĉiuj**

all alone **tutsole**

all together **sume**

alligator **aligatoro**

allow **lasi, permesi**

almost **preskaŭ**

alone **sola, sole**

along **laŭ**

along the river **laŭ la rivero**

aloud **laŭte**

already **jam**

also **ankaŭ**

although **kvankam**

always **ĉiam**

am **estas**

amaze **mirigi**

American **usonano, usona**

among **inter**

amusing **amuza**

amusingly **amuze**

ancestors **praavoj**

ancient **antikva, praa**

ancient history **prahistorio**

and **kaj**

and so on **kaj tiel plu (ktp)**

angry **kolera**

animal **besto**

annihilate **neniigi**

anniversary **jubileo, datreveno**

announce **anonci**

annoyance **ĉagreno**

annual **ĉiujara**

answer **respondi, respondo**

ant **formiko**

anthology **antologio**

anxious **maltrankvila**

any **ajn, ajna**

any kind of **ajna**

any time **iam ajn**

anybody **iu ajn**

anyone **iu ajn**

anything **io ajn**

apart from **krom**

apiece **po**

apologize **pardonpeti**

app **apo**

apparently **verŝajne**

appear **aperi, ŝajni**

appearance **aspekto**

apple **pomo**

apple juice **pomsuko**

apple tree **pomarbo**

appropriate **taŭga**

approximately **proksimume**

April **aprilo**

Arab **arabo**

Arabic **araba**

archaeology **arkeologio**

are **estas**

area of expertise **fako**

arm **brako**

army **armeo**

around **ĉirkaŭ**

arrange **aranĝi**

arrival **alveno**

arrive **alveni**

art **arto**

artwork **artaĵo**

as **kiel**

as if **kvazaŭ**

as regards **rilate**

as though **kvazaŭ**

as to **rilate**

ask **demandi**

ask for **peti**

assembly **kunveno**

association **asocio**

astonish **mirigi**

at **ĉe**

at a person's house **ĉe**

at all **ajn**

at first **komence**

at home **hejme**

at last **finfine**

at least **almenaŭ**

at no time **neniam**

at present **nuntempe**

at random **hazarde**

at the rate of **po**

at the same time **samtempe**

atmosphere **etoso**

attempt **provi**

August **aŭgusto**

aunt **onklino**

Australia **Aŭstralio**

author **verkisto**

autumn **aŭtuno**

available **havebla**

avid reader **legemulo**

avoid **eviti**

await **atendi**

awaken **veki**

away **for**

awfully **aĉe**

back **dorso**

background **fono**

bad **malbona**

bad person **aĉulo**

bad-tasting **malbongusta**

badly **malbone**

bake **baki**

bakery **bakejo**

ball **pilko**

ballad **kanzono**

banana **banano**

bank **banko**

bank note **monbileto**

bar **trinkejo, drinkejo, taverno**

barely **apenaŭ**

base **bazo**

basin **lavujo**

be able **kapabli**

be absent **foresti**

be alive **vivi**

be amazed **miri**

be angry **koleri**

be ashamed **honti**

be astonished **miri**

be born **naskiĝi**

be called **nomiĝas**

be changed **ŝanĝiĝi**

be entitled to **rajti**

be exhausted **lacegi**

be found **troviĝi**

be founded **fondiĝi**

be glad **ĝoji**

be hungry **malsati**

be ill **malsani**

be in agreement **akordi**

be in tune **akordi**

be interested in **interesiĝi pri**

be lacking **manki**

be located **troviĝi**

be possible **ebli**

be present **ĉeesti**

be right **pravi**

be scared **timi**

be sorry **bedaŭri**

be sure **certi**

be surprised **surpriziĝi**

be tired **laci**

be unwell **malsani**

be wrong **malpravi**

bear **urso**

beautiful **bela**

beautiful woman **belulino**

beautifully **bele**

beauty **belo, beleco**

because **ĉar**

because of **pro**

become **fariĝi, iĝi**

become better **pliboniĝi**

become engaged **fianĉiĝi, fianĉiniĝi**

become pale **blankiĝi**

become seated **sidiĝi**

become sick **malsaniĝi**

become tired **laciĝi**

bed **lito**

bedroom **dormĉambro**

beef **bovaĵo**

beer **biero**

before **antaŭ**

begin **komenciĝi**

begin learning **eklerni**

begin something **komenci**

begin to fear **ektimi**

beginner **komencanto**

beginning **komenco**

behind **malantaŭ, post**

behave **konduti**

behold **jen**

belief **kredo**

believe **kredi**

belly **ventro**

beloved **amata**

below **sub**

beneath **sub**

berry **bero**

beside **apud**

best wishes **bondezirojn**

best-selling **furora**

bestseller list **furorlisto**

better **pli bone**

between **inter**

beyond **preter**

bicycle **bicikli, biciklo**

big **granda**

biggest **plej granda**

bike **bicikli, biciklo**

biology **biologio**

bird **birdo**

birthday **naskiĝtago**

biscuit **biskvito, kekso**

bite **mordi**

black **nigra**

blow **blovi**

blue **blua**

blues **bluso**

blush **ruĝiĝi**

body **korpo**

boil **boli**

book **libro**

book service **libroservo**

booklet **libreto**

boring **enua, teda**

boss **ĉefo**

both **ambaŭ**

both ... and **kaj ... kaj**

bother **ĝeni**

bottle **botelo**

bow **klini**

box **skatolo**

boy **knabo**

boyfriend **koramiko**

brave **kuraĝa**

Brazil **Brazilo**

bread **pano**

break **rompi**

break-up **disiĝo**

breakfast **matenmanĝo**

bridge **ponto**

bridge language **pontlingvo**

bright **brila, hela**

bring along **kunporti**

Brit **brito**

Britain **Britio**

Briton **brito**

broadcast **dissendi**

broccoli **brokolo**

brochure **informilo**

broken **rompita**

bronze **bronzo**

brother **frato**

brother-in-law **bofrato**

brotherhood **frateco**

brown **bruna**

browser **retumilo**

brush **brosi, broso**

build **konstrui**

building **konstruaĵo**

burger **burgero**

burn **bruli, bruligi**

burned **bruligita**

bus **buso**

but **sed**

butter **butero**

buy **aĉeti**

by accident **hazarde, senintence**

by chance **hazarde**

Bye! **Ĝis!**

cabbage **brasiko**

café **kafejo**

cake **kuko**

California **Kalifornio**

call **telefoni, voki**

calm **kvieta, trankvila**

Cambridge **Kembriĝo**

Canada **Kanado**

Canadian **kanadano**

canal **kanalo**

cancel **nuligi**

candle **kandelo**

candle stick **kandelingo**

capable **kapabla**

capital city **ĉefurbo**

captive **kaptito, mallibera**

car **aŭto**

card **karto**

carrot **karoto**

carry **porti**

carry out **plenigi**

castle **kastelo**

cat **kato**

catch **kapti**

catch sight of **ekvidi**

category **kategorio**

cathedral **katedralo**

Catholic **katoliko, katolika**

cause **igi**

cease **ĉesi**

celebrate **festi**

celebration **festo**

celtic **kelta**

central **centra**

centre **centro**

century **jarcento**

certain **certa**

certainly **certe**

chance **ŝanco**

change **ŝanĝi, ŝanĝiĝi, ŝanĝo**

channel **kanalo**

charming **ĉarma**

charts **furorlisto**

chat **babili**

chatroom **babilejo, mesaĝejo**

cheap **malmultekosta**

cheese **fromaĝo**

chef **kuiristo**

cherry tree **ĉerizarbo**

chest **brusto**

chicken **kokaĵo, koko**

chief **ĉefo**

chiefly **precipe**

child **infano**

childhood **infanaĝo, infaneco**

children's film **porinfana filmo**

Chile **Ĉilio**

Chinese **ĉina**

chips **fritoj, terpomfritoj**

chocolate **ĉokolado**

choir **ĥoro, koruso**

choose **elekti**

chorus **refreno**

Christian **Kristana, Kristano**

church **preĝejo**

cinema **kinejo**

city **urbo**

clarify **klarigi**

classic **klasika**

classical **klasika**

close **proksima**

club **klubo**

club member **klubano**

co-worker **kolego**

cock **virkoko**

cockerel **virkoko**

cocktail **koktelo**

coffee **kafo**

coffee cup **kaftaso**

coffee pot **kafujo**

coin **monero**

cold **malvarma, malvarmumo**

collaborate **kunlabori**

collaboration **kunlaboro**

colleague **kolego**

collect **kolekti**

collection **kolekto**

colour **koloro**

come **venas**

come back **reveni**

come in **enveni**

come to an end **finiĝi**

comedian **komediisto**

comedy **komedio**

comic **komikso**

comic strip **bildstrio**

comma **komo**

command **ordoni, ordono**

commander **komandanto**

comment **komento**

common **komuna**

communist **komunista**

comparatively **kompare**

compatriot **samlandano**

compel **devigi**

competition **konkurso**

complain **plendi**

complainer **plendemulo**

complete **tuta**

completed **finita**

completely **tute**

complex **komplika, malsimpla**

complicated **komplika**

compose **komponi, verki**

composer **komponisto, verkisto**

compulsory **deviga**

compute **komputi**

computer **komputilo**

concerning **rilate**

concert **koncerto**

conference **kongreso**

confident **memfida**

confirm **konfirmi**

confirmation **konfirmo**

confirmation letter **konfirmilo**

confused **konfuzita**

congratulate **gratuli**

Congratulations! **Gratulon!**

congregate **kunveni**

consecutive **sinsekva**

consent **konsenti**

consider **konsideri**

contact **kontakti**

container **ujo**

content **enhavo, kontenta**

contest **konkurso**

continually **daŭre**

continue **daŭri**

contribute **kontribui**

contribution **kontribuo**

convention **kongresejo**

conversation **konversacio**

cook **kuiri, kuiristo**

cookie **kekso, kuketo**

cool **mojosa, mojose**

copy **fotokopio, kopii**

cordially **kore**

correct **ĝusta**

correctly **ĝuste**

correspond **korespondi**

correspondence **korespondado**

cost **kosti, kosto**

costly **multekosta**

Côte d'Ivoire **Eburbordo**

cougar **pumo**

cough **tusi**

countless **sennombra**

country **lando**

couple **duopo, geedzoj**

courage **kuraĝo**

courageous **kuraĝa**

course **kurso**

court **amindumi**

cousin **kuzo, kuzino**

cow **bovo**

cowboy **vakero**

crazy **freneza**

create **krei**

creator **kreinto**

credit card **kreditkarto**

crime **krimo**

criminal **krima**

crisps **ĉipsoj , terpomflokoj**

criticize **kritiki**

Croatia **Kroatio**

crocodile **krokodilo**

cross **transiri**

crown **krono**

cry **plori**

cry out **ekkrii**

crying **plorado**

Cuba **Kubo**

culture **kulturo**

cup **taso**

curious **scivolema**

currency unit **monunuo**

current **nuntempa, aktuala**

currently **nuntempe, aktuale**

curry **kareo**

cute **beleta**

cutlery **manĝilaro**

dad **paĉjo**

daddy **paĉjo**

damn **damne**

dance **danci**

dangerous **danĝera**

dangerously **danĝere**

dark **malhela**

darkness **mallumo**

date **amrendevui, dato**

daughter **filino**

day **tago**

day after tomorrow **postmorgaŭ**

day before yesterday **antaŭhieraŭ**

dead **mortinta**

dear **kara, multekosta**

death **morto**

debt **ŝuldo**

December **decembro**

decide **decidi**

definitely **nepre**

definition **difino**

degrees **gradoj**

delegate **delegito**

delicious **bongusta**

demand **postuli**

Denmark **Danio**

dentist **dentisto**

depressed **deprimita**

describe **priskribi**

desert **dezerto**

deserving **inda**

desire **deziri**

desk **labortablo**

desktop **labortablo**

dessert **deserto**

destroy **detrui**

detail **detalo**

diary **taglibro**

dictionary **vortaro**

die **morti**

difference **diferenco**

different **malsama**

difficult **malfacila, malsimpla**

diligently **diligente**

dining room **manĝejo**

directly **rekte**

director **reĝisoro**

disappear **malaperi**

disconnect **disigi**

discount **rabato**

discourage **malkuraĝigi**

disgusting **fia**

dishearten **malkuraĝigi**

dismiss **eksigi**

distance **distanco**

do **fari**

doctor **kuracisto**

document **dokumento**

documentary **dokumentfilmo**

dog **hundo**

dollars **dolaroj**

dolphin **delfeno**

domestic **hejma**

donkey **azeno**

don't mention it **ne dankinde**

door **pordo**

double **duobla**

doubt **dubi, dubo**

doubtful **malcerta**

dove **kolombo**

dragon **drako**

drama **dramo**

dress **vesti**

dress **vesti sin**

drink **trinki, trinkaĵo**

drop **faligi**

drown **droni**

dry **seka**

duck **anaso**

duckling **anasido**

during **dum**

duty **devo**

each **ĉiu**

each other **unu la alian**

eagle-owl **gufo**

ear **orelo**

early **frue**

earth **tero**

east **oriento**

easy **facila**

eat **manĝi**

eating **manĝado**

eating utensil **manĝilo**

edible **manĝebla**

educate **eduki**

Egypt **Egiptio**

eight **ok**

eighteen **dek ok**

eighty **okdek**

either … or **aŭ … aŭ**

elect **elekti**

electronic **elektronika**

elephant **elefanto**

elevator **lifto**

eleven **dek unu**

else **alie**

email **retpoŝto**

email address **retadreso, retpoŝtadreso**

embarrass **embarasi**

embarrassed **embarasita**

embarrassment **embaraso**

Eminence **moŝto**

emperor **imperiestro**

empire **imperio**

empty **malplena**

encourage **kuraĝigi**

end **fino**

ending **finaĵo**

enemy **malamiko**

England **Anglio**

English **angla**

enjoy **ĝui**

enjoy eating together **kunmanĝema**

enlarge **pligrandigi**

enormous **grandega**

enough **sufiĉe**

enter **eniri, enveni**

entertainingly **amuze**

entire **tuta**

entirely **tute**

entrance **enirejo, enirpordo**

envious **envia**

epoch **epoko**

equally **same**

error **eraro**

Esperanto **Esperanto**

Esperantoland **Esperantujo**

establish **fondi**

esteemed **estimata**

et cetera **kaj tiel plu (ktp)**

etc. **ktp**

Europe **Eŭropo**

Euros **eŭroj**

even **eĉ**

evening **vespero**

evening meal **vespermanĝo**

event **evento, okazo**

ever **iam**

every **ĉiu**

every day **ĉiutage**

every evening **ĉiuvespere**

every year **ĉiujare**

everyone's **ĉies**

everything **ĉio**

everywhere **ĉie**

evil **malbona**

ex– **eksa**

ex-husband **eksedzo (eks-edzo)**

example **ekzemplo**

Excellency, etc. **moŝto**

except **krom**

excited **ekscitita**

excitement **ekscito**

exciting **ekscita**

excuse me **pardonon**

exist **ekzisti**

exit **eliri, elirejo**

expect **atendi**

expensive **multekosta**

experience **sperto, travivi**

experienced **sperta**

expert **spertulo**

explain **klarigi**

explanation **klarigo**

express **esprimi**

extra **plia**

extremely **ege**

extremely beautiful **belega**

eye **okulo**

face **vizaĝo**

fact **fakto**

fair **foiro**

faith **kredo**

faithful **fidela**

fall **fali**

fall asleep **ekdormi, endormiĝi**

fall ill **malsaniĝi**

fall in love **enamiĝi**

false **malvera**

falsehood **mensogo**

family **familio**

family member **familiano**

famous **fama**

fantasy **fantasto**

fare **farti**

farthest **plej fora**

fast **rapida, rapide**

fastest **plej rapide**

fat **dika**

father **patro**

father-in-law **bopatro**

fatherland **patrujo**

fear **timi, timo**

feather **plumo**

February **februaro**

fee **kotizo**

feed **manĝigi**

feel **senti**

feel **senti sin**

feeling **sento**

female **virina**

female friend **amikino**

feminine **virina**

few **malmultaj**

fiancé **fianĉo**

fiancée **fianĉino**

fiction **fikcio**

fictional **fikcia**

fictitious **fikcia**

field **fako**

fifteen **dek kvin**

fifth **kvina, kvinono**

fifty **kvindek**

fight **lukto**

fill **plenigi**

film **filmo**

final **fina**

finally **finfine**

finance **financo**

financial **financa**

find **trovi**

finger **fingro**

finish **fini, finiĝi**

finished **finita**

Finland **Finnlando**

Finn **finno**

fire **fajro, eksigi**

first **unua**

fish **fiŝo**

fish meat **fiŝaĵo**

five **kvin**

fizzy water **gasa akvo**

flag **flago**

flash **ekbrili**

flight **flugo**

flirt **koketi**

flirting **koketado**

fluently **flue**

fly **flugi, muŝo**

follow **sekvi**

following **sekva**

food **manĝaĵo**

food coupon **manĝkupono**

foot **piedo**

football **futbalo, piedpilko**

football player **futbalisto**

for beginners **porkomencanta**

for example **ekzemple**

for nothing **senpage**

for the first time **unuafoje**

for this reason **tial**

forbid **malpermesi**

forearm **antaŭbrako**

foreground **malfono**

foreign **fremda**

foreigner **alilandano, fremdulo**

forest **arbaro**

forget **forgesi**

forgetful **forgesema**

fork **forko**

former **eksa**

forty **kvardek**

forwards **antaŭen**

found **fondi**

foundation **fondiĝo**

four **kvar**

fourteen **dek kvar**

fourth **kvara**

fox **vulpo**

France **Francio**

fraternity **frateco, ordeno**

free **libera, senpaga, senpage**

free of cost **senpaga**

free time **libertempo**

freedom **libereco**

freeze **frosti**

French **franca**

French fries **fritoj, terpomfritoj, frititaj terpomoj**

French person **franco**

frequency **ofteco**

Friday **vendredo**

friendless **senamika**

friends **geamikoj**

friendship **amikeco**

fright **timo**

frighten **timigi**

frightfully **timige**

frog **rano**

from **de, el**

fruit **frukto**

full **plena, sata**

full-time **plentempa**

fully **tute**

fulfil **plenigi**

fun **amuzado**

furthest **plej fora**

future **estonteco**

gallery **galerio**

gander **viransero**

garden **ĝardeno**

garlic **ajlo**

gas **gaso**

gasless water **sengasa akvo**

gate **pordego, pordo**

gather **kunveni**

gathering **kunveno**

general **ĝenerala**

genre **ĝenro**

geography **geografio**

Georgia **Kartvelio**

German **germana, germano**

Germany **Germanio**

gesture **gesto**

get angry **ekkoleri**

get better **pliboniĝi**

get bored **enuiĝi**

get engaged **fianĉiĝi, fianĉiniĝi**

get married **edziĝi**

get out of bed **ellitiĝi**

get to know **ekkoni**

get up **leviĝi**

ghetto **geto**

giraffe **ĝirafo**

girl **knabino**

girlfriend **koramikino**

give **doni**

give birth **naski**

glass **glaso**

glimpse **ekvidi**

global **tutmonda**

go **iri**

go away **foriri**

go back **reiri**

go in **eniri**

go on foot **piediri**

go on stage **surscenejiĝi**

go out **eliri**

go shopping **butikumi**

go through **trairi**

go to bed **enlitiĝi**

goal **celo**

god **dio**

Good day **Bonan tagon**

Good evening **Bonan vesperon**

Good morning **Bonan matenon**

Good night **Bonan nokton**

good-hearted **bonkora**

goodbye **adiaŭ**

goose **ansero**

gorgeous **belega**

govern **estri**

grandad **avĉjo**

grandchildren **genepoj**

granddaughter **nepino**

grandfather **avo**

grandmother **avino**

grandpa **avĉjo**

grandparents **geavoj**

grandson **nepo**

granny **avinjo**

grapes **vinberoj**

gratitude **dankemo**

great **bonege**

great-grandfather **praavo**

great-grandmother **praavino**

Greece **Grekio**

greedy **avara**

green **verda**

greenery **verdaĵoj**

greet **saluti**

greeting **saluto**

grey **griza**

group **aro, grupo**

group of colleagues **kolegaro**

grow **kreski**

Guatemala **Gvatemalo**

guest **gasto**

guide **gvidi**

guided tour **ĉiĉeronado**

guilt **kulpo**

guilty **kulpa**

habit **rutino**

hail **hajlo, hajli**

hair **haro, hararo**

half **duono**

half brother **duonfrato**

halt **halti**

ham **ŝinko**

hammer **martelo**

hand **mano**

handsome man **belulo**

happen **okazi**

happy **feliĉa**

harbour **haveno**

hard **malfacila**

hardly **apenaŭ**

hare **leporo**

harmony **harmonio**

have **havi**

have an opinion **opinii**

have on **surhavi**

have the right to **rajti**

have to **devi**

he **li**

head **kapo**

headache **kapdoloro**

headmaster **lernejestro**

health **sano**

healthy **sana**

heat **varmigi**

heap **aro**

hear **aŭdi**

heart **koro**

heart breaker **korrompulo**

heartily **kore**

hedgehog **erinaco**

hello **saluton**

help **helpi**

helpful **helpa, helpema**

hen **kokino**

her **ŝia**

here **ĉi tie**

here and there **dise**

here is / are **jen**

hero **heroo**

heroine **heroino**

hi **saluton**

high **alta**

Highness **moŝto**

hinder **malhelpi**

hip-hop **hiphopo**

his **lia**

history **historio**

hit **bati, furora**

hobby **hobio**

hold **teni**

holder **ingo**

holy **sankta**

home **hejmo, hejmen**

honestly **honeste**

honour **honoro, honori**

hope **espero, esperi**

hopefully **espereble**

hopeless **senespera**

horror **hororo**

horse **ĉevalo**

hospital **hospitalo, malsanulejo**

host **gastiganto, gastigi**

hot **varmega**

hotel **hotelo**

hour **horo**

house **domo**

house of ill repute **fidomo**

hovel **domaĉo**

how **kiel**

how many **kiom**

how much **kiom**

however **tamen**

hug **brakumi, brakumo**

huge **grandega**

human **homo**

humanity **homaro, homeco**

humour **humoro**

hundred **cent**

hunger **malsato**

hungry **malsata**

hunt **ĉasi**

hurt **dolori**

husband **edzo**

husband and wife **geedzoj**

I **mi**

I apologize **mi pardonpetas**

I like **plaĉas al mi, mi ŝatas**

ice cream **glaciaĵo**

Iceland **Islando**

idea **ideo**

ideal **idealo**

idealist **idealisto**

identifier **identigilo**

identify **identigi**

identity **idento**

idiom **idiotismo**

if **se**

ignorance **nescio**

ill **malsana**

imagine **imagi**

imitate **imiti**

immediately **tuj**

immoral person **fiulo**

impede **malhelpi**

impolite **malĝentila**

important **grava**

impossible **malebla**

improve **pliboniĝi, plibonigi**

in **en**

in advance **anticipe**

in all honesty **verdire**

in any case **ĉiaokaze, ĉiuokaze**

in exchange for **kontraŭ**

in fact **efektive, fakte**

in front of **antaŭ**

in love **enamiĝinta**

in mornings **matene**

in that way **tiel**

in the afternoon **posttagmeze**

in the beginning **komence**

in the evening **vespere**

in the meantime **dume, intertempe**

in the morning **matene**

in the vicinity **ĉe**

in total **sume**

in-laws **bogepatroj**

including **inkluzive de**

incorrectly **malĝuste**

increase **kreski, pligrandigi**

incredibly **nekredeble**

indeed **ja**

independence **sendependeco**

independent **sendependa**

India **Barato**

Indian **baratano**

indicate **indiki**

indicator **indikilo**

inexpensive **malmultekosta**

infamous **fifama**

infancy **infanaĝo, infaneco**

inform **informi, sciigi**

information **informoj**

inner **ena**

inquiry office **informejo**

inside **ena, ene**

instead of **anstataŭ**

instrument **instrumento, muzikilo**

insult **insulto, insulti**

intelligent **inteligenta**

intend **intenci**

intention **intenco**

interest **intereso**

interesting **interesa**

international **internacia**

internet **Interreto, reto**

interpret **interpreti**

interpreter **interpretisto**

into **en**

invade **invadi**

invite **inviti**

Iraq **Irako**

Ireland **Irlando**

Irish **irlanda**

Irish person **irlandano**

iron **fero**

ironic **ironia**

ironically **ironie**

irony **ironio**

irritate **ĝeni**

is **estas**

it **ĝi**

it is important **gravas, estas grave**

it is possible **eblas, estas eble**

it's my fault **kulpas mi**

Italian **itala, italo**

Italy **Italio**

item of clothing **vestaĵo**

item of cutlery **manĝilo**

its **ĝia**

it's about **temas pri**

it's already the time **jam temp' está**

it's raining **pluvas**

it's snowing **neĝas**

Ivory Coast **Eburbordo**

jaguar **jaguaro**

January **januaro**

Japan **Japanio**

Japanese **japana**

jazz **ĵazo**

jealous **ĵaluza**

Jew **judo**

job **laborposteno**

join **aliĝi**

joke **ŝerci, ŝerco**

joker **ŝercemulo, ŝercisto**

journal **ĵurnalo, taglibro**

joy **ĝojo**

jubilee **jubileo**

juice **suko**

July **julio**

jump **salti**

June **junio**

jungle **ĝangalo**

just **ĵus**

karaoke **karaokeo**

kennel **hundejo**

kill **mortigi**

kilo **kilogramo**

kilogramme **kilogramo**

kind **bonkora**

king **reĝo**

kiss **kisi, kiso**

kitchen **kuirejo**

kitten **katido**

knock down **faligi**

know **koni, scii**

knowledge **scio**

Korea **Koreio**

lady **damo**

ladies and gentlemen **gesinjoroj**

lamb **ŝafido**

lamp **lampo**

land **lando**

language **lingvo**

language knowledge **lingvoscio**

large **granda**

largest **plej granda**

last **daŭri, lasta**

late **malfrua**

laugh **ridi**

laughable **ridinda**

lead **estri**

leaf **folio**

leaf through **trafoliumi**

learn **ekscii, lerni**

learner **lernanto**

least **malplej**

leave **foriri, lasi**

leave the Esperanto movement **kabei**

lecture **prelego**

left **maldekstra**

leftwards **maldekstren**

leg **kruro**

legible **legebla**

legion **legio**

lemon **citrono**

length **longo, longeco**

lengthy **longe**

less **malpli**

let **lasi**

letter **letero, litero**

liberate **liberigi**

liberty **libereco**

lie **mensogi, mensogo**

life **vivo**

life story **vivrakonto**

lift **lifto**

light **lumo, malhela**

lightning **fulmo**

like **ŝati**

likewise **simile**

limerick **limeriko**

limit **limo**

lion **leono**

lip **lipo**

list **listigi, listo**

listen **aŭskulti**

literature **literaturo**

litre **litro**

little **malgranda**

little one **etulo**

live **loĝi, vivi**

live through **travivi**

load **ŝuti**

local **loka**

London **Londono**

lonely **sola**

long **longa**

longer **pli longe**

look **aspekti, rigardi**

look forward to **antaŭĝui**

look like **aspekti**

lots **multaj**

lottery **loterio**

loudly **laŭte**

lovable **aminda**

love **ami, amo**

loved **amata**

loving **amema**

low **malalta**

luck **ŝanco**

lucky **bonŝanca**

lunch **lunĉo**

machine **maŝino**

madam **sinjorino**

maestro **majstro**

magazine **gazeto**

maid **servistino**

mail **poŝto**

main **ĉefa**

main character **ĉefrolanto**

main square **ĉefplaco**

mainly **precipe**

Majesty **moŝto**

make **fari, igi**

make glad **ĝojigi**

make progress **progresi**

make someone run away **forkurigi**

male hedgehog **vira erinaco**

Mali **Malio**

man **viro**

manage **sukcesi**

mankind **homaro**

manner **maniero**

manual **mana**

many **multaj**

map **mapo**

March **marto**

march **marŝi**

marker **indikilo**

market **bazaro**

marvel **mirindaĵo**

master **majstro**

masterpiece **majstroverko**

masterwork **majstroverko**

May **majo**

maybe **eble**

mayor **urbestro**

mean **signifi, avara**

meaning **senco**

meanwhile **dume, intertempe**

meat **viando**

meet **renkonti**

meeting **kunveno**

melody **melodio**

member **membro**

menu **menuo**

message **mesaĝo**

messenger **mesaĝejo**

metre **metro**

metro **metroo**

Mexico **Meksiko**

midday meal **tagmanĝo**

middle **meza**

milk **lakto**

million **miliono**

minister **ministro**

minute **minuto**

mishear **misaŭdi**

mistake **eraro**

misunderstand **miskompreni**

moaner **plendemulo**

mobile phone **poŝtelefono**

modest **modesta**

mom **panjo**

moment **momento**

mommy **panjo**

Monday **lundo**

monetary unit **monunuo**

money **mono**

monkey **simio**

monolingual **unulingva**

month **monato**

monument **monumento**

mood **humoro**

moon **luno**

more **pli, plu**

more or less **pli-malpli**

moreover **plie**

morning **mateno**

Morocco **Maroko**

most **plej**

mother **patrino**

mother-in-law **bopatrino**

motherland **patrujo**

mountain **monto**

mountain lion **pumo**

mouse **muso**

mouth **buŝo**

move **movi**

movie **filmo**

movie theatre **kinejo**

Mr **sinjoro**

Mr and Mrs **gesinjoroj**

Mrs **sinjorino**

much **multa**

multilingual **plurlingva**

multiple **pluraj**

mum **panjo**

mummy **panjo**

murder **murdi**

museum **muzeo**

music **muziko**

Muslim **islamano**

must **devi**

my **mia**

mysterious **mistera**

name **nomo, nomi**

name badge **nomŝildo**

nation **nacio**

national **nacia**

national language **nacilingva**

native **denaska**

near **proksima**

necessary **necesa**

neck **kolo**

need **bezoni**

needlessly **senbezone**

neither … nor **nek… nek**

Nepal **Nepalo**

nephew **nevo**

nervous **nervoza**

net **reto**

never **neniam**

new **nova**

new age **novepoka**

new person **novulo**

New York **Novjorko**

new-age music **novepoka muziko**

news **novaĵo**

newspaper **gazeto, ĵurnalo**

newspapers **gazetaro**

next **sekva, venonta**

next to **apud**

nice **afabla**

niece **nevino**

Niger **Niĝero**

Nigeria **Niĝerio**

night **nokto**

nine **naŭ**

nineteen **dek naŭ**

ninety **naŭdek**

no **ne**

no doubt **sendube**

no longer **ne plu**

no more **ne plu**

no one's **nenies**

nobody **neniu**

nod **kapjesi, leveti/malleveti la kapon**

noise **bruo**

nonsense **sensencaĵo**

nonsensical **sensenca**

noon **tagmezo**

north **nordo**

nose **nazo**

not at all **tute ne**

notable **fama**

nothing **nenio**

notice **konstati, rimarki**

notorious **fifama**

novelty **novaĵo**

November **novembro**

now **nun**

nowadays **nuntempe**

nowhere **nenie**

nuisance **ĝenulo**

nullify **nuligi**

number **nombro, numero**

object **objekto**

obligation **devo**

obligatory **deviga**

obviously **evidente**

occasion **fojo**

occur **okazi**

October **oktobro**

of **da, de (with quantities)**

of course **kompreneble**

of that time **tiama**

offend **ofendi**

offer **oferti, oferto**

office **oficejo**

official **oficiala**

often **ofte**

oh **ho**

Oh no! **Ho ve!**

OK **en ordo, bone**

old **maljuna, malnova**

omnivore **ĉionmanĝanto**

on **sur**

on account of **pro**

on occasion **foje**

on one hand … on the other **unuflanke …
aliflanke …**

on paper **surpapere**

on the contrary **male**

on the left **maldekstre**

on the right **dekstre**

on time **ĝustatempe**

one **unu, oni**

one after the other **unu post la alia**

one another **unu la alian**

one to the other **unu al la alia**

one's own **propra**

oneself **si**

onion **cepo**

only **nur, sola, sole**

onto **sur**

onwards **antaŭen**

open **malfermi**

opinion **opinio**

opposite **male, malo**

or **aŭ**

orange **oranĝo, oranĝkolora**

orange juice **oranĝsuko**

order **mendi, mendo, ordoni, ordono,
ordo, ordeno**

order **mendi, ordoni**

organization **organizo**

organize **organizi**

organizer **organizanto**

original **originala**

originally **origine**

other **alia**

otherwise **alie**

our **nia**

out of **el**

outlive **postvivi**

outside **ekster**

over **super**

overwhelmed **superŝutita**

owe **ŝuldi**

owing to **pro**

owl **strigo**

owlery **gufujo**

own **posedi**

owner **posedanto**

page **paĝo**

pain **doloro**

paint **farbi, pentri**

painter **pentristo**

pair **duopo**

palace **palaco**

palm tree **palmo**

panda **pando**

panther **pantero**

paper **papero**

parents **gepatroj**

park **parko**

part **parto**

part-time **partatempa**

participate **partopreni**

particular **aparta**

particularly **aparte**

party **festo, festumi**

passionate **pasia**

past **pasinteco, preter**

pasta **pastaĵoj**

path **vojo**

patient **paciento, pacienco**

pause **paŭzo**

pavement **trotuaro**

pay **pagi**

pay attention **atenti**

payment **pago**

peace **paco**

pear **piro**

peas **pizoj**

pen **skribilo, plumo**

pen pal **plumamiko**

penguin **pingveno**

pepper **pipro, kapsiko**

perfectly **perfekte**

perhaps **eble**

period **epoko**

permission **permeso**

permit **permesi**

perplexed **konfuzita**

person **persono**

Peru **Peruo**

pest **ĝenulo**

pet **hejmbesto, dorlotbesto**

phone **telefoni, telefono**

photo **foti, foto**

photocopier **fotokopiilo**

physician **kuracisto**

physics **fiziko**

pie **torto**

pig **porko**

pigeon **kolombo**

pile **aro**

ping pong **tabloteniso**

pioneer **pioniro**

pizza **pico**

place **ejo, loko**

plan **plani**

plastic **plasto**

play **ludi**

pleasant **afabla**

please **bonvolu, plaĉi**

pleases me **plaĉas al mi**

pleasing **kontentiga, plaĉa**

pleasure **plezuro**

poem **poemo**

poet **poeto**

poetry **poezio**

point **punkto**

Poland **Pollando**

police **polico**

police officer **policano**

police station **policejo**

Polish **pola**

polite **ĝentila**

ponder **pripensi**

poor **malriĉa**

pop music **pop-muziko**

popular **populara**

pork **porkaĵo**

Portuguese **portugala**

possess **posedi**

possibility **eblo**

possible **ebla**

post **afiŝo, posteno, poŝto**

postage **afranko**

postage stamp **poŝtmarko**

postcard **poŝtkarto**

poster **afiŝo**

potato **terpomo**

pound **pundo**

practise **ekzerci sin**

pray **preĝi**

pre-order **antaŭmendi, antaŭmendo**

precisely **ĝuste, precize**

prefer **preferi**

preferably **prefere**

preference **prefero**

prepare **prepari**

prepay **antaŭpagi**

present **nuntempo**

president **prezidanto, prezidento**

press **gazetaro, premi**

presumably **supozeble**

pretty **bela, beleta**

previously **antaŭe**

price **kosto**

primal **praa**

prime minister **ĉefministro**

primeval **praa**

primeval forest **praarbaro**

primitive **praa**

primordial **praa**

principal **ĉefa**

principally **precipe, ĉefe**

prisoner **kaptito**

prize **premio**

problem **problemo**

problematic **problema**

produce **produkti**

producer **produktisto**

programme **programi**

programmer **programisto**

progress **progresi, progreso**

prohibit **malpermesi**

promise **promesi, promeso**

pronounce **prononci**

pronunciation **prononco**

properly **dece**

property **havaĵo**

propose **proponi**

proprietor **posedanto**

prose **prozo**

proverb **proverbo**

pub **trinkejo, drinkejo**

public **publika**

publish **eldoni, publikigi**

puma **pumo**

pumpkin **kukurbo**

punctually **ĝustatempe**

punk **punko**

puppy **hundido**

purchase **aĉeti**

purse **monujo**

put **meti**

quadruple **kvarobla**

quality **kvalito**

quarter **kvarono**

quartet **kvaropo**

queen **reĝino**

question **demando**

questionnaire **demandaro**

quick **rapida**

quickest **plej rapide**

quickly **rapide**

quiet **kvieta, trankvila**

rabbit **kuniklo**

race **raso**

raindrop **pluvero**

rap **repo**

raspberry **frambo**

rate **taksi**

rather **prefere**

re- **re-**

reach **atingi**

read **legi**

ready **preta**

real life **reala vivo, verviva**

reality **vero**

realize **ekscii**

really **vere**

reason **kialo**

receive **ricevi**

receive congratulations **gratuliĝi**

recently **lastatempe**

reception **akceptejo**

recognize **rekoni, agnoski**

recommend **rekomendi**

recommendation **rekomendo**

red **ruĝa**

redden **ruĝiĝi**

refuse **rifuzi**

regard **konsideri**

reggae **regeo**

registration form **aliĝilo**

regret **bedaŭri**

regrettably **domaĝe**

relation **parenco, rilato**

relative **parenco**

relaxed **malstreĉita**

religion **religio**

remain **resti**

remedy **kuracilo**

remember **memori**

remind **memorigi**

remove **forpreni**

renew **renovigi**

renovate **renovigi**

repeat **ripeti, ripeto**

repetition **ripeto**

report **raporti, raporto**

represent **reprezenti**

reputation **reputacio**

request **peti**

require **postuli**

reside **loĝi**

rest **ripozi**

restaurant **restoracio**

restless **maltrankvila**

restroom **necesejo**

result **rezulto**

return **reiri**

revolution **revolucio**

rhyme **rimo**

rhythm **ritmo**

rice **rizo**

rich **riĉa**

ride **veturi**

right **dekstra, ĝusta**

rightwards **dekstren**

rise **leviĝi**

risk **riski**

river **rivero**

rock music **rok-muziko**

Roman **romano**

romantic **romantika**

Rome **Romo**

room **ĉambro**

rooster **virkoko**

routine **rutino**

rude **malĝentila**

rugby **rugbeo**

ruin **ruino**

run **kuri**

run about **diskuri**

run away **forkuri**

Russia **Rusio**

Russian **rusa**

sacred **sankta**

sad **malfeliĉa, trista**

sadness **tristeco**

salad **salato**

salesman **vendisto**

saleswoman **vendistino**

salt **salo**

samba **sambo**

same for me **same por mi**

sandwich **sandviĉo**

satisfactory **kontentiga**

satisfied **kontenta**

Saturday **sabato**

sauce **saŭco**

saw **segi**

sawdust **segaĵo**

say **diri**

say goodbye **adiaŭi**

saying **diraĵo**

scabbard **glavingo**

scare **timigi**

scarily **timige**

scene **sceno**

schedule **horaro, plani**

school **lernejo**

science fiction **sciencfikcio**

scientist **sciencisto**

Scot **skoto**

Scotland **Skotlando**

scrawl **skribaĉo**

screen **ekrano**

scribble **skribaĉo**

search **serĉi**

season **sezono**

second **dua**

secretly **sekrete**

see **vidi**

see again **revidi**

See you later! **Ĝis poste!**

See you! **Ĝis revido!**

seem **ŝajni**

self **mem**

self-assured **memfida**

self-content **memkontenta**

self-satisfied **memkontenta**

sell **vendi**

send **sendi**

send out **dissendi**

Senegal **Senegalo**

sensation **sento**

sense **senco, sento**

senseless **sensenca**

sentence **frazo**

separate **disigi**

September **septembro**

series **serio**

serious **serioza**

servant **servisto, servistino**

service **servo**

set **aro**

set up **starigi**

seven **sep**

seventeen **dek sep**

seventy **sepdek**

several **kelkaj, multaj, pluraj**

shack **domaĉo**

shake **skui**

shake hands **manpremi**

shake one's head **kapskui**

Shame! **Fi!**

shameful **fia**

share **kunhavi, kunhavigi, dividi**

she **ŝi**

sheath **glavingo, ingo**

sheep **ŝafo**

sheet **folio**

shine **brili**

shiny **brila**

ship **ŝipo**

shirt **ĉemizo**

shop **vendejo, butiko, aĉetumi, butikumi**

short **malalta, mallonga**

shoulder **ŝultro**

shout **krii**

shout out **ekkrii**

show **montri**

shut **fermi**

shy **timida**

siblings **gefratoj**

sick **malsana**

side **flanko**

sidewalk **trotuaro**

sight **vidindaĵo, vido**

sight worth seeing **vidindaĵo**

similar **simila**

similarly **simile**

simple **simpla**

since **ekde**

sincerely **sincere**

sing **kanti**

sing along with **kunkanti**

singer **kantisto**

sink **lavujo**

sir **sinjoro**

sister **fratino**

sit **sidi**

sit down **sidiĝi**

six **ses**

sixteen **dek ses**

sixty **sesdek**

sleep **dormi**

Slovak **slovaka**

Slovakia **Slovakio**

slow **malrapida**

slowly **malrapide**

small **malgranda**

smash **disrompi**

smell **odori, odoro**

smoke **fumi**

smoker **fumanto**

snack **lunĉo**

sneeze **terni**

snow **neĝi**

snowflake **neĝero**

so **do, tial, tiel**

sociable **sociema**

society **socio**

socket **ingo**

soldier **soldato**

solely **sole**

solution **solvo**

somebody **iu**

somehow **iel**

someone **iu**

something **io**

something like that **io tia**

sometimes **foje**

somewhere **ie**

son **filo**

soon **baldaŭ**

sorry **pardonon, mi pardonpetas**

sound **sono**

soup **supo**

south **sudo**

South Africa **Sud-Afriko**

South Korea **Sud-Koreio**

Soviet **soveta**

spaceship **kosmoŝipo**

spaghetti **spageto**

Spanish **hispana**

sparkling water **gasa akvo**

speak **paroli**

speak a language besides Esperanto with
    Esperantists **krokodili**

speak someone else's language in an
    Esperanto environment **aligatori**

speak inaccurately **misparoli**

speaker **parolanto**

special **speciala**

specialty **fako**

spectate **spekti**

speech **parolado**

spend the night **tranokti**

spider **araneo**

spoken **parolata**

sport **sporto**

spot **punkto**

spread about **dise**

spring **printempo, fonto**

squeeze **premi**

stables **ĉevalejo**

stage **scenejo**

staircase **ŝtuparo**

stand **stari**

star **stelo, stelulo**

start **komenci, komenciĝi**

station **stacidomo**

statue **statuo**

stay **resti**

step **ŝtupo**

still **ankoraŭ**

still water **sengasa akvo**

stomach **ventro, stomako**

stomach ache **ventrodoloro**

stop **ĉesi, haltejo**

store **butiko, vendejo**

storm **ŝtormo**

story **rakonto, historio**

straight ahead **rekte**

strange **stranga**

strawberry **frago**

street **strato**

stress **streĉo**

stressed **streĉita**

stride **marŝi**

stroll **promenado, promeni**

strong **forta**

student **studento**

studious **studema**

study **studi**

study a little **studeti**

stupid **stulta**

style **stilo**

subway **metroo**

succeed **sukcesi**

success **sukceso**

such things **tiaĵoj**

suffer **suferi**

sufficiently **sufiĉe**

suffix **finaĵo**

sugar **sukero**

sugary **sukera**

suggest **proponi**

suitable **taŭga**

summer **somero**

sun **suno**

sunbathe **sunumi**

Sunday **dimanĉo**

sunglasses **sunokulvitroj**

supermarket **superbazaro**

supper **vespermanĝo**

supposably **supozeble**

suppose **supozi**

sure **certa**

surely **certe**

surf the web **retumi**

surface **supraĵo**

surprise **surprizo**

surprised **surprizita**

surprising **surpriziga**

surround **ĉirkaŭi**

survive **postvivi, travivi**

swear word **fivorto**

sweets **dolĉaĵo**

swim **naĝi**

swimming pool **naĝejo**

Swiss **sviso**

sword **glavo**

system **sistemo**

table **tablo**

table tennis **tabloteniso**

take along **kunporti**

take a shower **duŝi sin**

take away **forpreni**

talent **talento**

talk **paroli**

talkative **parolema**

tall **alta**

target **celo**

tart **torto**

task **tasko**

taste **gusto, gustumi**

tasty **bongusta**

taxi **taksio**

tea **teo**

tea lounge **gufujo**

teach **instrui**

teacher **instruisto**

technical **teĥnika, teknika**

tedious **teda**

telephone **telefoni, telefono**

telephone call **telefonvoko**

television **televido**

tell **rakonti**

tell the truth **verdire**

ten **dek**

ten thousand **dek mil**

tennis **teniso**

tenth **deka**

terrible **terura**

terribly **terure**

testament **testamento**

textbook **lernolibro**

than **ol**

thank you **dankon**

thanks **dankon**

thanks to **dank' al**

that **ke, tio, tiu**

the **la**

the more … the more **ju pli … des pli**

The Netherlands **Nederlando**

theatre **teatro**

their **ilia**

theme **temo**

then **tiam**

theory **teorio**

there **tie**

these days **nuntempe**

they **ili**

thick **dika**

thin **maldika**

thing **afero, aĵo**

think **opinii, pensi**

think about **pripensi**

third **tria, triono**

thirst **soifi, soifo**

thirteen **dek tri**

thirty **tridek**

this **ĉi tiu**

this evening **ĉi-vespere**

this month **ĉi-monate**

this week **ĉi-semajne**

this year **ĉi-jare**

thought **penso**

thought-provoking **pensiga**

thousand **mil**

three **tri**

three hundred **tricent**

through **tra**

thunder **tondro**

Thursday **ĵaŭdo**

thus **tiel**

ticket **bileto**

ticket machine **biletvendilo**

tiger **tigro**

time **tempo**

timely **ĝustatempe**

timetable **horaro**

timid **timema**

tiny **eta**

tip **dankmono**

tired **laca**

tiring **laciga**

to **al**

to another country **alilanden**

to be sick **malsani**

to the left **maldekstren**

to the right **dekstren**

today **hodiaŭ**

together **kune**

Togo **Togolando**

toilet **necesejo**

tomato **tomato**

tomorrow **morgaŭ**

tone **tono**

tongue **lango**

tonight **ĉi-vespere**

too **ankaŭ, tro**

tool **ilo**

tooth **dento**

toothache **dentdoloro**

top **supraĵo**

torrent **torento**

total **tuta**

totally **tute**

touch **tuŝi**

Toulouse **Tuluzo**

tour guide **ĉiĉerono**

tourism **turismo, turismado**

tourist **turisto**

tourist information **turistinformejo**

tower **turo**

town hall **urbodomo**

toy **ludilo**

tragedy **tragedio**

train **trajno**

translate **traduki**

translation **traduko**

travel **vojaĝi**

tree **arbo**

tribe **tribo**

trio **triopo**

triple **triobla**

true **vera**

truly **vere**

trustworthy **fidinda**

trusty **fidela**

truth **vero**

try **provi**

Tuesday **mardo**

tune **melodio**

Tunisia **Tunizio**

twelve **dek du**

twenty **dudek**

twenty-one **dudek unu**

twenty-two **dudek du**

twice **dufoje**

two **du**

two hundred **ducent**

two thousand **du mil**

type **tajpi**

ufo **NIFO**

ugly **malbela**

um **nu**

unbelievably **nekredeble**

uncertain **malcerta**

uncle **onklo**

under **sub**

under pressure **streĉita**

underground **metroo**

underneath **sub**

understand **kompreni**

undoubtedly **sendube**

unfair **maljusta**

unfortunately **bedaŭrinde**

unhappy **malfeliĉa**

unhealthy **malsana**

unification **unuiĝo**

unimportant **malgrava**

unintentionally **senintence**

unity **unueco**

university **universitato**

unjust **maljusta**

unnecessarily **senbezone**

unnecessary **malnecesa**

unpleasant **malafabla**

unsuccessfully **sensukcese**

unsure **malcerta**

unsurprisingly **sensurprize**

until **ĝis**

untrue **malvera**

untruth **malvero**

upset **ĉagrenita**

US citizen **usonano**

USA **Usono**

use **uzi**

useful **utila**

usefully **utile**

useless **malutila**

usually **kutime**

vase **floringo**

vegan **vegano**

vegetable **legomo**

vegetarian **vegetarano**

vendor **vendisto**

verbally **voĉe**

verse **strofo**

very **tre**

Vietnam **Vjetnamio**

view **vido**

villager **vilaĝano**

vision **vido**

visit **viziti**

visual **vida**

visually **vide**

vixen **vulpino**

vocally **voĉe**

voice **voĉo**

vote **voĉo, voĉdoni**

wait **atendi**

waiter **kelnero**

wake up **vekiĝi**

Wales **Kimrio**

walk **marŝi, piediri, promenado, promeni**

wall **muro**

wallet **monujo**

want **voli**

war **milito**

warm **varma, varmigi**

warmly **varme**

warn **averti**

warrior **militisto**

wash **lavi**

watch **spekti**

water **akvo**

way **vojo**

way of thinking **pensmaniero**

we **ni**

weak **malforta**

wear **surhavi**

weather **vetero**

website **retejo**

wedding **nupto**

Wednesday **merkredo**

week **semajno**

weekend **semajnfino**

weeklong **unusemajna**

weep **plori**

weeping **plorado**

weigh **pezi**

welcome **bonvenon, bonvenigi**

welcoming **bonveniga**

well **bone, nu**

well-behaved **bonkonduta**

well-known **konata**

well-wishes **bondeziroj**

Welsh **kimra**

west **okcidento**

wet **malseka**

whale **baleno**

what **kio**

What a pity! **Domaĝe!**

What a shame! **Domaĝe!**

what else **kion alian**

what kind of **kia**

what time **kioma horo**

when **kiam**

where **kie, kien**

whether **ĉu**

whether … or **ĉu … ĉu**

which **kiu**

while **dum**

white **blanka**

whiten **blankiĝi, blankigi**

whither **kien**

who **kiu**

whole **tuta**

whose **kies**

why **kial**

wife **edzino**

will **testamento**

wind **vento**

window **fenestro**

wine **vino**

wing **flugilo**

winter **vintro**

wish **deziro**

with **kun**

with pleasure **plezure**

with respect to **rilate**

within **ene de**

without **sen**

without a problem **senprobleme**

woe **ve**

woman **virino**

womanly **virina**

wonder **mirindaĵo**

wood **arbaro, ligno**

word **vorto**

word list **vortolisto**

word order **vortordo**

work **labori, laboro, verki, verko, funkcii**

work hard **laboregi**

worker **laboristo**

works **verkaro**

workspace **labortablo**

world **mondo**

world language **mondlingvo**

world war **mondmilito**

worldwide **tutmonda**

worth seeing **vidinda**

worthy **inda**

worthy of thanks **dankinde**

wrestling **lukto**

wretchedly **aĉe**

write **skribi**

writer **verkisto**

writing **skribo**

year **jaro**

yearbook **jarlibro**

yellow **flava**

yes **jes**

yesterday **hieraŭ**

yet **ankoraŭ**

you **vi**

young **juna**

your **via**

youth **junulo, junularo, juneco**

you're welcome **ne dankinde**

zebra **zebro**

zero **nul**

dolĉâ pomo

pomo dolĉa

Sweet apple

Kaj = and

la = definite article
leaf or a leaf
la folio
laj folioj

Kato granda

big cat

PRESENT = (as) ending

Ni estas feliĉaj.

We are happy.

mi = I
vi = You (sing or plural)
li = he
ŝi = she
ĝi = it (thing or animal)
ni = we
ili = they

can't be made plural
rapide = quickly
facile = easy

esti = to be
flugi = to fly
kuri = to run
(marchy) marŝi = to walk
dormi = to sleep